THE TYRANNY OF RESOLUTION

SOCIETY
OF BIBLICAL
LITERATURE

DISSERTATION SERIES

Saul M. Olyan, Old Testament Editor
Mark Allan Powell, New Testament Editor

Number 181

THE TYRANNY OF RESOLUTION
I Corinthians 7:17–24

by
Brad Ronnell Braxton

Brad Ronnell Braxton

THE TYRANNY OF RESOLUTION
I Corinthians 7:17–24

Society of Biblical Literature
Atlanta

THE TYRANNY OF RESOLUTION
I Corinthians 7:17–24

by
Brad Ronnell Braxton
Ph.D., Emory University, 1999
Carl Holladay, Dissertation Advisor

Library of Congress Cataloging-in-Publication Data

Braxton, Brad Ronnell.
    The tyranny of resolution : 1 Corinthians 7:17–24 / Brad Ronnell Braxton
      p. cm — (Dissertation series ; no. 181)
    Includes bibliographical references.
    ISBN 0-88414-031-8
    1. Bible. N.T. Corinthians, 1st VII, 17–24—Criticism, interpretation, etc.
    I. Title: First Corinthians seven seventeen to twenty-four. II. Title.
    III. Dissertation series (Society of Biblical Literature) ; no. 181.

    BS2675.2 .B736 2000
    227'.207—dc21   00-045627

08 07 06 05 04 03 02 01 00   5 4 3 2 1

Printed in the United States of America
on acid-free paper

TABLE OF CONTENTS

CHAPTER 3
CIRCUMCISION IN THE GRECO-ROMAN WORLD

CHAPTER 4
SLAVERY IN THE GRECO-ROMAN WORLD

Table of Contents vii

CHAPTER 5
IDEOLOGY AND INTERPRETATION

ACKNOWLEDGMENTS

In the African American Christian tradition, there is a song that queries, "If it had not been for the Lord on my side, where would I be?" Had it not been for divine assistance, I know that I would never have come to the end of this project. The Apostle Paul was right when he declared in Romans 8 that the Holy Spirit helps us in our weakness. God's Spirit was operative in so many people and in so many ways during my research and writing.

Every sentence of this dissertation was written while I served as the full-time Senior Pastor of Douglas Memorial Community Church, a 600-member African American congregation in the urban heart of Baltimore, Maryland. While completing this dissertation, I preached nearly two hundred Sunday sermons, officiated eighteen weddings and over seventy funerals, taught two Bible classes every Wednesday with over one hundred students, and made hundreds of visits to hospitals. Even as I poured myself into the lives of my parishioners, God always insured that my intellectual and emotional cup was never empty when I found those scarce moments to read and write.

Furthermore, I am indebted to the New Testament faculty of the Graduate Division of Religion at Emory University. In every phase of this doctoral program, they equipped me to be a responsible New Testament scholar and a thoughtful member of the intellectual community. Moreover, in a difficult period during my qualifying examinations, the New Testament faculty demonstrated ἔλεος (compassion) and showed me great grace. I am especially grateful to my dissertation adviser, Professor Carl Holladay. Professor Holladay's unrelenting insistence on solid argumentation significantly enhanced this project. He has indelibly etched on my mind the importance of caution when attempting to make credible scholarly assertions. Also, I am deeply appreciative of Dr. Steven Kraftchick who nurtured this dissertation in its embryonic stage.

I am truly thankful for my devoted and indefatigable staff at Douglas Memorial Community Church. I am particularly grateful to the Assistant Pastor, the Reverend Chester France, Jr. and to the Church Administrator, Ms. Kathe Hammond, for their Christian professionalism. Their diligent efforts provided me with time and peace of mind to do serious scholarly work. Also, the lay leaders of Douglas Church, especially Mr. Paul Scott and Mr. Carl Adair, have consistently encouraged me in my quest to bridge the gap between church and academy. Furthermore, I appreciate the members of Douglas Church who ministered to me in so many ways during this process. Some saints offered encouraging words; others cooked meals, and countless persons sent prayers to heaven with my name on them.

So many friends and colleagues have cheered me on during this project, but of the many, there is one I must mention, Dr. Peter Henry. His abiding friendship, perceptive intellect, and gentle spirit have nurtured and enriched me in ineffable ways. In physical stature, Peter is well over six feet tall, but he is taller still because of his integrity. In those periods of my research when exhaustion and frustration were about to consume me, I heard from him our battle cry, "Write them chapters, Doctor!"

Also, several persons have poured over my manuscripts, lending to me their editorial prowess. My editors include: Gwendolyn Barbour, Professor Steven Fine, Pamela Johnson, Mary Lee, Catherine Luckett, Sharon Lewis, Elizabeth Parker, Michael Scott, Ted Smith, Joanne Swanson, and Brad Tharpe. They rescued me from many egregious errors. I am solely responsible for any errors that persist.

I have been blessed with a wonderful wife, Lazetta, whose physical beauty is only surpassed by her inner beauty. Lazetta's laughter—at me, at herself, and at us—compelled me not to take myself too seriously. She has also reminded me that when I sweep through the pearly gates, God's first question will *not* be, "Were you a good graduate student?" Moreover, our friendship has made our home a "safe place" to dream, reflect, and write. Without Lazetta in my corner, this dissertation would still be on my "Things To Do List."

Finally, I will spend the balance of my days thanking God for my parents, the Reverend James and Mrs. Louise Braxton. Of all my many teachers, they still rank number one on my list. The integrity of their Christian witness is light in a dark world. The Apostle Paul may have been ambiguous about some things, but without a doubt, my parents' love for me has always been *abundantly clear*. With profound gratitude, I dedicate this dissertation to them.

INTRODUCTION

In this dissertation, I will argue that ambiguity is an irreducible and even original feature of 1 Corinthians 7:17-24. Many previous interpretations of this passage have prematurely resolved the ambiguous features, rendering them as self-evident. This is a form of exegetical tyranny where the text is made to subserve preconceived notions of its meaning. If, however, we resist the premature resolution of complexity and ambiguity, we will do greater justice to the interpretive richness of this text. This study will attempt to explore the text's ambiguity on a variety of levels.

First, there is the ambiguity that results from various textual features. Thus, in chapter one I will take the reader on an exegetical tour of the textual features of 1 Corinthians 7 that contribute to complexity and ambiguity. My analysis will demonstrate how certain lexical, semantic, and argumentative features of this passage lend themselves to polyvalence. Because of this potential polyvalence, the flow of Paul's overall argument in chapter seven is sometimes difficult to discern. Also, the internal connections between various sections of the chapter are not always evident. Rather than honor these tensions in the text, some interpreters have labeled this text as a "theoretical digression." Such an interpretive move may be another example of the premature resolution of ambiguity. Vv. 17-24 may not be a theoretical digression but instead an integral part of the passage's rhetoric, and the issues discussed in vv. 17-24 may relate directly to concrete concerns in the Corinthian community.

My attention in chapter one to textual features will necessitate a discussion of Paul's notion of calling, which is a central and repetitive motif of the passage. Some exegetes have overlooked the integral role of the concept of calling in 1 Corinthians in general and our passage in particular. Other exegetes who have treated Paul's notion of calling have, nevertheless, robbed this concept of its apparently complex and dynamic nature. These interpreters contend that the call of God creates fixed social states in which believers are to remain. This imposition of a doctrine of the status quo does not honor the richness of this important concept in 1 Corinthians.

In chapter one, I will offer a reading of Paul's call language that attempts to respect the complexity of this concept. I will also suggest that an underlying feature of chapter seven may be Paul's reflection on the (radical) nature and (social) implications of the call of God. In 1 Corinthians 7, Paul may still be sorting out the consequences of the call of God upon the lives of his converts. Thus, I will conclude chapter one by suggesting that some of the ambiguity of this text may result from Paul's ambivalence on the role of the call.

The second level of ambiguity I will explore is that which may have resulted from certain features of the social and cultural worlds of first century Corinth. Thus, an examination of certain elements of the social location of this text will be the task of chapter two. My basic contention in chapter two is that the ambiguity of this passage is not merely a function of textual features; it is also an outgrowth of larger social realities. Rather than engage the vast realities of social life in the first century CE Mediterranean world, I will focus primarily on ethnicity and social status, the two social motifs that figure most prominently in vv. 17-24. In my discussion of ethnicity and social status, I will enlist certain insights of sociology and social anthropology. By means of these tools, I hope to reconstruct some of the plausible frameworks that may have informed both Paul's writing and the Corinthians' hearing of this passage. Additionally, in chapter two I will explore the factors that shaped Paul's understanding of his social identity.

Having established the analytical frameworks of ethnicity and social status in chapter two, I will provide closer readings of Paul's appeals to circumcision, uncircumcision, slavery and manumission in vv. 17-24. Chapter three will explore circumcision and uncircumcision, and chapter four will treat slavery and manumission. In my estimation, language about circumcision and uncircumcision encompasses issues of ethnic identity broadly configured, and language about slavery and manumission encompasses issues of social status broadly configured.

Circumcision and the language used to describe this practice functioned in very interesting and complex ways in the first century CE world. I will offer an overview of the role of circumcision in establishing Jewish identity, especially in the Diaspora. I will discuss the Greco-Roman antipathy for this rite, as well as one intriguing Jewish response to this antipathy, namely, epispasm. Furthermore, I will also investigate the ways in which Jews used metaphor and allegory to speak of the importance (or perhaps even dispensability) of this ethnic rite. As I discuss the role of circumcision in Jewish identity, I will appeal to Philo of Alexandria. As a first century CE Diaspora Jew, Philo serves as a useful foil by which we may examine issues of ethnic identity that may have obtained in other Diaspora locations such as Corinth. Some of Philo's comments on circumcision will be examined.

Finally in chapter three, this rich social data will be brought to bear on the exegesis of 1 Corinthians 7:17-24. On those occasions when exegetes have considered this passage to reflect actual socio-historical realities in Corinth, they have treated only slavery and manumission as potentially concrete concerns. Since Paul's language about circumcision and uncircumcision seems out of place, it has been treated as an illustrative digression. Endeavoring to honor the passage's complexity, I will suggest the possibility that issues of circumcision and uncircumcision (i.e., ethnic identity and ethnic alterations) may be equally real concerns of Paul and of the Corinthians. In particular, I will maintain the plausibility that Paul may be "in competition" with two important and alluring institutions, the gymnasium and the synagogue. Thus, even though Paul's words concerning circumcision and uncircumcision are apparently straightforward, it is possible that his hearers may have come to different conclusions concerning the implications of circumcision and uncircumcision being "nothing" (v. 19).

Similarly, slavery, and language associated with that institution, functioned in multiple ways in the first century CE world. For an exceptional minority, slavery was a potential avenue for upward mobility. Nevertheless, for the vast majority of Roman slaves, slavery was "social death." Orlando Patterson has exhaustively researched this concept of slavery as social death. In chapter four, I will use Patterson's concept of the social death of slavery as a heuristic device to describe first century CE Roman slavery. I will amplify this description with relevant examples from primary sources.

Interestingly, a discussion of Roman slavery necessarily entails an exploration of manumission, since manumission was a constituent feature of Roman slavery. I will treat the mechanisms of manumission and some of the groups in the first century world that may have assisted slaves in obtaining their freedom. A discussion of manumission, however, is in order for a more obvious reason. In vv. 17-24, Paul, perhaps, hints at (concrete) manumission for the slaves in the Corinthian congregation.

After amassing and analyzing the relevant materials on Roman slavery, I will bring the data to bear on an exegesis of 1 Corinthians 7:17-24. I will suggest that Paul's ambiguity concerning whether slaves should seek manumission or remain in slavery is intentional. Unable or unwilling to take sides on this controversial issue at this particular moment, Paul travels the middle way of ambiguity. Thus, some of the ambiguity, which has been treated in the history of interpretation as a *problem in the text*, may actually be an *inherent feature of the text*.

In the first four chapters of this dissertation, I will come full circle. In chapter one I will begin with a textual analysis. In chapter two I will expand my scope to include an investigation of the social world, and in chapters three and four I will return to the text for a closer analysis. In this interpretive journey, I will demonstrate that complexity and ambiguity, be they incidental or intentional, are irreducible aspects of this passage.

Finally, in chapter five I will explore the ideological dimensions of the ambiguity of this text. I will investigate the role of this passage in the intense cultural debates in nineteenth century America concerning the perpetuation or abolition of chattel slavery. There is no greater practical demonstration of this text's irreducible ambiguity than its simultaneous use by two ideologically opposed factions to support mutually exclusive social purposes.

Lest one think that the premature resolution of ambiguity evident in the nineteenth century has been overcome by the critical exegetical methodologies of the twentieth century, I conclude the dissertation by examining how certain ideological presuppositions of historical criticism actually perpetuate the tyranny of resolution. The recognition of ambiguity as an important hermeneutical category will enrich our interpretive practices and will remind us of the difficult, yet rewarding, work of textual interpretation and ethical discernment.

Chapter 1

EXEGETICAL OVERVIEW

INTRODUCTION

After translating the text, I will offer an exegetical survey of the passage and, in the process, make suggestions about alternative ways to read the text which are exegetically plausible. This demonstration of alternative readings is not necessarily meant to suggest the "correctness" of them over against other readings. Rather, its purpose is to show how complexity and ambiguity exist in this text.

A TRANSLATION OF 1 CORINTHIANS 7:17-24

17. But[1] to each as the Lord assigned, each as God has called,[2] thus let him walk. Thus, in all the churches I command this.

---

[1] In the Greek, this is εἰ μή. How the interpreter understands εἰ μή affects her perception of the relationship between vv. 17-24 and vv. 1-16. Is Paul now signaling that he is about to pinpoint what is essential in the preceding verses? In other words, after all is said and done, this is what is really important. Or is Paul addressing a new topic? Archibald Robertson and Alfred Plummer argue that v. 17 "reads better as a fresh starting point," but they, nonetheless, admit that "this verse may be taken either as a summing up of what has just been said, or as a fresh starting point for what is to follow (18-24)." See Robertson and Plummer, *The First Epistle of St. Paul to the Corinthians* (Edinburgh: T & T Clark, 1914), 144-145.

[2] In the Greek, κέκληκεν is the perfect tense which generally denotes a completed past action whose effects continue in the present. See F. Blass and A. Debrunner, *Greek Grammar of the New Testament and Other Early Christian Literature* (Chicago: University of Chicago Press, 1961), 175-176. (The references to Blass and Debrunner are to page numbers.) I will discuss below if the verb tense sheds light on the complex notion of calling in Paul's arguments.

18. If anyone was circumcised when he was called, let him not remove the marks of circumcision. If anyone was called in the state of uncircumcision, let him not be circumcised.

19. Circumcision is nothing, and uncircumcision is nothing, but keeping (the) commandments of God.[3]

20. Each in the calling in which he was called, in this let him remain.

21. Were you a slave when called? Let it not be a care to you, but even if you are able to become free, use it all the more.[4]

22. For the slave called in the Lord is a freedman of the Lord; likewise the free person called is a slave of Christ.

23. You were bought with a price; do not become slaves of humans.

24. Each in the calling[5] in which he was called, brothers, in this let him remain before God.

---

[3]The elliptical phrase ("but keeping the commandments of God") will be discussed fully below.

[4]Many studies have been devoted to the interpretive problems surrounding v. 21. Most notably, see S. Scott Bartchy, Μαλλον Χρησαι: *First Century Slavery and the Interpretation of 1 Corinthians 7:21* (Missoula: Society of Biblical Literature Dissertation Series, 1973). For a more recent treatment of these problems, see J. Albert Harrill, *The Manumission of Slaves in Early Christianity* (Tübingen: J. C. B. Mohr, 1995). In approach and perspective, there are similarities between Harrill's work and mine, especially as it relates to the importance of an adequate investigation of social context for the proper exegesis of this passage. In spite of these similarities, there are several differences which will be noted.

[5]The grammatical difficulty of this verse will be discussed below.

THE ARGUMENT IN 1 CORINTHIANS 7?

In this dissertation, I will investigate what an interpretation of 1 Corinthians 7:17-24 looks like if the exegete does not treat the meaning of this passage as self-evident. If one refuses to conceal the complexity and ambiguity[6] and instead exposes them in full view, what are the interpretive consequences? Many previous attempts to interpret this passage, be they historical-critical or ideological, have ignored various enigmas. The complexity and ambiguity in this passage are thoroughgoing, existing both at the level of its composition and of its subsequent receptions by various reading communities.

This study is designed to investigate whether it is possible to resist the tyranny of the premature resolution of complexity and ambiguity. It will also show how the text has been exploited when the complexity and ambiguity have not been honored. The ability to live with ambiguity might expand our interpretive horizons, but this remains to be seen. The first task of this dissertation will be an in-depth exploration of the features in the text itself which contribute to ambiguity, that is, ambiguity created by Paul in the process of composition.

The interpreter of 1 Corinthians 7:17-24 finds herself *in medias res*. A responsible interpretation attempts to situate a passage contextually. One of the first questions which emerges is, what is the relationship of this passage to the preceding and succeeding verses in 1 Corinthians 7 and to the letter as a whole? The relationship of 1 Corinthians 7:17-24 to chapter

---

[6]Concerning this passage, Antoinette Wire remarks, "First Corinthians 7. . . shows Paul's *ambiguous* response to a pattern of withdrawing from long-term sexual relationships in the Corinthian church. Some people have remained formally married, others have left believing spouses, still others have left non-believing spouses." See Wire, *The Corinthian Women Prophets: A Reconstruction through Paul's Rhetoric* (Minneapolis: Fortress Press, 1990), 72 (emphasis mine). As this dissertation will show, the ambiguity of 1 Corinthians 7 extends far beyond Paul's responses concerning marriage and sexuality.

seven will occupy us now, with consideration being given later to the relationship of this passage to the entire letter.

In 1 Corinthians 7:17 Paul writes, "But to each as the Lord assigned, each as God has called, thus let him walk. Thus, in all the churches I command this" (Εἰ μὴ ἑκάστῳ ὡς ἐμέρισεν ὁ κύριος, ἕκαστον ὡς κέκληκεν ὁ θεός, οὕτως περιπατείτω. καὶ οὕτως ἐν ταῖς ἐκκλησίαις πάσαις διατάσσομαι). Notwithstanding the awkward syntax of this verse, in the first words of our passage, one is faced with an immediate interpretive problem. What is the intended nuance of εἰ μή?

Contrary to the opinion of some interpreters,[7] the decision one makes may affect one's understanding of the relationship of 7:17-24 to the rest of chapter seven. By εἰ μή Paul may be indicating that vv. 17-24 constitute the essence of what he has said in the preceding verses. In effect, Paul would be saying, "I have addressed specific concrete concerns that you have posed, *but* what I really want you to learn from these examples is this: each should conduct himself according to the call with which he has been called." Therefore, by using εἰ μή Paul could be signaling that this notion of living according to one's calling is the core of his message.

Some exegetes have argued that vv. 17-24 constitute a digression from the major thrust of the argument in chapter seven.[8] Thus, they contend that in vv. 17-24 Paul is assuming a new line of thought. In effect, Paul would be saying, "But, in spite of my preceding instructions, this is what I really want you to know and do." Depending upon how one understands εἰ μή, one may view this section as a summary of Paul's argument or a digression from it. Of course, in order to determine if εἰ μή in v. 17 summarizes or diverts from the argument, one must identify,

---

[7]For example, Hans Conzelmann remarks, "Arguing whether v. 17 sums up the foregoing or represents a new beginning is an idle matter." It may be idle, however, only if one assumes that the meaning of this passage and its relationship to the preceding verses are self-evident. See Conzelmann, *A Commentary on the First Epistle to the Corinthians* (Philadelphia: Fortress Press, 1975), 125.

[8]For a nuanced version of the argument that vv. 17-24 are a digression, see Gregory W. Dawes, "But if you can gain your freedom (1 Corinthians 7:17-24)," *Catholic Biblical Quarterly* 52 (1990): 681-697.

if only generally, the thrust of the argument in 1 Corinthians 7. To this, we now turn our attention.

According to scholarly consensus, in 1 Corinthians 7 Paul is responding to concerns expressed by some in the Corinthian community. Throughout his letter, Paul has addressed concerns in the Corinthian community, be they real or imagined by him. A classic historical reconstruction suggests that the means by which Paul receives information about the Corinthian community take at least two forms, oral and written. For instance, some information may have reached him orally via Chloe's people (1:11).[9] Other information, such as that in ·chapter seven, has reached him via written form (περὶ δὲ ὧν ἐγράψατε, 7:1).

Just as the phrase περὶ δὲ ὧν ἐγράψατε in 7:1 may indicate that Paul is responding to a letter from the Corinthians,[10] so too, other textual features reveal that in chapter seven he is addressing particular groups within the Corinthian community. Consequently, chapter seven can be divided without much difficulty into the following sub-sections:

vv. 1-7: Advice to the married

vv. 8-9: Advice to the unmarried and widows

vv. 10-11: Advice to the married

---

[9]In other places in 1 Corinthians, Paul gives evidence that he has received some kind of report about matters in the Corinthian community. See, for example, 4:18, 5:1, and 6:1. In the history of scholarship on the Corinthian correspondence, much ado has been made about Paul's possible receipt of information via oral *and* written sources. Subsequently, this hypothesis has been used to support various partition theories (i.e., the notion that the Corinthian correspondence is a composite of different letters written at various times). See John Coolidge Hurd, Jr., *The Origin of 1 Corinthians* (New York: Seabury Press, 1965), 43-58.

[10]Margaret Mitchell contends that the function of the phrase "περὶ δέ . . . " is to refocus the discussion or to signify that a new topic is about to be introduced. See Mitchell, *Paul and the Rhetoric of Reconciliation: An Exegetical Investigation of the Language and Composition of 1 Corinthians* (Tübingen: J. C. B. Mohr, 1991), 235.

vv. 12-16: Advice to those in "mixed marriages"

vv. 17-24: Digression or statement of principle

vv. 25-28: Advice to the unmarried

vv. 29-35: Apocalyptic rationale

vv. 36-40: Advice concerning one's betrothed and remarriage

Difficulties arise, however, when one attempts to interpret these sub-sections. I shall now examine these difficulties closely.

vv. 1-7: Advice to the Married

The attempt to reconstruct historically the concerns and actions of the Corinthians based upon the responses of Paul is precarious at best. Nevertheless, when Paul writes in 7:1, "It is good for a man not to touch a woman" (καλὸν ἀνθρώπῳ γυναικὸς μὴ ἅπτεσθαι), scholars[11] generally assume that he is merely repeating one of the formulas of certain Corinthians (who were thought to be of an ascetic persuasion) and that Paul is not offering his own opinion. According to the logic of this scholarly assumption, after quoting the Corinthians' slogan in 7:1, Paul in vv. 2-7 exhorts the married persons in the community to avoid sexual asceticism as a regular practice because it increases the likelihood of *porneia*. Attempting to uncover ambiguity cloaked in scholarly consensus, one must raise this question: Is the meaning of 7:1-7 (and of the entire chapter) altered, or can it be read another way if one does not

---

[11]See Conzelmann, 115. Also see, C. K. Barrett, *The First Epistle to the Corinthians* (New York: Harper & Row, 1968), 154. Barrett acknowledges the possibility that 7:1 is not a quotation but Paul's own opinion. Barrett writes, "*Some difficulty is alleviated* if these words [it is good for a man not to touch a woman] are regarded as a quotation from the Corinthian letter" (emphasis mine). Barrett, 54.

automatically assume that 7:1 is a quotation, but instead Paul's own statement?

Additionally, Paul's rationale for the necessity of sexual relations among married persons in vv. 2-5 is not incongruous with the (or his) ascetic statement in v. 1. Unlike the Genesis accounts of creation that celebrate and even encourage[12] the sexual love of husband and wife, and of which Paul is undoubtedly aware,[13] Paul's justification for sexual love in marriage does not extol the intrinsic worth of such love but views it merely as a guard against temptation. He exhorts husbands and wives to avoid long periods of abstinence "lest Satan tempt you on account of your lack of self-control" (ἵνα μὴ πειράζῃ ὑμᾶς ὁ Σατανᾶς διὰ τὴν ἀκρασίαν ὑμῶν). Perhaps, in vv. 1-7 Paul opts not to appeal to the Genesis account because it does not support his own preference for celibacy, which he states in v. 1.

Whether v. 1 contains a Pauline quotation is not the only ambiguity of v. 1. Another issue to be adjudicated is: What nuance is Paul (or are the Corinthians) intending by the use of καλόν? By saying that not touching a woman is καλόν does he (or do they) mean that avoiding sexual activity is noble, virtuous, desirable, advisable? The adjective καλόν can have many shades of meaning.

Also, there appears to be an incongruity between Paul's relative tentativeness in v. 6 and his relative assertiveness in v. 7. In v. 6 Paul readily acknowledges that the preceding words are his opinion (συγγνώμην) and not a command (ἐπιταγήν) from the received tradition.[14] Throughout the letter, Paul has

---

[12]In the Priestly version of the creation, see Genesis 1:27-28, and in the Yahwistic account of the creation, see Genesis 2:24. Of course, these distinctions between the Priestly and Yahwistic versions are the result of modern, historical-critical analysis and would not have been applicable to Paul's reading of Genesis. For a concise treatment of the documentary hypothesis, see E. A. Speiser, *Genesis* (Garden City: Doubleday, 1983), xxii-xxxvii.

[13]In 1 Corinthians 6:16 Paul quotes verbatim from the LXX of Genesis 2:24.

[14]In 7:10 Paul says that he has a command of the Lord, and in other places in 1 Corinthians he indicates that he is the recipient of

strongly asserted his views,[15] but by calling attention to his words as an *opinion* and not a command in v. 6, he seems almost apologetic. Does Paul's tentativeness in v. 6 reflect his own ambiguity about the matter at hand, or is it a tacit admission that some will disagree with and disobey his counsel?

In v. 7a Paul says more assertively, "I wish that all people were as I myself am. . . ." (θέλω δὲ πάντας ἀνθρώπους εἶναι ὡς καὶ ἐμαυτόν). This call to imitation does not appear for the first (or the last) time in chapter seven[16] but in fact begins earlier in the Corinthian correspondence.[17] Moreover, some scholars contend that the call to imitation takes several forms and carries out various rhetorical functions.[18] Having introduced earlier in the letter his desire for the Corinthians to imitate him, Paul reiterates this theme in 1 Corinthians 7. Yet, the assertiveness of v. 7a is partially eclipsed by the concessions he offers in v. 7b. He writes, "But each has his own gift from God, one of this kind and one of another" (ἀλλὰ ἕκαστος ἴδιον ἔχει χάρισμα ἐκ θεοῦ, ὁ μὲν οὕτως, ὁ δὲ οὕτως). What is the relationship between Paul's desire for all to be like him and his concession of the different gifts given to each believer?

---

important traditions. For instance, in 11:23 and 15:3 he speaks of passing on traditions which he has received. For a discussion of Paul's use of the technical terms of receiving (παραλαμβάνειν) and passing on a tradition (παραδιδόναι), see Conzelmann, 195-196.

[15]See, for example, 1:10, 5:1-5, and 6:1-8.

[16]Even though Paul does not use the explicit language of imitation (e.g., μιμητής) in 1 Corinthians 7, imitation of him is certainly in view in 7:7-8. Also, depending upon how one renders the clause in 7:26 ὅτι καλὸν ἀνθρώπῳ τὸ οὕτως εἶναι, Paul may be encouraging imitation of himself there. Conzelmann notes that the phrase οὕτως εἶναι in 7:26 can be rendered three ways: a) remain as one is; b) remain as I am [which is tantamount to imitate me]; c) remain as the virgins are. See Conzelmann, 132. The subtlety of the exhortation for imitation in vv. 7-8 (and possibly v. 26), as opposed to the direct call to imitation in 4:16, may be a keen indicator of Paul's own ambiguity on the topics being discussed.

[17]1 Corinthians 4:16. Also, see 11:1.

[18]See Elizabeth A. Castelli, *Imitating Paul: A Discourse of Power* (Louisville: Westminster/John Knox Press, 1991), 59-117.

C. K. Barrett notes the possibility of an unresolved tension between Paul's wish in 7:7a ("I wish that all people were as I myself am") and the concession in 7:7b ("but each has his own gift from God"). Barrett writes, "When Paul intends to express a wish he knows to be unattainable, he rightly uses the imperfect tense of the verb. . . . When he uses the present tense as here [in v. 7a] he intends to express a wish that is capable of realization and ought to be realized. . . almost a command."[19] If Barrett is right, the interpreter of vv. 1-7 might have to contend with a split between what Paul *says* and what Paul *means*.[20] Paul says that each has his own gift. That is, he allows a concession. Perhaps, the meaning of this section (vv. 1-7) is to suggest gently to his readers that there is a better form of existence, and of course, Paul is the model of that better existence.

It appears that the substance of the argument in 1 Corinthians 7 is a recitation of Paul's apostolic responses to a host of concrete concerns. Seemingly, both the concerns and the responses are bound by the common thread of sexual and marital ethics. Closer inspection, however, might reveal another way of reading the textual evidence. I contend that the focus in 1 Corinthians 7 may not be abstinence,[21] or marriage and sexual ethics per se; rather, the force of the argument may be to enjoin the Corinthians to remain as they are. Since, however, in the divine scheme, people have different gifts, acceptable concessions are suggested by Paul.

Lest we lose our way in an increasingly puzzling labyrinth, let us remember that the attempt to identify the basic argument

---

[19]Barrett, 158.

[20]This distinction between *expression* (i.e., what one says) and *meaning* is not new but has been at the heart of many discussions of New Testament hermeneutics. Most notably, see Rudolf Bultmann "The New Testament and Mythology" in *Kerygma and Myth*, ed. Reginald Fuller (London: SPCK, 1953), 1-44.

[21]O. Larry Yarbrough also suggests that it is misguided to place too much emphasis in chapter seven on the theme of sexual abstinence. He contends, "The emphasis is on *remaining as you are*, not on abstinence from sexual intercourse." See *Not Like the Gentiles: Marriage Rules in the Letters of Paul* (Atlanta: Scholars Press, 1985), 94.

of 1 Corinthians 7 resulted from the ambiguity of εἰ μή in 7:17. Depending on how one translates the ambiguous εἰ μή, vv. 17-24 might be a *summary* of the preceding argument or a *digression* from the argument. In order to determine if it summarizes or digresses from the argument, one needs, as best as possible, to determine the argument.

The attempt to ferret out the force of the argument in chapter seven has led us to further ambiguities. Paul's argument in 1 Corinthians 7 is not self-evident. Past interpreters have treated this chapter as a more-or-less straightforward apostolic response to the questions of some in the Corinthian community. The argument is more complex than previously acknowledged and could, in fact, be Paul's attempt to work out the relationship between membership in the ἐκκλησία and other social realities.

My point is not to assert the superiority of one reading over another. Rather, I am attempting to demonstrate the possibility of other plausible ways of construing Paul's argument when one does not consider that the text is inherently lucid. Are the first seven verses of the chapter practical answers to specific questions posed to Paul by the Corinthians? Or is Paul less interested in the specific social-ethical questions in Corinth and more interested in using these issues as a platform to proclaim and explain the important principle of remaining as one is? Is there some relationship between the social-ethical questions and Paul's principle? If there is, does Paul explicate that relationship *clearly*? These questions must be borne in mind as we proceed.

vv. 8-9: Advice to the Unmarried and Widows

Having dealt with the married persons, Paul now addresses the unmarried and widows.[22] He says, "It is good for them if they

---

[22]The Greek of 1 Corinthians 7:8 reads, λέγω δὲ τοῖς ἀγάμοις καὶ ταῖς χήραις, καλὸν αὐτοῖς ἐὰν μείνωσιν ὡς κἀγώ. One could legitimately translate the datives in this verse as "concerning" instead of "to." That is, the verse could be rendered, "I say *concerning* the unmarried and the widows. . ." Rather than addressing these groups directly, Paul may be talking about them. Regardless of the nuance given to the dative, the basic meaning appears to be unaltered.

remain as I myself am" (καλὸν αὐτοῖς ἐὰν μείνωσιν ὡς κἀγώ). Notice the similar syntactic structures in v. 8 and v. 1.[23] In v. 8, Paul writes, "It is good for them. . . ." and then states his preference, namely, it is good if the unmarried and the widows imitate Paul (ἐὰν μείνωσιν ὡς κἀγώ), which presumably means remaining celibate.[24]

Paul's use of a similar syntactic structure in v. 8 and v. 1 might be a clue that in v. 1 he is not merely quoting the ascetics in the community but is also stating his own preference. In v. 1 as in v. 8, Paul uses καλόν and the person(s) to whom the statement is directed in the dative case. As such, there is a parallel structure between vv. 1-2 and vv. 8-9. In v. 1 and v. 8 Paul states the preference. In v. 2 and v. 9 Paul offers the concessions. The link between the preference in v. 1 and the preference in v. 8 is the strong wish or subtle command for the Corinthians to be like Paul.

Similarly, the link between the concession in v. 2 and the concession in v. 9 is Paul's prohibition against sexual immorality.[25] In v. 2 Paul calls it πορνεία and suggests that even his ascetic principle can and should be superseded if the possibility of πορνεία exists. Likewise, with more colorful language, Paul concedes in v. 9 that there is a "principle" even higher than remaining as one is. That principle is avoiding πορνεία, which in v. 9 is euphemistically referred to as a "lack of self-control" (ἐγκρατεύονται) or as "being aflame with passion" (πυροῦσθαι).

---

[23]In a recent monograph, *Paul on Marriage and Celibacy*, Will Deming thinks that the syntax is not as similar as scholars contend. He maintains that in 7:1 Paul does not merely say, "it is good," but says, "it is good *for a man*." In other words, Paul has, "it is good" plus a noun in the dative case. Deming's observation would seem to me, ironically, to argue in favor of a similar syntax between 7:1 and 7:8. Although different wording is used in 7:8, Paul does use "it is good" with a noun in the dative. This time Paul uses αὐτοῖς. See Deming, *Paul on Marriage and Celibacy* (Cambridge: Cambridge University Press, 1995), 110.

[24]1 Corinthians 7:1.

[25]Although complexity and ambiguity attend many of Paul's statements in chapter seven, he *is* consistently clear concerning his prohibition of sexual immorality. Also, see my discussion of Paul in chapter two.

In the first nine verses, Paul has stated *clearly* his ascetic preference, yet offered concessions to believers whose gifts are different than his. In order to avoid the risk of πορνεία, Paul has also *clearly* stated that when given the choice of remaining as one is or falling into πορνεία, one should *not remain as one is* but instead marry. Perhaps, Paul's message is not so *clear* after all.

vv. 10-11: Advice to the Married

It would appear that this structure of preference and concession is broken in v. 10 as Paul addresses those who are already married but perhaps contemplating divorce. Paul writes, "To[26] those who have been married, I command, not I but the Lord, that a woman should not divorce her husband" (τοῖς δὲ γεγαμηκόσιν παραγγέλλω, οὐκ ἐγὼ ἀλλὰ ὁ κύριος, γυναῖκα ἀπὸ ἀνδρὸς μὴ χωρισθῆναι). This is one of the rare moments in the Pauline corpus when Paul appeals to words spoken by Jesus.[27] Yet, even the command of the Lord is subject to conditions and concessions. Paul interrupts the command of the Lord with a conditional clause. In v. 11 he writes, "But if she does separate, let her remain unmarried or let her be reconciled to her husband" (ἐὰν δὲ καὶ χωρισθῇ, μενέτω ἄγαμος ἢ τῷ ἀνδρὶ καταλλαγήτω).

Then, presumably, Paul continues with the command of the Lord and says that "the husband should not divorce his wife" (καὶ ἄνδρα γυναῖκα μὴ ἀφιέναι). This concession of divorce

---

[26] Again, this dative could be translated "concerning." See my discussion above.

[27] Also, see 1 Corinthians 9:14. For a full discussion of Paul's use of the words of Jesus, see David L. Dungan, *The Sayings of Jesus in the Churches of Paul: The Use of the Synoptic Tradition in the Regulation of Early Church Life* (Philadelphia: Fortress Press, 1971). Dungan argues that although there may not be many explicit quotations of Jesus' sayings in Paul's writings, Paul was, nonetheless, thoroughly familiar with these sayings and may have alluded indirectly to them more than previous interpreters have realized.

which Paul allows[28] seems all the more important because it is made over against a known command of the Lord.[29] One should be cautious about making too much of this, but it is no small move for Paul to set himself up as one who can offer practical advice that contravenes even the words of Jesus.[30] In the concessions in vv. 8-11 Paul is asserting himself as one who can

---

[28]Interestingly, Jerome Murphy-O'Connor believes that Paul actually refuses the divorce. See Murphy-O'Connor, "The Divorced Woman in 1 Cor 7:10-11," *Journal of Biblical Literature* 100 (1981): 601-606.

[29]Dungan remarks, "Whatever the case may have been [as to why this woman alluded to in 1 Corinthians 7:11 may have wanted a divorce], the fact remains that Paul *permits the divorce if it has taken place*: 'let her remain unmarried.' " Dungan, 92. Dungan suggests, however, that even in this "concession," Paul remains close to Jesus' teaching on divorce. According to Dungan, Jesus' teaching on this matter was not as much a prohibition of divorce as it was a prohibition against remarriage. Thus, by prohibiting the remarriage of the women in v. 11, Paul actually upholds the teaching of Jesus. Notwithstanding Dungan's careful argumentation, one must still ask, if in v. 10 *and 11,* Paul is actually following the intent of the original command of Jesus, why does he feel the need now to emphasize that the command against divorce is from the Lord. On other occasions, Paul has felt quite confident that his apostolic authority was enough in itself to carry the day, without his making appeals to traditions about Jesus. Very simply, without adducing complicated arguments about Paul and the Synoptic tradition as Dungan does, one can contend that Paul in v. 10 mentions the command of the Lord not to add to the authority of his (i.e., Paul's) teaching but precisely because Paul in the next breath is planning to modify the teaching of Jesus. On this matter, Paul assumes the authority to adapt the received tradition to fit the exigencies in his congregation.

[30]Without stretching the evidence too far, one can suggest that just as the Matthean Jesus offers halakah or reinterprets the known traditions in the so called "Antitheses" in Matthew 5:21-48, so too, Paul assumes the right of offering his own rules of conduct on marriage in 1 Corinthians 7, reinterpreting even the known tradition. For an exhaustive study of divorce and remarriage in the New Testament, see Craig S. Keener, *And Marries Another: Divorce and Remarriage in the New Testament* (Peabody: Hendrickson Publishers, 1991), especially 50-82. Keener intimates that Paul in 1 Corinthians 7:11 is offering exceptions to the teaching of Jesus. Also, see Peter Richardson, " 'I Say not the Lord': Personal Opinion, Apostolic Authority, and the Development of Early Christian Halakah," *Tyndale Bulletin* 31 (1980): 65-86.

make programmatic statements even in the face of the known tradition.

vv. 12-16: Advice to Those in "Mixed Marriages"

Turning next to marriages of believers with unbelievers, Paul begins, "To the rest I, not the Lord, say. . . ." Paul groups those believers who do not fall in the categories previously discussed and addresses them as "the rest" (τοῖς δὲ λοιποῖς).[31] Before giving his instructions, he again distinguishes between himself and Jesus and emphatically states that what is being said are his own words. He writes, "To[32] the rest I, not the Lord, say that if any brother has a wife who is an unbeliever, and she agrees to live with him, he should not divorce her" (τοῖς δὲ λοιποῖς λέγω ἐγὼ οὐχ ὁ κύριος· εἴ τις ἀδελφὸς γυναῖκα ἔχει ἄπιστον καὶ αὕτη συνευδοκεῖ οἰκεῖν μετ' αὐτοῦ, μὴ ἀφιέτω αὐτήν).

Some commentators imply that Paul's attempt to distinguish his command from that of the Lord is an act of deference. Paul's instructions should be taken seriously but are not, however, to be compared with the Lord's commands. Conzelmann writes, "The regulation given by the historical Jesus is also that of the exalted Lord. It is a supra-temporal command. The historic character of the command is not canceled."[33] Is it not also possible that in contradistinction to Conzelmann's claim, Paul in v. 12 is subtly setting himself alongside Jesus as one possessing authority[34]—authority even to offer concessions and qualifications to commands of the Lord?

Paul's advice in vv. 13-14 seemingly supports the command of the Lord in v. 10 against divorce. If the unbelieving partner desires to live in harmony with the believing partner, there should be no divorce. Paul in v. 14 offers an additional

---

[31] Dungan argues that by using this phrase (τοῖς δὲ λοιποῖς) Paul really has the non-Christian spouses in mind. That is, "the rest" is a Pauline term for unbelievers. Dungan, 93.

[32] Again, this dative could be translated "concerning." See my discussion above.

[33] Conzelmann, 120.

[34] 1 Corinthians 7:40.

reason against divorce. He contends that the unbelieving spouse does not defile the believing spouse but is made holy (ἡγίασται) by the believing spouse.

In the history of interpretation of 1 Corinthians 7, vv. 14-16 have been another *crux interpretum*. One of the first riddles the interpreter must solve is deciphering what Paul intends by his use of the verb ἁγιάζω.[35] The use of this verb raises questions of both means and ends.

With respect to means, what is the mechanism by which the believing spouse effects this sanctification? In other places in 1 Corinthians,[36] Paul speaks of sanctification as a state effected by Jesus Christ in the life of the believer. In 7:14 the process of sanctification occurs in a non-believer and is effected by another human being.[37] With respect to ends, how does one define the state of sanctification for the non-believer? Moreover, Paul asserts that the children of such a union are also rendered holy. What is shrouded in mystery is how Paul understands the children of these mixed marriages to be holy. What form does this state of holiness take for the children involved? Since one's spouse and children can be sanctified if one remains in the marriage, Paul discourages believers from seeking divorce.

In the face of the arguments just marshaled against divorce, Paul, in contradistinction to the command of the Lord, declares in v. 15 that divorce is not only permissible but even

---

[35]For a discussion of the family of words related to ἅγιος, see Otto Procksch, "ἅγιος" in *Theological Dictionary of the New Testament*, vol. 1 (Grand Rapids: William B. Eerdmans Publishing Company, 1964), 88-97, 100-115.

[36]See 1:2 and 6:11.

[37]Jerome Murphy-O'Connor argues that this sanctification is the result of the action of the non-believing spouse, whose willingness to remain in the marriage is the means by which the sanctification occurs. This argument is faulty on several grounds. First, it does not do justice to the passive voice of ἡγίασται in v. 14. Second, in this section of 1 Corinthians 7, Paul is concerned with the behavior of the *believers* and not so much with the behavior of the unbelievers. Shifting the emphasis to the behavior of the unbelievers is to miss the point of the passage. See Murphy-O'Connor, "Works Without Faith in I Cor. VII 14," *Revue Biblique* 84 (1977): 349-361.

desirable if the unbelieving partner no longer wants to remain married. He writes, "But if the unbelieving partner desires to separate, let it be so; in such a case the brother or sister is not bound"[38] (εἰ δὲ ὁ ἄπιστος χωρίζεται, χωριζέσθω· οὐ δεδούλωται ὁ ἀδελφὸς ἢ ἡ ἀδελφὴ ἐν τοῖς τοιούτοις). Divorce is permissible in this case because ultimately the call of God is a call to peace not disharmony (v. 16). Once again, Paul permits and even encourages a change of status. The change this time is advocated in order to avoid disharmony.

Although a Christian spouse may sanctify one's unbelieving spouse, Paul raises a query[39] in 1 Corinthians 7:16 about the salvation of one's spouse. The sanctification spoken of in v. 14 may be something different from the state of salvation spoken of in v. 16. Paul's belief that an unbelieving spouse is sanctified seems to have more to do with his desire to have the fruit of this union, the children, be holy and not impure.[40] The sanctifying effect of a believing spouse on an unbelieving spouse is enough to make the children holy but not enough necessarily to secure the salvation of that unbelieving partner.

Paul's use of the verb σῴζω may add to the ambiguity of v. 16. In its New Testament usage, the verb σῴζω carries several

---

[38]Paul's use of the verb δουλεύω (to be bound) in v. 15 itself raises questions. The Christian husband or wife who acquiesces to the divorce is not bound to what?: the marriage?; the command of the Lord prohibiting divorce? See P. Dulau, "The Pauline Privilege: Is It Promulgated in the First Epistle to the Corinthians?," *Catholic Biblical Quarterly* 13 (1951): 146-152.

[39]In the history of interpretation, there has been considerable debate concerning whether Paul's question in v. 16 should be understood optimistically (i.e., how do you know that you will not save your husband?, with a yes answer being implied) or pessimistically (i.e., how do you know that you will save your husband?, with a no answer being implied). Regardless of how one renders this verse, it is clear that the sanctification of v. 14 and the salvation implied in v. 16 are thought to be different states. See Sakae Kubo, "I Corinthians VII. 16: Optimistic or Pessimistic," *New Testament Studies* 24 (1978): 539-544.

[40]In v. 14 it almost seems as if the holiness of the children is for Paul a foregone conclusion. He appears to start with this premise and then reason backwards.

shades of meaning,[41] including making healthy or whole[42] and rescuing one from being lost.[43] Paul often uses σῴζω in an eschatological sense to depict the ultimate rescue of the believer from sin and God's wrath,[44] but he also uses this verb to describe the goal of his missionary activity. For example, in 1 Corinthians 9:22 he talks about "saving" people which in this context must mean winning their allegiance to the ἐκκλησία. Thus, one could interpret Paul's use of salvation language in 1 Corinthians 7:16 in several ways. When Paul speaks of spouses saving one another, he could have in mind the goal of winning the unbelieving spouse's allegiance to the ἐκκλησία, or he could be alluding to the ultimate eschatological salvation of the unbelieving spouse. Perhaps, both nuances of σῴζω are intended.

vv. 17-24: Digression or Statement of Principle

Since I will analyze closely the difficulties of vv. 17-24 later in this chapter, I will offer no extended exegetical comments here. In these verses, Paul reflects on the relationship of the call to various social realities.

vv. 25-28: Advice to the Unmarried

After vv. 17-24, Paul again instructs the unmarried (τῶν παρθένων).[45] Before offering his advice, he reasserts his

---

[41]For a fuller treatment of the meanings of σῴζω in the New Testament, see Werner Foerster, "σῴζω" in *Theological Dictionary of the New Testament*, vol. 7 (Grand Rapids: William B. Eerdmans Publishing Company, 1971), 989-998.

[42]See, for example, Mark 3:4, 5:23, 5:28, and 5:34.

[43]See, for example, Luke 19:10.

[44]See, for example, Romans 5:9 and 1 Corinthians 1:18.

[45]In the history of scholarship on 1 Corinthians 7, there has been much discussion concerning the identity of the virgins (τῶν παρθένων). Probably, Paul has in mind here the young, unmarried persons in the community. This debate is not necessarily germane to our present

trustworthiness. Although possessing no command of the Lord, Paul, in this affirmation of trustworthiness, continues to cultivate the Corinthians' appreciation of and respect for his views.

In v. 26 we encounter a syntactic structure similar to that found in v. 1 and v. 8.[46] Paul uses the adjective καλόν and the person to whom his words are addressed in the dative case. He writes, "I think, therefore, that in light of the impending distress, that it is good for a person to remain as he is"[47] (Νομίζω οὖν τοῦτο καλὸν ὑπάρχειν διὰ τὴν ἐνεστῶσαν ἀνάγκην, ὅτι καλὸν ἀνθρώπῳ τὸ οὕτως εἶναι). Paul's exhortation in v. 26 is similar to the ones in vv. 7-8. In vv. 7-8 there is a direct call for the unmarried and the widows to be as Paul is, followed by the concession for each believer to use his own gifts. In v. 26 the call to imitate Paul is subtle. He says that the believer should remain as he (i.e., the believer) is. Since in vv. 25-26 Paul is talking to the unmarried (τῶν παρθένων), for the unmarried person "to remain as he is" would be tantamount to imitating Paul.

In v. 27, as Paul presents two concrete scenarios, it would appear that he is no longer speaking exclusively to the unmarried. He writes, "If you are bound to a wife, do not seek to be free. If you are free from a wife, do not seek a wife" (δέδεσαι γυναικί, μὴ ζήτει λύσιν· λέλυσαι ἀπὸ γυναικός, μὴ ζήτει γυναῖκα). In v. 26 Paul's trustworthy opinion for the unmarried is to remain as they are, namely, unmarried. Then, in v. 27 Paul clarifies the notion of remaining as one is with an exhortation about being married and remaining thus or being unmarried and remaining thus. In other words, v. 27 can be read as an

---

discussion. For an investigation of various views on this topic, see J. F. Bound, "Who are the 'Virgins' Discussed in 1 Corinthians 7:25-38?," *Evangelical Journal* 2 (1984): 6-7 and J. M. Ford, "Levirate Marriage in St. Paul (1 Cor vii)," *New Testament Studies* 10 (1963): 361-365.

[46]The frequency with which Paul has exhorted various groups to adopt a sexually ascetic lifestyle (e.g., v. 1, vv. 7-8, and v. 26) might be a subtle indicator that the exhortation for the sexually ascetic lifestyle is not merely a Corinthian slogan but Paul's own thoughts on the matter.

[47]Literally, the Greek says, "it is good for a person *to be thus.*" For possible ways to render this ambiguous phrase ὅτι καλὸν ἀνθρώπῳ τὸ οὕτως εἶναι, see footnote sixteen.

explication of remaining as one is. It is unclear why Paul would include an exhortation about married persons remaining married when he is giving advice to the unmarried in vv. 25-28.[48]

In spite of the exhortation in v. 26 for the unmarried "to remain as he is," Paul again presents concessions in v. 28. "But if you marry, you do not sin, and if a girl marries, she does not sin" (ἐὰν δὲ καὶ γαμήσῃς, οὐχ ἥμαρτες· καὶ ἐὰν γήμῃ ἡ παρθένος, οὐχ ἥμαρτεν). Presumably, Paul writes this in order to address both the male and female. The "you" in the first part of the clause (ἐὰν δὲ καὶ γαμήσῃς, οὐχ ἥμαρτες) is a male. Then, in order to treat this situation with some parity, he addresses the female, who here is referred to as ἡ παρθένος. In v. 28 Paul assures those who do not remain as they are that such behavior does not constitute sin. This statement might be Paul's attempt to contravene teaching in the Corinthian community that to marry was tantamount to sin.

Although those who marry do not sin, Paul, nevertheless, clearly indicates the negative consequences that may accompany choosing to marry. Those who choose not to remain as they are but rather to marry will have trouble or distress in the flesh. In the last half of v. 28 he writes, "Such ones will have trouble in the flesh, and I would spare you that" (θλῖψιν δὲ τῇ σαρκὶ ἕξουσιν οἱ τοιοῦτοι, ἐγὼ δὲ ὑμῶν φείδομαι). The word θλῖψιν can denote usual suffering or difficult times, but it also can be used to denote the troubles and suffering that were to accompany the end time.[49] Paul's use of this word raises the following questions, what kind of distress does Paul have in mind, and is it apocalyptic in nature?

---

[48]Deming attempts to solve this riddle by suggesting that Paul is using a diatribe style of argumentation. In such a case, Paul uses both parts of the statement (i.e., if you are bound to a wife, do not seek to be free; if you are free from a wife, do not seek a wife), but, in actuality, for the sake of his argument Paul is only interested in the second part, namely, if you are free from a wife, do not seek a wife. See Deming, 173-177.

[49]See, for example, Daniel 12:1 (LXX) and Mark 13:19, 13:24.

vv. 29-35: Apocalyptic Rationale

Paul's intent to clarify the statement in the last half of v. 28 is indicated by the phrase in v. 29, "what I mean is this" (τοῦτο δέ φημι). Presumably, in the following verses Paul will explicate "trouble in the flesh" (θλῖψιν δὲ τῇ σαρκί).

Some interpreters[50] suggest that θλῖψιν, in this instance, carries apocalyptic overtones because of what Paul says in v. 26 about the present distress (ἐνεστῶσαν ἀνάγκην[51]). These exegetes understand the "present distress" to be Paul's way of talking about the imminent end of history. Such interpreters bolster their argument by means of what Paul says in v. 29, "I mean, brothers, the appointed time is short" (τοῦτο δέ φημι, ἀδελφοί, ὁ καιρὸς συνεσταλμένος ἐστίν). Thus, for such interpreters, ἐνεστῶσαν ἀνάγκην of v. 26 and the phrase ὁ καιρὸς συνεσταλμένος ἐστίν in v. 29 are two ways of talking about the same reality. In vv. 26-32, Paul uses several words that in the first century CE Greco-Roman world could carry apocalyptic nuances.[52]

When these verses are viewed apocalyptically, Paul is suggesting that, of all the options available to the believer, marriage is a viable one which does not constitute sin. Marriage, nonetheless, is an option that carries with it a considerable tax (i.e., θλῖψιν δὲ τῇ σαρκί). In light of the tumult that was to accompany the end times,[53] Paul wants to spare the Corinthian converts from additional troubles.

---

[50]See, for example, Barrett, *The First Epistle to the Corinthians*, 174-176.

[51]ἀνάγκη also can be used in an apocalyptic context to describe the distress and calamities associated with the end time. See, for example, Luke 21:23.

[52]In particular, ἀνάγκη, θλῖψις, and καιρός. See the note above. Also, for examples of the use of θλῖψις in an apocalyptic context, see Matthew 24:9, 24:21, and 24:29. For examples of the use of καιρός in an apocalyptic context, see Mark 13:33 and Luke 21:8.

[53]See, for example, Mark 13:3-27.

Other exegetes,[54] however, do not hear apocalyptic overtones in this section and render ἐνεστῶσαν ἀνάγκην as "present necessity," which is taken to mean some present crisis in the Corinthian congregation (e.g., issues surrounding marriage and celibacy). θλῖψιν, for such interpreters, carries no apocalyptic overtones and simply denotes worldly anxieties and troubles. Those scholars who opt for a non-apocalyptic interpretation of these terms note that in v. 37 ἀνάγκην is used again in what appears to be a non-apocalyptic manner.

In v. 37 Paul writes, "Whoever stands firm in his own heart, *having no necessity*, but he has control over his own will, and he has decided in his own heart to keep his betrothed, he does well" (ὃς δὲ ἕστηκεν ἐν τῇ καρδίᾳ αὐτοῦ ἑδραῖος μὴ ἔχων ἀνάγκην, ἐξουσίαν δὲ ἔχει περὶ τοῦ ἰδίου θελήματος καὶ τοῦτο κέκρικεν ἐν τῇ ἰδίᾳ καρδίᾳ, τηρεῖν τὴν ἑαυτοῦ παρθένον, καλῶς ποιήσει). Those favoring a non-apocalyptic rendering understand the phrase "having no necessity" (μὴ ἔχων ἀνάγκην) in v. 37 to be the antithesis to the phrase ἐὰν ᾖ ὑπέρακμος in v. 36 which refers to the man who does not have his passion under control.[55] For some interpreters, "necessity" in these verses has more to do with issues of sexuality than with the apocalyptic passing away of the world. This inability to determine with certainty whether vv. 26-28 are undergirded by an overt[56] apocalyptic understanding of the world only compounds the ambiguity of vv. 29-31.

---

[54]See, for example, John G. Gager, "Functional Diversity in Paul's Use of End Time Language," *Journal of Biblical Literature* 89 (1970): 325-337. For a critique of Gager, see Deming, 177-197 and especially note 270.

[55]For the ambiguities surrounding ὑπέρακμος, see Gordon Fee, *The First Epistle to the Corinthians* (Grand Rapids: William B. Eerdmans Publishing Company, 1987), 349-352.

[56]I say "overt" here because in the history of New Testament scholarship some exegetes have contended that even in the absence of ostensible apocalyptic terminology, the framework for Pauline thought is apocalyptic, nevertheless. For example, in a classic essay Ernst Käsemann wrote, "The apocalyptic question 'To whom does the sovereignty of the world belong?' stands behind the resurrection theology of the apostle, as behind his parenesis which centers around the call to obedience in the body. Apocalyptic even underlies the particular shape of Pauline anthropology. . . . I hope I have made it clear

In vv. 29b-31 Paul engages in another rhetorical flourish to elucidate principles by which believers are to govern themselves from now on (τὸ λοιπόν). The phrase τὸ λοιπόν (i.e., from now on) represents the period in which the believers are now living— a period which itself is short or has been shortened (ὁ καιρὸς συνεσταλμένος ἐστίν)—until the consummation of the age. The principle that should govern believers could be called the "as if not" (ὡς μή) principle.

Paul writes, "Let those who are married live as if they have no wife. Let those who are weeping as if not weeping, and those rejoicing as if not rejoicing, and those buying as if not possessing, and those using the world as if they had no dealings with it. For the form of this world is passing away" (ἵνα[57] καὶ οἱ ἔχοντες γυναῖκας ὡς μὴ ἔχοντες ὦσιν, καὶ οἱ κλαίοντες ὡς μὴ κλαίοντες καὶ οἱ χαίροντες ὡς μὴ χαίροντες καὶ οἱ ἀγοράζοντες ὡς μὴ κατέχοντες, καὶ οἱ χρώμενοι τὸν κόσμον ὡς μὴ καταχρώμενοι· παράγει γὰρ τὸ σχῆμα τοῦ κόσμου τούτου.).

Even if there is little agreement among exegetes about the presence and influence of apocalyptic on vv. 26-28, few would deny the presence of apocalyptic language in vv. 29-31. For instance, in other contexts, Paul uses καιρός to refer to the consummation of the age.[58] Moreover, this notion of "the short time before the end" appears elsewhere in the New Testament

---

why I describe apocalyptic as the mother of Christian theology." See Käsemann, "On the Subject of Primitive Christian Apocalyptic" in *New Testament Questions of Today* (London: SCM Press, 1969), 135-137. Or more recently, see J. C. Beker who suggests that "apocalyptic defines the network of symbolic relations within which Paul's thought moves." *Paul the Apostle: The Triumph of God in Life and Thought* (Philadelphia: Fortress Press, 1980), xix. For a classic rebuttal of Käsemann's position, see Rudolf Bultmann, "Ist die Apokalyptik die Mutter der christlichen Theologie?: Eine Auseinandersetzung mit Ernst Käsemann" in *Apophereta Festschrift für Ernst Haenchen zu seinem siebzigsten Geburtstag am 10. Dezember 1964* (Berlin: Verlag Alfred Töpelmann, 1964), 64-69.

[57]My translation reflects the fact that ἵνα in Hellenistic Greek can be a substitute for the imperative. See Blass and Debrunner, 195.

[58]See, for example, Romans 13:11, 1 Thessalonians 5:1.

in apocalyptic contexts.[59] Finally, this passage ends with the proclamation that the form (σχῆμα)[60] of this world is passing away. The idea that the ages or epochs of humankind are divided into segments is a salient characteristic of apocalyptic literature.[61]

Since we are unclear as to the importance of apocalyptic on vv. 26-28, yet relatively clear as to its presence and importance in vv. 29-31, do we superimpose vv. 29-31 onto vv. 26-28 and thus read vv. 26-31 in the light of apocalyptic, or do we only allow the apocalyptic imagery to influence its immediate context, namely, vv. 29-31? Moreover, why is apocalyptic imagery present only in this section (vv. 26-31) and not the rest of the chapter?

Though the meaning of this flourish in vv. 29-31 seems obvious (i.e., wear one's status in the world loosely in light of the imminent end of the world), these "as if not" statements create a number of difficult dilemmas,[62] not the least of which is this question, what, if any, is the relationship between the "as if not" statements in vv. 29-31 and vv. 17-24?[63] Moreover, the

---

[59]See, for example, Romans 13:11-12, Mark 13:20.

[60]Vincent Wimbush suggests that σχῆμα means "the distinctive manifestations—institutions, morals, ideals—that characterize the κόσμος." See Wimbush, *Paul, The Worldly Ascetic: Response to the World and Self-Understanding according to 1 Corinthians* (Macon: Mercer University Press, 1987), 34.

[61]See Klaus Koch, "What is Apocalyptic? An Attempt at a Preliminary Definition" in *Visionaries and Their Apocalypses*, ed. Paul Hanson (Philadelphia: Fortress Press, 1983), 16-36.

[62]Vincent Wimbush, who devotes an entire chapter to the explication of the ὡς μή statements, remarks, "But the *vagueness* of the ὡς μή expressions forces us to ask whether it could not be understood— especially in light of the fact that an eschatological affirmation regarding the imminence of the Parousia precedes it—as a summons to physical withdrawal from the world, namely, from worldly ties and involvements." See Wimbush, 30 (emphasis mine). For critiques of Wimbush, see David Cartlidge, "Review of *Paul, The Worldy Ascetic*," *Journal of Biblical Literature* 108 (1989): 355-357, and Deming, 9-10.

[63]For Wimbush, there is a self-evident link between vv. 17-24 and vv. 29-32. For him, vv. 17-24 are an extended analogy which have little or nothing to do with concrete social matters in Corinth. Vv. 17-24 articulate the principle of remaining, and vv. 29-32 provide additional

attempt of some of the Corinthians to live "as if not" a part of
the world has apparently already caused confusion in the
congregation—so much confusion that Paul has had to address
it in 1 Corinthians 5:9-13. It stands to reason that a similar
confusion would be engendered among the Corinthians by
means of these ὡς μή statements. For ancient Christian
converts enmeshed in the institutions and mores of a bustling
Greco-Roman city such as Corinth, what were the practical
implications of the impractical suggestion to live "as if not" in
the world?

Although we have not yet offered a full-blown, systematic
exegesis of vv. 17-24, the plain[64] sense of those verses is "remain
as you are." In three different ways Paul says this (vv. 17, 20, 24).
How does one remain as one is but still live as if not married, or
how does one live as if not crying or as if not invested in the
world? The commands that Paul gives in vv. 17-24 vis-à-vis
those given in vv. 25-31 do not necessarily complement one
another. The rationale Paul gives for the Corinthians living "as
if not" comes in v. 32. He writes, "I want you to be free of
anxiety" (θέλω δὲ ὑμᾶς ἀμερίμνους εἶναι). Then, he contends
that those who are married are, of necessity, beset with the
cares of how they should please their spouses. Such a person,
Paul believes, is divided (καὶ μεμέρισται. v. 34). Why is it

---

rationale concerning how and why worldly status should be minimized
in light of the things of the Lord. See Wimbush, 14, 69-71. That vv. 17-24
and vv. 29-32 are so clearly linked for Wimbush may result from the fact
that he attempts to reduce the complexities of 1 Corinthians 7 to one
main issue. He writes, "Paul argues throughout chapter seven that one's
condition or status in the world has no power to affect for good or ill
status with God." But is this really what Paul argues? In chapter seven
Paul seems to suggest that there are certain states and conditions (e.g.,
πορνεία 7:2, and δουλεία, "do not become slaves of humans" 7:23),
which are detrimental. In light of this, Paul does not always enjoin the
Corinthians to remain as they are, but in some instances, encourages
them to make changes if changes will prevent them from falling into
detrimental states. Of course, Paul's instructions concerning changes in
marital status seem somewhat clearer than his instructions concerning
slavery.
[64]The use of words such as "plain" and "clear" becomes
increasingly more ironic the further we investigate 1 Corinthians 7.

important for Paul that the Christian believer be free of the cares of the world or be undivided? Is such a believer less of an asset to the ἐκκλησία? In an earlier chapter (and in a different context), Paul chided the Corinthians for their extreme behavior that resulted from their misunderstanding of his instructions.[65] Why should the Corinthians now believe that such extreme behavior is useful?

Paul says in v. 35 that his instructions have been for the benefit of the Corinthians and that he does not want to lay any restraint upon them. Paul's detailed response to the Corinthians' letter may be a subtle indicator that he *does* want to lay upon them the "restraint" of his views and that he hopes that his views are taken seriously and heeded.[66] The ultimate goals of these suggestions made for the Corinthians' benefit are said to be good order and their undivided devotion to the Lord (ἀλλὰ πρὸς τὸ εὔσχημον καὶ εὐπάρεδρον τῷ κυρίῳ ἀπερισπάστως).

Even in this section (vv. 29-35), Paul's attempt to create space for his opinion is most evident. Is he merely answering the practical questions posed to him and then elaborating upon them, or is he using this practical moment as a way of suggesting that his opinion is one that should be taken seriously?

---

[65] 1 Corinthians 5:9.

[66] Concerning the rhetorical situation of this letter, Elisabeth Schüssler Fiorenza writes, "In 1 Corinthians *stasis* seems to be understood best as *status translationis* that is given when the speaker's/writer's *auctoritas* or jurisdiction to address or settle the issue at hand is in doubt and needs to be established." See Schüssler Fiorenza, "Rhetorical Situation and Historical Reconstruction in 1 Corinthians," *New Testament Studies* 33 (1987): 394. For other investigations of the role of rhetoric in Pauline (and specifically 1 Corinthians) exegesis, see, for example, W. Wuellner, "Greek Rhetoric and Pauline Argumentation" in *Early Christian Literature and the Classical Intellectual Tradition: In Honorem Robert M. Grant*, ed. W. R. Schoedel and R. L. Wilken (Paris: Editions Beauchesne, 1979), 177-188; Wire, *The Corinthian Women Prophets*; Mitchell, *Paul and the Rhetoric of Reconciliation*; Ben Witherington, *Conflict & Community in Corinth: A Socio-Rhetorical Commentary on 1 and 2 Corinthians* (Grand Rapids: William B. Eerdmans, 1995).

The force of the argument and the function of chapter seven upon ever closer inspection are not readily clear.

vv. 36-40: Advice concerning One's Betrothed and Remarriage

Ambiguity is also a hallmark of vv. 36-38. The first difficulty the exegete encounters is precisely how to render the verses. One may translate them, "If anyone thinks that he behaves improperly towards *his betrothed* (τὴν παρθένον αὐτοῦ), and if passion is strong (ἐὰν ᾖ ὑπέρακμος), and it has to be thus, let him do as he wishes; he does not sin; let them marry." Or without much difficulty these verses could also be rendered, "If anyone thinks that he behaves improperly towards his *unmarried daughter*, when she is past her bloom (ἐὰν ᾖ ὑπέρακμος),[67] and it has to be thus, let him do as he wishes; he does not sin; let them (i.e., the daughter and her suitor) marry."[68]

In v. 38 Paul gives a directive that is similar to previous ones in the chapter. He suggests that those who must marry do not sin if they wed. Paul, however, reiterates that though such behavior is permissible, there is a more preferred course of action. Consequently, in v. 38 Paul remarks, "So that he who marries[69] his betrothed does well, but he who refrains from marriage[70] will do better" (ὥστε καὶ ὁ γαμίζων τὴν ἑαυτοῦ παρθένον καλῶς ποιεῖ καὶ ὁ μὴ γαμίζων κρεῖσσον ποιήσει).

---

[67]Dale Martin argues that if the phrase ἐὰν ᾖ ὑπέρακμος refers to the unmarried woman and not her male suitor, it also carries connotations of (the dangers of) inordinate passion. That is, the longer a woman delayed the fulfilling of her sexual desires the more likely it was that she would fall prey to πορνεία. For a fascinating discussion of the role of (ancient and contemporary) sexual ideology in the interpretation of 1 Corinthians 7:36-38, see Dale Martin, *The Corinthian Body* (New Haven: Yale University Press, 1995), 218-228.

[68]The *New Revised Standard Version* translation does not even acknowledge the lexical difficulty of τὴν παρθένον αὐτοῦ in v. 36. This is a classic example of rendering the ambiguous as clear.

[69]Another lexical riddle is how to translate γαμίζων. It could refer to the father who is giving his daughter in marriage to another. Or it could refer to the male suitor who is being married.

[70]See note 69.

Paul concludes this discussion with a word about a Christian woman's right to remarry upon the death of her husband. She is supposed to remarry only in the Lord. This phrase "in the Lord" (ἐν κυρίῳ) can possess several nuances, and thus is ambiguous.[71] It could mean that if this woman remarries, her husband should be a Christian. However, when Paul uses such phrases as "in the Lord" or "in Christ," he seems to suggest that believers are to live in this world under the ruling authority of Christ. Even if a Christian woman married a non-Christian man,[72] she could still be marrying "in the Lord" as long as she realized that she was under the ultimate Lordship of Christ. Although we may not be able to ascertain the particular nuance of the phrase "in the Lord" in v. 39, the indisputable point is that Paul permits such remarriage. After granting this allowance, Paul, nevertheless, contends that if a woman remains unmarried, she is happier than if she remarries.

Paul concludes the chapter by declaring, "And I think that I have the Spirit of God" (δοκῶ δὲ κἀγὼ πνεῦμα θεοῦ ἔχειν). Yet, his claim to have the Spirit is certainly not strengthened by his choice of the rather weak verb δοκέω which could easily be rendered, "I suppose." In light of the complexity and ambiguity of the entire chapter, it is fitting that Paul ends the chapter with the less than clear declaration, "I *suppose* I have the Spirit of God."

We began this exploration of chapter seven because the first two words in v. 17 εἰ μή warranted it. In order to determine if vv. 17-24 complement and restate the preceding material or represent a digression from it, one needs to establish the parameters and thrust of the argument. More traditional approaches to this passage have suggested that Paul is merely responding to questions posed to him by some in the Corinthian

---

[71]I will discuss the phrases "in Christ" and "in the Lord" more fully in chapter two.

[72]One should note that in 1 Corinthians 7:12-16 Paul does not seem particularly bothered by "mixed marriages." He becomes concerned when disharmony threatens to upset such marriages. See above my discussion of vv. 12-16.

congregation—questions having to do with marital and sexual relations. In the reckoning of more traditional approaches, the main point of the argument concerns Paul's preference for celibacy.

Yet, as I have attempted to show, the exegetical evidence can support other (compelling) ways of rendering the text. The initial attempt to sort out the ambiguities in vv. 17-24 is complex because one cannot state clearly what the force of the argument is in 1 Corinthians 7. Perhaps, in this instance, the larger context of the chapter will become clear once we tunnel more deeply into vv. 17-24.

A CLOSER READING OF VV. 17-24

Textual Analysis

Before proceeding with an in-depth investigation of vv. 17-24, a lexical analysis of the passage will prove helpful. First, I will display the passage in Greek:

7:17 Εἰ μὴ **ἑκάστῳ** ὡς ἐμέρισεν ὁ κύριος, **ἕκαστον** ὡς **κέκληκεν** ὁ θεός, οὕτως περιπατείτω. καὶ οὕτως ἐν ταῖς ἐκκλησίαις πάσαις διατάσσομαι.

7:18 περιτετμημένος τις **ἐκλήθη**, μὴ ἐπισπάσθω· ἐν ἀκροβυστίᾳ **κέκληταί** τις, μὴ περιτεμνέσθω.

7:19 ἡ περιτομὴ οὐδέν ἐστιν καὶ ἡ ἀκροβυστία οὐδέν ἐστιν, ἀλλὰ τήρησις ἐντολῶν θεοῦ.

7:20 **ἕκαστος** ἐν τῇ **κλήσει ᾗ ἐκλήθη**, ἐν ταύτῃ **μενέτω**.

7:21 δοῦλος **ἐκλήθης,** μή σοι μελέτω· ἀλλ᾽ εἰ καὶ δύνασαι ἐλεύθερος γενέσθαι, μᾶλλον χρῆσαι.

7:22 ὁ γὰρ ἐν κυρίῳ **κληθεὶς** δοῦλος ἀπελεύθερος κυρίου ἐστίν, ὁμοίως ὁ ἐλεύθερος **κληθεὶς** δοῦλός ἐστιν Χριστοῦ.

7:23 τιμῆς ἠγοράσθητε· μὴ γίνεσθε δοῦλοι ἀνθρώπων.

7:24 **ἕκαστος** ἐν ᾧ **ἐκλήθη**, ἀδελφοί, ἐν τούτῳ **μενέτω** παρὰ θεῷ.

Even a quick glance at this passage reveals an obvious repetitive structure. Certain key words (ἕκαστος, καλέω) and a recurring principle (walking or remaining in one's calling)[73] constitute what Gregory Dawes calls a "constant refrain."[74] This note of remaining in one's calling is sounded in v. 17. It is repeated in v. 20 with a slight variation, and it brings the passage to a finale in v. 24, but once again with a slightly different nuance. In this passage the word ἕκαστος in v. 17 and v. 24 functions as parentheses to enclose the passage as a sense-unit, and ἕκαστος occurs in the middle of the sense-unit as well (v. 20).[75]

Walking or remaining in one's calling is vitally important for Paul. He says it three times and in three different ways. In v. 17 he exhorts them to walk in the calling (ἕκαστον ὡς κέκληκεν ὁ θεός, οὕτως περιπατείτω). In v. 20 he tells them to remain in the calling (ἕκαστος ἐν τῇ κλήσει ᾗ ἐκλήθη, ἐν ταύτῃ μενέτω), and in v. 24 he encourages them to remain in the calling before God (ἕκαστος ἐν ᾧ ἐκλήθη, ἀδελφοί, ἐν τούτῳ μενέτω παρὰ θεῷ). If the rhetorical function of vv. 17, 20, and 24 is to convey the principle of walking or remaining in the call, how are the other verses functioning?

If v. 17 states the principle, v. 18 can easily be seen as an illustration or explication of the principle. The circumcised person is admonished not to seek uncircumcision, and the uncircumcised person is admonished not to seek circumcision.

---

[73]These words and this principle have been highlighted in bold type in the Greek text.

[74]Dawes, 684.

[75]For a discussion of repetitive and opening-middle-closing textures in socio-rhetorical criticism, see Vernon Robbins, *Exploring the Texture of Texts: A Guide to Socio-Rhetorical Interpretation* (Valley Forge: Trinity Press, 1996), 8-9, 19-21.

7:18 presents "pictures" of walking in the calling. Given the intriguing and complex history of the relationship between Judaism and Hellenism,[76] Paul could not have chosen a more culturally accessible and (as we shall argue later) ambiguous set of illustrations[77] than circumcision and uncircumcision. If v. 17 states the principle, and v. 18 is the illustration of that principle, v. 19 is the "theoretical" rationale of the principle. With this in mind, vv. 17-19 can be summarized as follows:

v. 17: The Principle: Walking in the calling
v. 18: Illustration of the principle: Circumcision/Uncircumcision
v. 19: The Rationale: Circumcision and uncircumcision are de-emphasized in light of the calling.

---

[76]The literature on the relationship between Judaism and Hellenism is vast, and this question has engaged generations of biblical scholars. Much of the scholarship on this topic in the last twenty years has been in conversation with Martin Hengel's classic *Judaism and Hellenism* (Philadelphia: Fortress Press, 1974). Hengel's basic thesis is that Palestine by the middle of the third century BCE was thoroughly hellenized. On the other side of the debate, there are scholars who contend that the hellenization of Palestine was minor and superficial. A champion of this view is Louis Feldman. See Feldman, "How Much Hellenism in Jewish Palestine?," *Hebrew Union College Annual* 57 (1986): 83-111. Myriad positions between these two exist contending that Judaism was hellenized in lesser or greater degrees. Carl Holladay maintains that scholars must not approach the subject of Hellenistic religion and culture as if there were only "fundamentally two options: acceptance or rejection of Greek culture." See Holladay, "Jewish Responses to Hellenistic Culture in Early Ptolemaic Egypt" in *Ethnicity in Hellenistic Egypt*, ed. Per Bilde, Troels Engberg-Pedersen, Lise Hannestad, and Jan Zahle (Aarhus: Aarhus University Press, 1992), 145. One of the tasks of chapter three of this dissertation will be an investigation of literary evidence concerning circumcision. This evidence provides an entree to the larger question of social identity and social ambiguity in the first century CE Greco-Roman world.

[77]By referring to v. 18 as an illustration, I am *not* implying that circumcision and uncircumcision are not actual concerns for Paul and those in the Corinthian community. In fact, as my argument develops, I will contend that these "illustrations" in v. 18 (and vv. 21-23) might indeed be *concrete* concerns in the Corinthian ἐκκλησία.

In vv. 20-23 we see a similar pattern. In v. 20 Paul reiterates the principle. This time he uses the verb μένω instead of the verb περιπατέω. He exhorts them to *remain* in the calling. In vv. 21-22 Paul chooses slavery to illustrate the principle. As in the case of circumcision, Paul could not have chosen a more compelling and slippery illustration than slavery. According to Orlando Patterson, "Rome evolved the most complex slave system of all the peoples of the premodern world."[78] Accompanying the complexity of Greco-Roman slavery was a host of ambiguous legal, political, and philosophical[79] realities.

Undoubtedly, circumcision and slavery, two phenomena directly related to issues of social identity, could serve as telling examples of Paul's principle of remaining. Yet, in a Greco-Roman culture, which was thoroughly hierarchical and socially-stratified, but flexible enough to allow for occasional upward or downward mobility, the meaning of these phenomena was by no means monolithic. By using circumcision and slavery as his examples, Paul, perhaps unwittingly, destined this passage to a lifetime of ambiguity.

In v. 22 Paul develops the slavery illustration. V. 23 appears to function similarly to v. 19 in that it offers some rationale to the principle of remaining. Paul says, "You were bought with a price; do not become slaves of people." As v. 19 de-emphasizes circumcision and uncircumcision, so too, in v. 23 Paul re-configures slavery by suggesting that all are bought with a price. Finally, in v. 24, he reiterates the principle of remaining but adds the notion of doing so "before God." In light of this, vv. 20-24 can be summarized as follows:

v. 20:   The Principle: Remaining in the calling
vv. 21-22: Illustration of the principle: Slavery

---

[78]Orlando Patterson, *Slavery and Social Death: A Comparative Study* (Cambridge, MA: Harvard University Press, 1982), 88.

[79]In many philosophical treatises in the first century CE world, it was a standard topic to explicate what constituted genuine slavery and freedom. See, for example, Epictetus, *Discourses* 4.1.1-5; Dio Chrysostom, *Oration* 14, and Philo, *Every Good Man is Free*.

v. 23:   The Rationale: Slavery is re-configured
                in light of the calling.
v. 24:   The Principle restated

The argumentative structure of vv. 17-24, in the main,
appears simple and straightforward. Some interpreters have
suggested that ascertaining the *meaning* of this passage is as
simple and straightforward as identifying what the structure is.
For example, the meaning of this passage for Gordon Fee is
abundantly self-evident. With enviable interpretive optimism,
Fee writes:

> To make this point [i.e., that one is no better off in one
> social condition than another] Paul illustrates from two
> other kinds of social settings—circumcision and slavery.
> The very lack of urgency in these matters indicates that
> they are not an issue. What is at issue is the Corinthians'
> concern over change of status. The argument is structured
> around the single imperative "remain (walk) as one was
> when called," which both opens the paragraph (v. 17) and
> concludes the two illustrations (vv. 20, 24). . . . *The
> argument is easily traced.*[80]

Two of Fee's statements above almost undercut
themselves. First, he writes that circumcision and slavery were
not concerns. Second, he writes that the issue was change of
status.[81] In the Greco-Roman world, could there be two more
powerful topics with respect to change of status than
circumcision/uncircumcision and slavery/manumission? The

[80]Fee, 307-308 (emphasis added).

[81]For classic discussions about the social status of early Christians,
see Adolf Deissmann, *Light from the Ancient East* (New York: G. H.
Doran, 1927); E. A. Judge, *The Social Pattern of Christian Groups in the
First Century* (London: Tyndale, 1960). For more recent discussions,
particularly as it relates to 1 Corinthians, see, for example, Theissen,
especially 69-143; Wayne A. Meeks, *The First Urban Christians: The
Social World of the Apostle Paul* (New Haven: Yale University Press,
1983), especially 51-73; Dale B. Martin, *Slavery as Salvation: The
Metaphor of Slavery in Pauline Christianity* (New Haven: Yale
University Press, 1990). Also, see Dale Martin, *The Corinthian Body*. In
The Corinthian Body, Martin skillfully brings social and ideological
issues to bear on the exegesis of 1 Corinthians.

possibility may exist that Paul's appeals to circumcision and slavery are not merely examples. These issues may have also been concrete concerns along with marriage and sexual ethics. Paul's appeal to circumcision and slavery cannot be so easily dismissed.

As we have indicated above, the relationship between vv. 1-16 and vv. 17-24 is not at all clear. Moreover, based upon the evidence thus far, one ought not posit so quickly, as has Fee, that there is a continuity between the former and the latter. There is little indication in the text that Paul's jump from a discussion of marriage to a discussion of circumcision and slavery makes sense. At least in Paul's mind, if not in the minds of his hearers, there was some relationship between a discussion of marriage and sexual ethics and of circumcision and slavery. The common argument proffered by some exegetes is that Paul turns his attention to these subjects for illustrative purposes.[82] In order, however, for these appeals to circumcision and slavery to function as (useful) illustrations, they should lend support[83] to the force of the argument (which, as we have demonstrated, is not easily identifiable).

In addition to exploring why Paul would appeal to these social realities (i.e., circumcision and slavery) in the first place, there is another thorn which must be removed: what Paul means when he speaks of the *call of God*. In vv. 17, 20, and 24, Paul advocates walking or remaining in the calling. Several factors underscore the importance of the call of God in this passage: the repetition of words of calling in vv. 17-18, 20-22, and 24; the fact that the idea of calling occurs in the opening, middle, and closing of the passage, and the importance of the notion of the call to

---

[82]This argument appears in several different manifestations. Dawes contends that vv. 17-24 are a rhetorical digression (in the ancient technical sense). See Dawes, 683, 697. Moreover, Bartchy submits that Paul appeals to circumcision and slavery because he has in mind the (baptismal) formula of Galatians 3:28. See Bartchy, 161-172. Few exegetes have given much credence to the fact that Paul, in discussing circumcision and slavery, might have been addressing people in those actual social states.

[83]Of course, illustrations can lend support to an argument by serving as "counter-examples."

the argumentative structure. The questions are, what is the call, and what does it mean to remain in it? To these and other questions we now turn our attention.

The Call of God

The discussion concerning what Paul means when he uses call language in 1 Corinthians has engaged many scholars, and a full rehearsal of the details has been skillfully accomplished by Bartchy.[84] A more thorough discussion of the plausibility of Bartchy's findings will not detain us here. The purpose of this chapter is to lay out in plain view the textual factors that contribute to ambiguity. I am attempting here only to identify factors that create ambiguity for which Paul, the author, is responsible.

I will examine the various uses of call language in 1 Corinthians to see if they shed any light on the uses of this type of language in our pericope.[85] Regardless of what this survey yields, one cannot be sure that even in the same passage Paul holds fast to any one nuance of a word or phrase about calling.[86] Outside of 1 Corinthians 7, the majority of Paul's uses of call language will be found in 1 Corinthians 1.

The first appearance of call language in 1 Corinthians occurs in 1:1. "Paul, *called* (κλητός) apostle of Christ Jesus through the will of God and Sosthenes the brother." In the beginning of his letter, Paul, in typical Greco-Roman fashion,[87] identifies himself by using the verbal adjective κλητός with the prepositional phrase "through the will of God" (διὰ θελήματος θεοῦ). The inclusion of this prepositional phrase indicates that,

---

[84]Bartchy, 132-159.

[85]Bartchy observes that "the verb καλέω dominates the eight verses in this pericope." Bartchy, 134, note 474.

[86]The desire to find in Paul some linguistic and conceptual consistency seems to be more a modern fixation than a concern of Paul's.

[87]For standard treatments of the features of Hellenistic letters, see William G. Doty, *Letters in Primitive Christianity* (Philadelphia: Fortress Press, 1973), and Stanley K. Stowers, *Letter Writing in Greco-Roman Antiquity* (Philadelphia: Westminster Press, 1986).

at least in this instance, the phenomenon of being called is a divine prerogative, an activity initiated by God's will.

In v. 2 Paul, again in good Greco-Roman fashion, identifies the recipients of his letter. "To the church of God in Corinth to those who have been sanctified in Christ Jesus, *called* saints, with all those who in every place *call*[88] upon the name of our Lord Jesus Christ, their (Lord) and our (Lord)" (τῇ ἐκκλησίᾳ τοῦ θεοῦ τῇ οὔσῃ ἐν Κορίνθῳ, ἡγιασμένοις ἐν Χριστῷ Ἰησοῦ, κλητοῖς ἁγίοις, σὺν πᾶσιν τοῖς ἐπικαλουμένοις τὸ ὄνομα τοῦ κυρίου ἡμῶν Ἰησοῦ Χριστοῦ ἐν παντὶ τόπῳ, αὐτῶν καὶ ἡμῶν). In v. 2 the perfect participle "having been sanctified" (ἡγιασμένοις) is passive and could legitimately be called a "divine passive" where God is the unspoken actor. Those in the church of Corinth have been sanctified by God and also called by God. Thus, in vv. 1-2, God *calls* Paul to be an apostle, and God *calls* the Corinthian converts to be saints.

The calling which Paul and the Corinthians have received brings them both into the ἐκκλησία. Both calls originate with God, but each call creates (in Paul's estimation) vastly different social arrangements. Paul's call makes him an apostle. The call of the Corinthians brings them into the ἐκκλησία or makes them Christians. The call does one thing for Paul, and it does another thing for the Corinthian community.[89] For Paul, the call works vertically. It places him atop the hierarchy or, in his words, makes him the father of the congregation.[90] Although there are other leaders in the Corinthian ἐκκλησία, Paul is the apostolic voice in the community. For the Corinthian converts the call works horizontally. It yokes together into a community

---

[88]Paul here uses the verb ἐπικαλέω which connotes prayer. For example, in the LXX see Genesis 13:4 and 21:33. Sometimes, ἐπικαλέω can connote calling out to a deity, especially in times of distress. For example, in the LXX see Job 5:1.

[89]Although Paul uses similar terminology to speak of his call and the call of the Corinthians, it appears that he understands these two callings in different ways. One could argue that Paul views his call as a unique event, one not repeatable in any meaningful way. On the other hand, the call which the Corinthians have received is available to all Christians. I will examine this point more in chapter two.

[90]1 Corinthians 4:15.

people who otherwise might not be together (e.g., Jews *and* Greeks[91]). In other words, the call creates an unusual fellowship.

In 1:9 Paul reflects upon this fellowship created by the call of God. He writes, "God is faithful through whom *you have been called* into the fellowship of his Son Jesus Christ our Lord" (πιστὸς ὁ θεὸς δι' οὗ ἐκλήθητε εἰς κοινωνίαν τοῦ υἱοῦ αὐτοῦ Ἰησοῦ Χριστοῦ τοῦ κυρίου ἡμῶν). In a way very similar to v. 2, Paul contends in v. 9 that the call of God is the mechanism which creates the church. The church in v. 9 is understood as those who partake in the fellowship of Jesus Christ.

In v. 9 Paul uses the verb καλέω in the aorist passive. Thus, the actual point of calling occurred in the past (i.e., they have been called). Yet, the reality of the fellowship of Christ (κοινωνία) should be an on-going reality. The fact that there are schisms (or at least Paul perceives that there are schisms) is ironic and, in Paul's estimation, unacceptable behavior for those who have been initiated into the κοινωνίαν τοῦ υἱοῦ αὐτοῦ Ἰησοῦ Χριστοῦ τοῦ κυρίου ἡμῶν.

The Corinthians' call occurred in the past. Paul's expectation, however, that their call is supposed to have enduring effects in the present is highlighted by his pointed question in 1 Corinthians 1:13, "Is Christ divided" (μεμέρισται ὁ Χριστός;)? The answer to this question should be no.[92] "Christ" should not be divided since the call of God creates fellowship in Christ. Yet, as far as Paul is concerned, the answer, in light of what he perceives to be the Corinthians' problematic behavior, is a disturbing "yes." In Corinth, Christ is divided. Such division is a distortion of the call.

---

[91] 1 Corinthians 1:24. Also, see my discussion below.

[92] This question, which is full of irony, is part of Paul's rhetorical technique. For a concise introduction to the importance of rhetoric in the Greco-Roman world and its influence on New Testament writings, see Burton L. Mack, *Rhetoric and the New Testament* (Minneapolis: Fortress Press, 1990). For more detailed insight on the ancient rhetorical uses of various kinds of questions, see Ronald F. Hock and Edward N. O'Neil, eds., *The Chreia in Ancient Rhetoric*, vol. 1 (Atlanta: Scholars Press, 1986), 84-87.

My analysis of vv. 2 and 9 reveals that the call of God is a divine initiative, occurring (for each believer) at some time in the past, which creates Christian fellowship—a fellowship which should have enduring present effects. The call of God creates a present reality, the ἐκκλησία. The saints are those who have been ushered into fellowship. Paul seems to be saying similar, if not the same, things in 1 Corinthians 1:2 and 1:9.

Thus far, all the uses of call language presuppose that the calling is done by God. One legitimately can raise a very important question. Although the call is a divine prerogative, does it involve any human agency? Without going too far afield, one can surmise that Paul would contend that the divine call which led to his being an apostle had little or nothing to do with human agency. In fact, in contradistinction to the Paul of Acts,[93] Paul in Galatians argues that "flesh and blood" played no role in his call. In Galatians 1:15-17 he actually uses the language of "calling." Paul writes:

> But when it pleased the one, who had set me apart from my mother's womb and who *called* me through his grace, to reveal his son in me in order that I might preach him among the Gentiles, I did not confer with flesh and blood, nor did I go up to Jerusalem to those who were apostles before me, but I went away into Arabia, and again I returned to Damascus.

Paul may have doubted that the call that made him an apostle had any agency other than God.[94] One wonders,

---

[93]In Acts there are several places where one sees the role of human agency in the midst of Paul's call. For instance, in Acts 9:17-18 Ananias lays his hand on Paul to relieve him of his blindness. Furthermore, in Acts 9:26-31 Barnabas acts as Paul's sponsor, presents Paul to the apostles, and interprets Paul's experiences on the Damascus road for the apostles. For a discussion of Luke's portrayal of Paul, see Alan Segal, *Paul the Convert: The Apostolate and Apostasy of Saul the Pharisee* (New Haven: Yale University Press, 1990), 3-11.

[94]For a striking parallel of the role of God in calling, see Epictetus, *Discourses* 3.22.1. Responding to a question about the calling of a Cynic philosopher, Epictetus declares, "The man who lays his hand to so great a matter as this [i.e., being a Cynic] without God is hateful to Him, and his wish means nothing else than disgracing himself in public. . . . So it

however, whether Paul understands the call of God that creates the ἐκκλησία to come at all through human agency. Is the call of God to be understood as the actual moment, for instance, that the Corinthians heard the kerygma as proclaimed by Paul or some other Christian herald? Even if Paul construes the Corinthians' call (which creates the ἐκκλησία) to have divine origin, does it come into reality through human agents? Does this call come through Christian apostles and through the proclamation of the Christian gospel?

The call of God creates κοινωνία. But κοινωνία for Paul and the Corinthians is not an abstract idea but a concrete, even corporeal reality. The ἐκκλησία is comprised of actual people with differing beliefs and social status. In fact, much of the interchange and correspondence between Paul and the Corinthians[95] is based upon the difficulties of specifying what it means for real people to have κοινωνία. In light of Paul's desire for κοινωνία among the Corinthians, it is reasonable to construe the call of God as the moment when the Corinthians heard the kerygma and responded to it.[96] Even though the call of God in 1 Corinthians 1 has been portrayed primarily as a divine

---

goes also in this great city, the world; for here also there is a Lord of the mansion [i.e., God] who assigns each and everything its place." Interestingly, in Epictetus's discussion of the calling of the Cynic philosopher, we see two basic ideas. First, the philosopher should not attempt the audacious task of being a Cynic unless he is called by God. Second, Epictetus suggests that God assigns everything and everybody to certain places and duties. When these things and people occupy their assigned places and execute their assigned duties, they are fulfilled and prosperous. Conversely, these things and people will meet ruin when they are in the wrong place.

[95]By Paul's own admission, he has written a previous letter to the Corinthians. See 1 Corinthians 5:9. Moreover, the scholarly debates still wage as to how many letters are contained in 1 and 2 Corinthians. For a useful summary of the partition theories, especially as it relates to 2 Corinthians, see Witherington, 328-333.

[96]In other places in 1 Corinthians, Paul adamantly reminds the Corinthians that their existence is the result of his labor among them. See, for instance, 2:1-4, 3:5-6, 3:10-11, and most pointedly 4:14-16. In 4:14-16, Paul emphatically declares that he "fathered" the Corinthians in Christ.

prerogative, this does not exclude the intervention and assistance of humans. I am suggesting that the call of God in vv. 2 and 9 has divine origins (and perhaps uses human agency). Moreover, the call creates a new, present reality, the ἐκκλησία or κοινωνία.

Call language appears again in 1:22-24. Paul writes, "Since also the Jews seek signs, and the Greeks seek wisdom, but we preach Christ crucified, on the one hand a stumbling block to Jews, and on the other hand foolishness to Greeks. *But to those who are called*, both Jews and Greeks, Christ the power of God and the wisdom of God" (ἐπειδὴ καὶ Ἰουδαῖοι σημεῖα αἰτοῦσιν καὶ Ἕλληνες σοφίαν ζητοῦσιν, ἡμεῖς δὲ κηρύσσομεν Χριστὸν ἐσταυρωμένον, Ἰουδαίοις μὲν σκάνδαλον, ἔθνεσιν δὲ μωρίαν, αὐτοῖς δὲ τοῖς κλητοῖς, Ἰουδαίοις τε καὶ Ἕλλησιν, Χριστὸν θεοῦ δύναμιν καὶ θεοῦ σοφίαν). Again, in 1:24, we encounter the verbal adjective κλητοῖς. In vv. 23-24 Paul distinguishes between those Jews and Greeks who find the proclamation of the crucified Messiah to be scandalous and foolish and those Jews and Greeks who are called. The Jews and Greeks who are called believe in the foolishness of the proclamation that in Christ, both the wisdom and the power of God are manifested(1:24).

In 1:18-25, it would appear that to be called is tantamount to believing the Christian proclamation. In v. 24 we learn quite specifically that the call of God shows no partiality; it gathers people from different ethnic groups. This usage of call language in v. 24 is consistent with the previous usage in chapter one. The call of God creates a present reality which includes both Jews and Greeks.

In 1:26, we encounter call language once more. Paul writes, "For consider your *call*, brothers, that not many were wise according to the flesh, not many were powerful, not many were well-born" (Βλέπετε γὰρ τὴν κλῆσιν ὑμῶν, ἀδελφοί, ὅτι οὐ πολλοὶ σοφοὶ κατὰ σάρκα, οὐ πολλοὶ δυνατοί, οὐ πολλοὶ εὐγενεῖς). In New Testament scholarship, especially those studies employing sociological methods,[97] this verse has been a touchstone with respect to the social status of the Christians in Corinth. Some scholars have argued that 1:26 is no theological truism but is actually a window into the social status of the Corinthian community. For instance, Gerd Theissen remarks, "There can be no doubt about the sociological implications of the language of 1 Cor. 1:26-29."[98] In spite of Theissen's assurance, there has been and continues to be considerable doubt and ambiguity about 1:26.

There is the debate about whether v. 26 should be translated as an indicative or, as Wilhelm Wuellner has argued, as an interrogative.[99] Wuellner contends that if the verse is read as an interrogative, Paul, ironically, is saying that many of the Corinthians *were*, in actuality, wise, powerful, and well-born. Thus, this reading of v. 26 turns the traditional sociological reading on its head.[100]

This on-going interpretive debate, the expansive studies on the influence of rhetoric on Paul's language, and the growing work on biblical intertextuality have made it virtually impossible for any exegete to read 1:26 as straight theology or straight sociology.[101] For instance, in a study of intertextuality,[102] Gail

---

[97]Most notably, see Gerd Theissen, "Social Stratification in the Corinthian Community" in *The Social Setting of Pauline Christianity: Essays on Corinth* (Philadelphia: Fortress Press, 1982), 69-119; Meeks, 51-73.

[98]Theissen, 72.

[99]See Wilhelm Wuellner, "The Sociological Implications of 1 Corinthians 1:26-28 Reconsidered," in *Studia Evangelica* VI, ed. E. A. Livingstone (Berlin: Akademie, 1973), 666-672.

[100]The traditional reading, which treats v. 26 as an indicative, suggests that many of the Corinthians *were not* wise, powerful, and well-born.

[101]Wilhelm Wuellner writes, "Rhetoric is not reducible to sociological or ideological studies, but both are indispensable for rhetoric—also, indeed especially, for the study of the rhetoric of religion." See Wuellner, "Biblical Exegesis in the light of the History and Historicity of Rhetoric and the Nature of the Rhetoric of Religion" in *Rhetoric and the New Testament: Essays from the 1992 Heidelberg Conference*, ed. Stanley E. Porter and Thomas H. Olbricht (Sheffield: Sheffield Academic Press, 1993), 499.

O'Day argues that the language in 1 Corinthians 1:26-31 is a type of haggadic exegesis on Jeremiah 9:22-23. O'Day's study raises once again the question of how much of a role 1 Corinthians 1:26-31 can play in a sociological approach to the Corinthian correspondence.[103] The above mentioned interpretive difficulties should be a caveat to the hasty exegete of 1 Corinthians 1:26-31.

Finally, in light of these difficulties, one is still left with the task of understanding Paul's injunction for the Corinthians to "consider their call." In its previous uses, it appears that the call of God is a divine action which creates a new (apocalyptic) reality.[104] Some exegetes[105] have argued that the use of call language in v. 26 seems to look backwards to the believer's previous social status. In other words, in asking the Corinthians to consider their call, Paul wants them to remember their past social circumstances. Interpretations which equate κλῆσιν in v. 26 with "social status" may not have paid enough attention to an important clue in vv. 27-28.

In those verses Paul writes, "But God chose the foolish things of the world in order to shame the wise, and God chose the weak things of the world in order to shame the strong, and God chose the insignificant and despised things of the world, the things not being, in order to nullify the things that are" (ἀλλὰ τὰ μωρὰ τοῦ κόσμου ἐξελέξατο ὁ θεός, ἵνα καταισχύνῃ τοὺς σοφούς, καὶ τὰ ἀσθενῆ τοῦ κόσμου ἐξελέξατο ὁ θεός, ἵνα καταισχύνῃ τὰ ἰσχυρά, καὶ τὰ ἀγενῆ τοῦ κόσμου καὶ τὰ

---

[102]Gail O'Day, "Jeremiah 9:22-23 and 1 Corinthians 1:26-31: A Study in Intertextuality," *Journal of Biblical Literature* 109 (1990): 259-267.

[103]In her article, O'Day writes, "The issue is not whether v. 26 has sociological content and import. Questions of social status divided the Corinthian community, and Paul's words in v. 26 reflect the complex reality of that social situation." O'Day, 264.

[104]Wolfgang Schrage suggests that in Paul's apocalyptic thought the believer is rescued from the sphere of power represented by the κόσμος and that the believer actually becomes a new creation. See Schrage, "Die Stellung zur Welt bei Paulus, Epiktet, und in der Apokalyptik: Ein Beitrag zu 1 Kor 7, 29-31," *Zeitschrift für Theologie und Kirche* 61 (1964): 126.

[105]See, for example, Fee, 79.

ἐξουθενημένα ἐξελέξατο ὁ θεός, τὰ μὴ ὄντα, ἵνα τὰ ὄντα καταργήσῃ). Paul uses the verb "to choose" (ἐξελέξατο[106]) three times to describe how God calls the ἐκκλησία into being. The proximity of the verb ἐξελέξατο to the word κλῆσιν may indicate that vv. 27-28 are an amplification of v. 26. When Paul asks the Corinthians to consider their call, he is again referring to the *divine* activity which created the ἐκκλησία. The call does not seem to be their former social status. The call is that which creates a new social reality. Thus, the call language in v. 26 appears to function in the same way as it did in vv. 2, 9, and 24.

In the relevant[107] uses of call language outside of 1 Corinthians 7, a theme does emerge. The call of God is a divine action which is perhaps mediated through human agents. On the one hand, the call bestows apostolic authority on Paul, and on the other hand it creates the reality of Christian fellowship and the ἐκκλησία. It seems clear that the call comes from God. What may be unclear for Paul and for the Corinthians is what impact this divine call should have on their existing social realities. A question which confronts Paul and the Corinthians is: In light of this divine call, how are believers to conduct their daily lives?

To Remain or Not to Remain. . . . This Is the Question?

We began the above discussion concerning calling because in vv. 17-24 Paul exhorts the believers to walk or remain in the calling.

---

[106]For a more detailed discussion of this verb, see G. Schrenk, "ἐκλέγομαι" in *Theological Dictionary of the New Testament*, vol. 4 (Grand Rapids: William B. Eerdmans Publishing Company, 1967), 168-192.

[107]Paul does use the verb καλέω in 10:27, but there it appears to bear its ordinary, non-theological meaning "invite." Paul also uses the verb καλέω in 15:9. He writes, "I am the least of the apostles who am not sufficient to be called (καλεῖσθαι) an apostle because I persecuted the church of God." Paul may be using the verb here to mean simply "named." In other words, he would be saying, "I am not sufficient to be *named* an apostle." Or he may be using the verb in a way similar to 1 Corinthians 1:1 where it is understood that the call bestows a certain authority. See the discussion above.

Before we could ascertain what walking or remaining *in* the calling meant, we needed to identify what the calling was. The question before us now is, is Paul advocating a principle of remaining?

In 7:17 Paul writes, "But to each as the Lord has assigned,[108] *each as God has called*, thus let him walk." In v. 17 Paul uses the perfect tense of καλέω.[109] One way of understanding this verb tense is that the κοινωνία created by the *past* call of God is supposed to have continuing effects among believers in the present.

Contrary to the consensus of many exegetes, on contextual[110] and grammatical grounds, there is nothing that *necessarily* dictates that Paul is advocating any "principle of remaining in a social status" in v. 17. Because of the prevalence of the verb μένω in vv. 20 and 24, exegetes traditionally have read that verb back into v. 17,[111] when in reality the verb μένω is not present in v. 17.

The call of God creates a new (apocalyptic) reality—a reality whose salient characteristic, according to v. 16, is *peace*. To walk in the calling might mean to walk in a *new* situation or in a new way, not to remain in an old one.[112] Also, in v. 17 Paul

---

[108]Another source of textual ambiguity is whether or not in v. 17 the two phrases ἑκάστῳ ὡς ἐμέρισεν ὁ κύριος, and ἕκαστον ὡς κέκληκεν ὁ θεός are synonymous. Or is Paul saying different things by means of each phrase? See Conzelmann, 126.

[109]See note two.

[110]In 1 Corinthians 7:1-16, when Paul uses "remain" language (i.e., the verb μένω or a cognate verb or idea) there is always an exception or a concession that he provides. See especially vv. 8-11.

[111]Bartchy, 135.

[112]The verb περιπατέω is a common Pauline verb with the connotation of "conducting one's life." This verb is used over thirty times in Paul's letters. See William F. Orr and James Arthur Walther, *1 Corinthians* (Doubleday: New York, 1976), 215. It is interesting to note that in Romans 6:4 Paul uses the verb περιπατέω precisely in the context of the exhortation to walk in a new way. (In Romans 6:4, Paul writes, "Therefore, we were buried with him through baptism into death, in order that as Christ was raised from the dead through the glory of the father, thus also we should walk in the newness of life.") In Romans 6, the ethical implications of the believer's life in Christ is tantamount to walking in a new manner. Furthermore, in Romans 6:15-23 Paul makes

contends that his command for believers to walk in the calling of God is not esoteric or isolated, but has been given in all his churches.

Paul elaborates in v. 18 on the implications of walking in the call from God. Paul says in v. 18, "If anyone was circumcised when he was called, let him not remove the marks of circumcision. If anyone was called in (the state of) uncircumcision, let him not be circumcised" (περιτετμημένος τις ἐκλήθη, μὴ ἐπισπάσθω· ἐν ἀκροβυστίᾳ κέκληταί τις, μὴ περιτεμνέσθω). Exegetes who have advocated that Paul is arguing for maintaining the social status quo have not paid enough attention to Paul's use of call language in 1 Corinthians 1, which is an important contextual key.

Another way of reconfiguring or rendering 7:18 would be, "Was anyone a *Jew* when he was called, let him not seek to be a *Gentile*. If anyone was a *Gentile* when he was called let him not seek to be a *Jew*."[113] Previously, in the letter, Paul juxtaposed call language and the terms Jew and Greek, most notably in 1:24. In 1:24 Paul argues that the call of God is inclusive of both Jews and Greeks (i.e., Gentiles).

To remove the marks of circumcision or to be circumcised as a condition of the call is an invalidation of the call of God. To take such action would suggest that God could not call one as a Gentile or as a Jew per se. Thus, rather than v. 18 being a simple illustration of staying in one's place or social condition, it could be a justification for or rationale of the radical nature of the call of God. In 7:18 Paul might be exploring the radical nature of the call as well as discussing its practical implications for believers (i.e., whether or not one should change social conditions).

---

liberal (and metaphorical) use of slave language. Sometimes, he uses slave language in a positive connotation. Other times he uses it negatively. Perhaps, Romans 6 might be a useful foil for the ways in which Paul uses slave language in 1 Corinthians 7.

[113]The equation of circumcision with Jewish ethnic status and uncircumcision with Gentile ethnic status will be explored fully in chapter three.

One thing is for sure; changes of social positions are *not condemned*[114] throughout 1 Corinthians 7. What Paul may be condemning is a change of status as a *precondition* for the call, since the call has already happened on a basis ultimately outside of human contingency. The call is a divine prerogative. Also, Paul may be suggesting that change, at least of the sort just mentioned (i.e., changing ethnic identity) is not an inevitable *consequence* of the call.

Change of social status is not a precondition of the call, nor is change a natural consequence of the call. To place such emphasis on social status in relation to the call would grant more of a role to human contingency in the process of calling than seemingly Paul wants to allow. To say that change of status as a precondition of the call is discouraged by Paul is quite another thing from saying that Paul is unilaterally opposed to change. The preponderance of exegetical evidence thus far proves that Paul is not opposed to social change as such.

The fact that change of social status is ἀδιάφορος[115] or is irrelevant *as it relates to the call of God* seems to be emphasized again by Paul in v. 19. He writes, "Circumcision is nothing,[116]

---

[114]See, for instance, 7:9, 7:11, and 7:15. Bartchy rightly remarks, "It was not Paul's intention in 1 Cor. 7 to urge the Christians in Corinth to 'stay as you are' as if there were some Christian value in maintaining the status quo as such." Bartchy, 153.

[115]ἀδιάφορος can be defined as that which does not matter or make a difference. It is that which is neither good nor bad. It was a favorite topic of Stoic philosophers. In another research project, it would be fascinating to explore ways in which Paul in 1 Corinthians 7 is in conversation with Stoic teachings concerning matters which are ἀδιάφορα. Will Deming has shown how Paul's thoughts on marriage and sexual ethics are shaped by Stoic and Cynic debates. It would be useful to investigate how Stoic debates might have influenced Paul's thinking on the role of social change. It is my contention that the discussion about marriage and sexuality in 1 Corinthians 7 may be a means and not an end unto itself. The end is Paul's larger reflection on the relationship between his construal of the ἐκκλησία and other social states and institutions.

[116]There are several occasions in other letters where Paul either redefines circumcision in some way or qualifies and reconfigures its importance. See, for example, Romans 2:25-29, Philippians 3:3, and Galatians 5:2-6.

and uncircumcision is nothing" (ἡ περιτομὴ οὐδέν ἐστιν καὶ ἡ ἀκροβυστία οὐδέν ἐστιν). Paul repeats in v. 19a the basic sentiment in v. 18. If, as it relates to the call, circumcision and uncircumcision are of no importance, then, what does matter as it relates to the call? The answer, according to Paul, is "keeping the commandments of God" (ἀλλὰ[117] τήρησις ἐντολῶν θεοῦ). This elliptical phrase has been a nuisance to interpreters who wanted prematurely to resolve the ambiguity of this passage.[118]

Several issues come immediately to mind. First, this de-emphasis of circumcision seems quite radical from the lips of Paul, a former Pharisee,[119] who by his own admission had followed the law blamelessly and had kept the traditions of the fathers with great zeal.[120] Second, if keeping the commandments is what counts, what commandments does Paul have in mind?

Will Deming contends that this elliptical phrase "keeping the commandments of God" is tantamount to "being a Christian."[121] This suggestion seems very plausible. Deming, however, strains the evidence when he contends that the *one* command that Paul specifically has in mind is Jesus' prohibition against divorce.[122] The quest to find any one command which stands behind ἐντολῶν in v. 19 is almost ruled out on lexical grounds by the omission of the definite article. Generally, in the LXX, when the word ἐντολή is used in the singular or plural to refer to the commandment(s) of God, it is accompanied by the

---

[117]The adversative conjunction ἀλλά implies that Paul is clearly distinguishing what comes after the conjunction (as being important) from that which has come before it.

[118]For a summary of some potential solutions to the ambiguity of v. 19b, see Deming, 169-170.

[119]Philippians 3:5, Acts 23:6, and 26:5. Paul's social identity will be discussed in detail in chapter two.

[120]Galatians 1:13-15.

[121]Deming, 171-172.

[122]Deming suggests this because of the discussion of marriage and sexuality in 7:1-16. Yet, the evidence of this chapter has shown that it is inconclusive as to what the relationship between vv. 1-16 and vv. 17-24 is. Furthermore, even when Paul does have a command from the Lord, we are not sure that he is necessarily beholden to it. See above my discussion of 1 Corinthians 7:10.

definite article.[123] The very fact that Paul does not use the definite article might indicate that he has no definite command in mind.

Therefore, in v. 19 Paul would be saying that circumcision and uncircumcision are irrelevant as preconditions or consequences of the call of God. What *is* relevant, as it relates to the call of God, is being a Christian, which here Paul labels as "keeping the commandments of God." Keeping the commandments of God is tantamount to remaining who one is as a result of the call, namely, a Christian. Paul appears to say the same thing in v. 17 and in v. 19: "Remain who you are, not in terms of social status, but in terms of membership in the ἐκκλησία. Remain who you are as a result of the call, that is, a Christian."

In order to emphasize this message of remaining a Christian, he then repeats himself in v. 20. He says, "Each in the calling in which he was called, in this let him remain" (ἕκαστος ἐν τῇ κλήσει ᾗ ἐκλήθη, ἐν ταύτῃ μενέτω). In other words, Paul is suggesting that to think that a change of status is a precondition for or direct consequence of the call is to misconstrue the call. With respect to the call, change of status is irrelevant. To say that change of status as it relates to the call is irrelevant is not, however, to say that change of status is prohibited, as the entire force of 1 Corinthians 7 implies. It very well could be the difference between the irrelevance of status as it relates to the call and the prohibition of change of status in general that Paul attempts to clarify in 7:21-23.

Ironically, in v. 21 where one would hope to find clarity, one instead finds considerable confusion. A celebrated attempt to dispel the confusion surrounding v. 21 has been made by S. Scott Bartchy.[124] In the main, his study attempts to deal with the

---

[123]See, for example, the LXX of Genesis 26:5; Exodus 12:17; Leviticus 4:13; Numbers 15:22, and Deuteronomy 4:2.

[124]Bartchy criticizes many previous New Testament scholars for making assertions about ancient slavery without themselves engaging in systematic investigations of the actual social phenomenon. In order to correct this mistake, Bartchy spends considerable time discussing manumission practices in Greco-Roman culture, since 1 Corinthians

crux interpretum created by the enigmatic phrase in 1 Corinthians 7:21d μᾶλλον χρῆσαι. Bartchy sets out to offer an interpretation of this elliptical phrase which is grammatically and semantically accurate as well as appropriate to the larger context of 1 Corinthians 7.[125]

Bartchy concludes that no convincing interpretation of 7:21d has yet been offered on the basis of syntax and grammar. This, in turn, has caused exegetes to lay greater stress on the context of the passage for interpretive clues. Bartchy faults interpreters for failing to consider the larger context of Paul's theology or the understanding of calling in Paul's theology and in the theology of the Corinthians.

Bartchy makes an important contribution by insisting that the interpretation of Pauline texts on slavery be done in the light of an actual investigation of the social structures of ancient Greco-Roman slavery. Moreover, he provides significant evidence about the manumission practices in first century Greco-Roman slavery. According to Bartchy, Paul in 7:17-24 is reflecting on statements he had made in the past about the

---

manumission practices in Greco-Roman culture, since 1 Corinthians 7:20-24 ostensibly deals with this aspect of slavery. As a result of his investigation, Bartchy stresses that in actuality the slave had little control over his manumission. The decision rested with the slaveowner, and if the owner decided for economic purposes to manumit his slave, the slave could not refuse the manumission. Bartchy also offers a detailed analysis of the factors that perhaps entered into the owner's decision to manumit slaves. In fact, the majority of slaves were manumitted because it was profitable for the slaveowner to do so. I will explore manumission in more detail in chapter four.

[125]An important issue to be solved is what object will be supplied after the phrase μᾶλλον χρῆσαι. Some in the history of scholarship have supplied the word δουλεία. In this case, Paul would be advocating that slaves who had the opportunity for manumission should rather forego such an opportunity and remain in slavery, knowing all the while, however, that they were "freedmen" in the Lord. Others in the history of scholarship have supplied the word ἐλευθερία in which case Paul would be advocating that slaves who had the opportunity for manumission should avail themselves of it. Bartchy says that generally scholars who have stressed grammatical considerations have preferred the "take freedom" interpretation, and those who have stressed the importance of context have preferred the "use slavery" interpretation. See Bartchy, 20-22.

overcoming of social divisions—statements like the one in
Galatians 3:28.

According to Bartchy, Galatians 3:28 is a fundamental
tenet of Paul's theology of calling and baptism. A scholarly
consensus suggests that this formula ("There is neither Jew nor
Greek, slave nor free, male and female") was a part of the early
Christian baptismal ritual.[126] Paul has incorporated it into his
argument in Galatians because it underscores his belief that in
light of one's entrance into the eschatological community via
God's call and the believer's baptism, certain social identity
markers lose their importance or at least become relatively less
important with respect to one's identity in Christ.

In the case of the Corinthian community, similar issues
have arisen concerning the continuing importance of certain
social arrangements in light of the call of God into the
fellowship of Jesus. Thus, when Paul was confronted with
questions about marital and sexual relations, in his response in 1
Corinthians 7, he also alluded to the Jew/Gentile controversy
about circumcision and to the problem of masters and slaves. In
the formula as it appears in Galatians, all three of these social
relations (male/female, Jew/Gentile, slave/free) are mentioned.

Bartchy seems to suggest that Paul wrote not out of real
concern for the actual slaves that undoubtedly were in the
Corinthian congregation but to illustrate an idea[127] which was

---

[126]For further discussion of how the formula "there is neither. . .
male and female" may have functioned in Pauline and other early
Christian communities, see Wayne A. Meeks, "The Image of the
Androgyne: Some Uses of a Symbol in Earliest Christianity," *History of
Religions* 13 (1973): 165-208.

[127]Bartchy himself is ambiguous as to whether 7:21 is an abstract
illustration or a statement directed to a concrete social situation. Thus,
he chooses the best of both worlds. Bartchy contends that in 7:21ab Paul
is offering an illustration. Paul, however, remembering that actual
slaves were in the Corinthian community, speaks in 7:21cd to those
slaves. Bartchy, 158. I agree with Bartchy that Paul may be clarifying his
notion of calling. Yet, I will suggest in chapters three and four that it
may have been the concrete exigencies surrounding institutions such as
the gymnasium and the synagogue and the "institution" of slavery that
necessitated this clarification from Paul. Thus, it is unlikely that Paul

central to his preaching, an idea which he expressed most succinctly in Galatians 3:28. This passage for Bartchy is a theoretical digression not related primarily to the social concerns (or institutions) in the Corinthian community. Yet, many scholars argue that the other concerns which Paul treats (e.g., eating food in 1 Corinthians 8-10 and spiritual gifts in 1 Corinthians 11-13) are not at all theoretical but the outgrowth of pragmatic issues which are creating problems in the community.

Why is 1 Corinthians 7:17-24 singled out as a theoretical digression having little to do with *social* issues in the community, while the other texts are seen by scholars as windows into the concrete social practices of the Corinthians? Bartchy's contributions are noteworthy, especially his attention to the importance of call language.[128] Yet, his contention that Paul only addresses the real slaves as an afterthought and his suggestion that the circumcision and uncircumcision language is purely illustrative, perhaps, conceal some of the social complexity which informs Paul's rhetoric.[129] Even if Bartchy is

---

begins a "theoretical" discussion of the call and then remembers that some slaves may be listening to him.

[128]With respect to the treatment of call language in this passage, Bartchy's work is superior to the recent treatment of slavery by Harrill. I disagree with Harrill's understanding of call language in this passage. For Harrill, such language means the previous social status of the believer. Part of the inherent ambiguity of this passage may result from ascertaining the impact of one's call upon the various social positions one may occupy. Furthermore, Harrill's study offers no extended reflection about the call of God (which is a salient rhetorical feature in the passage) nor about that social reality which the call creates, the ἐκκλησία. Because of this neglect, Harrill then does not give adequate emphasis to a central theme of vv. 17-24, which is not just social status, but social status *in light of one's membership in the ἐκκλησία*.

[129]In the final analysis, Bartchy supplies τῇ κλήσει as the object of μᾶλλον χρῆσαι. His rendering of 7:21cd is, "If you are able to become free, by all means, live according to your calling." Bartchy also implies that Paul favored manumission if it were offered to slaves. Such a rendering may be closer to the overall import of the passage than interpretations which have Paul proffering a doctrine of maintaining the status quo. Yet, even if one supplies the object τῇ κλήσει, the ambiguity of the verse remains. The question could be raised by slaves and masters, what precisely does it mean to live according to your

correct, and Paul in 7:17-24 is alluding to and filling out Galatians 3:28, the social and rhetorical ambiguities that would have attended circumcision and slavery may have, nevertheless, been perplexing realities in Pauline communities. Persons in Paul's churches may have grappled with the relationship between their divine call and various social practices.

If one assumes that in vv. 21-23 Paul is addressing the issue of concrete slavery, compelling rationales can be offered for the "take freedom" or the "use slavery" interpretation of 7:21d. For the sake of argument,[130] let us take as a given that the object to be supplied after μᾶλλον χρῆσαι should be "take freedom" (τῇ ἐλευθερίᾳ). That is, 1 Corinthians 7:21 would be rendered, " Were you a slave when called? Let it not be a care to you, but if you are able to become free, use it (i.e., freedom) all the more."[131]

The fact that Paul might exhort actual slaves in Corinth to seek freedom does not contravene the tenor of 1 Corinthians 7.

---

calling in light of the concrete circumstance of slavery? Does that necessarily imply manumission, or does that necessarily entail one remaining in slavery?

[130]As suggested earlier, those who have favored the "use slavery" interpretation have often made their arguments on contextual grounds, that is, on the basis that Paul in 1 Corinthians 7 supposedly advocates a socially conservative philosophy of maintaining the status quo. My analysis of the textual evidence has shown that in actuality there is no such philosophy advocated by Paul. 1 Corinthians 7 is a mélange of Paul's preferences, opinions, and concessions. As will be argued in chapter four, Paul may have purposefully intended for his readers to hear both the "take freedom" and the "use slavery" overtones in his ambiguous phrase μᾶλλον χρῆσαι. Proponents of the "use slavery" interpretation who claim that their reading has contextual support have, in effect, rendered the ambiguous as self-evidently clear. 1 Corinthians 7 is far more complex than it appears on the surface. In the following pages of this chapter, I use the "take freedom" interpretation as an example. This interpretation seems to resonate better with Paul's granting of concessions. Yet, as will be evident, even if one decides exclusively on the "take freedom" interpretation, the passage's ambiguity is not overcome.

[131]For a list of previous interpreters who have favored the "take freedom" rendering, see Bartchy, 6-7. For more recent support of the "take freedom" interpretation, see Fee, 317-318.

Paul does not seem opposed to concrete social changes. Instead, as we have argued above, he is, perhaps, opposed to changes when they are viewed as a precondition or an inalienable consequence of the call to be a Christian. If this is what Paul is suggesting, it might help us make some sense of what he is attempting to say in vv. 21-24.

In v. 21ab, Paul says, "Were you a slave when you were called? Let it not be a care to you" (δοῦλος ἐκλήθης, μή σοι μελέτω). In this verse Paul may have been influenced by the Stoic teaching about indifference, which suggested that a state like slavery, though unfortunate, would not ultimately destroy a person. If, as Bartchy has contended, one-third of the Corinthian population consisted of slaves, one wonders if certain persons in the Corinthian ἐκκλησία did feel as if the precarious[132] social institution of slavery[133] *would* ultimately destroy them?

---

[132]In *Slavery as Salvation*, Dale Martin makes a significant contribution to New Testament scholarship by explicating how the metaphor of slavery could have a positive, even soteriological, valence in antiquity. I will discuss Martin in more detail in chapter two. One should also keep in mind that the depictions of Greco-Roman slavery offered by other academic interpreters are not nearly as positive as Martin's. One such depiction is contained in the work of Orlando Patterson. See *Slavery and Social Death*, especially 35-101. Patterson analyzes slave regimes, including the Greco-Roman regime, and explores the rituals of enslavement that have been imposed upon slaves to dislodge them from their previous social ties, thereby creating in them a sense of social death. These rituals include the (re)naming of slaves and the adoption by the slave of the slave owners' religion or of the religion of the state. Furthermore, Patterson implies that, both in antiquity and in modernity, the very word "slavery" could well be a synonym for "social ambiguity." Roman slavery will be discussed more fully in chapter four of this dissertation.

[133]When discussing Paul's views on issues which might be problematic to the sensibilities of (post)modern American interpreters, one must be careful not to superimpose contemporary values and perspectives on Paul. There is always a danger of making Paul look like a contemporary liberation theologian. For an example of a rendering of Paul which unwittingly transforms him into a twentieth century liberation theologian, see Amos Jones, Jr., *Paul's Message of Freedom: What Does It Mean to the Black Church?* (Valley Forge: Judson Press, 1984). For a more critical attempt to grapple with the difficulties of a

What does Paul mean by, "let it not be a care to you?" Is he saying that the slave should not worry about being a slave? I do not think that this is the force of his statement. The key to what Paul means by "let it not be a care to you" is perhaps contained in v. 21a.

In v. 21a Paul juxtaposes two primary concerns, slavery and calling. He writes, "Were you a *slave* when you were *called*?" Then, in v. 21b he continues, ". . . let it not be a care to you." In other words, Paul is *not* saying do not worry about being a slave. On the contrary, he may be saying do not worry about being a slave *with respect to your calling*; this is what should not be a concern to the Christian slave. Perhaps, Paul does not want Christian slaves to become overly preoccupied with their status, when their focus should be upon their call to the ἐκκλησία. Yet, lest Paul's words (i.e., "let it not be a care to you") be mistaken for unadulterated acquiescence to slavery, he attempts to clarify himself in v. 21cd, "But if you are able to become free, use it all the more."

With respect to this interpretation, v. 22 could be understood as Paul's attempt to explain what he means in v. 21 and especially in v. 21b ("let it not be a care to you"). In v. 22 he writes, "For the slave called in the Lord is a freedman of the Lord; likewise the free person called is a slave of Christ" (ὁ γὰρ ἐν κυρίῳ κληθεὶς δοῦλος ἀπελεύθερος κυρίου ἐστίν, ὁμοίως ὁ ἐλεύθερος[134] κληθεὶς δοῦλός ἐστιν Χριστοῦ.). In other words, Paul intends in v. 22 to give insight on what the "it" is behind the third person imperative μελέτω in v. 21.

What should not be of concern to some of the Corinthians is that they were called into Christian fellowship as slaves. Paul is not saying to them that their slave status should not be of concern to them but only that their slave status as it relates to

---

modern appropriation of Paul, see Neil Elliott, *Liberating Paul: The Justice of God and the Politics of the Apostle* (New York: Orbis Books, 1994).

[134]For a discussion of the various connotations of ἐλεύθερος in its Hellenistic and New Testament uses, see Heinrich Schlier, "ἐλεύθερος" in *Theological Dictionary of the New Testament*, vol. 2 (Grand Rapids: William B. Eerdmans Publishing Company, 1964), 487-502.

the call into κοινωνία should not be a concern to them. By the same token, Paul tells the Corinthians that the one who was a free person when called is a slave of Christ. Therefore, v. 22 can be read as Paul's attempt to add nuance to v. 21, and especially to his exhortation μή σοι μελέτω.

If we posit that v. 22 is an attempt to clarify v. 21, and that v. 21 itself is supposedly a clarification or expansion of v. 20, what still is not clear is how Paul envisions slaves becoming freedmen of the Lord and free persons becoming slaves of Christ. In short, v. 22 is a labyrinth of literal and metaphorical pronouncements, and Paul, unfortunately, does not leave the exegete any cords by which to find her way out.

There is no textual reason to doubt that Paul is speaking to slaves in a literal manner in v. 22a. He writes, "For the slave called in the Lord is a freedman of the Lord" (ὁ γὰρ ἐν κυρίῳ κληθεὶς δοῦλος ἀπελεύθερος κυρίου ἐστίν). Yet, if Paul is speaking literally to slaves in v. 22a, even there a metaphor seems to be present. Paul says that the slave is a "freedman of the Lord" (ἀπελεύθερος κυρίου). It would appear that this phrase is metaphorical. No matter how badly a slave might want to be a freedman (i.e., juridically), Paul says that the slave is a freedman *of the Lord*. The obvious question for which there is no ready answer emerges, is the manumission alluded to here factual or fictional?

Then, in v. 22b Paul says, "Likewise the free person called is a slave of Christ" (ὁμοίως ὁ ἐλεύθερος κληθεὶς δοῦλός ἐστιν Χριστοῦ.). The phrase "slave of Christ" (δοῦλος Χριστοῦ) leads us to believe that we are again in the arena of metaphor; for no matter how "true" one's servitude or obedience might be to Christ, such a relationship (i.e., being a slave of Christ) lacks the real, factual stuff (e.g., a corporeal master to whom one owes tangible signs of homage) which constituted ancient slavery, even in its most benevolent manifestations. Thus, even if the interpreter of this passage can articulate an exegetical logic as to the internal relationship among vv. 20-22, one is still left with what appears to be a hopeless riddle of literal and figurative statements juxtaposed one to the other.

This puzzling juxtaposition of the literal and the metaphorical continues even in v. 23. Paul writes, "You were bought with a price; do not become slaves of humans" (τιμῆς ἠγοράσθητε· μὴ γίνεσθε δοῦλοι ἀνθρώπων). In light of both Paul's metaphorical use of δοῦλος Χριστοῦ in v. 22 and of his use of the identical construction τιμῆς ἠγοράσθητε in 1 Corinthians 6:20 (which in that particular context seems to have little, if anything, to do with actual Greco-Roman slavery), the phrase, "you were bought with a price" appears to be a metaphor, obviously rooted in the institution of slavery. This metaphor is depicting the believer's relationship and responsibility to Christ.

Also, the interpreter must sort out whether v. 23b is also metaphorical, or if it has some link to actual Greco-Roman slavery. Paul's exhortation is, "Do not become slaves of people." Contextually, it seems clear that Paul is comparing and contrasting being a δοῦλος Χριστοῦ with being a δοῦλος ἀνθρώπων. We suggested above that δοῦλος Χριστοῦ appeared to be metaphorical. Even if there is some comparison between δοῦλος Χριστοῦ and δοῦλος ἀνθρώπων, one need not understand Paul's prohibition against becoming δοῦλοι ἀνθρώπων as simply metaphorical.

If by means of μᾶλλον χρῆσαι in v. 21, Paul is hinting at concrete manumission, the prohibition μὴ γίνεσθε δοῦλοι ἀνθρώπων could be read, without much effort, very literally. In other words, in spite of Paul's desire for the Corinthians to imitate him, he realizes that some states[135] or positions are detrimental to the well-being of the believer. It is very possible that Paul viewed concrete slavery as such a (detrimental) state. Consequently, he gives the prohibition in v. 23b.

---

[135]In 1 Corinthians 7, some of these states would include πορνεία in v. 1; extended celibacy, even if by mutual agreement, in v. 5; those who "burn" or are unable to exercise self-control in vv. 8-9. And in light of this reading of 7:21-23, Paul would add to that list of detrimental states being a slave of humans in the concrete sense.

Furthermore, taking seriously that Paul has slavery in mind in the concrete sense, one recent interpreter[136] has even argued that behind v. 23 stands the practice of ecclesial manumission, whereby those enslaved in the Corinthian church would have the price of their manumission paid by other members in the congregation. The analysis of this exegetical suggestion is beyond the scope of this chapter,[137] but the suggestion would give new (tangible) meaning to the phrase, "you were bought with a price" in v. 23. Such a suggestion also underscores how difficult it is in these verses to disentangle literal statements from metaphorical ones.

Finally, we come to v. 24 where Paul says, "Each in the calling in which he was called, brothers, in this let him remain before God" (ἕκαστος ἐν ᾧ ἐκλήθη, ἀδελφοί, ἐν τούτῳ μενέτω παρὰ θεῷ). It is virtually impossible to overlook the parallel structure in v. 17 and v. 24. In v. 17, there is ἕκαστον, and v. 24 begins with ἕκαστος. Also, the parallels continue with the use of the verb καλέω and the noun θεός in both verses. Some commentators believe that these parallels in v. 24 are meant to signal the end of a digression.[138]

Identifying the parameters of this pericope by means of linguistic parallels is fairly straightforward. What is open to question is how one renders the relative clause in v. 24 ἐν ᾧ ἐκλήθη. Literally, it could be read, "each in the thing in which he was called." If one attempts to add nuance to this translation, should one render this, "each in the *state* in which he was called," or "each in the *calling* in which he was called"?

In Greek grammar, the relative pronoun ᾧ can be a neuter. According to C. F. D. Moule, there are occasions when "a neuter relative is used where strictly a masculine or feminine might have been expected."[139] The demonstrative pronoun (τούτῳ) which follows the relative clause in v. 24 can also be

---

[136]Allen Callahan, "A Note on 1 Corinthians 7:21," *The Journal of the Interdenominational Theological Center* XVII (1990): 110-114.

[137]This suggestion will be explored more fully in chapter four.

[138]See Dawes, 681-684.

[139]C. F. D. Moule, *An Idiom Book of New Testament Greek* (Cambridge: Cambridge University Press, 1953), 130. Also, see Bartchy, 135.

understood as a neuter. If this neuter relative pronoun (ᾧ) can stand in for a masculine or feminine antecedent, it is possible that κλῆσις is the antecedent. Such a rendering seems to correspond to the general notion of the passage and to the idea expressed in v. 20. Moreover, this rendering avoids the awkward and problematic interpretation "each in the *state* in which he was called. . ." As we demonstrated earlier, the call of God is understood primarily by Paul to be that divine action which creates the ἐκκλησία. The call is not equated with social states; rather, it creates a new social reality and a new identity for the believer. V. 24 may be yet another exhortation for the believer to remain what he is before God as a result of his call, namely, a Christian.

In light of this way of reading v. 24, is Paul attempting to compare and contrast being slaves of *humans* in v. 23 (δοῦλοι ἀνθρώπων) with remaining *before God* in v. 24 (παρὰ θεῷ)? Some exegetes[140] infer that Paul's use of the phrase "before God" is an attempt to redeem, as it were, the (negative) social status in which a believer might find himself, by contending that such a status is noble or at least bearable because it is in the presence of God. The natural corollary of this interpretation is that such a believer then need not seek outward change.

We, however, have demonstrated the dubious nature of interpretations which depict Paul in this passage as the defender of the social status quo. Rather than reading παρὰ θεῷ as the theological justification of maintaining the status quo, is it not possible that Paul, in his reflection on the radical nature of the call of God, ends this discussion in the same manner he began it, namely, talking about God? The call which makes one a believer starts with God and ends with God, and the only real context in which it ultimately has significance is in the presence of God.

If the call of God places one's existence before God, it is not exactly clear what Paul envisions. With the dative case, the preposition παρά usually connotes location. The phrase παρὰ θεῷ occurs frequently in the New Testament,[141] and in most

---

[140]See, for example, Barrett, 172.

[141]See, for example, Matthew 19:26 (and parallels), Luke 1:30, 2:52, Romans 2:11, 2:13, and 1 Corinthians 3:19.

instances it seems to mean something like "in the sphere of God." If Paul's use of the vague phrase παρὰ θεῷ in v. 24 is akin to the notion of "in the sphere of God," he does not explicate how the believer lives in the sphere of God while still being enmeshed in a variety of concrete social relationships. As should be evident, v. 24, in many regards, is as puzzling as other aspects of the passage.

CONCLUSIONS

The relationship of 1 Corinthians 7:17-24 to the rest of chapter seven is not at all clear, and this is partly the case because the argument in chapter seven itself is not clear. Moreover, a closer look at vv. 17-24 has yielded a host of unsolved interpretive problems. Finally, one might ask, is there any relationship between 1 Corinthians 7:17-24 (or chapter seven itself) and the rest of the letter?

A full exploration of this topic is a separate study in itself and thus is far beyond the scope of this dissertation. Nevertheless, I want to make an exegetical suggestion concerning a probable rhetorical function of 1 Corinthians 7:17-24. This suggestion might provide some insight into the relationship between chapter seven and the rest of 1 Corinthians.

In recent rhetorical and ideological studies on 1 Corinthians, exegetes have shown us that what Paul *says* in 1 Corinthians may be a vehicle to arrive at what he *means*. By the same token, the meaning of a Pauline passage may not be what it says but what the passage *does*. In the wake of rhetorical analysis, we can no longer view texts as innocent. Texts (and the authors who pen them) have agendas. They seek to do something. Aristotle reminds us, "Rhetoric then may be defined as the faculty of discovering the possible means of persuasion in reference to any subject whatever."[142] Furthermore, Dale Martin has shown us that one meaning of Paul's use of slave language is to *persuade* lower-status members in the Corinthian congregation that he is their defender, and higher-

---

[142] Aristotle, *Art of Rhetoric* 1.2.

status members that they should be willing to relinquish certain rights. Martin writes, "The final goal of Paul's rhetoric in 1 Corinthians is the unity of the church, a theme that pervades the entire letter."[143]

In another study,[144] Abraham Malherbe argues that in 1 Corinthians 8 and 9 Paul uses the discussion of meat offered to idols to explore the theme of freedom, to influence the behavior of the Corinthian converts, and to add his own peculiar twist to prevailing philosophical (i.e., Stoic) doctrines. Malherbe contends that Paul's argument on freedom runs from 1 Corinthians 8:1 to 11:1. Malherbe's study provides useful evidence that in 1 Corinthians Paul uses an actual social issue affecting the Corinthian congregation (e.g., food offered to idols) as an opportunity to adapt or clarify his kerygma. Just as Paul uses the practical questions posed to him about food offered to idols as the context to reflect on freedom, so too in 1 Corinthians 7, he may be using the practical issues of marriage, sexuality, circumcision, and slavery as the contexts to reflect on the role of change in the ἐκκλησία.

In spite of the many complexities and ambiguities of chapter seven, a general topic appears to hold all of the issues together, that is, *change of status* in light of one's membership in the ἐκκλησία. In the chapter Paul reflects on various kinds of change. For the sake of clarity, one could divide the changes Paul discusses into three broad categories: 1) changes in social status; 2) changes in ethnic status, and 3) changes in religious orientation.

With respect to changes in social status, Paul deals with whether or not married couples should be sexually active or celibate. He also treats whether single persons should marry, whether widows should remarry, how persons in mixed marriages should comport themselves, and how persons who are betrothed to one another should view marriage.

---

[143]Martin, *Slavery as Salvation*, 142.

[144]Abraham J. Malherbe, "Determinism and Free Will in Paul: The Argument of 1 Corinthians 8 and 9" in *Paul in His Hellenistic Context*, ed. Troels Engberg-Pedersen (Minneapolis: Fortress Press, 1995), 231-255.

Furthermore, with respect to social status, Paul offers (ambiguous) advice concerning whether Christian slaves should seek manumission.

Not only does Paul reflect upon social changes, he also reflects upon changes in ethnic identity. By virtue of the Corinthians' accepting the kerygma, they have already engaged in some form of ethnic alteration. No longer are they simply Gentiles or Jews. They are now *Christians*. Their call to the ἐκκλησία may create a new "ethnic" identity. Yet, as we will argue in chapter two, Paul may not have been clear about the relationship between one's previous ethnic identity and the new identity in Christ.

Finally, Paul seems to reflect on changes in spiritual orientation. Regardless of decisions made in the social and ethnic arenas, believers are urged to locate the center of their religious orientation "in the Lord" or in the ἐκκλησία. Whatever else believers do, they must remember that their lives are now being played out in the presence of God (παρὰ θεῷ).

Although the notion of various kinds of change may be a common denominator that (loosely) holds together the chapter, one is hard pressed to find any unifying features in Paul's responses to these changes. On certain occasions, he discourages changes. For example, married persons are urged not to alter the frequency of their sexual relations, and if there must be a period of celibacy, it should be short. On other issues, Paul encourages changes. It is better for single persons to marry than to fall into πορνεία. On still other issues, Paul urges persons to accept things as they are. As long as an unbelieving spouse is content to remain in the marriage with the believing spouse, there should be no change. With respect to ethnic identity, Paul discourages believers from seeking circumcision or uncircumcision, not because such practices are inherently evil, but because such practices are irrelevant in light of the call. As will be shown later, Paul's directions concerning the slave's change of social status are shrouded in ambiguity. Yet, regardless of how one understands Paul's opaque words to slaves, he seems to suggest that all believers have a new patron or a new master, Christ.

The many (and sometimes ambiguous) positions that Paul assumes on the topic of change may reflect that he is still sorting out the concrete implications of what it means to be "in Christ." Of course, for every position that Paul took on various kinds of change, the Corinthians may have taken a different position. As Paul and his congregation attempt to integrate their experience with Christ with various ethnic and social realities, complex issues are emerging—issues which Paul struggles to address. We will better appreciate (if not understand) some of Paul's answers to these issues, especially those in 1 Corinthians 7:17-24, if we take more seriously the social world surrounding the composition and initial reception of our text. An investigation of the wider socio-historical context of the Corinthian community and of the social identity of Paul will be the task of chapter two.

Chapter 2

THE SOCIAL WORLD OF
THE CORINTHIANS AND OF PAUL

INTRODUCTION

In chapter one, I examined the textual features which contribute to the passage's complexity and ambiguity. Scholars of semiotics[1] and practitioners of social scientific criticism[2] have recently reminded exegetes that textual meaning (or in our case textual ambiguity) never exists in isolation.[3] Textual features only have meaning in relation to a social environment. We have investigated the *content* of 1 Corinthians 7, especially vv. 17-24. Now, we must analyze the *context* of 1 Corinthians 7.

We move outward from the text itself to a description and analysis of features in the society and culture from which Paul and the Corinthians would have taken their social and cultural cues. Such an analysis is not a misappropriation of the text but

---

[1]For a recent example of a semiotic exegesis of Pauline letters, see Hendrikus Boers, *The Justification of the Gentiles: Paul's Letters to the Galatians and Romans* (Peabody: Hendrickson Publishers, 1994).

[2]For a succinct, yet very useful introduction to social scientific criticism with an exhaustive bibliography, see John H. Elliott, *What Is Social Scientific Criticism?* (Minneapolis: Fortress Press, 1993). Another helpful synopsis can be found in Carolyn Osiek, *What are they saying about the social setting of the New Testament?* (New York: Paulist Press, 1992).

[3]Explaining the methodological underpinnings of his socio-rhetorical criticism, Vernon K. Robbins writes, "Underlying the method is a presupposition that words themselves work in complex ways to communicate meanings that we only partially understand. It [socio-rhetorical criticism] also presupposes that meanings themselves have their meanings by their relation to other meanings." See Robbins, *Exploring the Texture of Texts*, 4.

rather an acknowledgment of the social nature of texts. John Elliott remarks:

> Texts are meaningful social discourses in either oral or written forms. Meaningful social discourse presumes a shared system of signification. Both the capacity of a text to serve as a medium of communication and the meanings communicated are determined by the conventions and constraints of the social and cultural systems in which the text and the communicators (senders and receivers) are based.[4]

In light of the social and cultural nature of texts and in light of the importance of analyzing social environments,[5] two questions arise: What are the social and cultural features which are operative in 1 Corinthians 7:17-24, and how do they contribute to the complexity and ambiguity of the passage?

These questions must be further delineated. What are the social and cultural features extrinsic to the text (i.e., those features that exercise influence on aspects of the text but do not appear explicitly in the texts)? And what are the social and cultural features embedded in the text itself? In short, a principal task of this chapter is to identify and analyze the social location and situation of 1 Corinthians 7:17-24.[6]

---

[4]Elliott, *What Is Social Scientific Criticism?*, 49-50.

[5]For a discussion of the importance of socio-linguistic worlds in sociological and rhetorical exegesis, see Stephen M. Pogoloff, *Logos and Sophia: The Rhetorical Situation of 1 Corinthians* (Atlanta: Scholars Press, 1992), 26-35.

[6]Any social description and analysis of an ancient text is heuristic, indirect, and hypothetical. It is heuristic in that such an investigation is designed to provide additional, plausible frameworks in which to understand this material. It is indirect in that unlike modern sociologists who analyze the group dynamics of living people, "sociologists" of New Testament texts must work with traces of past activity recorded in static, ancient documents. It is hypothetical in that it is impossible to specify with absolute accuracy that all people in a given social location thought alike or subscribed to the same or even similar ideologies. Discussing the challenges of identifying social location, Vernon Robbins remarks, "Tracing correlations between thought and social context, however, is a notoriously difficult task in the sociology of knowledge. We can never assume that all persons in a given context

THE SOCIAL LOCATION

In chapter one, we demonstrated how ambiguity abounds in this text when its multiple features are not isolated from one another and treated as self-evident. We explored the textual features in their rich complexity. Similarly, in this chapter, we will endeavor to honor the complexity of first century CE social life and social identity.

Of the many factors that combined with and played off one another to create social identity in the first century Mediterranean world, two factors occupy a prominent place in 1 Corinthians 7:17-24: ethnicity and social status. In this chapter, we will be content to offer descriptions of these social factors, and in subsequent chapters, we will incorporate these descriptions into an exegetical analysis. The question that occupies us now is, what constituted ethnic identity and social status in the first century Mediterranean world?

The Corinthians

Corinth, by any estimation, was one of the most important urban centers of the Greco-Roman world.[7] Much of its importance stemmed from its ideal geographical location on the

---

thought alike. Nor is there any necessary causality linking context and ideas. It is much more likely that a range of ideas will appear as plausible alternatives to people who share a given social location." See Robbins, "The Social Location of the Implied Author of Luke-Acts" in *The Social World of Luke-Acts: Models for Interpretation*, ed. J. H. Neyrey (Peabody: Hendrickson Publishers, 1991), 306.

[7]Strabo, *Geography* 8.6.20-23. Strabo, the famous ancient geographer whose dates are approximately 64-63 BCE to 21-22 CE, passed through Corinth in 44 BCE and actually visited the city in 29 BCE. For a useful anthology of ancient authors who comment on Corinth, see Jerome Murphy-O'Connor, *St. Paul's Corinth: Texts and Archaeology* (Wilmington: Michael Glazier, Inc., 1983). For more succinct studies on the city of Corinth and what archeology has revealed to modern exegetes, also see, Murphy O'Connor, "The Corinth that Saint Paul Saw," *Biblical Archaeologist* 47 (1984): 147-159, and Murphy-O'Connor, "Corinth" in *Anchor Bible Dictionary*, vol. I. (1992), 1134-1139.

isthmus that formed the bridge between the mainland of Greece and the southern peninsula, the Peloponnesus. This prime location made Corinth an important post for internal trading within Greece, and it was also a crossroads for commerce moving between Rome and the east.

In its history, Corinth had at least two distinct phases. Until the middle of the second century BCE, it had flourished as a Greek city, but in 146 BCE it was sacked by the Roman military led by the consul Lucius Mummius. Lying in ruins for over a century,[8] Corinth was rebuilt by Julius Caesar in 44 BCE as a Roman province. Emphasizing the "Romanization" of this Greek city, Ben Witherington writes, "The architecture would take on a Roman look. . . . It would be ruled by a Roman form of government with Roman officials and. . . The city would be colonized by Romans. . . . Roman Corinth was certainly never simply a Hellenistic city."[9] This issue concerning whether Corinth was Hellenistic or Roman positions us nicely for a serious discussion of ethnicity, one of the factors of social location and identity.

Ethnic Composition

Ethnicity Re-Examined

A category or feature of the social location of any New Testament writing or writer, which in the last century has gone

---

[8]Richard E. Oster has cautioned New Testament scholars about overemphasizing the degree to which Corinth lay in ruins in the period between 146 BCE and 44 BCE. See Oster, "Use, Misuse and Neglect of Archaeological Evidence in Some Modern Works on 1 Corinthians: (1 Cor 7,1-5; 8; 10; 11,2-16; 12,14-26)," *Zeitschrift für die Neutestamentliche Wissenschaft* 83 (1992): 52-73. Interestingly and ironically, Oster strongly criticizes the *religionsgeschichtliche Schule* (RGS) for casting its net too widely in its search for parallels to and backgrounds for Pauline statements. In this article, Oster seems to commit the same error, the only difference being that he is interested in archeological parallels and the RGS was more interested in literary parallels.

[9]Witherington, *Conflict & Community*, 6-7.

unnoticed at worst and underdeveloped at best, is the concept of ethnicity. Ferdinand Christian Baur,[10] the founder of the Tübingen School and the pioneer of "historical theology," in the nineteenth century argued that the prime mover in the development of early Christianity was the controversy between Jews and Gentiles or more specifically the controversy between Jewish Christianity and Gentile Christianity.[11]

As history would show, Baur's insights, though seminal and in many regards correct, were too narrowly configured and thus too myopic. In his emphasis on Jewish Christianity and Gentile Christianity, he was more interested in the *theological* differences of each version of Christianity than he was in the question of ethnicity per se. Moreover, Baur had not accounted for other factors that had influenced both the shape and the direction of early Christianity.[12]

Other scholars, in their attempt to modify or correct Baur's overemphasis, recognized the ethnic distinctions between Jewish and Gentile Christianity, but the ethnic distinction for these scholars was always a means to an end and never an end

---

[10]For succinct treatments of the place and impact of F. C. Baur on the history of New Testament interpretation, see William Baird, *History of New Testament Research: From Deism to Tübingen*, vol. 1 (Minneapolis: Fortress Press, 1992), 258-269; Hendrikus Boers, *What is New Testament Theology?* (Philadelphia: Fortress Press, 1979), 39-42; Robert Morgan with John Barton, *Biblical Interpretation* (Oxford: Oxford University Press, 1988), 65-76; Robert Morgan, "New Testament Theology" in *Biblical Theology: Problems and Perspectives*, ed. Steven J. Kraftchick, Charles D. Myers, Jr. and Ben C. Ollenburger (Nashville: Abingdon Press, 1995), 104-130; Peter Hodgson, *The Formation of Historical Theology* (New York: Harper & Row Publishers, 1966).

[11]Commenting on the growing schism between Jewish and Gentile Christianity in the first century, Baur wrote, "They [Jewish Christians] could not look on with indifference when they saw a Gentile Christian church arising over against the church of Jerusalem in utter disregard of the ordinances and privilege of Jerusalem, and yet putting forth a claim to equal place and dignity with themselves." See Baur, *The Church History of the First Three Centuries* (London: William & Norgate, 1878), 51-52.

[12]Robert Morgan remarks, "By making this conflict [between Paul and some Jewish Christians] the key to the whole development [of early Christianity], Baur failed to give due weight to other factors." See Morgan, *Biblical Interpretation*, 72.

unto itself. That is, the ethnic distinction between Jewish and Gentile Christianity was in service of a discussion of history.[13]

The primary agenda of these scholars was not an analysis of the complex ways that these ancient groups defined themselves and others but rather a historical construct of the stages and developments of primitive Christianity. For example, to the degree that the *religionsgeschictliche Schule* was interested in exploring and tracing the development of Christianity as a living religion, it failed to account fully for the concept and role of ethnicity.

In the current milieu of New Testament scholarship, where interdisciplinary approaches to exegesis are gaining credibility and wider application,[14] insights from social anthropologists and sociologists have awakened New Testament scholars to the importance of ethnicity.[15] Previous New Testament scholars may have avoided the concept of ethnicity because it is notoriously difficult to define. It is mainly the difficulty of defining ethnicity and of distinguishing ethnic groups and boundaries in the New Testament social matrix which contributes to the thick social and cultural texture of the Corinthian correspondence, in general, and of our passage, in particular. Before engaging, the topic of ethnicity any further, however, a brief discussion differentiating between older approaches to ethnicity and newer, emerging approaches will be helpful.

---

[13]For example, Wilhelm Bousset, a member of the *religionsgeschictliche Schule*, in his classic work *Kyrios Christos*, traced the changes that the religion of Jesus and of Palestinian Christianity underwent as it moved into new geographic and ethnic boundaries. Yet, this investigation was not so interested in issues of ethnicity per se, as it was in tracing historical developments. The title of Bousset's book is telling: *A History of the Belief in Christ from the beginning of Christianity to Irenaeus*, trans. John E. Steely (Nashville: Abingdon Press, 1979) [emphasis mine].

[14]Vernon Robbins, *The Tapestry of Early Christian Discourse: Rhetoric, Society and Ideology* (New York: Routledge, 1996), 15-16.

[15]A testimony to this awakening is the scholarly conference in Denmark (1990) which produced the book *Ethnicity in Hellenistic Egypt*, ed. Per Bilde et. al. (Aarhus: Aarhus University Press, 1992).

Typically, in more dated discussions of the role and import of ethnicity, the approach could be labeled as "essentialist." In an essentialist approach, there are thought to be relatively fixed, sometimes observable qualities or characteristics that define one ethnic group over against another. Such an approach is designed to locate the "essence" of what it means to belong to a particular ethnic group.

In the wake of the growing realization gained from the social sciences that both group and individual identity is a social construction, the criteria for establishing ethnic boundaries have changed. Social anthropologists are insisting that group and individual identities should be explored on a variety of levels, including the *subjective* evaluations of group members themselves.[16] That is, social anthropology encourages complex, subjective analysis in addition to simple, objective analysis.

A chief architect of this shift in the study of ethnic identity is the Norwegian social anthropologist Fredrik Barth. Barth argues, "The symbolic and social construction of people's realities entail the necessity of comprehending interpersonal events by interpreting them, on many simultaneous levels of meaning and significance, by means of the codes and keys employed in their own culture as well as analyzing them by canons which we can accept as objectively, materially adequate."[17]

In addition to calling for a greater appreciation of complexity in ascertaining ethnic identity, Barth also contends that scholars have not paid enough attention to the construction and maintenance of ethnic boundaries.[18] Boundary maintenance

---

[16]Jonathan Smith contends that the notion of essence is inappropriate for the discussion of group boundaries in religions. Instead of a "monothetic" approach to mapping the boundaries of religious groups, he calls for a more complex, "polythetic" approach. See Smith, "Fences and Neighbors: Some Contours of Early Judaism" in *Imagining Religion: From Babylon to Jonestown* (Chicago: University of Chicago Press, 1982), 1-18.

[17]Fredrik Barth, "Introduction" in *Process and Form in Social Life: Selected Essays of Fredrik Barth*, vol. 1 (London: Routledge & Kegan Paul, 1981), 8.

[18]Fredrik Barth, "Ethnic Groups and Boundaries" in *Process and Form in Social Life*, 198.

among ethnic groups is complicated and problematic. In the social mechanisms of an ethnic group, there are particular roles, functions, and cultural features that lead to the creation of boundaries around the group. Yet, the boundaries created by these roles, functions, and cultural features are neither impervious nor absolute. The cultural features which identify an ethnic group may change according to various circumstances.[19]

In light of the volatile nature of those ethnic boundaries based on cultural features, social anthropologists have looked to another important and overlooked feature of ethnic boundaries, namely, self-identification, or what group members are *saying* about themselves. What individuals and groups say about themselves gives insight into the attitudes of groups members.

Privileging self-identification as a primary criterion of ethnic identity, social anthropologists have discovered that a person in ethnic group "A" may actually adopt cultural features which generally typify ethnic group "B." Yet, this person continues to identify himself as a member of group "A."[20] Ethnicity is as much a function of attitudes[21] expressed in discourse as it is an analysis of observable cultural features.

Thus, there must be a shift from an infatuation with "objective" reports from readers distant in time and space from those being investigated to an attentive investigation to what these (ancient) groups are saying about themselves. The

---

[19]Fredrik Barth remarks, "It is thus inadequate to regard overt institutional forms as constituting *the* cultural features which at any time distinguish an ethnic group—these overt forms are determined by *ecology* as well as by transmitted culture." Barth, "Ethnic Groups and Boundaries," 202 (emphasis mine).

[20]Barth, "Ethnic Groups and Boundaries," 213.

[21]For a succinct and useful treatment of (ancient Jewish) ethnicity from the perspective of cultural constructs and attitudes rather than "ethnic essentialism," see Hayim Lapin, "Locating Ethnicity and Religious Community in Later Roman Palestine" (paper presented at the Annual Meeting of the Society of Biblical Literature in the Constructs of Social and Cultural Worlds of Antiquity Group, San Francisco, CA, November 22-25, 1997). This paper was the preliminary draft of the introduction to *Religious and Ethnic Communities in Later Roman Palestine*, ed., Hayim Lapin (Potomac: University Press of Maryland, 1999).

proponents of this new approach to ethnicity realize the precarious nature of the shift to a focus on attitudes. Yet, in spite of the quantitative and analytical difficulties inherent in this boundary approach to ethnicity, advocates of this approach contend that boundary mechanisms for ethnic groups are expressed frequently, but certainly not exclusively, in words.

Admittedly, this focus on discourse as an ethnic symbolic boundary marker is cyclical. Ethnicity is a part of one's social context, and ethnic groups mark off their "territories" with the symbolic boundaries of language. Language receives its meanings from social context. The circle[22] created between the interaction of language and society,[23] however, is not to be lamented, cannot be avoided, and can enrich our understanding of both text and context.

Working from the assumption that ethnicity is more about attitudes than essential characteristics, Koen Goudriaan in a recent article[24] summarizes the implications of this new approach to ethnicity in six points. These six points will be borne in mind as we progress, and they will enhance our ensuing discussion of the import of ethnicity in first century Corinth. Goudriaan's six points[25] are:

1. "Ethnicity is looked at from the inside."[26]

---

[22]John Elliott maintains, "Analysis of biblical texts requires attention to the research and conclusions regarding their social contexts. These contexts, in turn, are further clarified by the evidence supplied by the texts." Elliott, *What Is Social Scientific Criticism?*, 33.

[23]Vernon Robbins says, "Language always emerges out of particular locations of the body in social, cultural and historical situations. Yet language is also an ingredient that 'makes' these circumstances social, cultural and historical. In other words, language is an integral, constitutive and cognitive feature of human society, culture and history." See Robbins, *Tapestry*, 8.

[24]Koen Goudriaan, "Ethnical Strategies in Graeco-Roman Egypt" in *Ethnicity in Hellenistic Egypt*, ed. Per Bilde et. al. (Aarhus: Aarhus University Press, 1992), 74-99.

[25]Goudriaan's points are in bold type. My clarification of his points are in brackets.

[26]Goudriaan, 75.

[Goudriaan argues that the categories used by insiders to describe themselves and to describe others become normative for ethnic boundaries.]

2. "Ethnicity, as a way of organizing cultural differences, implies that specific features of culture (in the broad sense) are singled out as ethnically significant, while others are neutral."[27]

3. "Ethnicity is an independent dimension of social life."[28]

[Goudriaan contends that the ethnicity of a group can never be reduced to any particular cultural feature of the society. Moreover, it could be said that ethnicity is greater than the sum of various cultural parts.]

4. "Survival of an ethnic identity group, in this view, is not the result of its biological reproduction, but the outcome of a continued interest on the part of its members in maintaining the boundaries."[29]

[In light of this point, Goudriaan introduces the concept of "ethnical strategy" which is the "policy adopted by an individual or a group for applying ethnical categories to themselves and others in a range of different circumstances."[30]]

5. "Ethnicity is a normal feature of social life. It does not automatically entail tension between the ethnic groups. So long as these are in agreement on the roles they have to play in society, they may live peacefully together."[31]

---

[27]Goudriaan, 76. The implications of this second point will be discussed in some detail with respect to circumcision.
[28]Goudriaan, 76.
[29]Goudriaan, 76.
[30]Goudriaan, 76.
[31]Goudriaan, 76. I will discuss below factors which may indicate whether there will be cooperation or conflict between ethnic groups.

6. "This marking off of [ethnic] boundaries is a universal trait of human experience. The way in which it manifests itself may, of course, vary greatly through the ages."[32]

[For Goudriaan, point six is the heuristic *raison d'être* which allows him and other scholars to employ the social category of ethnicity in diachronic analysis. That is, regardless of the culture and time period (be it twentieth century northern European culture or first century Mediterranean culture), groups distinguish themselves from one another ethnically. How groups distinguish themselves may differ, but that this differentiation occurs is a social constant. Thus, whereas the category of ethnicity as discussed above is, in some sense, a modern scholarly construct, the social phenomenon entailed in or meant by this construct will (or did) occur in actual social life, even ancient social life.]

Before leaving this abstract discussion of ethnicity, let us note the important distinction Goudriaan makes between culture and ethnicity. A boundary approach to ethnicity presupposes the presence of cultural features and even allows for the presence of a shared culture between ethnic groups. Since, however, ethnicity emphasizes some features of culture as more or less important than others, it is possible for groups to share the *same culture* yet understand themselves to belong to totally different *ethnic* groups. Goudriaan writes, "It can be seen that for the working of ethnicity the content of the shared culture is largely irrelevant so long as a [ethnic] filter is blocking certain elements from filtering through; these are the cultural traits that serve as boundary makers."[33] This being the case, new light must be shed on the age-old debate concerning the Hellenization of Judaism. If Hellenization was about the spreading of Greek *cultural* institutions and mores, to what degree did Jewish people in the Hellenistic period remain a

---

[32]Goudriaan, 77.
[33]Goudriaan, 77.

distinct *ethnic* identity in spite of sharing, sometimes to a large degree, in Hellenistic *culture*?[34]

Ethnicity Applied to 1 Corinthians

Roman control of Corinth played a decisive role in determining the demographics of the city. As a relatively new Roman colony, Corinth would have been an enormously eclectic place. There may have been a few Greeks there who could have made an ancestral claim to the Corinth before the days of its decimation in 146 BCE.[35] Yet, even for such people, one wonders how persuasive ancestral claims would have been in such a "new" city. At the time of Paul's apostolic activity, hardly anything in this city was more than a hundred years old.[36] Moreover, even though Corinth was geographically in the heart of Greece, the principal language of this colony was Latin, another attestation of Roman influence.

More than likely, Roman Corinth housed a sizable military presence. In addition to the imperial army which was a given in Roman provinces, a host of military veterans would have undoubtedly inhabited Corinth.[37] One of the fringe benefits of Roman military veterans was that they could settle in the

---

[34]Goudriaan argues forcefully that Hellenization was about *culture* not *ethnicity*. See Goudriaan, 77. The implications of the distinction between culture and ethnicity will be explored in my discussion of circumcision in chapter three.

[35]In his *Description of Greece,* Pausanias writes, "Corinth is no longer inhabited by any of the old Corinthians, but by colonists sent out by the Romans." See *Description of Greece* 2.1.2. Although historians and archeologists have relied on Pausanias's reports, one must bear in mind that he visited Corinth around 165 CE, more than a century after Paul was there.

[36]Theissen, *Social Setting,* 99.

[37]Concerning Roman military presence in newly founded colonies, Plutarch writes, "And in the effort to surround himself with men's good will as the fairest and at the same time securest protection, he [Julius Caesar] again courted the people with banquets and distributions of grain, *and his soldiers with newly planted colonies, the most conspicuous of which were Carthage and Corinth.*" See *Life of Caesar* 47.8 (emphasis mine).

coloniae civium romanarum (colonies of Roman citizens)[38] and perhaps receive exemption from taxation. We learn from Strabo that another large portion of the Corinthian population would have consisted of freedmen.[39] Upon their manumission, these freedmen, who hailed from diverse regions throughout the Mediterranean world, fled to Corinth with the hopes of carving out a new existence.

In addition to the ethnic diversity resulting from ancestral Greeks, Roman soldiers, veterans, and freedmen from all over the Mediterranean basin, one must add to this ethnic equation the Jewish population in Corinth. In the history of scholarship on 1 Corinthians, the question concerning the presence or absence of a sizable Jewish population has spawned considerable debate. Archeological evidence has been at the center of the discussion.

Archeologists discovered an epigraphical fragment in Corinth which they have reconstructed as "Synagogue of the Hebrews" ([Συνα]γωγὴ Εβρ[αίων]).[40] Motivated by the possibility that this was the synagogue mentioned in Acts 18, earlier scholars contended that this synagogue was contemporaneous with the Corinthian correspondence. More recent and critical archeological judgments[41] have dated this

---

[38]See Everett Ferguson, *Backgrounds of Early Christianity*, 2d edition (Grand Rapids: William B. Eerdmanns Publishing Company, 1993), 39.

[39]Strabo remarks, "Now after Corinth had remained deserted for a long time, it was restored again, because of its favorable position, by the deified Caesar, who colonized it with people who for the most part belonged to the *freedman class.*" *Geography* 8.6.23 (emphasis mine).

[40]See Inscription 718 in *Corpus of Jewish Inscriptions*, ed., Jean-Baptiste Frey, revised by Baruch Lifshitz (New York: Ktav, 1975), 518.

[41]One indicator of the possible lateness of this fragment is the style of the lettering. See Victor Paul Furnish's informative article, "Corinth in Paul's Time—What Can Archaeology Tell Us?," *Biblical Archaeolgy Review* XV (1988): 14-27. For further information on Diaspora synagogues, see A. T. Kraabel, "The Diaspora Synagogue: Archaeological and Epigraphic Evidence since Sukenik" in *Aufstieg und Niedergang der Römische Welt* (New York: Walther de Gruyeter, 1979), 19.1:479-510; Michael L. White, "The Delos Synagogue Revisited: Recent Fieldwork in the Graeco-Roman Diaspora," *Harvard Theological Review* 80 (1987):

epigraphical fragment as late as the fourth or fifth century CE, thereby rendering it of no consequence as to the presence and size of the Jewish population in Corinth during the time of Paul's apostolate.

Just as the presence of archeological evidence should not be used unilaterally or uncritically to prove the existence of a Jewish community in first century Corinth, Richard Oster cautions historians and exegetes against uncritically disproving such a Jewish community in Corinth because of a lack of epigraphical or archeological remains.[42] Although archeological and epigraphical studies offer no real assistance in this matter, ancient literary texts do fill the gap to a limited degree. Commenting on the various geographical locations to which Jews were sent as a result of the pogrom of Gaius Caligula, Philo remarks that Jewish colonists were sent to "Thessaly, and Boeotia, and Macedonia, and Aetolia, and Attica, and Argos, *and Corinth*, and all the most fertile and wealthiest districts of Peloponnesus."[43]

Other important pieces of literary evidence concerning the Jews in first century Corinth come from the New Testament itself. In Acts 18, Luke records that after Paul left Athens he traveled to Corinth and found there the Jews, Aquila and Priscilla. Because Paul shared with them the tentmaking trade, he resided with them.[44] Luke attempts to account for the

---

133-160; Michael L. White, *Building God's House in the Roman World* (Baltimore: Johns Hopkins University Press, 1990).

[42]Oster, 57. Moreover, John Barclay speaks soberly concerning the dearth of literary or archeological evidence by which to analyze Diaspora Jewish communities. He remarks, "There are, in fact, only five locations in the Mediterranean Diaspora in this period [323 BCE to 117 CE] where our literary and/or archaeological evidence is sufficient for us to describe the Jewish Diaspora in any depth: Egypt, Cyrenaica, the province of Syria, the province of Asia and the city of Rome. Only in these locations can we provide a coherent account of the history of the Jewish communities over an extended period of time, and only here does our literary and non-literary evidence combine to give us a moderately full view of Diaspora life." Barclay, *Jews in the Mediterranean Diaspora*, 10.

[43]Philo, *On the Embassy to Gaius*, 36.281 (emphasis mine).

[44]In assessing the historical dependability of the Lukan evangelist, we must keep in mind Luke's theological *Tendenz*, one of which is to

presence of Aquila and Priscilla and other Jews in Corinth by means of the Edict of Claudius[45] which expelled Jews from Rome.

Also, in Acts 18 the most obvious literary evidence of an active Jewish community in Corinth is the mention of the synagogue. Luke suggests that Paul regularly visited the synagogue in an attempt to win converts. Although it must be analyzed critically, there is literary evidence to support the hypothesis of Jewish presence in Roman Corinth. Even if the case for Jewish presence in Corinth is debatable, first century Corinth can still be seen as an ethnically diverse city.[46]

---

demonstrate that Paul regularly began his apostolic work among the Jews and then turned to the Gentiles upon Jewish rejection or persecution. Nonetheless, Luke's theological tendencies do not preclude him from using history to create verisimilitude. Luke Johnson remarks, "There is, therefore, the stuff of genuine history within Luke's account [of Paul's activity in Corinth]. But his narrative is not itself a critical history. It is an *apologia* for God's action in history, and Luke provides the sort of literary touches required to shape the story in that direction." See Johnson, *The Acts of the Apostles* (Collegeville: Liturgical Press, 1992), 325. One such literary touch which adds historical verisimilitude is Luke's description of Paul, Priscilla, and Aquila as tentmakers. As discussed above, in a city like Corinth which was a crossroads of the ancient world, tents would have been in great demand. Ronald Hock suggests that "Paul's customers were more likely to have been civilians—persons whose occupations entailed much travel, such as the oarsmen who pitched tents for several days while their ship was in port." See Hock, *The Social Context of Paul's Ministry: Tentmaking and Apostleship* (Philadelphia: Fortress Press, 1980), 33-34.

[45]The veracity of the Edict of Claudius is corroborated by the Roman historian Suetonius in his *Life of Claudius* 25.4. Suetonius writes, "Since the Jews constantly made disturbances at the instigation of Chrestus, he expelled them from Rome." Also, papyrological studies have yielded important evidence of Claudius's attempt to deal with the Jews and the Alexandrians in Alexandria. See "The Letter of Claudius to the Alexandrians," in *Corpus Papyrorum Judaicarum*, vol. II, ed. Victor A. Tcherikover and Alexander Fuks (Cambridge, MA: Harvard University Press, 1960), 36-55. I will further discuss "The Letter of Claudius to the Alexandrians" in chapter three.

[46]There is also substantial archeological evidence suggesting the presence of Egyptian cults in Corinth. For example, archeologists have discovered what appears to be a sanctuary of Isis. For a detailed study of

Sociological and social scientific models attempt to identify and analyze the social and cultural features which are embedded in the text. Gerd Theissen has helped an entire generation of New Testament exegetes see that textual features in 1 Corinthians, heretofore investigated only theologically, actually contained valuable sociological insights concerning status or class divisions in the Corinthian congregation.[47] As mentioned in chapter one, there has been no lack of discussion about the sociological import of 1 Corinthians 1:26-28. By placing the exegetical spotlight on 1:26-28, some other important sociological features embedded in 1 Corinthians 1, suggestive of a Jewish presence in Corinth, have remained unilluminated.

For instance, as Paul explicates his theology of the cross, he writes in 1:22, "For Jews demand signs and Greeks seek wisdom, but we preach Christ crucified, a stumblingblock to Jews and folly to Gentiles, but to those who are called, both Jews and Greeks, Christ the power of God and the wisdom of God." In a recent article,[48] Christopher Stanley has argued that exegetes often miss the *ethnic* implications of Paul's use of the terms "Jews and Greeks." He writes, "Christian commentators have routinely overlooked the ethnic implications of such juxtaposed references to 'Jews' and 'Greeks' in early Christian literature due to their theological (and ahistorical) assumption that 'Greek' means the same as 'Gentile' wherever the term occurs."[49]

In 1 Corinthians 1:22-24, at one point Paul does use the term Gentile (ἔθνεσιν in v. 23) which, according to Stanley, is a Jewish ethnocentric term.[50] Paul, however, refers twice to the

---

this evidence, see D. E. Smith, "The Egyptian Cults at Corinth," *Harvard Theological Review* 70 (1977): 201-231.

[47]See, for example, Theissen, *Social Setting*, 145-174.

[48]Christopher Stanley, " 'Neither Jew nor Greek': Ethnic Conflict in Graeco-Roman Society," *Journal for the Study of the New Testament* 64 (1996): 101-124.

[49]Stanley, 123, note 71.

[50]Stanley writes, "The use of the term 'Gentiles' (ἀλλοφύλοι or ἔθνη) to designate all non-Jews represents a 'social construction of

Jews (vv. 22, 24) and twice to the Greeks (vv. 22, 24). Are these references to be viewed merely as theological abstractions summarizing Paul's preaching in other locales? Or are these verses windows into the concrete practices of Paul in Corinth?

In his initial preaching in Corinth, Paul encountered resistance and questions from various ethnic groups (i.e., "the Jews demand signs, and the Greeks seek wisdom"), and yet, in spite of their questions and protestations, the power (or folly) of the early Christian message was manifested in that it brought together *ethnic* groups which traditionally were estranged from one another.[51] In other words, in 1 Corinthians 1:24, the coordinating particles τε καί[52] in the phrase "both the Jews and the Greeks (Ἰουδαίοις τε καὶ Ἕλλησιν) are emphasizing the radical nature of the call which creates the church—a church of *both Jews and Greeks*.

The preaching about the cross simultaneously drives some Jews and Greeks away while compelling other Jews and Greeks to come together. This "gathering" which Paul calls the ἐκκλησία is not just a theological reality (i.e., it is called into existence by God), but it is also a social reality (i.e., it consists of different *ethnicities*). Even if archeological evidence is inconclusive, there are perhaps neglected features in the text[53]

---

reality' developed by a particular people-group (the Jews) in a concrete historical situation." Stanley, 105.

[51]See Stanley for a synopsis of the hostility between Jews and Greeks in the first century world. Also, see Barclay, *Jews in the Mediterranean Diaspora*, 48-81.

[52]According to Blass and Debrunner, in Greek grammar, "τε... καί [which is often written without an intervening word as in 1 Corinthians 1:24] provides a closer connection than simple καί." See Blass and Debrunner, 230.

[53]In chapter one, I alluded to the fact that in the history of scholarship on 1 Corinthians, interpreters have (arbitrarily) contended that certain textual features are windows into the concrete social practices of Paul or of the Corinthians, while other features (which might offer similar, if not more extensive, sociological insight) have gone unnoticed. One wonders if certain important social and cultural features (e.g., the role of ethnicity) have gone unnoticed because interpreters of various passages have not been interested in finding that kind of information. The questions one asks will dramatically shape the kind of answers one receives. If one were looking for textual traces or

which suggest the presence of a Jewish population in first century Corinth.

Ethnic Cooperation or Ethnic Conflict?

The social interaction of various ethnicities in an ancient Mediterranean city would not necessarily have created social disharmony.[54] The presence or absence of certain factors would serve as a catalyst for either interethnic cooperation or interethnic conflict. Christopher Stanley, using the insights of contemporary studies on the interaction of different ethnicities, contends that ethnic conflict is more likely in places:

> where groups are competing for scarce social, economic or territorial resources; where there are discrepancies or changes in the size or political power of competing groups; where one group has migrated into the territory of another; where there is a history of conflict between groups; or where groups in the same geographical area possess discordant systems of personal and social values.[55]

---

hints of Jewish presence in Corinth, one might find some fascinating data if one were to pay attention to the social and cultural texture of 2 Corinthians 3:12-18. For instance, in 2 Corinthians 3:15, Paul writes, "Yet, to this day whenever Moses is read a veil lies over their minds, but when a man turns to the Lord the veil is lifted." This passage has been such the focal point of the theological discussion of Paul's understanding of and relationship to the law that its sociological hint about Jewish synagogue practice (i.e., the reading of the Torah in the synagogue or "whenever Moses is read") is practically ignored. 2 Corinthians 3:12-18 could be a window into the synagogue experience of Jews in Corinth during the time of Paul.

[54]In contrast to this point, Josephus records incidents of great hostility between the Jews and other ethnic groups. For hostility between the Jews and the Alexandrians, see, for example, Josephus, *Antiquities* 18.257-260; 19.278-291. A helpful discussion of the Alexandrian Pogrom is in Barclay, *Jews in the Mediterranean Diaspora*, 48-81. For hostility between the Jews and the Selucians, see, for example, *Antiquities* 18.371-376. Josephus also mentions the severe enmity between the Jews and other ethnic groups during the time of the war with Rome. See, for example, *War of the Jews*, 2.457-512.

[55]Stanley, 115.

It might prove fruitful to analyze (or hypothesize about) the ethnic situation in Corinth in light of these factors. Although some exegetes have built elaborate anthropological models on the notion of Mediterranean culture being "agonistic,"[56] with persons competing for scarce tangible and intangible goods, one might contend that the intensity of this perpetual ancient contest might have been lessened in Roman Corinth. According to Stanley, economic and social resources were the first factor affecting interethnic cooperation or conflict. Yet, all indications are that financial opportunities were burgeoning in Corinth. These economic opportunities were not necessarily restricted to certain people by hundreds of years of tradition in the way in which such opportunities might have been restricted in a city like Athens or Rome.

Our ability to check the second factor of interethnic cooperation or conflict, namely, changes in the political power of competing groups, is limited. Much detailed work has been done on the inscriptional and literary evidence, especially on the names of persons who, according to Paul, may have held some political offices. Yet, it has been difficult to determine the actual offices that such persons held[57] or what ethnicity such persons were. For instance, one could possess a Greek name and be Jewish. For that matter in the ancient Mediterranean world, one could subscribe in large part to Greco-Roman sensibilities and philosophies and still consider oneself *ethnically* to be a Jew.[58]

---

[56]See, for example, Bruce Malina, *The New Testament World: Insights from Cultural Anthropology* (Louisville:Westminster/John Knox, 1993), 37.

[57]For instance, in Romans 16:23, Paul, offering the greetings of Corinthian Christians, mentions an Erastus who is said to be οἰκονόμος τῆς πόλεως. There has been considerable discussion and disagreement concerning what office or administrative post is meant by this phrase. Is this a high-ranking position or a low-level bureaucratic post which could have been held by a slave? See Theissen, 75-83. Also, see H. J. Cadbury, "Erastus of Corinth," *Journal of Biblical Literature* 50 (1931): 42-58.

[58]Of course, a paradigmatic example of this is Philo of Alexandria. See above Goudriaan's six synopses about ethnicity, especially number two.

The third factor, the migration of one group into a territory, would not have been as much of an issue in Corinth since so many people in this reconstituted urban center would have migrated from elsewhere. For those living in Corinth, being a "native" Corinthian may have been the exception which proved the rule.

The fourth feature affecting the amount of interethnic cooperation or conflict is a history of conflict between or among ethnic groups. To be sure, at times there was enmity among the Greeks, Romans, and Jews throughout the Mediterranean world, but this macro-social reality did not unilaterally impose its pattern on every social situation and in every geographical locale. Archeological evidence and historical reconstructions have revealed no compelling evidence of large-scale, overt, politically-sponsored conflicts between these groups in Roman Corinth.[59]

The fifth determinant of interethnic cooperation or conflict, however, may be of some use to us. Scholars of ethnic studies contend that conflict is often sparked by different social values. Undoubtedly, in many instances, the Jews in an ancient Roman city and their Greco-Roman neighbors had enormous differences in their values. Yet, it was not so much the values that caused the antipathy between the Jews and their non-Jewish counterparts as much as it was the *practices* which gave expression to those values.[60]

---

[59]There was, however, a considerable anti-Jewish tradition among the Greeks and the Romans. For example, there was the first century CE Greek rhetorician Apion who lived in Alexandria. We primarily know of him because of Josephus's refutations of his ideas. See Josephus, *Against Apion*. Also, for an example of anti-Jewish rhetoric from a Roman author, see Tacitus, *Histories* 5.4-5. Tacitus remarked, "The Jews regard as profane all that we hold sacred; on the other hand, they permit all that we abhor." For a useful discussion of various aspects of the anti-Jewish tradition among Greeks and Romans, see Louis H. Feldman, *Jew and Gentile in the Ancient World: Attitudes and Interactions from Alexander to Justinian* (Princeton: Princeton University Press, 1993), 84-176.

[60]In "Thessalonica and Corinth: Social Contrasts in Pauline Christianity," John Barclay stresses that sociological studies of Pauline congregations should pay less attention to social status and more

Commenting on the social interaction of the Jews, the Greeks, and the Romans, Lawrence Shiffman writes:

> Many non-Jews [in the Hellenistic world] saw their Jewish neighbors as strangers and resented the special privileges[61] they enjoyed without becoming full members of the polis. Perhaps even more unacceptable was the Jewish refusal to worship the pagan gods, and therefore, to join in the local city cults.[62]

This refusal to participate in community activities, especially religious activities, would not have set well with many Greeks or Romans. Roman religion had a decidedly public nature.[63] The Greco-Roman gods were a pervasive feature in Corinth.[64] We

---

attention to *social interactions*. See Barclay, "Thessalonica and Corinth," *Journal for the Study of the New Testament* 73 (1992): 49-74. Sociologists and anthropologists have known for a while that belief and behavior operate almost cyclically; beliefs are expressed in behavior, and behaviors reinforce beliefs. Yet, in the Greco-Roman world, where philosophy and the practice of religion were viewed less as theory and more as therapy, one can assume that the point of contention between competing groups revolved as much around differing social *practice* as around ideological positions. On the importance of *behavior* in establishing Jewish identity, especially in the Diaspora, John Collins remarks, "Despite the persistent concern with matters of political allegiance and civil status, the dominant locus of Jewish identity was in the area of *ethics and piety*." See John J. Collins, *Between Athens and Jerusalem: Jewish Identity in the Hellenistic Diaspora* (New York: Crossroads, 1983), 130 (emphasis mine).

[61]For a succinct and useful discussion of some of the privileges afforded Jews in Hellenistic cities, see Victor Tcherikover, *Hellenistic Civilization and the Jews* (Philadelphia: Jewish Publication Society of America, 1959), 296-332.

[62]Lawrence H. Schiffman, *From Text to Tradition: A History of Second Temple and Rabbinic Judaism* (Hoboken: Ktav Publishing House, 1991), 91.

[63]Robert L. Wilken remarks, "It was in its public functions that Roman religion had its most characteristic *Sitz im Leben*." See Wilken, *The Christians as the Romans Saw Them* (New Haven: Yale University Press, 1984), 57.

[64]There seems to have been substantial religious diversity in Corinth. This fact, however, in a crossroads city like Corinth should come as no surprise. As noted above, archeologists and historians agree that Egyptian deities had a substantial number of devotees in Corinth. In

can imagine that Jewish refusal to participate in the rituals would have raised social tension.

For some Greeks and Romans, the Jews' lack of participation was a manifestation of their misanthropy.[65] For the Jews, the indulgence of the Greeks and Romans in the worship of these gods was proof of their idolatry. On occasion in his letters, Paul himself reveals the influence of Jewish morality on his thinking. For the Jew, the twin poles of Gentile moral depravity were idolatry and sexual immorality. For instance, in 1 Thessalonians, Paul typifies the Gentile converts' existence prior to their conversion as one marked by *idolatry*,[66] and in 1 Corinthians 5 Paul says that the *immorality* in the Corinthian church was worse than that found among the Gentiles.[67] It was the difference in social values which was evident in different social practices that provided the greatest source of tension between the Jews and other ethnic groups in the Mediterranean world.

---

addition to the Egyptian deities, the Greco-Roman gods were present and fully accounted for in Corinth. On the Acrocorinth, a steep mountain which dominated the city's horizon, there was a temple to Aphrodite. Also, there was a temple to Apollo. Concerning the worship of the gods in Corinth, Jack Sanders remarks, "The gods in Corinth, as in any similar city around the Mediterranean, were omnipresent and inescapable." See Jack Sanders, "Paul Between Jews and Gentiles in Corinth," *Journal for the Study of the New Testament* 65 (1997): 71.

[65]For example, in *Against Apion* 1.309, Josephus discusses a Lysimachus who contended that Moses instructed the Jews "to have no kind regards for any man, nor give good counsel to any but always to advise them for the worst; and to overturn all those temples and altars of the gods they should meet with." In the *Histories* 5.5, Tacitus writes, "Again, the Jews are extremely loyal toward one another, and always ready to show compassion, but toward every other people they feel only hate and enmity. They sit apart at meals, and they sleep apart, and although as a race, they are prone to lust, they abstain from intercourse with foreign women."

[66]1 Thessalonians 1:9.

[67]1 Corinthians 5:1.

Conclusions

In order to analyze the social location of the Corinthians, it has been necessary to introduce and explore in some detail the concept of ethnicity, a much overlooked social category in New Testament studies. The above discussion of ethnicity should caution us against superficial and monolithic interpretations of such complex and *ambiguous* cultural and ethnic terms (or allusions to them)[68] such as Ἕλλην, Ἰουδαῖος, and βάρβαρος in Pauline writings.

If ethnicity is a function of language as well as group dynamics, a host of difficult questions arise, not the least of which are: About whom is Paul talking when he employs such terms as Ἕλλην, Ἰουδαῖος, and βάρβαρος[69]? Would the persons or groups so labeled by Paul have used similar, identical or different terms by which to identify themselves? We should be aware that the social boundary markers which Paul uses to map his world may differ drastically from those used by persons inside and outside of his churches. In order to particularize this present discussion, let me offer an example.

In 1 Corinthians 1:22 Paul says, "For the *Jews* demand signs, and the *Greeks* seek wisdom (ἐπειδὴ καὶ Ἰουδαῖοι

---

[68]In chapter three, there will be a more extensive treatment of the Pauline *ethnic* allusions to Jews and non-Jews in 1 Corinthians 7:18: "If anyone was circumcised when he was called, let him not remove the marks of circumcision. If anyone was called in the state of uncircumcision, let him not be circumcised."

[69]With respect to ethnicity, it is fascinating that in Romans 1:14 Paul says that he is ready to preach to the Ἕλλησίν τε καὶ βαρβάροις (to the Greeks and to the barbarians). Just as the phrase τὰ ἔθνη ("the Gentiles") became a socially-constructed, Jewish, linguistic way of dealing with "otherness," so too the word βάρβαρος was a socially-constructed Greek or (Greco-Roman) linguistic way of dealing with "otherness." In Romans 1:14, Paul, the Jew, speaks about preaching to the barbarians, and by using such language he places himself on the Greco-Roman socially-constructed map (i.e., in this symbolic world there are Greeks and Romans and the rest of the world is lumped under the label "barbarians"). Yet, by the coordinates of that same socially-constructed map, many "Greeks," in fact might have considered Paul to be a *barbarian*. In the socially-constructed realm of ethnicity, *ambiguity* abounds!

σημεῖα αἰτοῦσιν καὶ Ἕλληνες σοφίαν ζητοῦσιν). As suggested above, Christopher Stanley urges exegetes not to empty Jew-Greek terminology of its *ethnic* import. In the interpretation of this verse (and similar verses), serious and overlooked questions are, who is a Jew, and who is a Greek in the social world of 1 Corinthians?

The simple fact that Paul speaks separately about each group is evidence that in his estimation Jews and Greek constitute two separate groups or ethnicities. Would others in Roman Corinth, however, have shared Paul's ethnic assessments? What, in the first instance, makes one a Ἰουδαῖος? Is it circumcision? As we shall explore in chapter three, the role and import of circumcision in establishing Jewish identity had a complex history itself.

Furthermore, if one were circumcised, yet a fluent Greek speaker, a participant in Greek institutions (e.g., the gymnasium) and sympathetic, for instance, to Stoic teachings, would one be a Ἰουδαῖος or a Ἕλην? As Stanley has contended, in the ancient world, more often than not, the term Ἕλην was reserved for those who "could still trace their family tree back to Hellas when required, as when the wealthier families went to enroll their sons in the local gymnasium."[70]

On the other hand, centuries earlier, the Athenian orator Isocrates remarked, "He who shares in our *paideia* is a Greek in a higher sense than he who shares in our descent."[71] To be sure, these words of Isocrates pre-date the composition of 1 Corinthians by more than three centuries. Did, however, the residue of this way of thinking still linger in the minds of some in the first-century world, namely, that being a Greek was more about *paideia* than family history?

If ancient Greek ethnicity was more about sharing in *paideia* than family history, would the person described above— a circumcised man who spoke Greek fluently and who was sympathetic to Greek institutions and philosophies—be a Hellenized Jew, that is a Jew *acculturated* to Hellenism, but not

---

[70]Stanley, 113.
[71]Isocrates, *Panegyricus* 50. Quoted in Barclay, *Jews in the Mediterranean Diaspora*, 89.

assimilated by Hellenism ethnically?[72] Or would such a person consider himself to be ethnically a Ἕλλην? Moreover, even if such a person considered himself a Ἕλλην, there would still be others (Greeks or Romans) who would label such a person a βάρβαρος. In light of the antipathy that existed between Greeks and Jews in the ancient world—an antipathy which brought with it persecutions (although we have no evidence that such persecutions occurred in Corinth)—what internal or external pressure might have been exerted on a Ἰουδαῖος to become a Ἕλλην or on a Ἕλλην to become a Ἰουδαῖος?[73]

When viewed from the perspective of a boundary approach, issues of ethnicity, which are present in 1 Corinthians in general and in 7:17-24 in particular, become increasingly more complex, and, at times, ambiguous. In the face of such complexity, Christopher Stanley rightly wonders "whether Paul really understood the power of ethnic identity to shape the attitudes and actions of both groups and individuals?"[74] This question will be borne in mind as we further expand our description of the social location of this text.

---

[72]Barclay makes the keen distinction between *acculturation* and *assimilation*. For him, acculturation is "the linguistic, educational and ideological aspects of a given cultural matrix." By contrast, assimilation "may be taken to refer to social integration (becoming similar to one's neighbors): it concerns social contacts, social interaction and social practice." Although acculturation might lead to assimilation, it need not in every case. Thus, it is possible for an ethnic group to be acculturated without being assimilated. See Barclay, *Jews in the Mediterranean Diaspora*, 92.

[73]On account of the privileges and accommodations that were granted by the Romans to the Jews who lived not only in Israel but also in the Diaspora (e.g., freedom from military conscription, the right to send tribute to Jerusalem, the right to assemble for sacred purposes), one can imagine that becoming a Ἰουδαῖος might have had many practical benefits. For Josephus's rendering of Jewish privileges granted by the Romans, see *Antiquities* 10.185-267 and 16.27-65.

[74]Stanley, 124.

Social Status

Economic Factors

The importance (and ambiguity) of social status in the first century Mediterranean world is now an axiom of sociological and social scientific criticism. Wayne Meeks contends that the category of status is "the most generally useful one for forming a picture of stratification in the Greco-Roman cities."[75] There has also been considerable work on the multi-dimensional nature of social status.

In the first century Mediterranean world, one's social status was the composite of many features.[76] It was quite possible to have high status as it pertained to certain markers while concomitantly possessing low status as it related to other markers. Occupying simultaneously two locations on the social stratification map led to "status dissonance" or "status discrepancy."[77] As a city on the make, as it were, Corinth would have had at least two groups who would have experienced significant status discrepancy, the *noveau riche* and the freedmen.

According to John Stambaugh, the imperial Roman world consisted of two basic strata, the ruling classes and those on the fringes of the power structure. Many of those in the ruling classes possessed "old money," having acquired their wealth through inheritances.[78] By contrast, much of the wealth in Corinth consisted of "new money."

---

[75]Meeks, 54. For a helpful discussion concerning the appropriateness of analyzing Roman society in terms of *class* divisions or *status* distinctions, see Peter Garnsey and Richard Saller, *The Roman Empire: Economy, Society and Culture* (London: Duckworth, 1987), 109-112.

[76]Recently, social scientific critics have distinguished between social status that was ascribed (i.e., granted naturally by birth) and social status which one acquired. See Malina, 33-37.

[77]John E. Stambaugh, "Social Relations in the City of the Early Principate," in *Society of Biblical Literature Seminar Papers* (Chico, CA: Scholars Press, 1980), 76.

[78]Stambaugh, 77.

As Roman Corinth was rebuilt, it became a magnet for new "capitalists." A noted example of the transformation of Corinth from "ruins to riches" is provided by an inscription[79] which tells of the benefaction of L. Castricus Regulus who served as the president of the Isthmian Games[80] between 7 BCE and 3 CE, a task which would have required enormous financial means. Prior to the resumption of the Isthmian Games in Corinth, the games had been held in Sicyon, but their return to Corinth in the late first century BCE and a Corinthian citizen's ability to serve as president of the games reveal that economic prosperity was returning to Corinth.

A sizable percentage of the *noveau riche* in Corinth would have been freedmen. When Corinth was re-established by the Romans, many of its new residents would have been slaves.[81] As much as one-third of Corinth's population in the first century CE consisted of slaves,[82] and manumission[83] was a regular part of Roman social practice. Consequently, the infusion of freedmen into the population would have been no social anomaly, but a standard procedure.

Many of these freedmen, believing that they had much more to gain than to lose, became the "venture capitalists" of the ancient world. A mere fifty years after its Roman resettlement, Corinth was well on its way to being a major financial center. The rapid rise of Corinth as an economic center of the first century CE Greco-Roman world is attested to by

---

[79]For the inscription and an analysis of its significance, see John Harvey Kent, *The Inscriptions, 1926-1950, Corinth* (Princeton: American School of Classical Studies at Athens, 1966), 70-73.

[80]For a dated, but intriguing account of the significance of the Isthmian Games in Pauline writings, see Oscar Broneer, "The Apostle Paul and the Isthmian Games," *Biblical Archaeologist* XXV (1962): 3-31.

[81]Strabo, 8.136.

[82]Bartchy, 58.

[83]S. Dill writes, "Frequent manumissions were swelling the freedmen class to enormous dimensions." Dill, *Roman Society from Nero to Marcus Aurelius* (New York: Meridian Books, 1956), 117. In 2 BCE, legislation had been passed in Rome to discourage indiscriminate manumission, but large numbers of slaves were, nonetheless, regularly manumitted in Rome and the provinces. See Keith Bradley, *Slavery and Society at Rome* (Cambridge: Cambridge University Press, 1994), 10.

Plutarch, the first and early second century philosopher, who in the *Moralia* alludes to the financial brokers of Corinth.[84] The lucrative financial opportunities afforded by Roman Corinth served as a magnet drawing many freedmen to this "boomtown" of the ancient world.

Classicists and New Testament scholars often discuss the fictitious freedman Trimalchio of Petronius's *The Satyricon*.[85] Trimalchio, a new freedman, who by means of his "venture capitalism" acquires enormous wealth, is a literary caricature of the self-made man whose wealth grants high-financial status. Mitigating against this high financial status is his position as a freedman.

Also, well-documented among classicists and New Testament scholars is the vitriolic contempt for the "newly-rich" freedmen frequently expressed by traditional Roman aristocrats. Perhaps, the hostility felt for the freedmen of Corinth was lessened for at least two reasons. First, the number of traditional Greek or Roman aristocrats would presumably have been smaller in a "new" city such as Corinth[86] than it would have been in a city such as Athens. Second, the freedmen would have comprised a substantial portion of the city's population, and by their very size they may have gained in political strength. Nonetheless, even in a relatively new city like Roman Corinth, the *noveau riche* and the freedmen would have experienced status dissonance.

---

[84]Plutrach, *On Borrowing* [*Moralia* 831A] and Murphy O'Connor, *St. Paul's Corinth*, 105.

[85]Petronius, *The Satyricon* (London: Penguin Books, 1986), 51-91. For a succinct discussion and analysis of the Dinner with Trimalchio in *The Satyricon*, see S. Dill, 121-137.

[86]Wayne Meeks remarks, "To be a freedman in the early years in Roman Corinth, a colony whose first settlers were mostly freedmen, would surely have been less of a social disability than it would have been in Rome or Antioch." Meeks, 55.

The Roman Orders

Although thus far we have focused on the economic factors contributing to social status, it should be clearly understood that one's social status could never be reduced simply to economics. In the world of the late republic and early empire, one's social status, more than anything, was a by-product of one's *dignitas* or honor, and one's honor was "a claim to worth along with the social acknowledgment of that worth."[87] On the Greco-Roman scale of values, *dignitas* ranked extremely high. Some of the sources of honor included "character, birth, office, [and] wealth."[88]

As suggested earlier, there was honor which was ascribed. This was the honor that was naturally granted by virtue of birth into an honorable family or through the inheritance of a large amount of wealth. There was also honor which came as a result of one's own actions. This was acquired honor. In the late republican and early imperial world, one could gain significant acquired honor, for example, by moving through the *cursus honorum*, the socially-prescribed progression of political offices. Before discussing the *cursus honorum*, a sketch of the orders of the Roman world will prove beneficial.

The Roman social world consisted of orders which were "social categories defined by the state through statutory or customary rules."[89] There were basically four orders: Senators, Equestrians, Decurions, and Plebeians.

The Senators: The senatorial order consisted of a very elite group of Roman families. In the time of Augustus, the number of senatorial families was reduced to a meager 600.[90] Moreover, in the time of Augustus, substantial barriers were placed around the senatorial order. In the first instance,

---

[87]Malina, 31.

[88]Peter Garnsey, *Social Status and Legal Privilege in the Roman Empire* (Oxford: Clarendon Press, 1970), 234.

[89]Garnsey, *The Roman Empire*, 112.

[90]In the *Res Gestae* 8, Augustus says that he revised the roll of the Senators three times. See Naphtali Lewis and Meyer Reinhold, ed., *Roman Civilizations: Selected Readings*, vol. 1, 3d edition (New York: Columbia University Press, 1990), 564.

membership in the Senate required the payment of one million sesterces,[91] and senatorial men were not allowed to marry freedwomen. Although membership in the Senate was not hereditary, sons of senators were allowed to wear the *latus clavus* (i.e., the purple stripe), and senatorial distinction and privilege extended to the third generation of a senator's family.

The Equestrians: The second order, the equestrians, was much larger than the senatorial order (perhaps numbering in the thousands), but in many other respects it closely resembled the senatorial order. Although substantially less than that of the senators, there was a monetary requirement of 400,000 sesterces levied against the equestrians. It has been suggested that the distinction and privileges associated with the equestrian order may have only extended to the first generation of an equestrian family.[92]

The Decurions: The decurions comprised a third order in the Roman world. Decurions were local magistrates who gained entrance into their order by means of "their social background and financial situation."[93] Free birth was an additional requirement, although sons of freedmen could enter this order. Decurions often funded local building projects, municipal maintenance, and entertainment. Thus, they were required to be men of financial means. It has been suggested that the financial requirement for decurions was 100,000 sesterces.[94]

These three orders, the senators, the equestrians and the decurions, constituted the *honestiores*. For members of these "higher" orders who already possessed some degree of *dignitas*, another avenue for them to acquire even more *dignitas* was to progress through the *cursus honorum*. The *cursus honorum* was the series of public offices that a Roman citizen, usually of the equestrian order, held en route to being a consul or a senator. The political process of the *cursus honorum* demonstrates that Roman life, both in the republic and the empire, was highly structured with respect to social status.

[91]Garnsey, *The Roman Empire*, 113.
[92]Garnsey, *Social Status and Legal Privilege*, 242.
[93]Garnsey, *Social Status and Legal Privilege*, 243.
[94]Garnsey, *The Roman Empire*, 114.

A prevalent Roman sentiment was that particular classes of people occupied certain positions or performed certain tasks based on "nature." The Romans, who were famous for borrowing ideas and practices from other peoples and placing on such ideas and practices their own stamp,[95] effectively borrowed this belief in the natural position of various social groups from Aristotle[96] and other Greek thinkers. In Roman society, the concept of a *novus homo* was not valued. Rather, the person who had access to leadership and, by extension, *dignitas* was the one who had been "in the system" for some time. The concept of the *cursus honorum* raises the issue of social mobility in the period of the Roman empire.

Undoubtedly, there were ample opportunities for upward mobility in the Roman Empire. Social change was the order of the day.[97] Upward social mobility, more often than not, was the privilege of the *honestiores*. Generally, a Roman man preparing to proceed through the *cursus honorum* was a member of the equestrian order, thereby already possessing some *dignitas*. If in our contemporary market culture, "nothing succeeds like success," in ancient Mediterranean culture, "nothing brought honor like honor." Historians, however, urge caution with respect to over-generalizations about the widespread prospects for upward social movement. Garnsey and Saller write:

> It has been suggested that for a traditional, pre-industrial society imperial Rome allowed great upward movement to an unusual degree. Such a generalization needs to be qualified: mobility in certain sectors of the population may have been common, while for others the prospects were virtually hopeless.[98]

Let us now turn to that portion of Roman society where hopelessness concerning upward mobility abounded.

---

[95]Ferguson, 20.

[96]For an example of Aristotle's appeal to what is "natural," see *Politics* 7.3.4.

[97]The title of Ovid's influential work *Metamorphoses* is quite telling of a prevailing attitude about change in the early imperial period.

[98]Garnsey, *The Roman Empire*, 123.

In contrast to the *honestiores*, there were the *humiliores* (or plebeians). In this group, one found the majority of persons in the Roman empire. Concerning the demographics of this group, Stambaugh remarks, "This category [*humiliores*] included a wide variety of economic situations, from the relatively prosperous to the relatively poor to the truly destitute."[99] In the *humiliores*, one could find shop keepers and craftspersons of an assorted variety. One would also find persons attending to their patrons.[100] Still others spent time on the streets of the urban centers of the empire[101] in abject poverty.

The vertical links between the *honestiores* and the *humiliores*, to the degree that they existed at all, were provided by the patron-client system. There is considerable evidence, however, that substantial *horizontal* links among the *humiliores* were established by associations and *collegia*.[102]

It is important to remember that the people who comprised the *collegia* generally were not the poorest members of the Greco-Roman world. In terms of social rank, the members of *collegia* were modestly well-off. The poorest people

---

[99]Stambaugh, 81.

[100]For a thorough study of the role of patronage in Roman Corinth, see John K. Chow, *Patronage and Power: A Study of Social Networks in Corinth* (Sheffield: JSOT Press, 1992).

[101]For a dated, but nonetheless, vivid account of life on the streets of Rome in the period of the empire, see J. Carcopino, *Daily Life in Ancient Rome* (New Haven: Yale University Press, 1940), 22-51.

[102]*Collegia*, in the main, were mutual aid societies formed to meet the basic needs of their members. The fundamental services provided by a *collegium* included the insurance of a decent burial at the death of one of its members, an occasional festive dinner, and an opportunity for general fellowship among its members. There were three basic types of *collegia*: First, there were *collegia* formed around professions or trades. For instance, there might be a *collegium* of shipowners or wool-workers. Second, there were associations, as mentioned above, that provided for the burial of members. Third, there were religious associations consisting of the devotees of a deity. For example, there was a society of the Bacchi which was a cult devoted to the worship of Dionysius. These categories were not rigid, and on many occasions a *collegium* might serve all three functions: professional, burial, and religious. See, for example, Wilken, 31-47. For a thorough investigation of *collegia*, see John S. Kloppenburg and Stephen G. Wilson, *Voluntary Associations in the Graeco-Roman World* (London: Routledge, 1996).

in the Greco-Roman world would not have even possessed enough money to pay the requisite dues to belong to a *collegium*; thus, when they died, they would have been buried in unmarked mass graves.

Even though there is evidence of frequent links between the *honestiores* and the *humiliores* through patronage and evidence of strong horizontal links among the *humiliores* through the *collegia*, the gulf separating the *honestiores* and the *humiliores* was wide. In most instances, not even Roman citizenship was a guaranteed way to bridge this gap. Some scholars[103] contend that from the second century CE onwards there was a general devaluing of Roman citizenship, but in the first century CE Roman citizenship did afford important privileges.[104] Yet, as important as citizenship was, possession of it did not prevent one from being a member of the *humiliores*. As Garnsey remarks, "The *honestiores/humiliores* distinction cuts across the citizen/alien distinction: there were citizens (and aliens) on both sides of the dividing line."[105]

Such was the highly-stratified world of the early empire—on the one hand, the *honestiores*, on the other, the *humiliores*. Finally, in the social world of the early empire, there was a group which, certainly in theory and quite regularly in practice, did not even appear "on the screen" of the values of the Greco-Roman world, the slaves.[106] In recent New Testament

---

[103]See, for example, A. N. Sherwin-White, *The Roman Citizenship* (Oxford: Clarendon Press, 1939).

[104]An important privilege of Roman citizens was the right to appeal to Rome in legal matters, thus removing one from the jurisdiction of the local authorities. For the appearance of this right in the New Testament, see, Acts 25:10-12. For a further discussion, see A. N. Sherwin-White, *Roman Society and Roman Law in the New Testament* (Oxford: Oxford University Press, 1963), 57-70.

[105]Garnsey, *Social Status and Legal Privilege*, 266.

[106]The literature on Greco-Roman slavery is copious. Some representative treatments of this institution include: J. Vogt, *Ancient Slavery and the Ideal of Man* (Oxford: Basil Blackwell, 1974); Keith Hopkins, *Conquerors and Slaves: Sociological Studies in Roman History* (Cambridge: Cambridge University Press, 1978); M. I. Finley, *Ancient Slavery and Modern Ideology* (New York: Viking Press, 1980); T. Wiedemann, *Greek and Roman Slavery* (Baltimore: Johns Hopkins

scholarship much ado has been made about the possibility of upward mobility afforded to socially well-placed slaves. A ground-breaking monograph on ancient Roman slavery and slavery metaphors in Pauline texts is Dale Martin's *Slavery as Salvation: The Metaphor of Slavery in Pauline Christianity*. Martin explores in detail the theme of the upwardly mobile slave.

In some ancient Greco-Roman texts, metaphors concerning slavery have negative valences which, in light of the indignities and loss of privileges which typified much of Greco-Roman slavery, would seem to make sense. In other contexts, however, slavery metaphors seem to have positive valences. The attempt to understand those instances when slavery metaphors in Pauline texts have seemingly positive valences is the launching point of Martin's study.

The perplexing question that drives Martin's study is, "How do we explain the positive soteriological use of slavery as a symbol for the Christian's relationship to God or Christ?"[107] Like Scott Bartchy, Martin understands the importance of an actual socio-historical investigation of the phenomenon of slavery in the proper exegesis of such texts. Martin's work incorporates his investigation of ancient inscriptions, novels, and handbooks in his exegesis of 1 Corinthians 9. Moreover, Martin's study is a step forward from Bartchy's in that it explores, with some sophistication, issues of rhetoric and recognizes that issues of power are at work in Paul's use of this problematic metaphor.

There are, however, difficulties with Martin's project. As he himself mentions, the vast majority of Greco-Roman slaves would not have heard slavery metaphors in terms of soteriology and *upward social mobility*. Instead, according to Orlando Patterson, the overwhelming majority of slaves would have

---

University Press, 1981); G. E. M. de Ste. Croix, *The Class Struggles in the Ancient World from the Archaic Age to the Arab Conquest* (London: Duckworth, 1981); Keith Bradley, *Slavery and Society at Rome*; Orlando Patterson, *Slavery and Social Death*; Patterson, *Freedom in the Making of Western Culture*, vol. I (New York: Harper Collins, 1991). Greco-Roman slavery will be explored in detail in chapter four.

[107]Martin, *Slavery as Salvation*, xiv.

heard in such language *social death*.[108] As Patterson has persuasively argued, slavery in most cultures, both ancient and modern, has been that ambiguous situation where a human being is physically alive but socially dead, having been (violently) denied the rights of heritage or progeny. Perhaps, a small percentage of the imperial slaves or middle managerial slaves might have heard Paul's language about slavery in 1 Corinthians positively. We must realize, however, that the inscriptional evidence is only partial. The voices of the majority of slaves are simply unavailable to us.

Martin is captivated by the fact that some slaves in their funerary inscriptions referred to themselves as slaves with seemingly no embarrassment. Some slaves also liked to identify themselves as the "slave of such and such a person." For Martin, the proud recording of their social status as the slave of this distinguished owner or patron can be interpreted to mean that in some circles slave status, slave names, and slave metaphors were not construed negatively but were (high) status indicators. Martin remarks, "Naming oneself the slave of an important person was a way of claiming status for oneself."[109] Again, we must realize that such a phenomenon may have only been valid for socially well-situated slaves.

Martin's book has moved the study of slavery and Christianity forward by addressing both the problem of social status and the problem of the metaphor of slavery in Pauline texts. Yet, as will be discussed in chapter four, even socially well-situated slaves were not immune from many of the indignities of slavery. Even if the masters of managerial slaves did not visit these indignities regularly upon their slaves, the

---

[108]See Patterson, *Slavery and Social Death*, 35-76. In this chapter entitled "Authority, Alienation and Social Death," Patterson analyzes slave regimes, including the Greco-Roman regime. Moreover, he explores the rituals of enslavement that have been imposed upon slaves to dislodge them from their previous social ties, thereby creating in them a sense of social death. These rituals include the (re)naming of slaves and the adoption by the slave of the slave owners' religion or of the religion of the state.

[109]Martin, *Slavery as Salvation*, 48.

legal right and privilege to do so, nevertheless, belonged to the masters. Thus, even among the upwardly mobile slaves, slavery could have conflicting meanings.

Moreover, in spite of those relatively well-positioned slaves who were able to leave some trace of their existence through inscriptions and the interpretations of their dreams recorded in handbooks, the majority of slaves in the imperial world hovered meagerly above the level of subsistence. One would be hard pressed to plot the "coordinates" of such slaves on the map of the imperial world. Such slaves possessed no coordinates because they were considered the quintessential outsiders. Slaves were outside of any established social designation—certainly not *honestiores* and even lower than the *humiliores*. If the *honestiores* were the epicenter of the social map, and the *humiliores* were on the margins of the map, the majority of slaves would not have even been on the page.

Conclusions

As if issues of ethnicity were not enough to complicate the social situation of Roman Corinth, one must also consider the equally complex arena of ancient social status. Economic factors and the stratification that resulted from the Roman orders were just two of the coordinates on the social map of ancient Corinth, and with respect to this map, a person could be two or more places at the same time. Social status was anything but a firmly-fixed reality. Yet, even though the concept of status was multi-dimensional, fluid, and even ambiguous, the concept, nonetheless, was a real, even if intangible, dividing line of Roman society. Garnsey is right when he says:

> Citizens of high status and citizens of low status were at no stage in the period on equal footing. Gradations within the body of citizens [let alone within the masses of the marginalized] made equality, whether political or judicial or economic, impossible to attain. . . . In Roman society legal and political capacity depended, not only upon the *persona* or character of the individual as defined or

recognized by the civil law (free or slave, citizen or alien), but also upon his background or status.[110]

It is precisely these gradations resulting from factors of ethnicity and social status that would have contributed to a complex and perhaps ambiguous hearing of Paul's words in general in 1 Corinthians 7:17-24 and of his allusions to circumcision and slavery in particular. Yet, a fuller analysis of circumcision and slavery and Paul's allusion to them will be more profitable once we have attempted to locate Paul on the social map. More than likely, we will find that the complexities and ambiguities that characterize the Corinthians' social location will also be present in Paul.

Paul

Introduction

Having attempted to situate the Corinthians provisionally on a social map, we now turn to Paul. The task in the case of Paul, however, is different and perhaps more difficult because of the nature of the evidence. In the case of the Corinthians, we possess data from a variety of sources. On the contrary, there is little corroborating evidence about Paul outside of the New Testament itself. In the main, we only know Paul through Paul's words.[111]

---

[110]Garnsey, *Social Status and Legal Privilege*, 270-271.

[111]There is, however, some useful evidence that we might glean from Paul's "biographer," the Lukan evangelist, who presents a substantial amount of material on Paul in Acts. One can also consult apocryphal traditions such as the *Acts of Paul and Thecla* in New *Testament Apocrypha*, vol. II, ed. Wilhelm Schneemelcher (Philadelphia: Westminster Press, 1964), 353-364. Additionally, there is very little evidence in the canonical New Testament concerning Paul's physical appearance. Some interpreters have taken Paul's comments, for example, in Galatians 4:12-20 or 2 Corinthians 12:1-12 as evidence of physical maladies suffered by Paul. For more on Paul's physical appearance, see Abraham J. Malherbe, "A Physical Description of Paul," *Harvard Theological Review* 79 (1986): 170-175.

The seemingly sparse evidence about Paul and a burning desire of many exegetes to know what made Paul "tick" have resulted in various psychological studies of Paul in the history of scholarship.[112] Critics of these kinds of studies began to realize that if psychological analysis of contemporary persons could not be accomplished without complications, how much more riddled with difficulties and conjecture were psychological studies of an *ancient* figure like Paul.

In the last decade, with the meteoric rise of rhetorical criticism in New Testament studies, Pauline scholars have recognized that instead of trying to get behind Paul's words in order to psychoanalyze him, they should analyze Paul's words (or more generally Paul's use of language) as a way of locating Paul on the social map. With this realization, psychoanalysis has given way to *rhetorical* analysis.

Detailed examination of Paul's rhetoric[113] has revealed clearly the enormous complexity of social identity in the ancient world. Moreover, such studies have also exposed the spurious nature of the rigid distinction between Hellenism and Judaism.[114]

---

[112]See, for instance, Gerd Theissen, *Psychological Aspects of Pauline Theology* (Philadelphia: Fortress Press, 1987), and C. H. Dodd, "The Mind of Paul: I and II" in *New Testament Studies* (Manchester: Manchester University Press, 1953), 67-128.

[113]For extensive, useful, and up-to-date bibliographies on Paul and rhetoric, see Witherington, 57-60; Rollin A. Ramsaran, *Liberating Words: Paul's Use of Rhetorical Maxims in 1 Corinthians 1-10* (Valley Forge: Trinity Press, 1996), 149-159; Pogoloff, 283-313, and Anders Eriksson, *Traditions as Rhetorical Proof: Pauline Argumentation in 1 Corinthians* (Stockholm: Almqvist & Wiksell International, 1998), 318-346.

[114]In the history of Pauline interpretation, the attempt to locate Paul's primary cultural and ethnic background has greatly exercised scholars. For instance, in the early twentieth century, Albert Schweitzer, operating with the historical reconstruction of the Tübingen School, contended that there were "watertight" compartments between Palestinian Judaism and Hellenistic Judaism. On the basis of this, Schweitzer argued that Paul's mysticism was a direct outgrowth of Palestinian eschatology. See Schweitzer, *The Mysticism of Paul the Apostle* (New York: Seabury Press, 1931). W. D. Davies later attempted to situate Paul against the background of Rabbinic thought. Davies argued that there were important aspects of Paul's thought that could only be explained in terms of Paul's Pharisaic background. More importantly,

For example, those interpreters who contend that Judaism was the primary well from which Paul drew[115] have to acknowledge that, in many instances, Paul's rhetorical moves were as involved and sophisticated as any Greco-Roman rhetorician.[116] Thus, with confidence we may presume that Paul was the beneficiary of a solid Greco-Roman education which could be acquired in a culturally diverse, "university town" like Tarsus or in an equally diverse city such as Jerusalem.[117] Ben Witherington remarks, "We must, therefore, assume that he [Paul] had a considerable Greek education. Rhetoric, unlike philosophy, was

---

Davies recognized that Schweitzer's rigid categories represented a methodological straightjacket, restricting interpreters from appreciating the rich complexity of the varied cultural influences upon Paul. Davies remarked, "The old dichotomy between Palestinian and Diaspora Hellenistic Judaism is no longer tenable. . . . The lines between Hellenism and Judaism by the first century were very fluid. . . . The Judaism with which he [Paul] grew up, even in Jerusalem, was largely Hellenized, and the Hellenism he encountered in his travels largely Judaized." See Davies, "Paul and Judaism" in *The Bible in Modern Scholarship*, ed. J. Philip Hyatt (Nashville: Abingdon Press, 1965), 180, 181-182.

[115]See, for example, Brad H. Young, *Paul the Jewish Theologian: A Pharisee among Christians, Jews, and Gentiles* (Peabody: Hendrickson Publishers, 1997). Young's attempt to firmly situate Paul in a Pharisaic context is noteworthy. One senses, however, that Young's motivation is not simply a historical reconstruction of Paul, but instead a "rehabilitation" of Paul for the purposes of the contemporary Jewish-Christian dialogue. This motivation is laudable, but in the service of it, Young overstates evidence. For instance, his insistence that Paul's Bible is the *Hebrew* scripture does not take into consideration Paul's use of the Septuagint. See my discussion below.

[116]Even when Paul denies that he is using rhetoric, ironically, he is using rhetoric; it is just a different kind of rhetoric. See H. D. Betz, "The Problem of Rhetoric and Theology according to the Apostle Paul" in *L'Apotre Paul: Personnaliteé, Style et Conceptions du Ministere*, ed. A. Vanhoye (Leuven: Leuven University Press, 1986), 16-37, especially 36-37.

[117]Witherington, 2. There has been considerable debate in the history of Pauline scholarship concerning precisely where Paul was raised, Tarsus or Jerusalem. For a classic treatment of this problem, see Willem C. van Unnik, *Tarsus or Jerusalem: The City of Paul's Youth* (London: Epworth Press, 1962). van Unnik believes that Paul was raised in Jerusalem.

at the very heart of education, even secondary education during
the empire, and Paul is likely to have learned more rhetoric than
philosophy in his schooling."[118]

On the other hand, an analysis of Paul's rhetorical
techniques also reveals that his tactics of persuasion were not
merely Greco-Roman but also, at times, distinctively Jewish.
Paul's Bible, more than likely the LXX, informed his symbolic
world[119] and provided him a source of rhetorical tropes[120] which
could be adapted or transformed to fit and speak to new settings
and circumstances. In exegetical discussions, Paul's use and
adaptation of antecedent Biblical traditions usually are grouped
under the headings of intertexuality or inner biblical exegesis.
Such terminology, however, should not obscure the reality that
Paul's use and adaptation of antecedent traditions were
effective and long-standing *Jewish rhetorical* practices.[121] Thus,

---

[118]Witherington, 3.

[119]Richard Hays remarks, "The vocabulary and cadence of
Scripture—particularly of the LXX—are imprinted deeply on Paul's
mind, and the great stories of Israel continue to serve for him as a fund
of symbols and metaphors that condition his perception of the world, of
God's promised deliverance of his people and of his own identity and
calling." See Hays, *The Echoes of Scripture in the Letters of Paul* (New
Haven: Yale University Press, 1989), 16.

[120]Discussing Paul's use of Scripture, Hays suggests that "Paul's
citations of Scripture often function not as proofs but as tropes: they
generate new meanings by linking the earlier text (Scripture) to the later
(Paul's discourse) in such a way as to produce unexpected
correspondences, correspondences that suggest more than they assert."
Hays, 24.

[121]In his groundbreaking study, *Biblical Interpretation in Ancient
Israel* (Oxford: Clarendon Press, 1985), Michael Fishbane overturns the
belief that Israelite scribes were passive tradents who merely handed on
the biblical tradition without interpolations. In fact, Fishbane argues that
the scribes were people of political savvy. He remarks, "Trained in the
forms and *rhetoric* and international diplomatic correspondence, and
thus kept abreast of internal and external affairs, many of these court
scribes—as individuals and as family guilds—were directly caught up in
religious and political affairs affecting the nation as a whole." Fishbane,
26 (emphasis mine). Moreover, Fishbane discusses in sophisticated
detail the exigencies which would have motivated the scribes in ancient
Israel to use or adapt the inherited traditions. To say that in rhetorical
terms, Fishbane contends that scribal activity was a response to a

in an analysis of Paul's rhetoric, one finds oneself simultaneously in the Greco-Roman *and* Jewish cultural worlds, and one discovers that in Paul, "Athens has much to do with Jerusalem" and vice-versa.[122]

As useful as it is to analyze the possible influence of Hellenism, of rabbinic Judaism or of Paul's hometown upon his social location, such analyses do not adequately account for the primary determinant of Paul's social identity. It was neither "Athens" nor "Jerusalem," that would provide Paul's ultimate source of identity. His (new) identity was rooted in his experience with Christ. Christ's impact upon Paul is unmistakably clear. This experience with Christ compelled Paul to re-evaluate radically every aspect of his identity and to re-plot the coordinates of his symbolic world.[123] Often, as Paul attempts to articulate the *social* implications of being "in Christ,"[124] certain ambiguities emerge. These ambiguities may be

---

rhetorical situation. See Fishbane, 409. My point is not to compare Paul with the ancient Israelite scribes. Instead, I am suggesting that when Paul adapted antecedent biblical traditions, he was engaging in a time-honored, Jewish rhetorical practice.

[122]The African Christian apologist Tertullian, in his *Presciptions against the Heretics,* suggested that Athens and Jerusalem had little, if anything, to do with one another. See *A New Eusebius: Documents illustrating the history of the Church to AD 337,* ed. J. Stevenson (London: SPCK, 1987), 166-167.

[123]A symbolic world according to Luke Johnson, "is not an alternative, ideal world removed from everyday life. To the contrary, it is the system of meaning that anchors the activities of individuals and communities in the real world." See Johnson, *The Writings of the New Testament: An Interpretation* (Philadelphia: Fortress Press, 1986), 12. For a classic discussion of symbolic universes, see Peter L. Berger and Thomas Luckmann, *The Social Construction of Reality* (Garden City: Doubleday & Company, 1966), 85-118.

[124]The formulation "in Christ" (ἐν Χριστῷ) [and the corresponding formulation "in the Lord" (ἐν κυρίῳ)] is a characteristic Pauline phrase which occurs well over a hundred times in his letters. This phrase has been the subject of much scholarly debate. In the earlier part of the twentieth century, interpreters such as Adolf Deismann and Albert Schweitzer contended that the phrase contained vestiges of mysticism. It was argued that by this phrase Paul was suggesting that believers could effect some kind of mystical union with Christ. In more recent scholarship, exegetes have begun to see in the phrase various

the result of Paul's genuine struggle to integrate his "Christ experience" with the exigencies of concrete social life. We will now discuss Paul's experience with Christ and some of its implications.

---

notions of corporate salvation. That is, the phrase may denote that Christ is the means or the instrument by which believers are brought into right relationship with God, or it may attempt to encapsulate some of the ethical implications of (communal) existence under the lordship of Christ. M. A. Seifrid remarks, "The phrases [in Christ/in the Lord] therefore became a vehicle for Paul to describe the life of faith under Christ's lordship in a world where other powers and temptations were present. To act 'in Christ' is to act in faith and obedience in the face of false alternatives. . . ." See Seifrid, "In Christ," in *Dictionary of Paul and His Letters*, ed. Gerald F. Hawthorne, Ralph P. Martin, and Daniel G. Reid (Downers Grove, IL: Intervarsity Press, 1993), 436. Wayne Meeks has also called our attention to the *social* connotations of the phrase "in Christ." Meeks writes, "It can also be said with some confidence that all attempts to make "mysticism" the center of Pauline Christianity have failed. Categories which have seemed to many readers 'mystical' such as the pregnant phrase 'in Christ' turn out to have largely *social* and cultic significance." See Meeks, "The Christian Proteus" in *The Writings of St. Paul* (New Haven: Yale University Press, 1972), 441 (emphasis mine). In this dissertation, I am especially interested in exploring Paul's difficulty in expressing the social implications of being "in Christ." For further discussion of the formulation "in Christ," see A. J. M. Wedderburn, "Some Observations on Paul's use of the Phrases 'in Christ' and 'with Christ,' " *Journal for the Study of the New Testament* 25 (1985): 83-97.

Paul's Experience with Christ

For Paul, Christ changed everything—everything in Paul[125] and everything in the world.[126] Before his encounter with Christ,[127] Paul's Pharisaic heritage had been his source of identity and pride. His experience with Christ provided him with a new system of valuation. The extent to which Paul has recalculated his identity is clearly seen, for example, in Philippians 3. First, in Philippians 3:4-6 Paul reviews his Jewish badges of honor. He writes:

> If anyone thinks he has reason to be confident in the flesh, I have more: circumcised on the eighth day, from the race of Israel, of the tribe of Benjamin, a Hebrew of Hebrews, with respect to the law a Pharisee, with respect to zeal one persecuting the church, with respect to righteousness in the law blameless (εἴ τις δοκεῖ ἄλλος πεποιθέναι ἐν σαρκί, ἐγὼ μᾶλλον· περιτομῇ ὀκταήμερος, ἐκ γένους Ἰσραήλ, φυλῆς Βενιαμίν, Ἑβραῖος ἐξ Ἑβραίων, κατὰ νόμον Φαρισαῖος, κατὰ ζῆλος διώκων τὴν ἐκκλησίαν, κατὰ δικαιοσύνην τὴν ἐν νόμῳ γενόμενος ἄμεμπτος.).

Undoubtedly, each of the (Jewish) epithets in Philippians 3:4-6 could be the subject of close scrutiny,[128] but the clear,

---

[125]Philippians 3:8.

[126]2 Corinthians 5:19.

[127]Scholars have expended considerable effort to understand the nature of Paul's encounter with Christ. Several factors have been of particular interest. First, there has been the attempt to compare and contrast Paul's depiction of his encounter with Luke's depictions in Acts. Second, scholars have debated whether Paul's encounter with Christ constituted a "call" or a "conversion." A third topic of concern has been ascertaining the degree to which this encounter with Christ influenced Paul's overall theology. For representative studies in this vast and contested area of Pauline scholarship, see James D. G. Dunn, " 'A Light to the Gentiles,' or 'The End of the Law': The Significance of the Damascus Road Christophany for Paul" in *Jesus, Paul and the Law: Studies in Mark and Galatians* (Louisville: Westminster/John Knox, 1990), 89-107; Segal, 117-183; and S. Kim, The *Origin of Paul's Gospel* (Grand Rapids: William B. Eerdmans Publishing Company, 1982).

[128]For a closer reading of these epithets, see, for example, Gordon D. Fee, *Paul's Letter to the Philippians* (Grand Rapids: William B.

overall rhetorical effect of vv. 4-6 is that Paul was a man firmly anchored in the world of Judaism. Yet, vv. 4-6 are the rhetorical foil for vv. 7-9. In vv. 7-9 Paul suggests that he is now *more* than a Jew because of his encounter with Christ. He writes in Philippians 3:7-9:

> Whatever was for me gain, these things I have considered loss on account of Christ. Much more, I count everything as loss because of the surpassing value of the knowledge of Christ Jesus my Lord. For his sake, I have suffered the loss of all things, and I consider them as dung in order that I may gain Christ, and be found in him, not having a righteousness of my own that comes from the law, but one that comes through faith in Christ, the righteousness of God based on faith ([ἀλλὰ] ἅτινα ἦν μοι κέρδη, ταῦτα ἥγημαι διὰ τὸν Χριστὸν ζημίαν. ἀλλὰ μενοῦνγε καὶ ἡγοῦμαι πάντα ζημίαν εἶναι διὰ τὸ ὑπερέχον τῆς γνώσεως Χριστοῦ Ἰησοῦ τοῦ κυρίου μου, δι' ὃν τὰ πάντα ἐζημιώθην, καὶ ἡγοῦμαι σκύβαλα, ἵνα Χριστὸν κερδήσω καὶ εὑρεθῶ ἐν αὐτῷ, μὴ ἔχων ἐμὴν δικαιοσύνην τὴν ἐκ νόμου ἀλλὰ τὴν διὰ πίστεως Χριστοῦ, τὴν ἐκ θεοῦ δικαιοσύνην ἐπὶ τῇ πίστει).

Paul's previous reasons for confidence (e.g., vv. 4-6) have been eclipsed by his "Christ experience." Formerly, his Jewish attributes were real privileges and badges of honor worth lauding. Peter O'Brien comments, "These [Jewish credentials] were not simply 'advantages' on a human plane; they were for Paul the Pharisee, zealous for God, gains at the divine level."[129] However, because of his provocative encounter with Christ, the coordinates of Paul's map have changed. Christ is now the epicenter of Paul's symbolic world. As noted above, Paul is now more than a Jew. He is now "in Christ"—one could even call him a "Christian."[130]

Eerdmans Publishing Company, 1995), 305-311, and Marcus Bockmuehl, *The Epistle to the Philippians* (London: A & C Black, 1997), 194-203.

[129]Peter T. O'Brien, *The Epistle to the Philippians* (Grand Rapids: William B. Eerdmans Publishing Company, 1991), 384.

[130]Paul never uses the term "Christian" (Χριστιανός) to describe his (or others') relationship to Christ. By using this terminology, I am simply connoting how influential Christ was to Paul's way of living and

The enormous importance of Paul's Christian identity led E. P. Sanders to his famous argument that the (Christian) solution is Paul's theological antecedent from which all else emanates.[131] Sanders contends that in Paul's thought the understanding of humanity's plight does not lead to an articulation of a solution, but conversely the understanding of the solution (that is, Christ) leads to an articulation of humanity's plight. So determinative is Christ to Paul that Paul reasons "backwards" from Christ. Concerning the dominance of Christ for Paul, Ben Witherington asserts, "Paul's thought world had a dominant sun—the son of God, Jesus Christ. Paul's thoughts about Christ inform and transform the entire rest of his thought, sometimes even absorbing aspects of his thought that one might have expected would have gone relatively untouched by christological reflections."[132]

Yet, if one analyzes some of the salient autobiographical references in Paul's letters,[133] one will also discover that Paul considers himself to be more than just a Christian. His call was not the usual call to Christian fellowship experienced by anyone who accepted the kerygma. As a result of his experience with Christ, Paul had received an important new commission. He was the "Apostles to the Gentiles."

---

thinking. Paul certainly believed that the "Christ event" created for him and for all of Christ's adherents a new identity.

[131]E. P. Sanders, *Paul and Palestinian Judaism* (Philadelphia: Fortress Press, 1977), 442-447.

[132]Ben Witherington, *Paul's Narrative Thought World: The Tapestry of Tragedy and Triumph* (Louisville: Westminster/John Knox Press, 1994), 81.

[133]For example, see Romans 11:13, Romans 15:14-21, 1 Corinthians 9:1-2, 1 Corinthians 15:8-10, and Galatians 1:12-16. For a recent study of Paul's understanding of his own identity, see James D. G. Dunn, "Who Did Paul Think He Was?: A Study of Jewish-Christian Identity," a paper presented at the Society for New Testament Study, Copenhagen, Denmark, July 1998. Also, Carl Holladay explores how Paul and other Hellenistic authors would have construed ethnic identity. See Holladay, "Paul and His Predecessors in the Diaspora: Some Reflections on Ethnic Identity in the Fragmentary Hellenistic Jewish Authors," a paper presented at the Society for New Testament Study, Copenhagen, Denmark, July 1998. Also, see Barclay, *Jews in the Mediterranean Diaspora*, 381-395.

Paul's belief that he was on special assignment is clearly indicated in Galatians 1:12-16. He writes:

> For I want you to know, brothers, that the gospel which was proclaimed by me is not from human origins. For I did not receive it from a human source, neither was I taught it but through a revelation of Jesus Christ. . . . But when it pleased the one, who had set me apart from my mother's womb and who called me through his grace, to reveal his son in me in order that I might preach him among the Gentiles, I did not confer with flesh and blood, nor did I go up to Jerusalem to those who were apostles before me, but I went away into Arabia, and again I returned to Damascus (Γνωρίζω γὰρ ὑμῖν, ἀδελφοί, τὸ εὐαγγέλιον τὸ εὐαγγελισθὲν ὑπ' ἐμοῦ ὅτι οὐκ ἔστιν κατὰ ἄνθρωπον· οὐδὲ γὰρ ἐγὼ παρὰ ἀνθρώπου παρέλαβον αὐτὸ οὔτε ἐδιδάχθην ἀλλὰ δι' ἀποκαλύψεως Ἰησοῦ Χριστοῦ . . . . ὅτε δὲ εὐδόκησεν [ὁ θεὸς] ὁ ἀφορίσας με ἐκ κοιλίας μητρός μου καὶ καλέσας διὰ τῆς χάριτος αὐτου ἀποκαλύψαι τὸν υἱὸν αὐτοῦ ἐν ἐμοί, ἵνα εὐαγγελίζωμαι αὐτὸν ἐν τοῖς ἔθνεσιν, εὐθέως οὐ προσανεθέμην σαρκὶ καὶ αἵματι οὐδὲ ἀνῆλθον εἰς Ἱεροσόλυμα πρὸς τοὺς πρὸ ἐμοῦ ἀποστόλους, ἀλλὰ ἀπῆλθον εἰς Ἀραβίαν καὶ πάλιν ὑπέστρεψα εἰς Δαμασκόν.).

Commentators have often surmised that Paul's mention of receiving the revelation through Jesus Christ is an allusion to his "conversion" experience.[134] Many exegetes consider the phrase "through a revelation of Jesus Christ" (δι' ἀποκαλύψεως Ἰησοῦ Χριστοῦ) to be primarily an objective genitive. In other words, the purpose of the revelation was to reveal to Paul the object or the content of his message to the Gentiles. Paul was to preach Jesus among the Gentiles. According to Richard Longenecker, when Paul speaks of his revelation of Jesus Christ, "in all probability [he] had his encounter with Christ on the Damascus road in mind, with that revelation including (at least embryonically) a mission to the Gentiles."[135]

It appears that Paul primarily thought of himself as a missionary who had been entrusted by Christ with the "gospel

---

[134]See, for example, Hans Dieter Betz, *Galatians* (Philadelphia: Fortress Press, 1979), 62-66.

[135]Richard Longenecker, *Galatians* (Dallas: Word Books, 1990), 24.

for the uncircumcised."[136] Noting the centrality of this "apostolic mission" to Paul's identity, James Dunn writes:

> When we include Paul's self-introductions in his letters, the most striking feature to emerge from these passages is Paul's sense of his identity as an apostle (to the gentiles). The dynamic of that self-identification is clear: it was Paul's asserting his authority in relation to his churches and in the face of those (within the churches or coming from without, usually other Jewish missionaries) who questioned it. *Paul's identity as a Christian was obviously closely bound up with his sense of apostolic calling.*[137]

Paul felt as if his apostolic commission had come directly from Christ.[138] Moreover, by taking the gospel to the Gentiles, Paul believed that he was completing the work of Christ. According to Paul's theology (especially in Galatians), the Gentiles were always included in the original covenant promises to Abraham. Therefore, one of Christ's purposes was to restore those promises to their original design. In Galatians 3:13-14, Paul remarks:

> Christ redeemed us from the curse of the law by becoming a curse for us—for it is written, 'Cursed is everyone who hangs on a tree'—in order that in Christ Jesus the blessing of Abraham might come to the Gentiles, so that we might receive the promise of the spirit through faith (Χριστὸς ἡμᾶς ἐξηγόρασεν ἐκ τῆς κατάρας τοῦ νόμου γενόμενος ὑπὲρ ἡμῶν κατάρα, ὅτι γέγραπται, Ἐπικατάρατος πᾶς ὁ κρεμάμενος ἐπὶ ξύλου, ἵνα εἰς τὰ ἔθνη ἡ εὐλογία τοῦ Ἀβραὰμ γένηται ἐν Χριστῷ Ἰησοῦ, ἵνα τὴν ἐπαγγελίαν τοῦ πνεύματος λάβωμεν διὰ τῆς πίστεως).

Paul's work among the Gentiles was a pragmatic implementation of Christ's mission.[139]

---

[136]See, for example, Galatians 2:7 and Romans 15:16.

[137]Dunn, "Who Did Paul Think He Was?," 3 (emphasis mine).

[138]Paul had neither walked with Jesus during Jesus' ministry nor been an original witness to the resurrection of Jesus. Nonetheless, in 1 Corinthians 15:3-11, he claims to have had his own experience with the resurrected Christ.

[139]Romans 15:17-18.

In fulfillment of his apostolic calling, Paul admits that flexibility (or some would say ambivalence) had become his *modus operandi*. For example, in 1 Corinthians 9:19-23 Paul remarks:

> For though I am free from all people, I have made myself a slave to all, that I might win the more. To the Jews I became as a Jew, in order to win Jews; to those under the law I became as one under the law—though not being myself under the law. To those outside the law I became as one outside the law—not being without law toward God but under the law of Christ—that I might win those outside the law. To the weak I became weak, that I might win the weak. I have become all things to all people, that I by all means may save some. I do it all for the sake of the gospel, that I may share in its blessings (Ἐλεύθερος γὰρ ὢν ἐκ πάντων πᾶσιν ἐμαυτὸν ἐδούλωσα, ἵνα τοὺς πλείονας κερδήσω· καὶ ἐγενόμην τοῖς Ἰουδαίοις ὡς Ἰουδαῖος, ἵνα Ἰουδαίους κερδήσω· τοῖς ὑπὸ νόμον ὡς ὑπὸ νόμον, μὴ ὢν αὐτὸς ὑπὸ νόμον, ἵνα τοὺς ὑπὸ νόμον κερδήσω· τοῖς ἀνόμοις ὡς ἄνομος, μὴ ὢν ἄνομος θεοῦ ἀλλ᾽ ἔννομος Χριστοῦ, ἵνα κερδάνω τοὺς ἀνόμους· ἐγενόμην τοῖς ἀσθενέσιν ἀσθενής, ἵνα τοὺς ἀσθενεῖς κερδήσω· τοῖς πᾶσιν γέγονα πάντα, ἵνα πάντως τινὰς σώσω. πάντα δὲ ποιῶ διὰ τὸ εὐαγγέλιον, ἵνα συγκοινωνὸς αὐτοῦ γένωμαι.).

Although an exhaustive examination of this much-discussed passage is beyond the scope of this chapter,[140] there are several important elements in this passage (and its immediate context) which shed light on the implications of Paul's experience with Christ.

Paul begins 9:19-23 by asserting his freedom. Yet, paradoxically, he is free to all people because he considers himself to be a *slave of Christ*. In 1 Corinthians 9:1-18 Paul

---

[140]The exegetical literature on this passage is copious. For more detailed discussions, see, for example, H. Chadwick, "All Things to All Men," *New Testament Studies* 1 (1955): 261-275; Fee, *1 Corinthians*, 422-433; P. Richardson, "Pauline Inconsistency: I Corinthians 9:19-23 and Galatians 2:11-14," *New Testament Studies* 26 (1979): 347-362; Martin, *Slavery as Salvation*, 77-85, 117-135; and Wendell Willis, "An Apostolic Apologia: The Form and Function of 1 Corinthians 9," *Journal for the Study of the New Testament* 24 (1985): 33-48.

depicts his apostolic commission as a form of slavery.[141] Like a slave unable to exercise his will, Paul, in his missionary efforts, is motivated by the divine necessity of his slave master, Christ. Paul's understanding of his ministry as slavery to Christ is evinced in 1 Corinthians 9:17.[142] He suggests that since his missionary efforts are against his will he does not receive a reward for his labor. Instead, like a slave steward, he has been entrusted with a commission (οἰκονομίαν). Οἰκονομία often connoted the management of household affairs—a duty frequently discharged by a slave.

The rhetorical effect of 9:1-18 is clear. Paul is a slave of Christ. The great paradox of his slavery to Christ is that it enables him to be free with respect to all people. In other words, Paul's slavery *liberates* him to engage in a variety of practices in order to win persons for his master, Christ.

Thus, in vv. 19-23 Paul indicates that his missionary adaptability is not an end unto itself but rather a means to win people to Christ. In vv. 19-23 Paul uses the verb "to win" (κερδαίνω) five times. In order to win persons for Christ, or bring them into the ἐκκλησία, Paul engages in different social conduct in different social settings. In the majority of his examples in these verses, Paul says that he became like (ὡς) the particular group.[143] The word ὡς may be crucial to a proper understanding of Paul's missionary tactics.

Paul could accommodate, for example, the salient practices of Jews, or Gentiles because he believed that these practices were not the source of a right relationship with God. In this regard, he could even live momentarily *as* a Jew or *as* a Gentile. In Paul's estimation, a right relationship with God now

---

[141]Dale Martin argues that 9:1-18 should be understood as the rhetorical foil to 9:19-23. See Martin, *Slavery as Salvation*, 83.

[142]In 1 Corinthians 9:17 Paul writes, "If I do this of my own will (i.e., preach the gospel), I have a reward. If I do this against my will, I am entrusted with a commission" (εἰ γὰρ ἑκὼν τοῦτο πράσσω, μισθὸν ἔχω· εἰ δὲ ἄκων, οἰκονομίαν πεπίστευμαι).

[143]Only in the case of the weak does Paul say that he actually became weak, and not simply *like* the weak. For further discussion of some of the implications of this point, see Richard B. Hays, *1 Corinthians* (Louisville: John Knox Press, 1997), 154-155.

could only come from being in Christ, and the social manifestation of being in Christ was membership in the ἐκκλησία. As long as various groups recognized that the ultimate identity marker was being in Christ, they could, within some limits,[144] freely engage in certain social practices that had defined them. Thus, in some sense, the Pauline ἐκκλησία welcomed a variety of social practices. Such practices could co-exist with one's identity as a Christian as long as they did not usurp the ἐκκλησία as one's primary identity marker.

Paul was a Jew who had encountered Christ in a decisive manner. On the one hand, this encounter did not preclude Paul from continuing as a Jew in a limited way. On the other hand, because of the encounter Paul was more than a Jew. Additionally, Paul's ministry among the Gentiles was based on a similar contention, namely, that Gentiles should enter the ἐκκλησία as Gentiles. Yet, in Christ, Gentiles were more than Gentiles.

Paul seems to suggest that membership in the ἐκκλησία creates a third social identity which surpasses, but does not necessarily obliterate, one's previous social (and especially ethnic) identity. The guiding reality for Paul is no longer ethnic identity, but the "law of Christ"[145] or the "commandments of God."[146] It would appear that Paul's references to the "law of Christ" or the "commandments of God" are meant to imply that being in the ἐκκλησία does entail adhering to certain ethical imperatives.

As suggested above, there are some behaviors that Paul would consider absolutely incongruous with the "law of Christ"

---

[144]One of the limits that Paul seems to impose is whether or not the particular action infringes upon the conscience of a fellow believer. The relationship between a believer's freedom in conduct and his concern for the welfare of other members of the ἐκκλησία is one of the main topics of 1 Corinthians 8-10. It is also clear that Paul is unwilling to tolerate certain actions such as idolatry and πορνεία in the ἐκκλησία. For examples of Paul's aversion to idolatry, see 1 Corinthians 10:14 and 1 Thessalonians 1:9. Of course, 1 Corinthians 5-7 contains several examples of Paul's prohibitions against πορνεία.

[145]1 Corinthians 9:21.
[146]1 Corinthians 7:19.

(e.g., idolatry and πορνεία). Yet, in the main, the "law of Christ" does not appear to be a set of established rules to which Paul or any other Christian could readily appeal. This is precisely the point. Many of the rules of social conduct in the Pauline ἐκκλησία had not been firmly established. For Paul, the believer's experience with Christ is paramount, but the interaction between one's membership in the ἐκκλησία and one's previous social relationships and conduct involves some flexibility. This flexibility created the potential for social ambiguity in the Pauline ἐκκλησία.

E. P. Sanders captures nicely the ambiguity of Paul's conception of the ἐκκλησία. On this point, Sanders deserves to be quoted extensively:

> Nevertheless in very important ways the church was, in Paul's view and even more in his practice, a third entity. It was not established by admitting Gentiles to Israel according to the flesh (as standard Jewish eschatological expectation would have it), but by admitting all, whether Jew or Greek, into the body of Christ by faith in him. Admission was sealed by baptism, most emphatically not by circumcision and acceptance of the law. The worship of the church was not worship in the synagogue (though quite conceivably some members could have done both). The rules governing behavior were partly Jewish, but not entirely, and thus in this way too Paul's Gentile churches were a third entity. . . . Paul's view of the church, supported by his practice, against his own conscious intention, was substantially that it was a third entity, not just because it was composed of both Jew and Greek, *but also because it was in important ways neither Jew nor Greek.*[147]

I disagree with only one aspect of Sanders's observation. I do not think that Paul's creation of the ἐκκλησία as a third entity was against his conscious intention. In my estimation, Paul is quite consciously attempting to create a new social reality, and some of the ambiguity in passages such as 1 Corinthians 7 stems from the fact that Paul has not fully worked out the implications of his conscious efforts.

---

[147]Sanders, *Paul, the Law, and the Jewish People* (Minneapolis: Fortress Press, 1983), 178-179 (emphasis mine).

Perplexing questions are arising for Paul (and surely for the converts in his congregations). In every situation does one's identity as a Christian "trump" one's former social status? Is one's identity as a Christian in force practically only when the ἐκκλησία meets, or is this new (third) identity determinative even when one is in the "marketplace" of Greco-Roman culture? In some sense, Paul honors ethnic distinctions while simultaneously declaring that they have been replaced by a new distinction, membership in the ἐκκλησία.

Wayne Meeks has provocatively likened Paul to a figure in Homer's writings, Proteus, *a daimon* of the sea who could assume any form he chose.[148] In his missionary practices, Paul is Proteus. In order to win persons for Christ and to bring them into the ἐκκλησία, Paul accommodates one group one day, and he accommodates another group the next. With respect to building the ἐκκλησία, Paul is a man of many forms and considerable flexibility. Yet, once persons had accepted the kerygma and become part of the ἐκκλησία, questions of personal and social norms within and without the ἐκκλησία became crucial and potentially divisive issues.

In the realm of ethical mandates, Paul is no less like Proteus. On certain matters, he definitively commands a course of action. On another issue, he states his preference, while permitting a concession. On still another issue, he admits that he has no historical traditions to guide him, but he, nonetheless, offers an opinion informed by the Holy Spirit. Outside of Paul's emphatic prohibitions against idolatry and πορνεία and his equally emphatic insistence on a love ethic which concerns itself with the welfare of other believers,[149] one might be hard pressed to locate a consistent Pauline ethic.

Concerning the malleability of Paul's ethical mandates, Wayne Meeks writes:

> The question of norms, How can I know what I ought to do? is much less likely to receive a clear and helpful answer from Paul. One of the intriguing things about his responses to practical ethical dilemmas in his congregations is the

---

[148]Meeks, "The Christian Proteus," 438.
[149]See, for example, 1 Corinthians 12-14 and Galatians 6:1-2.

diversity of norms and guides that he employs. He appeals to catechetical rules of thumb—some practical harmony and "building up" of the congregation; to his own life-style. . . . To a rather general notion of "freedom." But one thing he never does: he never uses "the law," either the Torah of Moses or any Hellenistic substitute for it, to lay down regulations for the Christian community. What stands behind every Pauline admonition—and they are many and manifold!—is the requirement that the Christian be "transformed by the renewal of your mind" in order to "test what is the will of God". . . . Both Paul and the Stoics recommend and practice essentially conventional behavior while in principle relativizing the whole ordinary basis for that behavior. Both demand a constant, practiced "testing" of the immediate situation, in order to discover what is the "fitting" response to the ultimate reality that is only indirectly visible in that situation. But for Paul that ultimate reality is not discovered by the rational analysis of "what depends on yourself" (Epictetus). Rather it is determined by the complex of symbols clustering around one central event, the crucifixion and resurrection of God's Messiah. And the significance of that event is not discerned in the sage's heroic detachment from all things not under his inner control, any more than it is found in the mystic's transport. Rather, it has to be learned within the life of the community formed by that event through memory, faith, and hope, a community which Paul will not permit to segregate itself from "the world."[150]

Meeks correctly emphasizes Paul's convictions that the Christ event is central and that this event has created a new social constellation, the ἐκκλησία. The challenge facing Paul is the creation of the *real* rules of social conduct for believers when they are inside and outside of the ἐκκλησία. Thus, a passage such as 1 Corinthians 7 may at times be complex and ambiguous because the Corinthians are asking their apostle to teach them about the social implications of life in Christ, and Paul is still learning the lessons himself. Paul is "teaching on the fly," or as Meeks suggests, he is "always thinking under pressure."[151] The complexities and ambiguities of our passage may not be unfortunate interpretive problems to be explained away but

---

[150]Meeks, "The Christian Proteus," 443-444.
[151]Meeks, "The Christian Proteus," 438.

instead vestiges of the genuine struggles of a man who has had a profound religious experience. Briefly, let us return to some of the features in our passage where traces of this struggle are evident.

Paul's Experience with Christ and 1 Corinthians 7

The majority of 1 Corinthians could be understood as Paul's protracted attempt to translate the Corinthians' experience with Christ into rules for social conduct. Having (re)established his authority as their apostle in chapters one through four, Paul earnestly wrestles with concrete issues in the remainder of the letter. His teaching ranges from sexual conduct,[152] to the appropriateness of eating idol meat,[153] to the importance of disciplined giving for the financial collection for the saints.[154] In chapter seven, the apparent topic is marriage and sexual ethics, but, as suggested earlier, Paul "interrupts" this discussion with crucial and complex reflections upon the call to the ἐκκλησία and its implications on conduct.

In 7:17 Paul's use of the verb περιπατέω is an important clue that he continues to be concerned about the Corinthians' everyday conduct. Literally, this verb means "to walk." However, like its Hebrew equivalent הלך, περιπατέω carried connotations of one's ethical conduct in the world.[155] Thus, in v. 17 Paul submits that the guiding principle for the Corinthians' daily conduct should be their call into the ἐκκλησία. Paul amplifies this discussion in the following verses with appeals to ethnic and social realities.

Paul clearly dissuades his converts from altering their ethnic status as a condition for membership in the ἐκκλησία. The circumcised should not be uncircumcised, and the

---

[152]See, for example, 1 Corinthians 5-7.

[153]See, for example, 1 Corinthians 8-10.

[154]See, for example, 1 Corinthians 16.

[155]See "περιπατέω" in *The Vocabulary of the Greek New Testament*, ed. James Hope Moulton and George Milligan (Grand Rapids: William B. Eerdmans Publishing Company, 1930), 507.

uncircumcised should not be circumcised. Paul seems to suggest that the ἐκκλησία is formed on a basis other than ethnic association. There is nothing inherently good or bad about being either a Jew or a Gentile. The primary identity marker is now the call into the community created by Christ. Therefore, the salient rituals for entrance and acceptance into these ethnic communities are no longer relevant for the formation of the ἐκκλησία.

Although Paul urges his converts not to alter their ethnic status in order to participate in the ἐκκλησία, he also does not overtly prohibit such actions in general. Circumcision and uncircumcision are not inherently evil or undesirable practices. Membership in the ἐκκλησία just transcends ethnic affiliations.

For Paul the perplexing question may not be the role of ethnic identity per se, but instead the proper relationship between ethnic identity and membership in the ἐκκλησία. When Paul entered the ἐκκλησία, he did not relinquish his Jewish heritage; he redefined his Jewish heritage. As indicated above, Paul is still a Jew, but he is also more than a Jew. The tenuous relationship between Paul's Jewish identity (which to some degree is still operative) and his new, dominant Christian identity may be a source of some ambiguity in Paul's writings.

1 Corinthians 7:19 may be a telling example of Paul's struggle to integrate his previous Jewish identity and his new Christian identity. In the first half of v. 19 it is clear that Pharisaic Judaism is no longer Paul's point of orientation. He declares, "Circumcision is nothing. . ." It is highly improbable that an observant Pharisaic Jew would make this kind of claim. The Pharisees were known for their strict interpretation of the written and oral Torah.[156] Paul's declaration that circumcision, a chief sign of the covenant, is no longer a basis for community formation clearly indicates his break with his *Pharisaic* past.[157]

---

[156]Concerning the strictness of the Pharisees' interpretation, see Josephus, *The War of the Jews* 1.110.

[157]James Dunn argues that Paul did not abandon Judaism as much as he abandoned *Pharisaic* Judaism. See Dunn, "Who Did Paul Think He Was?," 9.

Yet, Paul in v. 19 also demonstrates no special fondness for Gentile culture. Uncircumcision, an important step in assimilation to a Gentile way of life, is considered equally irrelevant with respect to the calling to the ἐκκλησία. In terms of the social conduct in the ἐκκλησία, the ritual practices of neither the Jewish nor Gentile communities are normative.

However, at precisely the moment it appears that Paul has broken from his Jewish heritage, he asserts that the true norm in the ἐκκλησία is the "commandments of God" (ἐντολῶν θεοῦ). The phrase the "commandments of God" has a distinctively Jewish ring. Even as Paul struggles to articulate rules of practical conduct in the new community, his Jewish heritage disallows him to contemplate a community without a law. As suggested in chapter one, the phrase in v. 19 "keeping the commandments of God" may mean "being Christian." In essence, Paul may be suggesting that the identity marker that matters is being a Christian and that the ethics of the ἐκκλησία must generally be in line with the commandments of God. Yet, it is doubtful that these (unspecified) "commandments" are to be equated with those given to Moses for the Jewish community on Mount Sinai.

Although supposedly Paul's "rules of conduct" in the ἐκκλησία are neither Jewish nor Gentile, it is remarkable (and ironic) that in v. 19 he, nonetheless, talks about these rules in distinctively Jewish language. The ἐκκλησία has a new code of conduct which Paul elusively labels "the commandments of God," but of course, Paul does not specify what the rules for conduct are because he may not have specific rules.

Social existence in the ἐκκλησία is guided by the Lord. Because of these fluctuations in Paul—between his Jewish heritage and his Christian heritage and between a community governed by a new law, but a law with no specific commandments—John Barclay has labeled Paul as "anomalous." It is worth quoting Barclay at some length. Barclay writes:

> Here, then, we encounter the truly anomalous character of Paul. In his conceptuality Paul is most at home among the particularistic and least accommodated segments of the

Diaspora; yet in his utilization of these concepts, and in his social practice, he shatters the ethnic mold in which that ideology was formed. He shows little inclination to forge any form of synthesis with his cultural environment, yet he employs the language of a culturally antagonistic Judaism to establish a new social entity which transgressed the boundaries of the Diaspora synagogues. By an extraordinary transference of ideology, Paul deracinates the most culturally conservative forms of Judaism in the Diaspora and uses them in service of his largely Gentile communities. . . . The tensions created by this [i.e., Paul's synagogue] experience and by the anomaly of his own stance are reflected in Paul's varying description of his identity. On occasions he proudly asserts his Jewishness, proclaiming himself a Hebrew, an Israelite and of the seed of Abraham (2 Cor. 11.22). . . . Yet elsewhere he talks of his *former* (not his present) life in Judaism (Gal 1.13-14), and in Phil. 3.2-11 he lists his Jewish credentials only to declare them all "loss," indeed "dung" for the sake of knowing Christ. Obviously rhetorical factors influence such variant self-descriptions, but they also reflect the turmoil into which he was thrown by his mission and its rejection in the synagogues.[158]

Just as features in 1 Corinthians 7:17-19 bear the marks of Paul's struggle to integrate his former experience and his new experience, features in 1 Corinthians 7:20-24 provide insights into how influential Christ had become for Paul. In these verses, Paul turns his attention to the issue of Roman slavery and whether Christians caught in this lamentable institution should seek concrete manumission. Regardless of the contested interpretations concerning his advice to slaves in these verses, Paul in vv. 20-24 ultimately defines both free persons and slaves with respect to their relationship to Christ.

The slave who is called into the fellowship of the ἐκκλησία (ὁ γὰρ ἐν κυρίῳ κληθεὶς δοῦλος, v. 22) is a freedman *of the Lord* (ἀπελεύθερος κυρίου). The free person who is called into the fellowship of the ἐκκλησία (ὁ ἐλεύθερος κληθεὶς) is a slave *of Christ* (δοῦλός Χριστοῦ). Since the ἐκκλησία is the Lord's community, members of it are (or ought to be) defined by their relationship to Christ. For Paul, *in theory* it would appear

---

[158]Barclay, *Jews in the Mediterranean Diaspora*, 393-394.

that the believer's real social status, be it free or servile, is a penultimate concern—if a concern at all. Problems may be arising, however, because theory and (concrete social) practice are beginning to collide in the Corinthian ἐκκλησία.

In these verses, Paul clearly emphasizes that the Christian's true identity is derived from an existence lived before God (παρὰ θεῷ). Paul, however, is not clear concerning the *practical* implications of his belief. The actual slave who might have heard these words would have had little doubt that he was now the client of a new patron, Christ. Yet, that same slave may not have been able to derive from Paul's statements any clear indication of whether he (i.e., the slave) should still belong to his real, earthly master. On the question of actual manumission from slavery, Paul is tentative at best.

This is not the first time in chapter seven that we have witnessed a tentativeness in Paul. As noted earlier, Paul seems almost hesitant as he offers concrete instructions concerning marriage and sexuality in chapter seven. For example, he provides some ethical exhortations concerning the roles of sexuality and marriage for the believers, but almost immediately he interrupts these instructions with concessions. Paul *is* firmly persuaded that *porneia* and idolatry have no place in the ἐκκλησία. Concerning, however, other concrete practices—such as marriage, sexual activity, the role of ethnicity, slavery, and manumission—the rules of conduct are being written as Paul speaks.

Conclusions

Although Paul was a man seemingly at home in the Jewish and Greco-Roman worlds, his experience with Christ had provided him with a new source of identity. As an apostle (to the Gentiles), Paul made it his life's work to create a special community, the ἐκκλησία, in the various places he traveled. In his directives to his churches, Paul was abundantly clear that membership in this new community should serve as the primary identity badge for the believer.

Paul, however, was anything but clear concerning many of the concrete rules of behavior that would typify life in the ἐκκλησία. As Alan Segal suggests, Paul had a vested interest "in the consequences of his perception that the Torah was no longer valid in the way he had supposed. He tried to understand how moral behavior was to continue in the new community of faith."[159] Furthermore, Paul still appeared to be grappling with the relationship between one's former social status in the world and one's new status "in Christ." Like the Corinthians, Paul was struggling to make sense of the myriad (social) implications of his (and their) "Christ experience." The complexities and ambiguities that emerged in this process may be telling indicators of the genuine difficulty of Paul's struggle.

Having positioned both the Corinthians and Paul on the social map, we are better equipped to travel further into the interior of the social situation of our text. Close readings of Paul's (rhetorical) appeals to circumcision and slavery in 1 Corinthians 7:17-24 will occupy us in chapters three and four.

---

[159]Segal, 149.

Chapter 3

CIRCUMCISION IN
THE GRECO-ROMAN WORLD

INTRODUCTION

In chapter one, I provided an overview and explanation of various textual features that contribute to the complexity and ambiguity in 1 Corinthians 7 in general and vv. 17-24 in particular. The purpose of chapter two was to widen the angle of investigation in order to see certain social factors in the first century CE Mediterranean world that also would have exacerbated the complexity and ambiguity of Paul's words in our passage. The most notable social factors would have included ethnicity and social status. Both of these areas, as was demonstrated, were themselves riddled with social complexity. Yet, it is precisely these two areas, ethnicity and social status, to which Paul makes strong rhetorical appeal in 1 Corinthians 7:17-24 when he speaks about circumcision/uncircumcision and slavery.

The ultimate aim of chapters three and four is to investigate how the appeals to these complex social phenomena function in 1 Corinthians 7:17-24. Thus, chapters three and four will attempt to synthesize the data from chapter one (i.e., textual features) with the data from chapter two (i.e., social factors). In order to understand the role and import of circumcision and slavery in this passage, an overview of each of these social realities in the ancient Mediterranean world will precede our exegetical analysis of its role in 1 Corinthians 7. The focus of chapter three will be circumcision.

CIRCUMCISION

Origins

The fact that circumcision played a significant role in the social identity of ancient Jews is a truism. Specifying, however, the nature of the role of circumcision and just when it became for most Jews[1] (but, perhaps, not for all Jews) a *sine qua non* of Jewish identity is an altogether different and more complicated matter.

Circumcision, although vitally important in Jewish society, did not originate with Jewish society. The Hebrew scriptures are cognizant that Israel was not the sole practitioner nor the originator of circumcision. Jeremiah, in the sixth century BCE, bemoaning the inevitable judgment to fall upon Judah, writes, "Behold the days are coming, says the Lord, when I will punish all those who are circumcised, but yet uncircumcised: Egypt, Judah, Edom the son of Ammon, Moab and all who dwell in the desert that cut the corners of their hair."[2] This passage, written more than 600 years before the Corinthian correspondence, raises an important issue (which will be explored below), namely, the role of physical and/or "symbolic" circumcision in the establishment of Jewish ethnic identity. This passage in Jeremiah also indicates an awareness that physical circumcision was practiced by many of Israel's neighbors.

The fact that Jeremiah mentions Egypt first in the list of the circumcised nations which are "uncircumcised" may be quite telling historically. It was reported in antiquity that the practice of circumcision had originated with the Egyptians.[3] Scholars,[4]

---

[1]The question whether circumcision was indispensable for Jewish identity, especially in the Diaspora, is precisely one of the areas that adds complexity to any discussion of circumcision.

[2]Jeremiah 9:25-26.

[3]In *The Histories*, Herodotus writes, "They [the Egyptians] practice circumcision, while men of other nations-except those who have learnt from Egypt-leave their private parts as nature made them." See Herodotus, *The Histories*, trans. Aubrey de Sélincourt (New York: Penguin Books, 1972), 143.

nevertheless, have queried concerning the Egyptian origin of circumcision. Jack Sasson removes the origins of circumcision from the African continent and places it in North Syria. According to one scholar, the precise moment or place when various civilizations began practicing circumcision is "lost in the mist of prehistory."[5] Nevertheless, it is incontrovertible that other cultures were practicing circumcision long before Israel adopted it.

Reasons Why Circumcision Was Practiced

At some point in the life of Israel, the *raison d'être* for circumcision was that it was commanded in the Torah. Yet, before it became a sign of the covenant, circumcision served other purposes in Israel, and residual evidence of these purposes can be seen in Israel's textual tradition.

In many ancient societies, including Israel, circumcision functioned as a fertility rite and as a method by which one could ward off evil. Both of these functions appear to be inextricably linked in the enigmatic story of Moses and Zipporah in Exodus 4:24-26.[6] In this passage, having received his commission from God, Moses returns to Egypt to begin the liberation project. During his journey, Moses is attacked by a divine/demonic being. Apparently as a means of protection, Moses' wife, Zipporah, circumcises their son, allowing the blood from the procedure to touch Moses' phallus. Upon completing this act, Zipporah says to Moses, "You are a bridegroom of blood to me." Scholars contend that this enigmatic Hebrew phrase "bridegroom of blood" (חתן דמם) is a vestige from a time when circumcision was a fertility rite, performed possibly prior to a

---

[4]See, for instance, Jack Sasson, "Circumcision in the Ancient Near East," *Journal of Biblical Literature* 85 (1966): 473-476.

[5]Rudolf Meyer, "περιτέμνω" in *Theological Dictionary of the New Testament*, vol. 6 (Grand Rapids: William B. Eerdmans Publishing Company, 1968), 75.

[6]For further discussion of the interpretive difficulties of this story, see L. Kaplan, "And the Lord Sought to Kill Him" (Exodus 4:24) Yet Once Again," *Hebrew Annual Review* 5 (1981): 65-74.

couple's wedding. The final editor of the story in Exodus, however, sensing the potential confusion caused by the phrase "bridegroom of blood," inserts an explanatory gloss in Exodus 4:26. "Then it was that she said, 'You are a bridegroom of blood' *because of the circumcision.*"

The story in Exodus 4 also bears witness to another early feature of circumcision, its function as an apotropaic rite, or a performance that wards off evil. Prior to Moses' (or his son's) circumcision, this divine/demonic spirit sought to kill Moses. After the rite of circumcision, "he (i.e., the attacking spirit) let him alone."[7] Circumcision had protected Moses from this attack of evil.

Although circumcision as a marriage and fertility rite and as a protection from evil loomed in the background as reasons why circumcision was practiced by Israel, another reason (which would eventually become *the* reason) was that circumcision was a primary sign of the covenant and thereby a sign of Jewish ethnicity.[8] To be circumcised was to be a member of the covenant people of God.[9] A primary text declaring circumcision to be a sign of the covenant is Genesis 17:9-11:

---

[7]Exodus 4:26.

[8]See, in chapter two, my discussion of Goudriaan's six points concerning ethnicity, especially point two. Goudriaan remarks, "Ethnicity, as a way of organizing cultural differences, implies that specific features of culture (in the broad sense) are singled out as ethnically significant, while others are neutral." Goudriaan, 76.

[9]Undoubtedly, male circumcision as the sign of the covenant in Israel raises a host of gender questions about the covenant status of women. Concerning the inherent gender difficulties and inequalities in privileging circumcision as a sign of the covenant, Shaye Cohen remarks, "Even if circumcision is an indication of Jewishness, it is a marker for only half of the Jewish population (in the eyes of the ancients the more important half, of course, but still, only half). How you would know a Jewish woman, when you saw one, remains open." See Cohen, " 'Those Who Say They are Jews and Are Not': How Do You Know a Jew in Antiquity When You See One?" in *Diasporas in Antiquity*, ed. Shaye D. Cohen and Ernest S. Frerichs (Atlanta: Scholars Press, 1993), 12. For an intriguing treatment of the theological and social dilemmas that arise from the biblical concept of the "maleness of God," see Howard Eilberg-Schwartz, *God's Phallus: And Other Problems for Men and Monotheism* (Boston: Beacon Press, 1994).

> And God said to Abraham, "As for you, you shall keep my covenant, you and your descendants after you through their generations. This is my covenant which you shall keep between me and you and your descendants after you. Every male among you should be circumcised. You shall be circumcised in the flesh of your foreskins, and it shall be a sign of the covenant between me and you.

Source criticism helps us place the understanding of circumcision proffered in Genesis 17 in an appropriate historical framework. Although canonically, the supreme emphasis on circumcision as a sign of the covenant occurs early in the story of Israel, source criticism reminds us that this pericope (as well as large portions of the Pentateuch itself) is the work of the Priestly school. Many Hebrew scripture scholars date the flourishing of the Priestly tradition to exilic and post-exilic periods.

Thus, although circumcision was practiced for centuries by Israel, it was probably not until the seventh-sixth centuries BCE that circumcision was elevated to the status of the supreme Jewish ethnic marker. The elevation of circumcision to a level of utmost importance in marking off the people of Israel was certainly aided by the Priestly juxtaposition of the rite of circumcision and God's discussion of the covenant with Abraham.[10] As Rudolf Meyer correctly notes, " Circumcision [in Genesis 17:1-27] is integrated into the theological exposition of the priestly author."[11] Before the exilic and post-exilic theology, represented by the Priestly school, asserted its dominance, there was already a definitive intermingling in Israel between ethnic identity and theological beliefs. In Genesis 17, the Priestly author and his devotees made sure that Israel's ethnic identity

---

[10]With respect to the Priestly intertwining of covenant theology, ethnic identity, and circumcision, Lawrence Boadt writes, "The author goes on in the rest of [Genesis] chapter 17 to explain how the rite of circumcision will be a sign of the covenant. P is thus able to present a way of keeping the covenant which does not require an independent state to live in or even a temple building to worship in. We know that the practice of circumcision was especially important to Judaism after the Babylonian exile of the sixth century as a sign of membership in the community." See Boadt, *Reading the Old Testament: An Introduction* (New York: Paulist Press, 1984), 141.

[11]Meyer, 76.

and its theological presuppositions would be inextricably linked forever.

That a strong correlation occurred between circumcision and theological narrative during and after the exile should come as no surprise. Undoubtedly, from the time of Israel's settling in the land of Canaan through the period of the united and divided monarchies, Israel had to contend with other nationalities or ethnicities. At times, Israel's relations with these ethnic groups was marked by peace; other times by hostility. Yet, the possession of a "homeland," along with the temple cult, provided common denominators of ethnic identity for Jewish persons.

The cataclysmic events of the exile (most notably the fall of Jerusalem, the destruction of the temple in 586 BCE, and the creation of a large Diaspora population) threw the question of Jewish identity into extremely sharp relief.[12] Physically apart from homeland and temple cult, Diaspora Jews might have frequently asked, "what makes me a person of the covenant (i.e., a Jew) in this particular social setting"? One answer that Diaspora Judaism[13] would offer would be circumcision.[14]

The role of circumcision as a primary sign of Jewish ethnic identity was both aided and hindered by a general cultural aversion to circumcision in the wider Greco-Roman world. The fact that many persons in the Greco-Roman world considered circumcision an act of perversion was all the more reason why certain Jews would want to "wear" the badge of ethnic distinctiveness. Yet, in the face of such cultural antipathy for

---

[12]Meyer has noted that the LXX, itself a fascinating and complex Diaspora production, refers more to circumcision than does the Hebrew text. The greater frequency with which circumcision is discussed in the LXX reflects the heightened awareness of ethnic issues in the Diaspora. See Meyer, 74.

[13]Shaye Cohen warns us about the danger of defining one variety of Judaism as normative. See Cohen, *From the Maccabees to the Mishnah* (Philadelphia: Westminster Press, 1987), 135.

[14]My emphasis on circumcision in the Diaspora is not at all to say that circumcision was not important in the land of Israel. In the land of Israel, however, the very land itself and the temple cult provided additional ethnic markers.

circumcision, Jews, who dared wear the badge of circumcision, could (and very often did) pay dearly for their decision.

Scholars often comment upon the religious persecutions suffered by Jews under the hands of Antiochus IV.[15] Chief of these persecutions was the execution of women who had their children circumcised.[16] Obviously, this violence, sparked by a desire of the Jews to be circumcised in the Maccabean period,[17] falls two centuries before the Corinthian correspondence. Yet, more than half a century after the Corinthian correspondence, the Roman aversion to circumcision continued and was

---

[15]As a result of Alexander's conquest and the ensuing "wars of the successors," Palestine became a hotly contested area in the struggle between two great Hellenistic kingdoms, the Seleucids and the Ptolemies. In the face of the infusion of Hellenistic culture into the Jewish cultural world, one could argue that at the heart of the Maccabean revolt lay the question, "what does it mean to be a Jew?" or perhaps "what are the boundary markers that characterize the Jewish way of life?" The Maccabean revolt was a complex mixture of political power and intrigue, issues of ethnic boundaries, and religious practices. One of the major tasks of scholars interested in the Maccabean period has been that of sorting out the relationship among these various factors. One of the most provocative theses concerning the Maccabean revolt has been proffered by Elias Bickerman. Bickerman contended that the precipitating cause of the Maccabean revolt was not the religious persecutions of Antiochus Epiphanes but rather pre-existing, *intra-Jewish* civil unrest. Prior to Bickerman's watershed thesis, many scholars argued the contrary, namely, that the persecutions preceded the uprising and that the conflict was really between the "pagan" Seleucids and the Jews who remained faithful to their ancestral traditions. Bickerman's position represented a *tour de force* in Maccabean scholarship, and it offered a compelling account of the origins and development of the Maccabean uprising. See Bickerman, "The Maccabean Uprising: An Interpretation" in *The Jewish Expression*, ed. J. Goldin (New Haven: Yale University Press, 1976), 66-86; *The God of the Maccabees: Studies on the Meaning and Origin of the Maccabean Revolt* (Leiden: Brill, 1979). Also see, Tcherikover, 175-203.

[16]1 Maccabees 1:60-61.

[17]In an interesting historical twist, once the Hasmoneans gained political authority, they forced those under them to submit to circumcision. Undoubtedly, this is an ironic expression of people gaining political liberation and using the very tools (i.e., violence) which once made for their domination.

embodied in the emperor Hadrian who outlawed circumcision.[18] Thus, the Maccabean revolt on the one hand, and the Bar Kochba revolt on the other, form a kind of historical parentheses around the three-century long profound dislike in the Greco-Roman world for various practices of Judaism, most notably circumcision.

The vital role of circumcision is underscored by the fact that each revolt, although separated by nearly three centuries, could be viewed as Greco-Roman attempts to further acculturate Jews, or these revolts could be viewed as Jewish attempts to avoid ethnic assimilation.[19] In the face of the persecution created by a desire to circumcise, however, some Jews saw circumcision no longer as a badge of ethnic honor but as an expendable cultural liability. These Jews attempted to hide the evidence of their circumcision. The classic and often cited example of this is found in 1 Maccabees 1:11-15:

> In those days, lawless men came forth from Israel, and misled many saying, "Let us go and make a covenant with the Gentiles round about us, for since we separated from them, many evils have come upon us." This proposal pleased them, and some of the people eagerly went to the king. He authorized them to observe the ordinances of the Gentiles. . . . So they built a gymnasium in Jerusalem, and removed the marks of circumcision[20] and abandoned the

---

[18]For further discussion, see E. M. Smallwood, "The Legislation of Hadrian and Antoninus Pius against Circumcision," *Latomus* 18 (1959): 334-347. It is debated whether Hadrian's action provided the impetus for the Bar Kochba Revolt or was an imperial response to it.

[19]Notice that I said *assimilation* and not acculturation. As I discussed in chapter two, from the Jewish standpoint, it was possible to share some of the same cultural features with the Greco-Roman world and still maintain a separate ethnic identity. The maintenance of this separate identity for many Jews was the very purpose of circumcision.

[20]Literally, the Greek of 1 Maccabees 1:15 says καὶ ἐποίησαν ἑαυτοῖς ἀκροβυστίας ("and they made themselves uncircumcised"). For more information on the Greek word ἀκροβυστία, see K. L. Schmidt, "ἀκροβυστία" in *Theological Dictionary of the New Testament*, vol. 1 (Grand Rapids: William B. Eerdmans Publishing Company, 1966), 225-226.

holy covenant. They joined themselves with the Gentiles and sold themselves to do evil.

When reading the Maccabean literature in general and 1 Maccabees in particular, we must realize that the author has a strong ideological agenda, which perhaps leads to historical distortions in his account. Nonetheless, this text gives clear witness to the surgical procedure called epispasm (referred to in 1 Maccabees as "making themselves uncircumcised"), by which a man could "un-do" his circumcision. In 1 Maccabees 1:11-15 the Hasmonean author's juxtaposition of the building of the gymnasium in Jerusalem with the procedure of epispasm is evidence, irrespective of the book's ideological agenda, of an important socio-historical reality.

Whereas other markers of Jewish ethnic distinctiveness[21] were quite visible or public (e.g., the observance of the Sabbath, dietary laws, and temple worship), the mark of circumcision was hidden until exposed by nakedness. In the gymnasium in Greco-Roman culture, the athletes exercised in the nude.[22] Thus, it was precisely as Jewish men in the Maccabean period began to participate in important Greco-Roman institutions, most notably the gymnasium, that their heretofore hidden mark of Jewish identity was visible for all to see, bringing with it overt ridicule.

As one reads 1 Maccabees 1, there is no question as to whether epispasm was practiced by Jewish men. The fascinating and complex question is, did such men who submitted to epispasm still consider themselves to be Jewish? The Hasmonean author who penned 1 Maccabees no longer considered these men to be Jews, but instead apostates. Yet, according to the rubrics of ethnicity in a boundary approach,[23] one may suggest that some Jews who submitted to epispasm may have seen this procedure as a move of *acculturation*

---

[21] Although written from a negative standpoint, that is, from the standpoint of the things that the Jews were *not* to do, 1 Maccabees 1:44 offers an interesting catalog of the practices which made the Jews ethnically distinctive.

[22] The Greek word for naked, of course, is γυμνός.

[23] See my discussion of ethnicity in chapter two.

without its being an act of *assimilation*. That is, epispasm allowed such men to participate more fully in the cultural institutions of the Greco-Roman world without necessarily causing them to recant their Jewish ethnicity.

The Hasmonean author undoubtedly wants the reader to see circumcision as a *sine qua non* of Jewish identity. Yet, the agenda of the Hasmonean author should not be allowed to mask the very important social and ideological question being waged within Judaism at that time, namely, what constitutes being a Jew? 1 Maccabees is a response to this question, but the very presence of 1 Maccabees indicates that other answers were being offered.

In the above discussion, there is a great likelihood that a person in *Jerusalem* during the Maccabean revolt who submitted to epispasm would not consider himself ethnically to be a Jew, especially in light of the importance that circumcision had and would continue to have in the land of Israel. The likelihood that a person in the Diaspora who submitted to epispasm may have still considered himself a Jew (even though others may not have considered him thus) increases substantially. In other words, questions of ethnic identity were more acute and had more significance when the presence of alternative interpretations of what it means to be a Jew was increased.

The proverbial clash of "Athens and Jerusalem," may not (as proponents of the theory of the thorough Hellenization of Jewish culture contend) have caused Jews to abandon their Jewish ethnicity, but instead this clash may have caused them to configure their ethnicity differently. Exploring the complex issue of Jewish identity in the first century CE (Diaspora) world, Shaye Cohen remarks:

> The strange phrase "those who say they are Jews and are not"[24] may have well been a current expression in the first century. It will have applied originally to Gentiles who act the part of Jews but are not in fact Jews. . . . The phrase

---

[24]This enigmatic phrase ("those who say they are Jews and are not"), which is the launching point for Cohen's article, is found in Revelation 3:8-9.

illustrates the *ambiguities* inherent in Jewish identity and Jewishness, especially in the Diaspora. In the homeland (at least until the fourth century CE) Jewishness for Jews was natural, perhaps inevitable, but in the Diaspora Jewishness was a conscious choice, easily avoided or hidden, and at best tolerated by society at large.[25]

Cohen's quotation lends support to a basic argument of this entire dissertation, that is, many factors taken as self-evident in New Testament interpretation, such as ethnicity and social status, upon further and closer inspection become increasingly more complex and even ambiguous. In objection to my use of and affinity with Cohen's position, some may argue that Cohen's investigation deals primarily with issues of Jewish identity in the book of Revelation, which, by most scholarly reckonings, is dated to the last decade of the first century CE (more specifically during the reign of Domitian).[26] Some might contend that the issue of ethnicity as reflected in Revelation, a text written nearly two decades after the Jewish war (and nearly four decades after the Corinthian correspondence) does not reflect accurately the ethnic realities that obtained in other parts of the Diaspora (e.g., Corinth) in earlier parts of the century, when hostilities between Romans and Jews were not as pronounced.

On the one hand, this hypothetical objection to my affinity with Cohen's position has merit. It is most reasonable to think that Roman perceptions of Jews (and vice-versa) would have been (and were) markedly different after the Jewish War than they were before it. Especially after the Jewish War, an

---

[25]Cohen, "Those Who Say They Are Jews And Are Not," 3 (emphasis mine).

[26]In the history of scholarship on Revelation, there has been debate concerning dating this book to the time of Domitian. For a persuasive argument that Revelation should be dated during the time of the Jewish war and destruction of Jerusalem, see Christopher Rowland, *The Open Heaven: A Study of Apocalyptic and Judaism in Christianity* (London: SPCK, 1982).

individual's decision to be Jewish (however one determined that) could be quite costly.[27]

On the other hand, if hostilities were less apparent (although certainly not absent) in Diaspora communities between Jews, Greeks, and Romans prior to the Jewish war, one could surmise that intermingling and ethnic cooperation and curiosity were natural parts of daily life in Diaspora communities. With such intermingling and ethnic curiosity on the part of Jews, Greeks, and Romans, the question that was bound to be raised was, who is a Jew?,[28] especially in light of the fact that some Romans may have been strongly attracted to Jewish practices[29] (a point not frequently stressed in discussions about Judaism and Hellenism). For our purposes, a topic which

---

[27]Suetonius tells us that Domitian rigorously leveled a tax against the Jews. We also learn in Suetonius that some attempted to hide their ethnic origins in order to avoid payment of this tax. See Suetonius, *Domitian* 12.2.

[28]Discussions about the Hellenization of Jewish culture often depict the cultural and ethnic influence in a uni-directional way, that is, from the Greco-Roman world to the Jewish world. There is, however, evidence that the direction of influence was bi-directional. For example, the Roman literary tradition evinces knowledge about Jewish Sabbath practice and perhaps evidence that even some Romans observed the Sabbath themselves. For example, in *The Art of Love*, Ovid, encouraging the would-be lover to seek his beloved in a variety of places in Rome, remarks, "She [i.e., one's beloved] will not come floating down to you through the tenuous air, she must be sought, the girl whom your glance approves. . . . You too, who seek the object of a lasting passion, learn first what places the maidens haunt. . . . Walk leisurely beneath the Pompeian shade. . . . Nor should you avoid the Livian colonnade . . . *Nor the seventh day that the Syrian Jews hold sacred.*" See *The Art of Love* 1.41-76 (emphasis mine). Also, Philo informs us that Augustus had respect for the Jewish Sabbath so much so that when the imperial distribution of corn "fell on the day of their sacred Sabbath, on which day it is not lawful for them to receive any thing, or to give anything or in short to perform any of the ordinary duties of life, he [Augustus] charged the dispenser of these gifts, and gave him the most careful and special injunctions to make the distribution to the Jews on the day following." See Philo, *On the Embassy to Gaius*, 158.

[29]The Roman attraction to Jewish ways was viewed by some in Rome as a cause for great alarm. See Dio Cassius, *Roman Histories* 57.18.5a, who contends that an uprising against Jews in Rome in 19 CE was the result of Jews converting Romans to the Jewish way of life.

deserves some investigation is the degree to which Jews in the Diaspora considered circumcision indispensable for Jewish identity, especially among proselytes.

CIRCUMCISION: REALITY, METAPHOR, AND ALLEGORY

Evidence of the complexity concerning circumcision can actually be found in the Jewish literary tradition itself—a tradition which spoke both metaphorically and allegorically about circumcision. Upon first glance, a discussion about linguistic and rhetorical practices such as metaphor and allegory seems strangely out of place in an analysis of a corporeal practice such as circumcision. Yet, the discussion in chapter two of ethnicity from a boundary approach demonstrated that language can serve as symbolic ethnic boundary markers. Thus, the ways in which groups employ and reconfigure language (even language about concrete social practices) reveal much about their understanding of ethnic boundaries. Traces of the ambivalence concerning the role of circumcision in determining social identity can be seen in the rise of allegorical interpretation among some Jews, especially in Diaspora settings. A cursory analysis of metaphor, allegory, and the subtle differences between the two is now in order.

A common definition of a metaphor[30] is to speak of one thing as if it is another. Even six centuries before the Corinthian

---

[30]In the wake of the sophisticated and often tortuously complicated work of structuralists, semioticians, and literary critics, one hesitates to speak of metaphor for fear that even simple reference to this linguistic term will commit one to copious theoretical discussions. My use of the term "metaphor" here is quite modest. For more advanced discussions of this literary feature, see, for example, the foundational work of structuralist Ferdinand de Saussure, *Course in General Linguistics*, trans. Roy Harris (LaSalle, IL: Open Court, 1986). Also, for further insights on metaphor from literary critics, see J. David Sapir and J. Christopher Crocker, eds., *The Social Use of Metaphor* (Philadelphia: University of Pennsylvania Press, 1977); Sheldon Sacks, ed., *On Metaphor* (Chicago: University of Chicago Press, 1978), and David S. Miall, ed., *Metaphor: Problems and Perspectives* (Sussex, NJ: Harvester Press, 1982).

correspondence, Jews were employing metaphors about circumcision. For instance, the writer of Deuteronomy 10:16 has Moses say, *"Circumcise then the foreskins of your heart* and do not be stubborn."* In the verses preceding this passage, Moses implores the people to live according to the commandments of the Lord. One of the commandments (especially in the theology of the Priestly school and the Deuteronomic historian) is circumcision. But in Deuteronomy 10:16, ethical living, including the commandment not be stubborn, is spoken of as "circumcising the foreskin of the heart." Language about circumcision is used metaphorically as an equivalent for a call to ethical living.

In a metaphor there are two (but there could be more) items brought together in the same semantic space, and a metaphor works rhetorically because there is some equivalence between the two items. For instance, the metaphor "the heat of the moment" makes sense rhetorically because it is understood that there is some equivalence between heat (as a natural phenomenon of subatomic particles colliding into one another) and human passions of an assorted variety.

Likewise, in Deuteronomy 10:16, the comparison of language about circumcision with language about ethical living works metaphorically because there is an equivalence (in the covenant theology of the Deuteronomic historian) between ethical living and physical circumcision. The metaphor is effective precisely because of the importance of *physical* circumcision to the writer. Metaphors operate by means of comparison made possible by some equivalence in meaning. Ethical living can be spoken of in terms of circumcision because to be (physically) circumcised is to live ethically as a Jew.

Allegory, on the other hand, works quite differently from metaphor.[31] According to Hans Frei, allegory "is the attachment of a temporally free-floating meaning pattern to any temporal occasion, without any intrinsic connection between sensuous

---

[31]For a recent attempt to distinguish between metaphor and allegory, see David Dawson, *Allegorical Readers and Cultural Revision in Ancient Alexandria* (Berkeley: University of California Press, 1994). Dawson remarks, "Allegory bears the closest possible relationship to metaphor because, in a sense, it is composed of metaphors. But allegory and metaphor should not simply be identified." Dawson, 5.

time-bound picture and the meaning represented by it."[32] No sensible connection is required between the two items brought together in an allegory. In fact, the literal or tangible item usually is the springboard which catapults a reader to the *true* meaning of the expression or item.

Without being too reductionistic and simplifying complex social factors to abstract literary conventions, one can suggest that as Judaism developed in the Diaspora, there was a shift among some Jews from metaphorical language about circumcision (which was able to equate ethical living for physical circumcision and vice versa) to an allegorical understanding of circumcision, where "temporally free-floating meanings" were attached to the temporal (and corporeal) rite of physical circumcision. Such a switch then raised questions as to whether the physical rite of circumcision actually had meaning.[33] This confusion, coupled with other inherently complex factors of first century Diaspora social life, created a social situation where ambiguity was possible.

In a recent monograph on the cultural and social identity of Paul, Daniel Boyarin writes extensively on the (Pauline) allegorization of circumcision. According to Boyarin, this allegorization is a philosophical and methodological necessity for Paul's overall critique of Judaism—the aim of which is to create "a non-differentiated, non-hierarchical humanity."[34] By demonstrating the potential relationships between linguistic practices and social identity in the first century CE world, Boyarin's project is a meaningful contribution to Pauline exegesis. Nevertheless, Boyarin's treatment of Paul in general and his exposition on circumcision in particular, though substantive, are problematic.

---

[32]Hans Frei, *The Eclipse of Biblical Narrative: A Study of Eighteenth and Nineteenth Century Hermeneutics* (New Haven: Yale University Press, 1974), 29.

[33]As Dawson intimates, the sense that the "literal" meaning of something is inadequate or passé is the very reason that allegories come into existence. Dawson, 3.

[34]Daniel Boyarin, *A Radical Jew: Paul and the Politics of Identity* (Berkeley: University of California Press, 1994), 8.

Boyarin uses cultural criticism as a framework[35] in which to "reclaim Pauline studies as an important even integral part of the study of Judaism in the Roman period and late antiquity"[36] and to "reclaim Paul as an important Jewish thinker."[37] His heavy reliance on the constructs of cultural criticism, however, skews his exegesis and creates a Paul who is more platonic than Plato himself.[38] With respect to Paul's apostolic aim, Boyarin writes, "The very impulse toward universalism, toward the One, is that which both enabled and motivated Paul's move toward a spiritualizing and allegorizing interpretation of Israel's scripture and law as well."[39] Contrary to Boyarin's

---

[35]Boyarin, 4.

[36]Boyarin, 1-2.

[37]Boyarin, 2.

[38]For example, Boyarin rests nearly his entire belief of Paul's desire for a univocal humanity on Galatians 3:26-28 and on Paul's allegory of Hagar in Galatians 4:21-31. Commenting on the role of Galatians 4:21-31, Boyarin remarks, "We thus see the political and theological themes of the entire Pauline enterprise in this letter coming together here in one brilliant stroke." Boyarin's estimation of the role of Galatians 4:21-31 is an overstatement. See Boyarin, 34. Moreover, he fails to heed the wisdom of the famous "coherence /contingency" debate that has waged for years in Pauline exegesis, namely, that the attempt to locate the center of Paul's thought in any or all of his letters, without an appreciation for the ways in which Pauline expressions are drastically shaped by the contingent situation, is naive and ill-advised. For recent treatments of the intellectual challenges of locating a theological center in Paul, see J. Christiaan Becker, "Recasting Pauline Theology: The Coherence-Contingency Scheme as Interpretive Model" in *Pauline Theology: Thessalonians, Philippians, Galatians, Philemon*, vol. 1, ed. Jouette Bassler (Minneapolis: Fortress Press, 1991), 15-24; Jouette M. Bassler, "Paul's Theology: Whence and Whither" in *Pauline Theology: 1 & 2 Corinthians*, vol. 2, ed. David M. Hay (Minneapolis: Fortress Press, 1993), 3-17; Steven J. Kraftchick, "Seeking a More Fluid Model: A Response to Jouette M. Bassler" in *Pauline Theology: 1 & 2 Corinthians*, vol. 2, ed. David M. Hay (Minneapolis: Fortress Press, 1993), 18-34; Paul W. Meyer, "Pauline Theology: A Proposal for a Pause in its Pursuit" in *Pauline Theology: Looking Back, Pressing On*, vol. 4, eds. E. Elizabeth Johnson and David M. Hay (Atlanta: Scholars Press, 1997), 140-160.

[39]Boyarin, 8. In the first instance, allegory was not a *typical* rhetorical trope for Paul. Second, one wonders whether Paul had a philosophical bent toward "The One." The question is not whether Paul wanted to erase all human difference unilaterally. Instead, the question

claim, there seems to be an appreciable difference between Plato's concept of "The One" and Paul's monotheistic belief that the world stands under the sovereignty of the one God of Israel who has offered new revelation in Jesus Christ.

Also, Boyarin reads Paul's use of the verb ἀλληγορέω in Galatians 4:24 (itself the subject of much exegetical debate) as if Paul had a sophisticated doctrine of allegory[40] like that of the Alexandrian school which really flourished in the second and third centuries of the common era.[41] In the history of Christianity, it was precisely Paul's passing use of the verb ἀλληγορέω which gave impetus to the meteoric rise of the use of allegorical exegesis in the early church.[42]

Certainly, allegory predated Paul, but Paul's use of this verb surely helped to secure allegory's place in the Christian tradition. Boyarin has taken a fleeting reference to allegory in one passage in Galatians and read into it an understanding of and emphasis on allegory that would have been appropriate in a discussion of medieval or reformation[43] interpretive practices.

---

for Paul is, when do human differences matter, and when do they not matter? Boyarin fails to mention that in another *rhetorical situation*, Paul, speaking to a different audience, says that there is much advantage to being a Jew (i.e., Romans 3:1).

[40]Boyarin overstates the case when he writes, "We must realize the depth of Paul's understanding of allegory not as a rhetorical device of language but as a revelation of the structure of reality (including historical reality) itself in order to have an appreciation for this passage [Galatians 4:21-31] and his thought in general." Boyarin, 35.

[41]For a treatment of the so-called Alexandrian School, see Robert M. Grant, *A Short History of the Interpretation of the Bible* (Philadelphia: Fortress Press, 1984), 52-62.

[42]Grant, 64.

[43]For a historical treatment of late medieval and reformation hermeneutics, see Karlfried Froehlich, " 'Always to Keep to the Literal Sense in Holy Scripture Means to Kill One's Soul': The State of Biblical Hermeneutics at the beginning of the Fifteenth Century" in *Literary Uses of Typology*, ed. Earl Miner (Princeton: Princeton University Press, 1977), 20-48. For the philosophical foundation for much of the medieval and reformation practice of allegorical interpretation, see Augustine, *On Christian Doctrine*, especially Book Three.

Finally, Boyarin does not fully take into account the social[44] and rhetorical nature of allegory.

In contradistinction to Boyarin, in a recent article, Elizabeth Castelli offers an impressive and sophisticated discussion of allegory which further clarifies our distinction between metaphorical language about circumcision and an allegorical understanding of circumcision. Her discussion is worth quoting at some length. Castelli writes:

> Allegory as a rhetorical trope possesses a capacity to persuade its reader or hearer to reimagine the meaning of a text or tradition. Allegory draws the reader into the argument and constructs a kind of complicity between the interpreter and the reader. Like other forms of rhetorical persuasion, allegorical interpretation depends upon what is familiar to the reader. In the course of the interpretation, the familiar is refigured, and what is familiar is translated into something new, different and often remarkable. . . . Allegory often schematizes or reduces the original text or tradition it seeks to interpret. . . . Although allegory may appear to the uninitiated to be contrived, fundamental to its success is its claim that the meaning exposed by the allegory is the foundationally true and complete meaning. This aspect of allegory is crucial to a consideration of its effects, for the explicit claim articulated by allegory is that meaning is not negotiable, situational, or mediated by history or circumstance. . . . the irony of this process [of allegorical interpretation] is that allegory is itself a response to inevitable, normative fixed meanings—an attempt to speak otherwise, to say something else publicly and openly (allo + agoreuo).[45]

---

[44]It is in its attention to the *social* nature of allegory that Dawson's monograph is superior to Boyarin's. I, however, find at least two areas of Dawson's work to be problematic. First, his notion that true allegories must have narrative contexts seems arbitrary. Second, his contention that allegories are not inherently revisionary misses a crucial point. Even when an allegory "domesticates" a text which is shocking to contemporary cultural sensibilities, this is a *revisionary* move. Prevailing cultural values may be preserved by such an allegory, but the shocking "literal meaning" of the text has been, of necessity, revised. See Dawson, 10.

[45]Elizabeth A. Castelli, "Allegories of Hagar: Reading Galatians 4:21-31 with Postmodern Feminist Eyes" in *The New Literary Criticism and the New Testament*, ed. Elizabeth Struthers Malbon and Edgar V.

As Castelli has shown with some sophistication, allegories work ironically. They are linguistic and interpretive acts of resistance against pre-existing meanings. But in order to effect this resistance, the interpretations yielded by allegories must posture themselves as self-evident. In short, allegories claim that pre-existing meanings are ambiguous and non-essential. Consequently, allegorical interpretations replace the "ambiguous" meaning with one that is "self-evident."

In light of the above discussion of metaphor, allegory, and the importance of language as ethnic boundary markers, a subtle, yet integral distinction must be made between metaphor and allegory. I contend that metaphors are rhetorical devices which equate one referent with the other without calling into question the importance or *reality* of either referent. On the other hand, allegory is a rhetorical device which not only substitutes one referent for another, but in so doing potentially eliminates the reality of the first referent. The need to supersede and eliminate the primary referent in allegory is often a response to some (seeming) ambiguity of the first element. Allegory is a "supra-textual" and "supra-historical" rhetorical device. It attempts to persuade by locating meaning "above and beyond" the (literal) text and "above and beyond" concrete historical realities.

This above digression concerning the nature of metaphor and allegory has significance with respect to the ethnic boundary marker of circumcision. As discussed above, with metaphors, though one referent is equated with another, both referents are understood to be "realities." Thus, metaphor permits and even encourages polyvalence, as the potential meanings of each referent bounce one off the other. Therefore, when Jewish writers resident in *the land of Israel* employ metaphorical language about circumcision, there is no social ambiguity about the necessity of *physical* circumcision. The very reason metaphorical language about circumcision works is because in the concrete socio-historical world of the land of

---

McKnight (Sheffield: Sheffield Academic Press, 1994), 230-232, 238-239, 243.

Israel, circumcision is understood to be indispensable for Jewish ethnicity.

The self-evident nature of the ethnic boundary marker of circumcision for Jews living in Israel in the first and second temple period gives rise to multiple uses of metaphorical language about circumcision. Thus, writers in the Hebrew Bible can talk about "circumcising" fruit, trees, and even one's heart. To circumcise the fruit and trees of the land, of course, is a metaphor for harvesting. Language about circumcision can be a linguistic equivalent for harvesting precisely because both circumcision and harvesting are "concrete" social practices in Israel. Metaphors invite multivocality, and multivocality is welcomed and not considered problematic because there is little ambiguity concerning ethnicity[46] in the land of Israel. Circumcision was requisite for Jewish identity in the land of Israel.

---

[46]One could argue that in the land of Israel, especially in the first century CE, the question was not distinguishing who was a Jew per se but instead *which group of Jews* had the right interpretation of Torah. Even the schism between the Samaritans and the Jews can be understood as an internal dispute. James D. Purvis contends, "Both Jews and Samaritans understood themselves (first and foremost) as carriers of Israel's sacred traditions—not as representatives of Juda-*ism* or Samaritan-*ism* but as the latter-day representatives of Israel's religion. The two differed from each other in terms of the focus of *Heilsgeschichte*, but both the Jews and Samaritans understood their faith (ideally) as Israelite." See Purvis, "The Samaritans and Judaism" in *Early Judaism and Its Modern Interpreters*, ed. R. A. Kraft and G. W. E. Nickelsburg (Atlanta: Scholars Press, 1986), 91-92. Although there is ambiguity in Josephus concerning the Samaritans, there is, nonetheless, evidence in Josephus's accounts that the Samaritans looked upon themselves as Jews (which is what matters according to the boundary approach to ethnicity). For a summary and analysis of Josephus on the Samaritan question, see Louis H. Feldman, "Josephus' Attitude toward the Samaritans: A Study in Ambivalence" in *Jewish Sects, Religious Movements, Political Parties*, ed. Menachem Mor (Omaha: Creighton University Press, 1992), 22-45. Also, see Reinhard Plummer "Samaritan Synagogues and Jewish Synagogues: Similarities and Differences" in *Jews, Christians and Polytheists in the Ancient Synagogue: Cultural Interaction during the Greco-Roman Period*, ed. Steven Fine (London: Routledge, 1999), 118-160.

The situation changes drastically, however, with a change in social location. When Jews in the first century CE find themselves in Diaspora locations, where the sacredness and inevitability of circumcision is not sanctioned by their Greco-Roman counterparts,[47] metaphorical language about circumcision gives way, in some instances, to allegorical interpretations of circumcision. As suggested above, allegory often arises as a response to seemingly "fixed," or "normative" meanings in a text. In the social context of the Diaspora, however, some Jews raised questions concerning the normative nature of traditional Jewish boundary markers. Thus, in some Diaspora locations Jews began offering allegorical interpretations of previously sacrosanct Jewish boundary markers, chief of which was circumcision.

In short, in the Diaspora, allegorical understandings of circumcision may have cast doubt on the importance of physical circumcision. Allegorical interpretation of circumcision in the Diaspora was a response to the social pressure of living in a world less than sympathetic to this rite. The question was raised, is physical circumcision really important in the first place? In Diaspora settings where Jews were all but too aware of their tenuous social position, some Jews began to allegorize the Jewish boundary markers. The resulting allegorical interpretations only exacerbated the complexity of the already riddled question, who is a Jew (in the Diaspora)?

The tension and problems of maintaining certain Jewish boundary markers in the Diaspora can be seen paradigmatically in Philo's treatment of circumcision. In my estimation, Philo, with respect to circumcision, uses allegory to reduce the social ambiguity of Jewish identity in Alexandria. Yet, he is unwilling to surrender the importance of physical boundary markers in light of his allegorical interpretation. Philo straddles the fence. Such straddling, in the end, only adds to the complexity of questions of Jewish identity in the Diaspora. Let us turn to the relevant sections in Philo.

---

[47]For a concise and helpful treatment of the Greco-Roman antipathy for circumcision, see Peter Schäfer, *Judeophobia* (Cambridge, MA: Harvard University Press, 1997), 103-105.

PHILO ON CIRCUMCISION

Much scholarly work[48] has already been done on the cultural sensibilities and philosophical influences of Philo of Alexandria who, for countless generations of biblical scholars, has been the quintessential example of the "Hellenized Jew." By introducing Philo into this discussion, I do not intend in any thoroughgoing way to comment upon or augment the volumes of Philonic scholarship. My sole purpose is to explicate some of the substantive comments about the role of circumcision in Philo, a Diaspora Jew contemporaneous with Paul.[49] Such an explication will further illustrate the inherent ambiguity that likely would have attended Paul's rhetorical appeal to circumcision in 1 Corinthians 7.

The interpreter of Philo can approach his prolific writings from many angles, but for our purpose, the most fruitful entree is to investigate Philo, the exegete. Concerning the primacy of exegesis in the work of Philo, David Runia remarks:

> Philo is first and foremost an exegete of Scripture. . . . He is only interested in giving exegesis of the writings of the blessed lawgiver Moses. . . . From his general approach and from very many individual passages, it is possible to discern that he saw his task not only as an exegete but also as an apologist of scripture. For the Jews of Alexandria,

[48]For a useful survey of Philonic scholarship over the last five decades, see Peder Borgen, "Philo of Alexandria: A Critical and Synthetic Survey of Research since World War II" in *Aufstieg und Niedergang der römischen Welt*, 2.21.1 (New York: Walther de Gruyeter, 1984), 98-154.

[49]In the history of Philonic and Pauline scholarship, there have been several instances when scholars have used Philo to better understand Paul and vice versa. A notable example of the juxtaposition of Philo and Paul on the theme of circumcision is Peder Borgen's essay, "Observations on the Theme 'Paul and Philo': Paul's Preaching of Circumcision in Galatia (Gal 5:11) and Debates on Circumcision in Philo" in *The Pauline Literature and Theology*, ed. Sigfred Pedersen (Aarhus: Forlaget Aros, 1980), 85-102. In this article, with respect to Paul's view on circumcision, Borgen limits his analysis to Paul's comments in Galatians 5. Yet, in spite of the contribution of this article, it is still written in service of the theological theme of "Paul and the Law." It is not written with a view to plumbing the depths of the social complexities in first century Diaspora communities.

surrounded on all sides by the proud achievements of the dominant (and prestigious) Hellenistic culture, the preservation of their ethnic and cultural identity was not something that could ever be taken for granted. Assimilation and apostasy were ever present dangers. Philo passionately defends his religious and cultural heritage.[50]

Runia's observation that Philo was both an exegete and an ethnic apologist[51] buttresses the assumptions of a boundary approach to ethnicity, namely, that language practices and self-identification serve as markers to ascertain who is in and out of the ethnic group. Thus, exegesis, the "correct" exposition of the revealed word of God, most especially the law of Moses, would, for Philo, be more than an intellectual exercise; it would be a matter of ethnic survival. According to Runia, in Philo's understanding, "The law of Moses is not only *not* the curiously archaic and jumbled document that it might seem to the casual uninformed reader. It is far more than that. It is the repository of the highest wisdom that man can attain. If only all the world would read it and study it and understand it."[52]

In previous discussions of Philo's understanding of circumcision, scholars have argued concerning whether a passage in *Questions and Answers on Exodus*[53] can be interpreted as Philo's admission of the existence of

---

[50]David T. Runia, "How to read Philo" in *Exegesis and Philosophy: Studies on Philo of Alexandria* (Brookfield: Variorum, 1990), 189.

[51]What Runia calls "religious and cultural heritage" in the above quotation, I would prefer to collapse into one phrase "*ethnic* heritage."

[52]Runia, 189.

[53]Specifically, *Questions and Answers on Exodus* 2.2 reads, "He shows most clearly that he is a proselyte who is not circumcised in the foreskin but in pleasures, desires, and other passions of the soul. For in Egypt the Hebrew race was not circumcised. . . ."

uncircumcised proselytes. Articles written by Neil McEleney[54] and John Nolland[55] have framed this scholarly debate.

McEleney's analysis of Philo's understanding of the importance of circumcision, as thoughtful as it is, seems ultimately in service of a theological[56] exposition of Ephesians 2. Nolland's exposition of Philo's understanding of circumcision is, for the most part, a convincing point-by-point refutation of McEleney's article.

One clearly finds some ambivalence among Jews in our period concerning the importance of circumcision. Robert G. Hall[57] has shown that in the period from the Maccabean revolt until late in the first century CE, there was evidence, especially in the Diaspora, of Jews practicing a surgical removal of circumcision, epispasm. According to John Nolland, such Jews (i.e., those who submit to epispasm) would be apostates and not Jews. But the whole point of my discussion of ethnicity in chapter two was that it is not sufficient for us to offer an "etic" (i.e., outsider's) assessment of whether such persons who practiced epispasm were or were not Jews. The significant point is to look for an "emic" (i.e., insider's) assessment. In other words, did such persons still consider themselves to be Jews even if they surgically removed the marks of circumcision?

Hall offers several reasons why Jews in the Diaspora may have undergone epispasm, including "the severe social stigma against circumcision together with the societal expectation to participate in the bath and gymnasium,"[58] and the fact that in

---

[54]Neil J. McEleney, "Conversion, Circumcision and the Law," *New Testament Studies* 20 (1974): 319-341. McEleney believes that there were uncircumcised proselytes.

[55]John Nolland, "Uncircumcised Proselytes?," *Journal for the Study of Judaism* XII (1981): 173-194. Nolland contends that there was no group of "uncircumcised proselytes."

[56]By no means am I suggesting that a theological exposition is problematic. I am suggesting that his theological agenda precludes him from engaging the *social* complexities surrounding Philo's writing about circumcision.

[57]Robert G. Hall, "Epispasm and the Dating of Ancient Jewish Writings," *Journal for the Study of the Pseudepigrapha* 2 (1988): 71-86.

[58]Hall, 78.

Alexandria, "citizenship required the removal of circumcision."[59] Emphasizing the importance of physical circumcision in a first century CE Diaspora community like Alexandria, then, was an act of no little consequence. It was an exercise that bore considerable political and ethnic implications. Samuel Sandmel contends, "The social and religious problems which confronted an Alexandrian Jew such as Philo cannot really be separated from each other. Analytically we may perhaps view them separately, but they are intertwined."[60] It is against such an ethnic backdrop that we must investigate some of Philo's remarks on circumcision.

Philo does not spend inordinate time discussing circumcision in his writings. Other topics such as the nature of virtue[61] or the creation of the world[62] seem to hold more of his attention. Yet, on those occasions when he does address the topic, his explanations are not devoid of complexity. In his comments on circumcision, one senses that Philo is trying to

---

[59]Hall, 78. This question about citizenship among the Jews in Alexandria continues to be widely debated in Greco-Roman and Philonic scholarship. In "The Letter of Claudius to the Alexandrians," Claudius appears to preserve the Alexandrian citizenship of those "who have been registered as epheboi up to the time of my principate." After encouraging the Alexandrians to behave "gently and kindly" towards the Jews in Alexandria, Claudius, however, says, "The Jews, on the other hand, I order not to aim at more than they have previously had and not in the future to send two embassies as if they lived in two cities. . . and not to intrude themselves into the games presided over by the *gymnasiarchoi* and the *kosmetai*, since they enjoy what is their own, and in a city which is not their own (ἐν ἀλλοτρία πόλει), they possess an abundance of all good things." Concerning the important phrase ἐν ἀλλοτρία πόλει, Tcherikover and Fuks (in note 95) remark, "These words of Claudius rightly serve (in the view of the majority of scholars) as a decisive point in favor of the theory that Jews did not possess civic rights in Alexandria." See "The Letter of Claudius to the Alexandrians," in *Corpus Papyrorum Judaicarum*, vol. II, 36-55. John Barclay believes that Philo enjoyed Alexandrian citizenship. See, Barclay, *Jews in the Mediterranean Diaspora*, 60-71, 158-165.

[60]Samuel Sandmel, "Philo Judaeus: An Introduction to the Man, his Writings and his Significance" in *Aufstieg und Niedergang der römischen Welt* 2.21.1 (New York: Walther de Gruyeter, 1984), 15.

[61]See, for example, Philo, *On the Virtues*.

[62]See, for example, Philo, *On the Creation*.

navigate between the Scylla of an overemphasis on physical circumcision and the Charybdis of an overemphasis on "spiritual" circumcision. In his efforts, he employs a mixture of the literal, the metaphorical, and the allegorical. Let us now turn to the most relevant examples.

From Philo's perspective, the scriptural mandate for circumcision found in Genesis 17 warrants exposition. Thus, in *Questions and Answers on Genesis*, Philo offers clarification. He writes:

> What is the meaning of, "And every male of you shall be circumcised, and you shall circumcise, or you shall be circumcised in, the flesh of your foreskin" [Genesis 17:10]. I see here a twofold circumcision, one of the male creature, and the other of the flesh; that which is of the flesh takes place in the genitals, but that which is of the male creature takes place, as it seems to me, in respect of his thoughts. Since that which is, properly speaking, masculine in us is the intellect, the superfluous shoots of which it is necessary to prune away and to cast off, so that it, becoming clean and pure from all wickedness and vile, may worship God as his priest.
>
> This therefore is what is designated by the second circumcision, where God says by an express law, "Circumcise the hardness of your hearts," that is to say, your hard and rebellious thoughts and ambition, which when they are cut away and removed from you, your most important part will be rendered free.[63]

Philo's above reference to "twofold circumcision" is a signpost that he is about to enter the realm of allegorical exegesis. In other words, in this passage there is something occurring which is more than metaphor. Philo is not merely referring to physical circumcision as something else. He is not just equating one referent with another. He, in fact, says that there are two levels or two kinds of circumcision.

As is often the case in his exposition on Genesis, Philo treats the literal meaning of circumcision as self-evident (i.e., "that which is of the flesh takes place in the genitals"). Philo

---

[63]*Questions and Answers on Genesis* 3.46.

spends the majority of his energy explaining the circumcision of "the male creature" which he identifies as the intellect. In the second part of this twofold understanding of circumcision, circumcision becomes another way of talking about removing impure thoughts from the heart so that one may have a more free communion with God. It is unarguably clear that Philo strives in this answer to maintain physical circumcision as a reality even as he discourses about symbolic circumcision. The correlation between actual and symbolic circumcision, perhaps, reflects Philo's attempt to provide a middle of the road position between the extreme literalists and the extreme allegorists in Alexandria.[64]

As I have suggested above, whereas metaphorical language about circumcision in the land of Israel did not foster ambiguity with respect to physical circumcision, in the drastically different and socially tense setting of Diaspora communities like Alexandria, allegorical interpretation of

---

[64]In Alexandria, it is believed that there were Jews who were extreme literalists with respect to the interpretation of the Pentateuch. For example, we can detect traces of their beliefs in Philo's dismissal of their exegesis of Genesis 1. In *On the Creation* 26, Philo writes, "Moses says also, 'In the beginning God created the heaven and the earth:' taking the beginning to be, not as some men think, that which is according to time; for before the world time had no existence. . . . And to venture to assert that it [time] is older than the world is absolutely inconsistent with philosophy." In other words, Philo scoffs at those Jews who take creation as something that happened literally in time. Yet, on the other hand, Philo has little or no regard for the extreme allegorists. In *On the Migration of Abraham* 89-92, Philo remarks, "There are some who, regarding laws in their literal sense in the light of symbols of matters belonging to the intellect, are overpunctilious about the latter, while treating the former with easy-going neglect. Such men I for my part should blame for handling the manner in too easy and off-hand a manner: they ought to have given careful attention to both aims, to a more full and exact investigation of what is not seen and in what is seen to be stewards without reproach. . . . It is true that receiving circumcision does indeed portray the excision of pleasure and all passions, and the putting away of the impious conceit, under which the mind supposed that it was capable of begetting by its own power: but let us not on this account repeal the law laid down for circumcising (ἀνέλωμεν τὸν ἐπὶ τῇ περιτομῇ τέθεντα νόμον).

circumcision did create some confusion. For instance, the fact that Philo has to chastise his co-religionists for treating certain customs with "neglectful indifference" is evidence that some Jews in Alexandria, in their allegorical interpretations, were disallowing physical circumcision any importance in light of a higher, "spiritual" circumcision.

In countering the extreme literalists, Philo offers an allegorical reading of circumcision. In countering the extreme allegorists, Philo offers an allegorical understanding of circumcision in which the real, tangible first referent (i.e., physical circumcision) is *not* displaced by the second "spiritual" referent. That is, Philo's use of allegory against the extreme allegorists contains elements that are as much, if not more, metaphorical as they are allegorical.[65] To have used allegory in its usual sense against the extreme allegorists would have proved ineffective. Thus, against the extreme allegorists, Philo's interpretation is neither strictly literal, strictly metaphorical nor strictly allegorical. In Philo, there is both metaphor and allegory. Thus, occasionally, Philo employs allegories where the real, physical referent still bears considerable importance.[66]

---

[65]In her book, *Metaphor and Religious Language*, Janet Martin Soskice distinguishes, as I do, metaphor from allegory. Furthermore, she suggests that *metaphors* can be used *in* allegories. Similarly, I am suggesting that at times Philo's interpretations are allegorical in the usual sense, namely, the "spiritual" referent replacing the "physical" referent. At other times, Philo, because of his need to emphasize certain concrete Jewish boundary markers, employs allegories with a metaphorical flavoring. Philo cannot afford to have the physical replaced by the spiritual, especially in the case of a physical marker like circumcision. Thus, he brings physical circumcision and spiritual circumcision together in creative ways, thereby allowing the meaning of each to play off the other without eliminating the other. For further explanation of the difference between metaphor and allegory, see Soskice, *Metaphor and Religious Language* (Oxford: Clarendon Press, 1985), 54-66, especially 55-56.

[66]Of the interpreters of Philo, Dawson comes as close as any to acknowledging this unusual use of allegory. Dawson contends, "Philo does not wish to reject literal readings. He is equally reluctant, however, to sacrifice nonliteral readings in order to preserve literal meaning. Philo's dual allegiance requires him to convince his audience that both literal and nonliteral readings are plausible interpretations of the same

For someone so interested in maintaining the importance of actual circumcision,[67] Philo is equally, or even more, adamant to underscore the *ethical* significance of symbolic circumcision. A clear example of Philo stressing the *symbolic or abstract* nature of circumcision can be found in *On the Special Laws*. First, Philo offers four reasons[68] why circumcision should be practiced. According to him, circumcision prevents disease, promotes cleanliness, creates a similarity between "the circumcised member" and the heart, and increases fertility. Philo, then, provides two additional symbolic reasons why circumcision is and should be practiced. He writes, "To these [previous four reasons] I would add that I consider circumcision to be a symbol of two things most necessary to our well-being. One is the excision of pleasure which bewitches the mind. . . . The other reason is that a man should know himself and banish from the soul the grievous malady of conceit."[69]

Philo's emphasis on the ethical aspects of circumcision can be seen as an apologetic[70] move designed to reduce the tension felt by Jews who were ridiculed by their Greco-Roman counterparts.[71] From the Greco-Roman perspective, this ridicule of Jews was justified since the Jews prided themselves on a social identity which, by means of rituals (most notably circumcision, Sabbath, and dietary laws), set them apart from

---

text that do not cancel one another. Of course, if one tries to read a text allegorically and literally without provisionally suspending one reading or the other, *the two readings will indeed cancel one another, or at least create considerable confusion.* Philo seeks to avoid this outcome by correlating the two aspects of scriptural language as closely as possible." Dawson, 101 (emphasis mine).

[67]Frequently, Philo goes to great lengths to rationalize physical circumcision, suggesting that God or Moses commanded it for hygienic purposes and population control. See, for example, *Questions and Answers on Genesis* 3.48.

[68]Philo, *On the Special Laws*, 1.4-7.

[69]Philo, *On the Special Laws*, 1.8-10.

[70]John Collins contends, "Philo was an apologist for Judaism more profoundly than he was a philosopher." Collins, 112.

[71]Philo's exegetical moves were not divorced from social realities. Dawson appropriately notes that Philo's revisionary readings of culture "reflected the real-life activities of [his community] and were intended to have real-life consequences for [his] readers." Dawson, 19.

the wider Greco-Roman world. This insistence on Jewish particularity[72] was not well received in the world of the early empire where people were encouraged to be "citizens of the world" (that is, the world, of course, as defined by imperial Rome) and to find some common denominators of social identity under the aegis of the *Pax Romana*. Social commonality[73] (or desiring people to identify with Greco-Roman mores) and not ethnic particularity was what was valued in Greco-Roman cities. Obviously, in such a social setting those who held firmly to their Jewish identity encountered tension.

John Collins suggests that there were various ways for Jews to reduce this social tension.[74] First, a Diaspora Jew could make an outright rejection of Judaism (although this was not a widely exercised option). Second, a Diaspora Jew could become acculturated while still resisting the temptation to assimilate. This process of "acculturation without assimilation" often took the form of Jews emphasizing the philosophical aspects of Judaism that might resonate with Hellenistic culture.[75] Philo's writings are a classic example of rendering Judaism in philosophical terms, and this process was greatly assisted by allegorical interpretation. Collins remarks, "The allegorical interpretation of scripture by Philo and others is an evident method of reducing the dissonance between the Jewish scriptures and philosophical religion."[76] By means of allegory,

---

[72]As we speak about *Jewish* particularity, we must keep in mind that the proclivity of groups of people to emphasize certain cultural features as ethnic badges is not inherently a Jewish phenomenon, but instead one of the rubrics for the creation of ethnicity in a boundary approach to ethnicity.

[73]Ironically, this desire for so-called "social commonality" was itself both an ethnic boundary marker and a form of ethnocentrism and imperialism on the part of the Romans. That is, the desire for everyone to be like the Romans was itself a Roman ethnic distinctive.

[74]Collins, 8-10.

[75]According to Collins, many times Jews would "highlight the aspects of Judaism which were most acceptable to cultured Gentiles, e.g., by representing Judaism as a philosophy, while playing down the more peculiar customs and rituals." Collins, 9.

[76]Collins, 9.

Philo sought a common ethic among Jews and non-Jews, even in the unlikely arena of circumcision.

Furthermore, John Collins has argued that much energy was exerted in Jewish Diaspora communities to show the commonalities between Greco-Roman life and Jewish identity. Concerning this push for a "common ethic," Collins writes, "One of the best known characteristics of Hellenistic Judaism lies in the attempt to build bridges to Hellenistic cultures by affirming Jewish values which were also appreciated by enlightened Gentiles (e.g., rejection of idolatry and homosexuality) while playing down the more problematic rituals and observances."[77]

For instance, Philo's holding together references to physical circumcision and symbolic circumcision is an effort to establish a common ethic[78] between Judaism and Greco-Roman philosophy. Moreover, Philo's interpretation of circumcision is a middle-of-the-road philosophical and political position whereby he can claim, along with the literalists, the importance of physical circumcision. Simultaneously, his position allows him to agree (but not too openly) with the extreme allegorists that the deeper (or real) meaning of circumcision lies beyond the physical. For Philo, physical circumcision was necessary but not sufficient.

Although fascinating to contemporary scholars, Philo's attempt to keep physical and symbolic understandings of circumcision together may have been less than convincing to certain of his contemporaries in Alexandria. Philo does not explain the necessity of physical circumcision; he merely asserts it. Some Alexandrian Jews (e.g., the extreme allegorists) may have asked, if the real import of circumcision is ethical (a point

---

[77]Collins, 16.

[78]As noted above, in *Questions and Answers on Genesis,* Philo expounds on the command in Genesis 17:10-12 to circumcise the male child on the eighth day. He also makes several appeals to symbolic circumcision as a necessary procedure for people to recognize that *God is the true father of the universe and the genuine father of all, and the creator of the universe.* In other words, there is a preponderance of appeals to *universality* even as Philo speaks of circumcision, the badge of Jewish exclusiveness. See *Questions and Answers on Genesis* 3.48.

which Philo would support), then why the need for physical circumcision? Whereas one might suspect that Philo's program of placing Judaism within the framework of a common ethic would lead him to nullify the concrete particularities of Judaism, Philo adamantly refuses to do away with *physical* circumcision.

Our treatment of Philo is not an end unto itself but instead a means to an end, namely, that in Diaspora communities there were several approaches to the question, what makes one a Jew. I contend that at least three options were available:

1. Philo and, ironically, also the extreme literalists (whom he opposed) provided one option, that is, that physical circumcision is indispensable. Philo and the Alexandrian literalists may have come to this conclusion by different avenues, but for each of them, to be a Jew, even in the Diaspora, meant to submit to physical circumcision.

2. Others (e.g., the extreme allegorists in Alexandria) considered circumcision dispensable. Either they did not practice it or submitted to epispasm. By dispensing with physical circumcision, they, however, did not consider themselves to be any thing other than Jews. Interestingly, Philo does *not* refer to the extreme allegorists as apostates. But the issue is not simply what Philo thinks about them; the real point is how they label themselves. It is quite plausible that different groups could chose to emphasize different cultural factors by which to be Jewish. Although it was widely known in the Diaspora that circumcision was an ethnic distinctive of Jews, some Jews in various communities may have dispensed with this rite, while still considering themselves to be Jews.

3. A third option was taken by those who dispensed with circumcision (either not practicing it or submitting to epispasm), and consequently no longer consider themselves to be Jews.[79]

---

[79]I find it fascinating that one of the rationales that Philo gives for infant circumcision is that when a man is grown up he might delay the operation out of fear. Philo, more than likely, is referring to the fear of physical pain. An adult man in a Diaspora setting, however, might have

In light of these insights about circumcision, especially in the Diaspora, let us now turn to an investigation of 1 Corinthians 7.

IMPLICATIONS[80] FOR THE EXEGESIS OF
1 CORINTHIANS 7:17-24

As intimated in chapter one, in the history of interpretation of 1 Corinthians 7:17-24, many scholars have worked presumably from the following two intellectual presuppositions[81] (whether or not these scholars made their presuppositions clear). One presupposition is that vv. 17-24 are a hypothetical digression from the main argument (although there has been and is considerable disagreement concerning what the main argument is). In short, according to this view, vv. 17-24 are "disembodied." These verses do not have real persons or concrete social realities in mind when they speak of circumcision and slavery; this passage is just "rhetorical."[82]

---

other kinds of fear which might motivate his delay or avoidance of circumcision (e.g., fear of social ostracism). See Philo, *Questions and Answers on Genesis* 3.48.

[80]In this discussion, I have made a basic methodological decision. My discussion purposefully avoids the "Paul and the Law debate" which has (pre)occupied much of Pauline scholarship in the last two decades. This debate is more an attempt to correct modern (Lutheran) prejudice in Pauline exegesis (a correction which has its merits) than it is a debate about ancient ethnicity, the topic presently at hand. To superimpose this debate concerning the law upon every Pauline passage where circumcision or law appears is to predetermine one's exegetical results; for questions posed control answers given. For a recent synopsis of the "Paul and the law" debate, see Colin G. Kruse, *Paul, the Law, and Justification* (Peabody: Hendrickson Publishers, 1996), 24-53.

[81]Some exegetes have worked from both presuppositions; others have interpreted this passage with respect to one or the other presupposition.

[82]By "rhetorical" I mean ornamental or purely illustrative. For a concise, yet helpful discussion of the history of ancient rhetoric, see Pogoloff, 7-35. Pogoloff illumines the fact that in antiquity, rhetoric was more than ornate form; it was the important, highly-prized art of

A second, typical exegetical presupposition is that the call, of which Paul speaks in vv. 17-24, is one's station or social status in life as in the English word "vocation." Although the exegetes who work from this presupposition do not "disembody" the text in the way in which the former group does, they, nonetheless, approach the text as if Paul is the advocate *par excellence* of a socially conservative philosophy of maintaining the status quo.

Those interpreters who understand vv. 17-24 as a digression treat Paul as if he is concerned simply with the history of ideas and not with real people in concrete social circumstances. Those who understand vv. 17-24 to be a treatise on being called to particular social stations or vocations treat Paul as if he is a socially conservative ideologue.

My treatment of the social location of 1 Corinthians 7 has shown the unlikelihood that Paul in these verses retreats into the world of ideas, employing illustrations with no thought at all of their actual social content, value, and implications. The Paul who writes 1 Corinthians 7:17-24 is genuinely struggling to integrate practical, concrete realities with the implications of the kerygma. Many persons in Pauline communities (including Paul) may have grappled with the relationship among one's call to be a Christian and one's ethnic and social status.

With respect to those exegetes who espouse the second presupposition, namely, that Paul presents in this passage a socially conservative ideology of "staying in one's place," my alternative reading of call language in 1 Corinthians has demonstrated that by "call" Paul could ostensibly mean the divine act which creates the ἐκκλησία or makes one a Christian. Thus, "remaining in the call" could very well mean "remaining a Christian." Furthermore, if the point of vv. 17-24 is to proffer some philosophy of "staying in one's position," this would undercut the entire thrust of 1 Corinthians 7:1-16, where Paul not only permits but also recommends, in certain circumstances, social change.

---

creating "conviction" in one's hearers. For a discussion of the shades of meaning attached to the word "rhetoric," see Patricia Bizzell and Bruce Herzberg, eds., *The Rhetorical Tradition: Readings from Classical Times to the Present* (Boston: Bedford Books, 1990), 1-15.

Thus, my contention is that two of the major exegetical presuppositions which have buttressed the interpretation of this passage do little, if any, justice, to the rich complexity of this piece of early Christian rhetoric. We should resist the premature resolution of ambiguity unwittingly created by either of these presuppositions and approach this passage from the standpoints that:

a) vv. 17-24 are not Paul's tangential or hypothetical observations but are integral (if only in Paul's mind) to the overall working of the letter's rhetoric;

b) Paul is not presenting a philosophy of maintaining the status quo per se. Instead, he is reflecting on the radical nature of the call of God which creates the church.

In light of our above discussions, what happens if we "embody" our exegesis with the actual social data that we have yielded in the first two chapters of this dissertation? Why does Paul appeal to the social reality of circumcision in the first place? What role, if any, do change and difference (of opinion from Paul's) have in Paul's understanding of community boundaries? From the outset of the letter it is abundantly clear that division in the ἐκκλησία is negative for Paul. In 1:10-11 he refers to the "dissension" and "schisms" in the community. 1 Corinthians cannot, of course, be reduced to one theme, but an important question underlying the entire letter is, in Paul's understanding, can one have a different opinion of the implications of the kerygma[83] and still be inside the boundaries of the ἐκκλησία?

A different but related issue underlying the entire letter is that of the role of social change. What role does change play in the life of the community? Is change (not just internal, moral transformation, but concrete socio-cultural, ethnic alteration)

---

[83]The salient issue is not difference of opinion per se. To suggest that Paul was opposed to anyone who construed things differently would make Paul appear infantile. The issue is a difference of opinion with respect to foundational matters, such as the implications of the kerygma and the boundaries of the ἐκκλησία.

necessitated by an acceptance of the kerygma, or is it a precondition of acceptance, or in light of the kerygma is social change ἀδιάφορος, a matter of indifference left up to the conscience of the believer?

Interpreted in this manner, 1 Corinthians 7 is not just a treatise on marriage and sexual ethics; it is also Paul's attempt to grapple with the place of the change of social status in light of the kerygma. The issue of change is especially problematic since certain persons in the Corinthian church seemingly have strong differences of opinion with Paul concerning the implications of the kerygma.

Since a salient issue for Paul is the role of societal changes with respect to the boundaries of the ἐκκλησία, Paul deals with concrete social practices and institutions which involve, and are symbolic of, societal changes: marriage and sexuality, ethnicity (construed here as circumcision/uncircumcision), and social status (configured here in terms of slavery). My point is that there are exegetically plausible ways to understand the rhetorical situation of this text which honor the complexity of this passage and which may reveal that the appeals to circumcision and slavery are not hypothetical but concrete.

The mention of circumcision and slavery may not be arbitrary, but may be Paul's attempt to wrestle with how the Corinthian community should treat rituals of change or transition. Who better than Paul, the apostle to the Gentiles, could understand the social transition involved in circumcision and epispasm? It is not unreasonable to believe that some in the Corinthian church were concerned about the role of ethnicity with respect to the kerygma. Does the gospel encourage or require an ethnic transformation, or is it indifferent to such transformation? Before attempting to assemble a more holistic reading of vv. 17-19,[84] let us analyze the various social possibilities envisioned by Paul in 7:18.

---

[84]My study of this passage differs from Harrill's in that I consider 7:17-19 as an equally important component for understanding this passage. Given my emphasis upon the necessity of social context, it is as much incumbent upon me to situate vv. 17-19 in some plausible social context as it is to situate vv. 20-24 in some social context. Harrill offers

In 7:18ab, Paul writes, "If anyone was circumcised when he was called, let him not remove the marks of circumcision." The first concrete social scenario offered by Paul is that of a circumcised man wanting to submit to epispasm. An overlooked textual feature in v. 18 buttresses the claim that Paul has actual social practice and ethnic status in mind.[85] Paul uses the technical medical term for reversing circumcision, epispasm. Paul implores the circumcised man μὴ ἐπισπάσθω. Concerning Paul's use of this technical term, Robert Hall says:

> This technical term, corresponding to the rabbinic *msk*, occurs only here and in Soranus's *Gynecology*. Even if Corinthian Jews had not submitted to epispasm, this passage [1 Corinthians 7:18] shows how readily epispasm arose as an option for a first century (55 CE) Jew once Paul had placed the advantage of circumcision in doubt. . . . In any case, Paul's use of a medical technical term shows that the practice of epispasm as a means of removing circumcision was current when the letter was written.[86]

Since epispasm was a live option in Diaspora communities, what kind of person would fit the social profile of 7:18ab, that is, a circumcised person seeking epispasm? The most natural response would be a Jew. Yet, remembering the social description of Corinth offered above, we recall that Corinth was a highly eclectic place, serving as the home for a host of ethnicities, including quite possibly some Egyptians (who themselves practiced circumcision). Thus, if we truly honor the complexity of the social world of Corinth, we must admit that there were potentially more circumcised persons in Corinth than just Jews. Yet, there is an extremely high probability that a circumcised person in Corinth would have been a Jew. What

---

no serious treatment of the role of ethnicity in this passage nor of Paul's appeal to ethnic factors.

[85]From Hellenistic literature as early as 1 Maccabees, there is evidence that social pressure from those imbued with Greek culture was enough to motivate one to seek epispasm. See, for example, 1 Maccabees 1:11-15.

[86]Hall, 73.

kind of Jew would have wanted to remove the marks of circumcision and why?

Several options present themselves. The first option would be a man who still wanted very much to be a Jew ethnically but by the same token wanted full and unfettered access to the civic benefits, including Roman citizenship and upward social mobility in Corinthian institutions such as the gymnasium. This kind of a Jew might view himself with a double identity, Jewish and Roman. We have already cited evidence that such dual identity was not necessarily problematic for the Romans. In the eyes of the Romans, a person could be a Jew and observe Sabbath and send money to Jerusalem and still hold Roman citizenship or still move up the ladder of power and honor in a important provincial capital like Corinth. Such a person, perhaps, would not want the embarrassment of his circumcision when exercising nude in the gymnasium or enjoying a moment of relaxation in the baths.

If one was circumcised, it might be a great social hindrance, especially if a person had designs on some municipal office in Corinth. Yet, submitting to epispasm was not necessarily an indicator that a person had abandoned his Jewish ethnicity. In fact, a man in Corinth who was a "social climber" could concomitantly possess a host of social allegiances and identities. Even after submitting to epispasm, he could still claim to be a Jew. Yet, through his other cultural associations he could claim to be a Greek or a Roman. Furthermore, if this person had also accepted the kerygma, he could well have a third identity marker, namely, Christian. To employ the terminology from chapter two, this person would be highly acculturated but not necessarily assimilated, still maintaining an appreciation of himself as Jewish.

A second, equally live option would be that of a man who no longer wanted to be Jewish but instead wanted, in every way, to be identified with Greek or Roman customs *and* ethnicity. The Jewish man who submitted to epispasm as a way of denouncing his Jewish ethnicity would not just have been acculturated to Greek or Roman culture but also *assimilated* into Greek or Roman *ethnicity*. Without removing the marks of circumcision, a

Jewish man in Corinth may not have had full access to Corinthian social life and power, and he would also have been the object of potentially severe social ridicule.

The degree to which a circumcised Jewish man in a Diaspora setting might be the target of public scorn is clearly illustrated in a fragmentary text published in *Corpus Papyrorum Judaicarum*. Considerable debate[87] has surrounded this text as it relates to its date, provenance and particularities of its content. Yet, in a recent article, Allen Kerkeslager[88] has offered a new interpretation of this fragment which sheds substantive light on issues of ethnicity in first century Diaspora communities.

The basic discussion in the fragment is related to athletics and those things which might disqualify one from competing. Previous interpreters of this fragment have located its setting in the theater. Kerkeslager has argued persuasively that this fragment instead preserves a discourse given in the gymnasium. He writes, "Discourse and lectures were integral to the life of the gymnasium."[89] The lines of this fragment that are of particular interest to us occur in Fragment b column 2. These lines appear to open in the middle of a sentence. They read:

> . . . and this man carrying a Jewish load (Ιουδαικον φορτιον). Why do you laugh and why are some of you disgusted at what has been said or at the man whom you see?

Commentators have offered various explanations as to what this "Jewish load" could have been, including suggestions that it was a Torah scroll or a kind of tax. Kerkeslager identifies

---

[87]For a synopsis of the scholarly debate, see *Corpus Papyrorum Judaicarum*, vol. 3, eds. Victor A. Tcherikover and Alexander Fuks (Cambridge, MA: Harvard University Press, 1964), 116-117.

[88]Allen Kerkeslager, "Maintaining Jewish Identity in the Greek Gymnasium: A 'Jewish Load' in CPJ 3.519," *Journal for the Study of Judaism* XXVIII (1997): 12-33.

[89]Kerkeslager, 19. Moreover, concerning the multiple purposes of the gymnasium, Ferguson remarks, "The rooms in a gymnasium complex included bathing rooms, dressing rooms, and storage rooms. There could also be a lecture hall, for the gymnasium was the center of activities for the ephebes." Ferguson, 95.

the mysterious Jewish load as a circumcised phallus.[90] If Kerkeslager is right, and the real location of this text is the gymnasium, such a social setting would have provided a natural opportunity for the public display of nakedness, thereby exposing the Jewish man's circumcision.

The laughter and disgust from the crowd also support the known evidence of Greco-Roman antipathy for circumcision. Contrary to those who have dated this fragment as late as 200 CE, Kerkeslager contends that one could just as easily date it to the period between 20 BCE and 41 CE. Furthermore, he suggests that the known evidence about Jew and non-Jew relations in Alexandria in this period makes Alexandria a likely geographical setting. In summary, in some Diaspora community, possibly in the early to mid-first century CE, there is fragmentary literary evidence of a Jewish man entering the gymnasium, and the crowd's recognition of his "Jewish load" elicits laughter and scorn.

Commenting on the implications of this fragment, Kerkeslager remarks, "The papyrus implies a period and a setting in which some Jews had reconciled the marks of Jewish identity with participation in the institutions of Greek identity."[91] Whereas this may be the case, there is another distinct possibility. Perhaps, it is precisely the laughter and scorn of those in the gymnasium that is most telling—telling of social reasons why a Jewish man might want to submit to episasm.

---

[90]Kerkeslager writes, "The simplest explanation for the phrase [Ιουδαικον φορτιον] is that the text presents us with the image of a nude circumcised Jewish athlete in a Greek gymnasium." Kerkeslager, 23. In support of the theory that the "Jewish load" is a phallus, see Martial, *Epigrams* 7.35. This epigram refers to the sexual organs (*inguina*) of a male Jewish slave as a *Iudaeum pondus* (Jewish weight). Another possible interpretation of the phrase (Ιουδαικον φορτιον) is that this "load" may be some kind of covering for the penis or even an artificial penis meant to conceal the athlete's circumcision. In *Epigrams* 7.82, Martial discusses a singer, Menophilus, who wore a *fibula*, a device designed to prevent erections. Yet, Menophilus's *fibula* was large enough to cover his whole penis. When his *fibula* fell off, his circumcision became evident. For a very useful and succinct discussion of these epigrams of Martial, see Schäfer, 93-105.

[91]Kerkeslager, 32.

The Jewish interest in and commitment to Greek and Roman cultures (and ethnicities) may have exacerbated an awareness of the barriers created by an adherence to Jewish ethnicity. Kerkeslager remarks, "Our text presents the rather ironic image of a Jew whose very devotion to an expression of Greek identity [i.e., gymnasium] makes his Jewish identity all the more inescapably obvious."[92] For Jews in Diaspora communities such as Alexandria or Corinth, there was actually a way to escape or at least hide that aspect of one's Jewish identity, epispasm.

What kind of Jewish man would be an avid participant in the gymnasium and concerned about the social ridicule that his circumcision would create in such a social location? An obvious answer would be a "social climber"—a Jew who was thoroughly acculturated and on his way to thorough assimilation. Participation in the gymnasium was no superfluous luxury. In many Greco-Roman cities, the gymnasium was the ladder to upward social mobility. The *ephebeia*, another important Greco-Roman social and intellectual institution, was often connected with the gymnasium. Concerning the *ephebeia* Ferguson writes, "The *ephebeia* had greater social than intellectual significance, for graduation from it was essential for full acceptance into the social and political life of the Greek cities."[93] In light of the gymnasium and *ephebeia* serving as important steps in Greco-Roman social life, it is more than plausible that a Jewish man, eager to climb the social ladder, might want unencumbered access to and participation in the gymnasium and *ephebeia*. Epispasm might have provided that access.

Yet, as we assess the social data, we must remember that 1 Corinthians 7 is "insiders' rhetoric," written by a Christian apostle to a Christian community. Although the Jewish man in the Corinthian congregation who submitted to epispasm may have been denouncing his Jewish ethnicity, such a man would still have been a member of the ἐκκλησία. When Paul advocates that a circumcised man not seek uncircumcision, Paul's interest

---

[92]Kerkeslager, 33.
[93]Ferguson, 101.

lies not in privileging Jewish ethnicity over against Greek or Roman ethnicities. Instead, Paul is trying to preserve the primacy of the new community (i.e., ἐκκλησία) and the new identity of the Christian. The new community, the ἐκκλησία, as Paul understands it, provides an identity which surpasses the honor and power-mechanisms of Greco-Roman cities. Richard Horsley rightly captures the *social* dimension of Paul's conception of the ἐκκλησία which is often overlooked in theological discussions. Horsley writes:

> At several points in 1 Corinthians Paul articulates ways in which the assembly of saints is to constitute a community of a new society alternative to the dominant imperial society. . . . The assembly stands diametrically opposed to 'the world' as a community of saints. As often observed, in Paul holiness refers to social-ethical behaviors and relations.[94]

If we take Horsley's argument seriously, especially his emphasis on the importance of social-ethical behavior, it helps us to understand why sexual ethics are so prominent in 1 Corinthians 7. In 1 Corinthians 7, Paul is not merely responding to concerns in the Corinthian congregation. He is also providing, according to the dictates of deliberative rhetoric, concrete examples of the erosion of the boundaries of the symbolic world. For Paul, compelling examples of this erosion consists in πορνεία, in all of its manifestations, and also in the adoption of standards from the social world which cut against the grain of Paul's desire to make the Corinthian ἐκκλησία "an exclusive alternative community to the dominant society and its social networks."[95] For Paul, the means by which one is retained in the ἐκκλησία is not ethnic identity but holiness.

If holiness, and not ethnic status, is what characterizes existence in the ἐκκλησία, the circumcised person should not remove his circumcision. Furthermore, the one who was called

---

[94]Richard A. Horsley, "1 Corinthians: A Case Study of Paul's Assembly" in *Paul and Empire: Religion and Power in Roman Imperial Society* (Harrisburg: Trinity Press, 1997), 244, 246.

[95]Horsley, 249-250.

in a state of uncircumcision should not seek circumcision. Having investigated the first social scenario (i.e., the circumcised person attempting to remove his circumcision), let us now analyze the second alternative (i.e., the uncircumcised person contemplating circumcision). What kind of person in the Greco-Roman world who was uncircumcised would be seeking circumcision?

The obvious answer is a proselyte. In the history of Jewish/Greco-Roman encounters, there was sizeable evidence that not only were Jews attracted by Greco-Roman practices and institutions, but also that Greeks and Romans were drawn by Jewish practices and institutions. For instance, there is ample evidence of Greek and Roman benefaction with respect to the building and maintenance of Jewish synagogues.[96] Moreover, there is evidence that there existed a group of non-Jews who participated in synagogue worship and were sympathetic to Jewish customs, the so-called God-fearers.

In the history of New Testament scholarship (and especially Luke-Acts interpretation), fierce debates have been waged concerning the existence of these God-fearers. A. T. Kraabel[97] has argued that the so-called God-fearers are a complete theological and literary fiction of the Lukan evangelist. Luke has created them in support of his *Tendenz* that Christianity became a Gentile movement while never divorcing itself totally from its Jewish heritage. John Gager[98] and Tessa Rajak,[99] however, have provided evidence that the term

---

[96]Louis H. Feldman, "Diaspora Synagogues: New Light from Inscriptions and Papyri" in *Sacred Realm: The Emergence of the Synagogue in the Ancient World*, ed. Steven Fine (Oxford: Oxford University Press, 1996), 51-55. The New Testament contains an example of Roman benefaction for a Jewish synagogue in the land of Israel. See Luke 7:1-10.

[97]A. T. Kraabel, "The Disappearance of the 'God-fearers,' " *Numen* 28 (1981): 113-126.

[98]John G. Gager, "Jews, Gentiles, and Synagogues in the Book of Acts," *Harvard Theological Review* 79 (1986): 91-99.

[99]Tessa Rajak, "Jews and Christians as Groups in a Pagan World" in *"To See Ourselves as Others See Us": Christians Jews, "Others" in Late Antiquity*, ed. Jacob Neusner and Ernest S. Frerichs (Chico, CA: Scholars Press 1985), 245-262.

θεοσεβής could very well have referred to proselytes who were "less fully Jewish than the others,"[100] but on their way to being fully Jewish. It is possible, even quite probable, that there existed semi-proselytes.[101]

According to this line of reasoning, the uncircumcised man spoken of in 1 Corinthians 7:18c could be a non-Jew who has been (semi)proselytized to Judaism, stopping short of circumcision. It is possible, in a boundary approach to ethnicity, that such semi-proselytes considered themselves "Jewish" in some sense, although in this state of partial commitment, they would not have had legal standing in the Jewish community.[102]

Furthermore, our emphasis on ethnicity clarifies an important point in the debate concerning circumcision and its necessity with respect to Gentiles who wanted to enter the ἐκκλησία. Early in the development of Christianity, Jewish leaders in Jerusalem[103] accepted that Gentiles could remain uncircumcised and still enter the ἐκκλησία. The provisions of the Jerusalem conference left no room (at least theoretically) for ambiguity. Uncircumcised Gentiles would be entering the ἐκκλησία as Gentiles. We have suggested above that in Diaspora communities it was taken for granted by some, but, perhaps, not all, that circumcision was the *sine qua non* of Jewish ethnicity. An uncircumcised man seeking circumcision in 7:18cd would, in Paul's estimation, not be understanding his identity with respect to Christianity or the ἐκκλησία because there was already a standard practice in Pauline churches that the uncircumcised could enter the church without circumcision. The uncircumcised man seeking circumcision, although a

---

[100]Rajak, 257.

[101]Rajak, 258. Rajak's suggestion is based, in part, on her reading of a second or third century CE inscription from Aphrodisias. The inscription, which dedicates a memorial, applies the term θεοσεβής to a group of non-Jewish sympathizers who appear to be very involved in the life of this particular Jewish community.

[102]Schiffman, 38.

[103]Galatians 2:7-10. Notwithstanding Paul's rhetorical and theological agenda in Galatians 2, New Testament scholars generally accept the historicity of Paul's account of the so-called Jerusalem conference.

member of the ἐκκλησία, would be defining his identity with respect to the synagogue.[104] Such a man would feel the need to submit to circumcision, not to be more fully Christian, but to be more fully a Jew. For Paul, the problematic issue would not be becoming a Jew per se. Instead, the issue for Paul would be to allow becoming a Jew to supersede the identity bestowed upon the believer by virtue of the call, namely, membership in the ἐκκλησία. Thus, Collins argues that "Paul's rejection of circumcision[105] symbolized a rejection of the ultimate efficacy of the contemporary synagogue."[106]

In other words, Paul de-emphasizes Greek and Jewish ethnicity with respect to the identity that really matters, namely, being a Christian or being in the ἐκκλησία. In this passage, it would appear that membership in the ἐκκλησία creates a new identity.[107] The ἐκκλησία is comprised of Jews and Gentiles, but the sum of the ἐκκλησία is greater than its parts.

This de-emphasis on ethnic identity and its social implications is also seen in 1 Corinthians 9:19-23. As noted in chapter two, in this passage we clearly see a Paul who can move in and out of ethnic states precisely because he is not defined by

---

[104]John J. Collins remarks, "Conversion to Judaism involved joining a new community and being accepted as a member of a synagogue. We may assume that synagogues would normally have insisted on circumcision, but in a place like Alexandria there may have been exceptions." See Collins, "A Symbol of Otherness: Circumcision and Salvation in the First Century" in *"To See Ourselves as Others See Us": Christians Jews, "Others" in Late Antiquity*, ed. Jacob Neusner and Ernest S. Frerichs (Chico, CA: Scholars Press 1985), 176. My suggestion is that in Corinth there may have been persons who proselytized to Judaism, stopping short of circumcision. Some of these "semi-proselytes" may have felt the need to be more fully involved or accepted in the life of the synagogue by means of circumcision.

[105]Paul also rejects uncircumcision in 1 Corinthians 7:18. This is the unusual and often overlooked point. In light of his assertions in Galatians, we would expect a rejection of circumcision. It is the concomitant rejection of *uncircumcision* that adds complexity to 1 Corinthians 7:18.

[106]Collins, "A Symbol of Otherness," 185-186.

[107]For Paul, membership in the ἐκκλησία was to be *the* identity by which the believer organized his existence.

them (or so he would like us to think). In 1 Corinthians 9:19-23 Paul remarks:

> For though I am free from all people, I have made myself a slave to all, that I might win the more. To the Jews I became as a Jew, in order to win Jews; to those under the law I became as one under the law—though not being myself under the law. To those outside the law I became as one outside the law—not being without law toward God but under the law of Christ—that I might win those outside the law. To the weak I became weak, that I might win the weak. I have become all things to all people, that I by all means may save some.

For our purposes, what is most telling is the relationship between 9:21 (i.e., "To those outside the law I became as one outside the law—not being without law toward God but under the law of Christ—that I might win those outside the law") and 1 Corinthians 7:19 (i.e. "circumcision is nothing; uncircumcision is nothing, but keeping the commandments of God"). In 7:19, the norm for those in the ἐκκλησία is keeping the commandments of God. In 9:21, Paul says the norm for his own apostolic behavior is being under the "law of Christ." Ben Witherington surmises that the law of Christ consists of "those ethical imperatives imposed on Christians [i.e., members of the ἐκκλησία] by Christ or by his example."[108]

Furthermore, I contend that the "law of Christ" (9:21) and the "commandments of God" (7:19) are similar, if not identical, constructs for Paul. They are his way of saying that the rubric by which the believer is to measure his social existence in the world is membership in the ἐκκλησία. Such membership then obligates one to keep the commands of God or the law of Christ. For Paul, when one properly understands the importance of the ἐκκλησία in determining social existence, one sees the inherent futility of attempts to gain fuller access to the gymnasium or the synagogue.

To submit to epispasm in order to scale more swiftly the ladder of Greco-Roman life or to seek circumcision in order to be more fully incorporated into the synagogue are equivalent

---

[108]Witherington, *Conflict & Community*, 213.

actions for Paul. They are two manifestations of the same problem, a denial of the most important identity bestowed upon the believer by the call of God, membership in the ἐκκλησία. Since submitting to epispasm and circumcision are tantamount, Paul arrives at a bold and unilateral affirmation in v. 19. "Circumcision is nothing, and uncircumcision is nothing, but keeping the commandments of God." Then, as if to remind his hearers of the importance of the call that makes one a Christian, in v. 20 he reiterates that each believer is to remain in his call, that is, he is to remain in the ἐκκλησία.

In light of Paul's de-emphasis of ethnicity in vv. 17-19, I am led to ask the following questions: Did Paul underestimate the role of ethnicity in community formation? Did the fledgling Christian community have enough tradition and stability to compete with the attractions of the gymnasium and the synagogue? Why should one, who had entered the ἐκκλησία, feel that "membership" in the ἐκκλησία was sufficient to meet all social needs?

Each of these questions could generate voluminous answers, but in short, I believe that Paul underestimated the role of ethnicity in configuring social existence. Interestingly, in several places in his other writings,[109] Paul is unable to extricate himself from his own ethnic assumptions and biases. Yet, it was his belief and hope that these ethnic assumptions and biases in others could be held in abeyance, if not eradicated, so that a new social unit could be configured, the ἐκκλησία. Paul's goal may have been laudable, but his method of achieving the goal may have been at best naive and at worst ambiguous concerning the role (and power) of ethnicity.

---

[109]See, for example, Romans 3:1-4, Romans 9-11, Galatians 2:15, and 1 Thessalonians 1:9.

CONCLUSIONS

Dissatisfied with the suppression of social factors that contribute to this passage's complexity, I have attempted to explore in some detail the origin and functions of circumcision in determining Jewish ethnic identity. Although there was some divergence of opinion in the Jewish Diaspora concerning the indispensability of circumcision, this rite continued to be an important aspect of Jewish ethnic identity. In light of the role of language practices in determining social boundaries, I investigated how language about circumcision was expressed in metaphors and allegories. Most notably, we explored the role of circumcision in some of Philo's writings.

Based on the gathered data, I then attempted to offer socio-historical scenarios which may have given rise to the Pauline statements in 1 Corinthians 7:17-20. Two institutions, undoubtedly conspicuous features of the Corinthian landscape, came clearly into our view, the gymnasium and the synagogue. The weakness of my reading is one that is endemic to all socio-historical and social scientific exegesis. My reading depends substantially upon imaginative hypothesis.

The strengths of my reading, however are three-fold. First, this reading provides a plausible social context in which to interpret 1 Corinthians 7:17-24, without suppressing the rich social complexity of this passage. Second, in the spirit of the *religionsgeschictliche Schule*, this reading takes seriously that in vv. 17-24 Paul has in mind more than the history of ideas. He is concerned about concrete, "living" institutions such as the gymnasium and the synagogue. Third, this reading avoids the resolution of ambiguity by refusing to treat this passage as an unrelated, unimportant or hypothetical tangent.

As noted above, 1 Corinthians 7:20 rounds off the first section of this passage and launches another. As we have "embodied" Paul's appeals to circumcision/uncircumcision in vv. 17-19, so too, we must embody his appeals to slavery in vv. 21-23. This will be the task of chapter four.

Chapter 4

SLAVERY IN THE
GRECO-ROMAN WORLD

INTRODUCTION

As discussed in chapter three, although circumcision was practiced by other groups in the Mediterranean world, the Jews singled out this cultural practice and turned it into a quintessential ethnic boundary marker. So complete was the identification of the Jews with circumcision that the term circumcision could be used by first century CE writers as a synonym for Jewish people.[1] Thus, circumcision, though itself a practice rife with complexity, was considered by many in the first century world to be, in the main, a *Jewish* phenomenon.

Turning our attention in this chapter to the discussion of slavery in the first century CE world, we must widen our scope of investigation. In fact, our scope needs to be as wide as the Roman empire itself. When one thinks of imperial Rome, many distinguishing markers come to mind: the accomplishments of Augustus celebrated in the *Res Gestae*, chief of which may have been the *Pax Romana*; the proliferation of Roman law; the rise of rhetoric; the establishment of provincial capitals or even the frequently-granted privilege of Roman citizenship. Yet, arguably, the most salient and enduring legacy of imperial Rome was the institution of slavery.

Moreover, the institution of Roman slavery would directly or indirectly affect the aforementioned aspects of Roman life as

---

[1]For a discussion of first century CE writers who use "circumcision" in a synonymous way to refer to the Jews, see Schäfer, 96-99. Interestingly, in an ironic subversion of the term "circumcision," Paul in Philippians 3:2 contends that the Christian community now constitutes the "true circumcision."

well as many others. With respect to the influence of the slave system on Roman law, W. W. Buckland in his magisterial study on ancient slave law remarked, "There is scarcely a problem which can present itself, in any branch of the law, the solution of which may not be affected by the fact that one of the parties to the transaction is a slave."[2] Historians and sociologists of the ancient world contend that Rome constituted one of the few authentic slave societies ever to exist in world civilization.[3] So influential was slavery to the warp and woof of Rome and of the empire in general that Moses Finley has concluded, "In the end, therefore, a genuine 'synthesis' of the history of ancient slavery can only be a history of Graeco-Roman society."[4]

Writing a history of the Greco-Roman world is impractical for this study, and such projects have been attempted more skillfully by others.[5] The purpose of my investigation of Roman slavery is to give fuller explanation of the factors that impinge upon 1 Corinthians 7:17-24.

In chapter two, I delineated those factors into the broad categories of ethnicity and social status. Chapter three attempted to embody the ethnic factors in terms of circumcision and uncircumcision. Chapter four will attempt to embody social status in terms of slavery and manumission. Although slaves in Roman imperial law held no legal status, it was precisely the

---

[2]W. W. Buckland, *The Roman Law of Slavery* (Cambridge: Cambridge University Press, 1908), v.

[3]Finley, *Ancient Slavery and Modern Ideology*, 9. The other four societies would be ancient Athens, and in the modern era Brazil, the Caribbean, and the United States. Picking up where Finley left off, Keith Bradley provides sociological data concerning what it means to call Rome a genuine "slave society." He contends that Roman Italy was a slave society according to demographic tests and other qualitative measures. See Bradley, 12-13.

[4]Finley, *Ancient Slavery and Modern Ideology*, 66.

[5]See, for example, G. E. M. de Ste. Croix, *The Class Struggle in the Ancient Greek World: From the Archaic Age to the Arab Conquests*; Ramsey MacMullen, *Roman Social Relations, 50 B.C. to A. D. 284* (New Haven: Yale University Press, 1974); M. I. Rostovtzeff, *Social and Economic History of the Hellenistic World* (Oxford: Oxford University Press, 1986), and Barclay, *Jews in the Mediterranean Diaspora*.

slave's *social* status that, in many regards, threw into relief and thereby defined the status of other persons in the Roman world.

An analysis of Roman slavery can be and has been a scholarly end in itself. My discussion will attempt to be thorough but in no way exhaustive. The ultimate aim of this chapter is to understand the implications of the social data for an exegesis of 1 Corinthians 7:17-24. Toward this end, we now strive.

In order to describe adequately the role and scope of slavery in Roman life, without providing a history of Greco-Roman culture itself, one needs an organizing device by which one can sift through and systematize the overwhelming amount of primary and secondary material. In this chapter, I will use Orlando Patterson's definition of slavery as that device. Patterson's comprehensive definition was derived from a diachronic sociological study of slave systems in both the ancient and contemporary worlds. In his sociological study,[6] Patterson argues persuasively that whereas the geographical location and ethnic and cultural factors might change from society to society, there are certain enduring sociological factors that are necessary and sufficient conditions for genuine slave societies, such as ancient Rome, to emerge and flourish. According to Patterson, "Slavery is the permanent, violent domination of natally alienated and generally dishonored persons."[7] The sum total of each of the social constituents in this definition creates for the slave *social death*.

FROM DEFINITION TO DESCRIPTION

In Patterson's general definition of slavery, there are five constituent elements: A) the permanence of slavery; B) the violence of slavery; C) the personal domination of slaves; D) the natal alienation of slaves, and E) the dishonor of slaves. The purpose of this section is to explore and explain each of these constituent elements of first century Roman slavery. Moreover,

---

[6]See Patterson, *Slavery and Social Death*.
[7]Patterson, *Slavery and Social Death*, 13.

I shall attempt to illustrate each of the elements with relevant primary sources.

The Permanence of Slavery

The literary, papyrological, and epigraphical fragments bequeathed to us from Greece and Rome indicate that very often one who was enslaved or even born a slave did not have to remain a slave all of his life.[8] Manumission, ironically, was an integral part of the slave institution, especially in Rome. Although individual slaves may have achieved their freedom and even at times Roman citizenship, the institution of slavery was a permanent fixture of Roman society. By some estimations, for more than two centuries prior to Augustus' claiming of the title *Princeps*, Rome was a well-established slave system.[9] Moses Finley has argued that the vast number of prisoners of war captured by the Romans in the Punic Wars[10] were turned into slaves precisely because there was already a substantial need[11] among the Romans for slaves.[12]

By the first century CE, slavery was a well-oiled, lucrative institution as much associated with the Roman way of life as the emperor or the military. Furthermore, even as late as the fourth century CE, slavery was still very much a part of Roman society. After his conversion to Christianity, the Emperor Constantine urged slave masters not to be excessive in exercising *their right* to punish slaves.[13] Constantine's admonition to fourth century

---

[8]Manumission will be considered in some detail below.

[9]Finley, *Ancient Slavery and Modern Ideology*, 83.

[10]264 BCE is the traditional date of the start of the first Punic War against Carthage.

[11]For a succinct and useful discussion of how this need for slaves was met, see Patterson, *Slavery and Social Death*, 105-131. Also, see Bradley, 31-56.

[12]Finley, *Ancient Slavery and Modern Ideology*, 86.

[13]Constantine wrote, "If an owner has chastised a slave by beating him with sticks or whipping him or has put him into chains in order to keep him under guard, he should not stand in fear of any criminal execution if the slave dies; and all statutes of limitations and legal interpretations are hereby set aside. . . . But he should not make

CE slave masters for restraint was a far cry from overarching social reform, let alone a social revolution to terminate the institution of slavery itself.[14]

For well over seven centuries (approximately the second century BCE to the fifth century CE), the institution of slavery not only existed but also flourished in the Roman world. For all intents and purposes, the longevity of the institution of slavery, if nothing else, perhaps provided slavery with the appearance of being natural. In addition to sheer longevity giving Roman slavery the appearance of naturalness, Aristotle's theoretical justification of slavery contributed considerably to its permanence. Aristotle provided significant philosophical support to the claim that slaves were indispensable for proper political management.

As to its origins, Aristotle's theory of natural slavery was, in some regard, a response to fourth century BCE Greek thinkers such as the comic poet Philemon who were decrying slavery as unnatural.[15] Aristotle was not merely arguing *against* his opponents; he was arguing *for* his version of the *polis*—a version that would encourage and permit the virtuous to rule. For Aristotle, politics and ethics reinforced one another. They were two sides of the same coin. The one fit to rule in Aristotle's

---

excessive use of his rights. He will indeed be accused of homicide if he willingly kills him with a stroke of a cane or a stone, inflicts a lethal wound by using something which is definitely a weapon. . . ." Quoted in Wiedemann, 174. A few years before the imperial ruling just cited, Constantine also decreed that slaves should not be branded in the face *but* on the legs. See Wiedemann, 194.

[14]Constantine's comments concerning the treatment of slaves are but one piece of evidence that the emergence of Christianity brought no real, large-scale amelioration of Roman slavery. For discussions of the interface between Christianity (ancient and modern) and the slave system (ancient and modern), see Elliott, *Liberating Paul*, 3-54 and David Brion Davis, *The Problem of Slavery in Western Culture* (Ithaca: Cornell University Press, 1966), 165-222.

[15]In his essay, "Aristotle and Slavery," P. S. Brunt points out that although the thinkers whom Aristotle opposed maintained the unnaturalness of slavery at the philosophical level, these thinkers never themselves called for its concrete abolition. P. A. Brunt, "Aristotle and Slavery" in *Studies in Greek History and Thought* (Oxford: Clarendon Press, 1993), 345, 351-352.

scheme is virtuous.[16] Conversely, the one lacking virtue, or more specifically reason, is unfit to rule but fit to be ruled.[17] In *Politics* 1.5.7 Aristotle writes, "The ruler must possess intellectual excellence (διανοητικὴν ἀρετή) in completeness."

Ironically, or even paradoxically, there is in Aristotle's system of ethics an ambiguity as to whether ability is completely endowed naturally or whether it is acquired. In some instances, Aristotle intimates that the process of gaining ἀρετή is directly related to having enough independence from the sordid affairs of earning a living wage. This leisure gives one the requisite time to acquire excellence. The freedom to be *absent* from daily concerns is made possible, of course, by the *presence* of slaves. By the same token, however, although the rulers could acquire or at least enhance the ἀρετή necessary for being a ruler, the acquisition of ἀρετή was thought impossible for slaves. For Aristotle, slaves are naturally deficient in reason.[18]

To employ the modern psychological terminology of "nature vs. nurture," Aristotle's argument for slavery actually contains some elements of a "theory of nature" and some elements of a "theory of nurture." That is, there is an articulation of the belief that nature parcels out and determines certain states for people. Thus, for Aristotle, slaves intrinsically cannot obtain enough ἀρετή themselves to be free. Yet,

---

[16]See, for instance, *Politics* 1.5.6-7.

[17]In suggesting that the slave is one who is deficient in some moral and intellectual way, Aristotle was merely picking up where his teacher left off. Plato himself believed that the slave was naturally bereft of λόγος. For a classic discussion of Plato's views on slavery, see Gregory Vlastos, "Slavery in Plato's Thought" in *Slavery in Classical Antiquity: Views and Controversies*, ed. Moses I. Finley (Cambridge: W. Heffer & Sons, 1960), 133-149. Also, more recently, Marimba Ani has creatively and convincingly demonstrated the ideological links between Platonic thought and the oppressive European imperialism which created many of the modern slave states in the Caribbean and the Americas. See Marimba Ani, *Yurugu: An African-Centered Critique of European Cultural Thought and Behavior* (Trenton: African World Press, 1994).

[18]In *Politics* 1.2.13 Aristotle says, "For he is *by nature* a slave who is capable of belonging to another (and that is why he does so belong), and who participates in reason so far as to apprehend it *but not possess it*" (emphasis mine).

concomitantly, Aristotle posits that in order for a ruler to become virtuous (and to remain virtuous), he must be unencumbered by daily demands, and this unencumbered state is made possible by the presence of slaves. Therefore, it is possible for the ruler's ἀρετή to be nurtured, but by the same token, the slaves who afford the ruler the leisure to gain this ἀρετή are themselves "naturally" bereft of ἀρετή. The inconsistency of Aristotle, once detected, is glaring, but this inconsistency,[19] if undetected, creates an airtight argument for the "naturalness of slavery" as a philosophical principle.

In order to rule, you must have ἀρετή. In order to have ἀρετή, you must be unencumbered by daily work. In order to be unencumbered by daily work, you must have slaves. Slavery is a necessary precondition for virtuous (i.e., ruling) men. Ironically, the slave in Aristotle's system is the opposite of the virtuous man, but it is precisely the presence of the slave that makes possible the attainment of ἀρετή. The slave, though antithetical to the virtuous man, is, nonetheless, an integral element in creating the virtuous man. Theoretically, Greek and Roman slavery functioned by means of this interesting paradox.

For imperial Rome, however, the discussion concerning slavery was modified such that the distinction was not between those who were or were not virtuous; instead the distinction was between those who were and were not citizens. In Rome,

---

[19]Brunt aptly exposes many of the ambiguities of Aristotle's ethical/political system. Unfortunately, on occasion in this article, Brunt ceases to be an expositor of Aristotle and becomes instead an apologist for Aristotle, seemingly almost taking up for him. Orlando Patterson offers an even-handed judgment of Aristotle that avoids the two poles of overly harsh criticism on the one hand and sympathetic apology on the other. Patterson remarks, "I think far too much, in the way of moral judgment, has been made of Aristotle's comments on the institution [of slavery]. What he has left us is a first-rate sociology of it, written from the viewpoint of someone who, like nearly everyone else in his day, assumed that it was essential for economic and social life. He makes the case for a natural view of slavery; it is a very weak argument, and not only does one get the distinct impression that he is not persuaded by it himself, but it is often not clear whether he is merely reporting the views of others who defend slavery on natural grounds, or presenting his own views." Patterson, *Freedom*, 162.

the slave was antithetical to the citizen, but ironically, in many instances, defined the citizen.

By definition in Roman law, a citizen could not be a slave. If the value of Roman citizenship was underscored and even defined by the institution of slavery, then, in theory, slavery was a social necessity for the Romans as long as Roman citizenship was a reality.[20] Undoubtedly, in the height of its imperial expansion in the first two centuries of the common era, some may have thought that Roman citizenship would be a never ending phenomenon. The same may have been thought about citizenship's defining antithesis, slave status. Although in imperial Rome, citizenship and slavery were fundamentally different social positions, they reinforced one another. As will be discussed below, formal modes of manumission created at least the opportunity[21] for the granting of citizenship. Once one was lifted from the dregs of his servile status, he became at least a candidate for the privilege of citizenship.

The permanence of slavery was further guaranteed by its great benefit to the ruling classes. According to what Aristotle says about slavery, the master-slave relationship was beneficial for both parties. Aristotle writes, "For one that can foresee with his mind is naturally ruler and naturally master, and one that can do these things with his body is subject and naturally a slave; so that master and slave have the same interest (διὸ δεσπότῃ κὰι δούλῳ ταὐτὸ συμφέρει).[22] If one offers a straightforward, literal rendering of the Greek impersonal phrase Aristotle uses, the above quoted phrase would read, "Therefore it [i.e., slave-master relationship] is of the same advantage for the master and for the slave." It will become abundantly clear, as we continue our investigation, that nothing was farther from the truth.

Roman slavery brought to slaveowners two very important kinds of capital, one more tangible than the other, but

---

[20]Patterson contends that the generosity of the Romans in granting citizenship to so many had roots in a shrewd sociology whose goal was "an effective means of enlarging the size of the Roman state and of recruiting fiercely loyal outsiders." Patterson, *Freedom*, 229.

[21]Manumission did not automatically bestow Roman citizenship.

[22]Aristotle, *Politics* 1.1.4.

both equally important in the social world of imperial Rome: *wealth and status*. One could even argue that of these two kinds of capital, the more important was status. Often in order for slaveholding to bring considerable wealth, one needed to employ large numbers of slaves such that the return produced from their work would significantly outstrip the cost of maintaining them. Yet, even those who lacked the means to employ a large number of slaves would have a sufficient number of slaves to assist them with various domestic chores and the education of their children.

The reality that slaves, especially domestic ones, filled many roles in the Roman household is an indication of the status that slaveholding brought. In this status-oriented society, it was thought to be a lack of taste to have the same slave carry out more than one duty. One might employ a slave just for the purpose of remembering the names of those whom one met.[23]

Again, insofar as there was a need for wealth and status among the Romans, slavery was bound to be a permanent fixture on the social landscape. By framing the issue of the permanency of slavery in a discussion of Aristotle, I do not mean to overlook the obvious social and cultural developments that occurred between the fourth century BCE Greek slavery of which Aristotle wrote and the first century CE Roman slavery which is our interest. The appeal to Aristotle, however, does clearly indicate the operative ideological frameworks and symbolic worlds which made it possible for the Greeks and the Romans to believe that slavery was a matter of φύσις. And if slavery were a matter of φύσις, then surely it was thought that the institution would be permanent, although individual persons may, at any time, fall into or out of this lamentable state.

---

[23]See Seneca, *Letters* 27 quoted in Wiedemann, 126.

The Violence of Slavery

Even though slaves could move upward socially, and thereby escape the violence at the lower levels of slavery, this was the exception.[24] Much more normal within the imperial Roman world was the experience of slaves who lived with the perpetual threat, as well as reality, of violence against which there was no legal recourse.

One can find abundant reflection about the execution, beating, and torture of slaves in the Roman law codes. Much of book forty-eight of the *Digest*[25] is devoted to the punishment and execution of slaves. One form of punishment that could be used for slaves who were convicted of attempted murder was cremation. The *Digest* 48.19.28.11 reads, "Slaves who have conspired against the well-being of their masters are generally burned in the fire, as sometimes also are free plebeians and persons of low rank."[26]

Other forms of execution used against slaves included crucifixion[27] and being thrown to the beasts. An "indirect" form of execution for many slaves resulted from their working

---

[24]Keith Bradley contends, "There can have been little likelihood of social improvement from slaves arising from the non-elite sectors of society, because slavery's stigmatic connotations were too pervasive to allow any realizable vision of a new or a different social order to manifest itself." Bradley, 144.

[25]The *Digest* was published in 533 CE, under the auspices of the Emperor Justinian. Although it was published five centuries after the Corinthian correspondence, it contains excerpts and legal opinions contemporaneous with the first and second centuries CE. For more insight on the *Digest*, see *Oxford Classical Dictionary*, 3d edition (Oxford: Oxford University Press, 1996), 803-804.

[26]*Digest*, ed. Alan Watson (Philadelphia: University of Pennsylvania, 1985).

[27]Suetonius writes, " He [Domitian] put to death a pupil of the pantomimic actor Paris, who was still a beardless boy and ill at the time, because in his skill and his appearance he seemed not unlike his master; also Hermogenes of Tarsus because of some allusions in his History, besides crucifying even the slaves who had written it out." See *The Lives of the Caesars, Domitian* 10.

conditions, especially in the mines.[28] Furthermore, there is substantive discussion in Roman legal sources about the beating, abuse,[29] and torture of slaves. With an analysis of the torture of Roman slaves, the insidious nature of Roman imperial slavery is all too plain to see.

---

[28]Diodorus Siculus, a first century BCE historian from Sicily, wrote a universal history. One of the surviving fragments from his work gives us insight into the harsh conditions of the mines throughout the Mediterranean world in which slaves (and some free persons) often worked. Concerning the mines he wrote, "The men engaged in these mining operations produce unbelievably large revenues for the masters, but as a result of their underground excavations day and night they become physical wrecks and because of their extremely bad conditions, the mortality rate is high." See *Diodorus Siculus*, trans., C. H. Oldfather et al. (Cambridge, MA: Harvard University Press, 1933-1976), 38.1.

[29]Alan Watson points out that the *Digest* 47 offers recompense to a slave owner whose virgin slave is seduced. But the law codes are mysteriously silent about the sexual abuse of slaves by the masters themselves. See Watson, "Roman Slave Law and Romanist Ideology," *Phoenix* 37 (1983): 56. Also, in the *Satyricon*, Trimalchio seems relatively unembarrassed that he had been the male prostitute for his master prior to his manumission. Furthermore, historians and even New Testament scholars (e.g., Martin, *Slavery as Salvation*) have made frequent references to the interpretation of dreams by Artemidorus. Whereas Artemidorus interprets the dreams of people from all strata of society, his interpretations of those dreams emanate from a particular social location. One example that presupposes the standpoint of the ruling class is found in his interpretation of dreams about sexual intercourse. Interestingly, the interpretation about to be quoted falls under the rubric of those sexual liaisons which are "natural, legal and customary." Artemidorus writes, [A dream about] "having sexual intercourse with one's servant, whether male or female, is good; for slaves are possessions of the dreamer, so that they signify, quite naturally, that the dreamer will derive pleasure from his possessions, which will grow greater and more valuable. To be possessed by a household slave is inauspicious, for it signifies that the dreamer will be despised and injured by that slave." For many slaves, the master's dream of sexual intercourse with slaves was anything but a dream, but instead a concrete social nightmare. See Artemidorus, *The Interpretation of Dreams*, trans., Robert J. White (Park Ridge: Noyes Press, 1975), 58-59. For a recent treatment of the sexual exploitation of slaves, see Jennifer Glancy, "Obstacles to Slaves' Participation in the Corinthian Church," *Journal of Biblical Literature* 117 (1998): 481-501.

In the face of this violence, the slave had little legal recourse[30] because in the eyes of Roman law slaves had no legal standing. Alan Watson remarks:

> Slaves had no access to censors, or other elected public officials or judges. They had no standing, and no legally recognized avenue of approach to anyone in authority. No machinery was created by which their complaints could be heard. In addition, they were in the physical control of the master who could ill-treat even more those who might be tempted to complain of ill-treatment.[31]

Even slaves who experienced upward social mobility and who occupied managerial positions[32] still lived under the threat of violence. In many instances, slaves were responsible for superintending their master's estates and other financial affairs. Dale Martin's work focuses on many of these managerial slaves. He writes:

> Many slaves held positions as *pragmateutai* for their owners. The normal Latin equivalent is *actor*; the position was something like a business agent. As several scholars have noted, these slaves were employed by wealthy and powerful families to manage property and run their business activities. Therefore, such slaves were often quite influential persons within the local society.[33]

Yet, in spite of this potential upward mobility, the laws and customs regarding, for example, the torture of slaves, served as

---

[30]There is, however, some evidence in the law codes that on occasion a slave could seek the mediating influence of the friend of his master. For example, the *Digest* 21.1.43.1 reads, "A slave who takes himself off to a friend of his master to seek his intercession is not a fugitive; indeed, even if his thinking be that in the event of his not receiving assistance, he will not return home, he is not yet a fugitive."

[31]Alan Watson, "Roman Slave Law and Romanist Ideology," 54-55. The Roman law codes, mention, however, the possibility of third party manumissions. That is, on occasions, a third party could arbitrate with the master on behalf of the slave and assist the slave in fulfilling the conditions for his manumission.

[32]Bradley offers a useful table of the myriad occupations that both rural and urban slaves would have filled. Bradley, 59-60, 62-63.

[33]Martin, *Slavery as Salvation*, 17.

a grim reminder, even to the socially well-placed slave, that his status was precarious.

According to the Roman law codes,[34] the evidence of a slave was permissible in court only after the slave had been tortured. Customarily, the slave could testify only for and never against his master.[35] Let us investigate some disparate pieces of data to see if we might produce a picture of the frequent use of slaves in managerial positions which differs somewhat from Martin's.

Some slaves were promoted to high-level bureaucratic positions where they managed large sums of money and property for their masters. If ever there were infelicities in a slave master's financial records that allowed another free person to take the master to court, the slave of the indicted master could only testify for his master, only after having been beaten. As a result of this arrangement, slave masters would benefit by having skilled slaves run their affairs. Additionally, by turning his affairs over to slaves, the master would gain more leisure.

The employment of skilled slaves to handle pecuniary affairs was a "win-win" situation for the master. The positive effect for the slave was incidental rather than intentional. Watson correctly observes, "Suddenly the widespread use of slaves in business that has seemed to indicate, among other things, a recognition of slaves as human beings, is revealed as having horrifying undertones."[36]

Then, as if to add insult to injury, the Roman law codes[37] give evidence that Roman jurists were fully aware that torture

---

[34]See, for example, *Digest* 48.18.9 which dictates, "The deified Pius wrote in a rescript that interrogation under torture may be applied to slaves in a case involving money, if the truth cannot be found in any other way. . . . In those cases where the torture of slaves against their masters should not be employed, it has been stated that not even interrogation [without torture] is valid; much less admissible are [voluntary] informations laid by slaves against their masters."

[35]Watson, "Roman Slave Law and Romanist Ideology," 57.

[36]Watson, "Roman Slave Law and Romanist Ideology," 57.

[37]It is interesting to note that an entire section of the *Digest*, 48.18, is devoted to a discussion of the appropriate and inappropriate times

of slaves was not the most effective means of obtaining truth in juridical proceedings. *Digest* 48.18.1.23 remarks:

> It is stated in constitutions that reliance should not always be placed on torture—but not never, either; for it is a chancy and risky business and one which may be deceptive. For there are a number of people who, by their endurance or their toughness under torture, are so contemptuous of it that the truth can in no way be squeezed out of them. Others have so little endurance that they would rather tell any kind of lie than suffer torture; so it happens that they confess in various ways, incriminating not only themselves but others also.

In light of this overt admission of the possible ineffectiveness of torture, one must ask, was the violence toward and torture of slaves designed to elicit truth, or was it intended to reinscribe in the minds of both the slave and the free that each person in the Roman social order had a "natural" place and was supposed to stay in that place?

The Personal Domination of Slaves

Closely related to the violence suffered by slaves was their subjection to complete personal domination. An investigation of some important words and values in the Roman symbolic world reveals the extent to which slaves experienced personal domination by their masters.

In chapter two, we discussed the importance of *dignitas* to the Romans. On the Roman scale of values, *dignitas* was the "*princeps.*" Rome was one of the few authentic slave societies in world history because honor, so valued by the Romans, was intricately related to their concept of power. Patterson nicely elucidates this point. He contends "It is one's sense of honor that often drives one to acquire the instruments of power in the first

---

and means to use torture. The majority of these legal rulings deal with the torture of slaves.

place."[38] The claim to honor presupposes the ability of the claimant to defend his honor. In the words of Julian Pitt-Rivers, "The claim to honor depends always in the last resort upon the ability of the claimant to impose himself. Might is the basis of right to precedence which goes to the man who is bold enough to enforce his claim regardless of what may be thought of his merits."[39]

---

[38]Patterson, *Slavery and Social Death*, 80. New Testament scholars who discuss honor (and shame) pay homage to the theories of Julian Pitt-Rivers, the famous anthropologist. Yet, many of these scholars do not explore fully the issue of power, especially personal power as a means of gaining honor in the first place. For instance, in his article "Honor and Shame" Halvor Moxnes gives only nominal treatment to the importance of power in acquiring honor in the first place. See Moxnes, "Honor and Shame" in *The Social Sciences and New Testament Interpretation*, ed. Richard Rohrbaugh (Peabody: Hendrickson Publishers, 1996), 34-36. For further insight on the relationship of honor and power, see Patterson, *Slavery and Social Death*, 79-81.

[39]Julian Pitt-Rivers, "Honor" in *Encyclopedia of the Social Sciences*, 2d edition, vol. 6 (New York: Macmillan Company, 1968), 505, quoted in Patterson, *Slavery and Social Death*, 80. The complex and intricate relationship between honor and power in imperial Roman ideology is well illustrated in Augustus's *Res Gestae*. The *Res Gestae* is inherently a piece of imperial rhetoric designed to celebrate for all time the accomplishments of Augustus and his *dignitas* resulting from these mighty acts. In the *Res Gestae*, Augustus celebrates that one of his first acts was the mustering of an imperial army, his institutional demonstration of power. In *Res Gestae* 1 Augustus extols, "At the age of nineteen, on my own initiative and at my own expense, I raised an army by means of which I liberated the Republic, which was oppressed by the tyranny of a faction. For which reason the senate, with honorific decrees, made me a member of its order. . . giving me the imperium." Lewis, 562. Patterson mounts a most sophisticated argument that in imperial Rome the (plebeian) people were content to give up their civic freedom if it meant the security of their personal freedom and happiness. In other words, as long as Augustus insured that there was tranquillity and relative personal prosperity, Augustus's desire to wield sovereign imperial power was seen as no real threat to the people. (Some aristocrats, however, may have felt differently about Augustus's power.) Patterson calls this "the Augustus compromise." See Patterson, *Freedom*, 258-263.

Without an oversimplification of vastly complex social realities, in the Roman world *dignitas* presupposed *potestas*,[40] and *potestas* guaranteed *dignitas*. An undisputed manifestation of *potestas* was the ability to determine whether another person would live or die. The social context where this determination was often made was warfare. When the Romans decimated a foreign people, two options were usually available to the victorious general and army: they could either execute them or enslave them.

Even the nomenclature of slavery derived from the setting where victorious generals decided whether prisoners should live or die. This is especially seen in Digest 1.5.4.2 which reports, "Slaves (*servi*) are so called, because generals have a custom of selling their prisoners and thereby *preserving* rather than killing them: and indeed they are said to be *mancipia*,[41] because they are captives in the hand (*manus*) of their enemies." The reality of Roman slavery as a form of suspended death receives additional mention in *Digest* 35.1.59.2. This statute suggests that a legacy bequeathed to a person who has received a penalty entailing slavery becomes invalid; "for slavery is equated with death."[42] In short, having slaves or mancipia[43] (originally as a result of warfare) was a consequence of one's *potestas* which further solidified one's *dignitas*. In other words, the ideological substructures of the Roman imperial world made slavery seem

---

[40]That is, power or the ability to control.

[41]The Latin word *manceps* is a commercial term which connotes the bidder at an auction who raises his hand to place a bid on merchandise. See Charlton T. Lewis, *A Latin Dictionary* (Oxford: Clarendon Press, 1879), 1106.

[42]That slavery in its ancient and modern manifestation was a form of social death is, of course, the central thesis of Patterson's *Slavery as Social Death*. The apostle Paul is also clearly aware that slavery could connote death. See, for example, Philippians 2:6-8.

[43]Literally, *mancipium* means taking possession. Eventually, however, *mancipium* became legal shorthand for a slave, regardless of whether the slave was the booty from warfare or bought in the slave markets.

all the more like a natural social arrangement—natural, that is, from the viewpoint of the masters.[44]

Bradley's assessment of the total domination of the slave is instructive and worth quoting in full. He remarks:

> In no other circumstance [as in slavery] was power exercised by one over the other in such an all-embracing manner. The Roman emperor passed laws that affected all of his citizen-subjects, but his powers of enforcement were limited. The Roman father retained formal authority over his sons until his death, but in real life adult sons were in many respects fully independent.[45] The powers of the school teacher and military officer were also circumscribed by time and situation. In the master-slave relationship, however, there were no restricting factors: the slave was at the complete and permanent disposal of the master and except by an act of resistance could never find relief from the necessity of obeying because there were no countervailing rights or powers in the condition of slavery itself to which the slave had recourse.[46]

In his theory of natural slavery, Aristotle contended that a slave was a "live article of property."[47] One could surmise that for many Roman masters the emphasis was on the slave as "property" and not as a "live" human being. Even the *peculium*,

---

[44]In spite of the abundance of ancient evidence concerning Roman slavery, very little of the evidence offers to the contemporary historian the "view from below," that is, the slave's perspective. Dale Martin acknowledges this fact; yet, his depiction of the upwardly-mobile managerial slave obfuscates the sordid realities of slavery that would have been the lot of most of those enslaved in the Roman empire. Bradley also acknowledges the lack of the slave's perspective and offers a more imaginative historical reconstruction of what the majority of slaves would have experienced. To accomplish this, Bradley uses Roman legal material, fictional material, and techniques of comparative historiography. For a discussion of Bradley's method, see Bradley, 1-9.

[45]Both sons and slaves were under the *potestas* of the *paterfamilias*, but with respect to the effects of this *potestas* and ways to be released from it, sons differed from slaves in degree and in kind. See Gardner, 12-13.

[46]Bradley, 5.

[47]*Politics* 1.2.5.

an aspect of Roman slavery which superficially seemed to affirm the slave's humanity, was another indicator of the master's complete domination.

The *peculium* was money or property which legally was the absolute possession of the master. The master, however, often loaned the *peculium* to the slave for the latter's use. The *Digest* offers an exhaustive treatment of the *peculium*, devoting an entire book to this topic. The *Digest* 15.1.4 says:

> A thing does not become part of the *peculium* just because the slave keeps it in a separate account; the master himself must have allocated it to the slave's account rather than to his own. It is not the slave's conduct that counts but the conduct of the master in establishing the slave's *peculium*; for it is he [the master] who has the power to increase it or diminish it or to take it away altogether.[48]

On the surface, the granting of the *peculium* to the slave appears benevolent. The picture becomes more bleak when we realize that a majority or even all of the *peculium* could be required by a Roman slave master as a condition of manumission. In other words, the granting of the *peculium* was not a concession necessarily rooted in morality as much as it was an "insurance policy" for the master against the capital loss incurred when selling a slave. The price paid to the master by one slave for manumission could be reinvested in the purchase and maintenance of another slave.[49]

On some occasions, a master might free a slave and allow him to keep some of his *peculium*. But on other occasions, the master could both require all of the *peculium* and additional

---

[48]For another example of the master's control of the *peculium*, see *Digest* 41.1.10. It reads, "We [masters] can make acquisitions not only personally and directly but also through those whom we have in power, through slaves in whom we have a usufruct and through freemen and slaves of others whom we possess in good faith. . . . Anything which our slaves receive by delivery and anything which they acquire. . . is acquired by us; for a person in the power of another can hold nothing for himself."

[49]Hopkins, 134. For a critique of Hopkins's theory of the *peculium* as a source of recapitalization, see E. Badian "Figuring Out Roman Slavery," *Journal of Roman Studies* 72 (1982): 168.

labor from the would-be freedman after manumission.[50] For hundreds of years before the first century CE, masters who freed slaves were taxed at a rate of 5 percent of the value of a slave.[51] Masters may have figured the cost of this tax into the price for manumission or may have recouped some of the cost of this tax by mean of the duties (*operae*) which a freedman may have been required to perform after manumission. Thus, when investigated more closely, the "humaneness" of the *peculium* is more apparent than real. Even the *peculium* was ultimately for the benefit of the master and served in some instances to further underscore the personal domination of the slave.

The Natal Alienation of Slaves

In many regards, the signs and effects of the permanence, violence, and personal domination of slavery were very tangible and thus easily observable as regular features of Roman society. The next two factors, natal alienation and dishonor, were more intangible, but nonetheless very real for slaves. Natal alienation involved the denial of the rights and privileges of birth normally extended to free persons. To say that the Roman slave was natally alienated is not to say that he did not experience some communal or even familial bonds. The inscriptional and papyrological evidence has indicated that slaves and freedpersons did enjoy some of these bonds.

Instead, the notion of natal alienation suggests that such bonds, though occasionally enjoyed, were never seen as legitimate or legal. A primary manifestation of natal alienation was the fact that slave marriages were not considered legitimate.[52] Since the familial bonds of slaves were not legally

---

[50] *Digest* 38.1.

[51] Susan Treggiari, *Roman Freedmen during the Late Republic* (Oxford: Clarendon Press, 1969), 17.

[52] In a detailed discussion of various family relations, the *Digest* 38.10.10.5 reads, "We do not refrain from using these names, that is, the names of cognate relatives, even in the case of slaves; and so we talk about the parents and sons and brothers of slaves too, but *servile relationships do not belong to [the realm of] the laws*" (emphasis mine).

sanctioned, masters felt little compunction in breaking up families by selling women and children to different owners and/or killing the men of the family.[53]

A second indicator that slavery exposed persons to a state of natal alienation was that children born to slave mothers were automatically considered to have slave status. It should be noted that Roman law did show considerable flexibility in considering the children of a slave woman as freeborn if that woman at any time herself experienced freedom. If the mother was born free and then at some later time reduced to slavery, or if the mother was a slave when the child was conceived, yet a freedwoman when the child was born, the child would be free. The *Digest* 1.5.5 remarks:

> By the *jus gentium*, peoples become slaves on being captured by enemies or by birth to a female slave. The freeborn are those who are born of a free woman; it suffices that she was free at the time of birth, even though she was a slave at the time of conception. And in the converse case, if a woman conceives as a free person, then gives birth as a slave, it has been decided that her child is born free. . . .

What should one make of these legal statutes? The granting of free status to children of mothers who at some point in their lives experienced freedom speaks simultaneously of the high-value placed upon freedom and also the bitter contempt that the Romans had for slavery. The unspoken corollary of these statutes is that any slave woman who has not or does not taste freedom in some point in her life will, by definition, give birth to slave children.

One should remember that the majority of slaves never experienced manumission. In the imperial period, the enormous number of slaves necessary in the Roman empire was supplied by homegrown slaves[54] and not by the booty of the Roman wars of expansion. Thus, it is not unreasonable to think that many slave "families" (to the extent that these families stayed intact)

---

[53]For a discussion of the effects of Roman slavery on the family, see Richard Saller, "Slavery and the Roman Family," *Slavery and Abolition* 8 (1987): 65-87.

[54]The Latin term for homegrown slaves is *vernae*.

experienced generation after generation of natal alienation, never breaking free from the stigma of servile status.

A third telling indicator of the effects of natal alienation can be seen from studying the manumission formulas from Delphi.[55] In some detail, Hopkins has studied these inscriptions.[56] In spite of minor variations among the inscriptions, there tends to be a pattern for these manumission formulas. The formula includes the date of the fictitious sale of the slave to the god Apollo, giving religious sanction to the slave's freedom.[57] In the phrase that details the fictitious sale to the god, a telling indicator of the natal alienation of slavery emerges. For instance, in the manumission formula of a slave woman named Pistis, we read:

> Polemarchos, the son of Polemon, with the agreement of his son Polemon, sold to Phythian Apollo, the female body whose name is Pistis, homeborn, on the following conditions. . . .[58]

The free persons involved in the transaction are known by means of their familial connections. For example, Polemarchos is *the son of Polemon*. The slave woman Pistis cannot be said to be the daughter of anyone because slaves had no legal rights to family connections. She is simply known as a "female body" ($\sigma\tilde{\omega}\mu\alpha$ $\gamma\upsilon\nu\alpha\iota\kappa\tilde{\epsilon}\iota o\nu$). The historical fact that some slaves, on occasion, did eke out some family existence does not eclipse another brute fact that at any time those connections could be

---

[55]For the collection of inscriptions from Delphi, see *Sammlung der griechischen Dialekt-Inschriften*, ed. Hermann Collitz (Göttingen: Verlag von Vandenhoeck & Ruprecht), 1899. I am aware that many of these inscriptions predate the Corinthian correspondence by two centuries; nonetheless, they are instructive with respect to the ideology of Greco-Roman slavery. For example, inscriptions 1722 and 2029, which depict the sale of Jewish slaves to the god Phythian Apollo, date from approximately 170-156 BCE.

[56]Hopkins, 133-171.

[57]Hopkins, 142.

[58]Hopkins, 142. This is inscription 2187 in *Sammlung der griechischen Dialekt-Inschriften*.

destroyed; for in the eyes of the Roman masters, such relationships were not legitimate.

It is often noted that the sons of freedmen scaled great heights in the Roman political and social world. Yet, the freedmen themselves, though at times quite rich and even powerful, had difficulty overcoming the social stigma of their slave origins. An example of the first century CE aristocratic venom for freedmen can be found in Pliny the Elder, who complains of the infiltration of freedmen into the equestrian order. Pliny contended, "Even men who have been freed from slavery leap over these restrictions to obtain the symbols of equestrian status."[59]

A clear example of the alienation created by slavery is couched in the explication of the Roman law of persons offered by Gaius, a second century CE jurist. Gaius remarks:

> The principal distinction made by the law of person is this, that all human beings are either free men or slaves. Next some free men are free-born (*ingenui*), others are freedmen (*libertini*). The free-born are those who were free when they were born; freedmen are those who have been released from a state of slavery.[60]

In Roman law, even if a person had been born free and later reduced to slavery, that person would be counted no longer as free-born but as *libertinus*, that is a freedman. As Gardner remarks, for that person born free but then reduced to slavery, "the period of slavery produces a discontinuity, and their original free birth is lost sight of."[61]

As important as law (*lex*) was in Roman culture, there was another important social factor which also wielded enormous influence, *mos* or custom.[62] Though freedmen were juridically

---

[59]Quoted in Wiedemann, 69.

[60]Quoted in Wiedemann, 24.

[61]Gardner, 3.

[62]Gardner urges caution with respect to the use of Roman laws as a method of doing social history. Analysis of law codes must be balanced by an appreciation for social attitudes and customs as well. Gardner contends, "Roman law consists not only in rules, but also in cases, and it is that which makes it so valuable a source for the Roman social

free (free, that is, according to *lex*), the natal alienation of their slave experiences would serve as an albatross around their necks with respect to *mos*. In fact, occasionally, *mos* was so powerful that it actually affected *lex*.

In the first century BCE, there was considerable aristocratic disdain for freedmen in general and for mixed marriages between the free-born and freedpersons in particular. This custom and attitude of disdain, in the principate of Augustus, actually became *lex*. Augustus forbade men and women of senatorial rank to intermarry with freedpersons.[63]

Although both *lex* and *mos* forbade those of the senatorial order to marry freedpersons, both masters and patrons often took slaves as their concubines. Slaves were an easily exploited outlet for the sexual desires of the ruling class. Should these slave women become impregnated, the women (and their children) could make no legitimate claims upon the estate of the masters.[64] Slaves, as natally-alienated persons, possessed neither the right of property nor progeny.

The Dishonor of Slaves

As discussed in chapter two, of all the values in the Roman symbolic world, arguably, *dignitas* or honor was supreme. The above discussion of the definition of slavery has demonstrated that the Roman slave was the complete antithesis to the person of honor. It was not that the slave possessed little honor.

---

historian. Both aspects, however, must be considered. The rules taken alone give a false picture of the actual workings of the society, and of its attitudes; looking at the cases on their own runs the risk of misinterpretation or unjustified generalization." Gardner, 6.

[63]*Digest* 23.2.44 reads, "The *lex Julia* provides that: 'A senator, his son, or his grandson, or his great grandson by his son, shall not knowingly or fraudulently become betrothed to, or marry, a freedwoman, or a woman who is or has been an actress. . . . Nor shall the daughter of a senator, his granddaughter by his son or great-granddaughter by his grandson become betrothed to or marry, knowingly or fraudulently, a freedman, or a man who is or has been an actor. . . .'"

[64]Saller, 65 and 71-72.

Instead, the slave possessed no honor, either ascribed or acquired.

Ascribed honor normally came as a result of being born into a noble family, but as discussed above, one's slave status severed one from the residual ascribed honor that would come from carrying a proud family name and tradition. Additionally, the slave could not acquire *dignitas* by virtue of possessing an inherently moral or intelligent nature; it was believed that such inherent attributes were not granted to slaves by nature. A scene from Petronius's "Dinner with Trimalchio" gives expression to the belief of the inherent inferiority of slaves.

During the dinner party, the freedman Trimalchio provides for his guests lavish entertainment, including acrobats. As the dinner guests are being entertained, one of the acrobats, who is a slave, falls into Trimalchio's lap, creating a stir and possibly injuring Trimalchio. In the aftermath, Trimalchio manumits the slave acrobat "so that no one could say that such a great figure [i.e., Trimalchio] had been injured by a slave."[65]

Even for a freedman like Trimalchio, himself not too far removed from his slave days, it was unthinkable that he would be wounded by someone of such a low station. Not only were slaves believed to be of an inferior nature, they were also believed to be morally reprobate with a proclivity to steal[66] and to run away.[67] In the eyes of many Romans, slaves were anything but worthy of honor.

Not only were the means of ascribed honor barred to the slave, the means of acquired honor were severely limited as well. Much has been written about the potential upward-mobility of certain imperial slaves. Dale Martin remarks, "Naming oneself the slave of an important person was a way of claiming status for oneself."[68] Concerning this supposed

---

[65]*Satyricon*, 71.

[66]For example, see Pliny the Elder, *Natural History* 33.6. Quoted in Wiedemann, 93.

[67]Roman slave masters' fear of their slaves running away is substantiated by the fact that an entire section of the *Digest* is devoted to this topic. See *Digest* 11.4.

[68]Martin, *Slavery as Salvation*, 48. Also, see my discussion of Martin in chapter two.

upward-mobility, two points need to be remembered. First, this upward-mobility was the exception that proved the rule. Second, the status which may have resulted from belonging, for example, to a powerful, aristocratic master was status gained through the person of another and was not truly the *slave's* status. This intangible "status by association," like the tangible *peculium*, may have been in the "possession" of some slaves but was never truly under the "ownership" of the slave. Technically, the slave could own nothing, not even honor, since he was socially dead.

This "status by association," so publicized in New Testament scholarship, was secured by the slave through a heavy tax, namely, the slave's own social death.[69] Patterson contends, "The slave, as we have already indicated, could have no honor because he had no power, and no independent social existence, hence no public worth. *He had no name of his own to defend.*[70] He could only defend his master's worth and his master's name."[71] The slave stood altogether outside of the game of honor. In a society so conscious of honor, the greatest *dis*-honor was to find oneself completely outside of the parameters of the honor contest itself. Or in the words of Publilius, the first century BCE epigrammatist, "None ever loses honor save him who has it not."[72]

As discussed earlier, the different and more severe forms of punishments visited upon slaves clearly indicate the slave's lack of honor and status. Callistratus, a provincial Roman lawyer in the late second and early third centuries CE, wrote, "Our ancestors, whatever the punishment, penalized slaves more severely than freemen, and notorious persons more than

---

[69]Patterson writes, "The slave, as a socially dead person, existed in a permanent state of transition: socially dead, yet physically alive; an instrument, yet a vocal one; a two-legged beast, yet with a mind and a soul; a physically separate being, yet no more than a living surrogate of the master." Patterson, *Freedom*, 238.

[70]This is poignantly underscored by the fact that at the time of manumission many slaves took the names of their patrons. Thus, even as freedmen, their names were still not truly their own.

[71]Patterson, *Slavery and Social Death*, 10 (emphasis mine).

[72]Quoted in Patterson, *Slavery and Social Death*, 78.

those of unblemished reputation."[73] Simply because one was a slave, and thus devoid of honor, one could routinely expect to receive harsher treatment in the courts of justice. In the imperial Roman world, "Justice" made no pretense about being "blind." The eyes of "Justice" were keenly affixed to the status (or lack thereof) of those who came before it.

In some detail, I have attempted to fill out Orlando Patterson's general, diachronic definition of slavery with the particularities of slavery in its ancient Roman manifestation. With some possible exceptions, Roman slavery was a state from which there could be no significant change. From the perspective of both the slave master and the slave, it must have appeared that the institution of slavery would exist forever. The individual slave could only hope that in his lifetime he might receive the fortune of manumission. Of course, manumission is a central motif in 1 Corinthians 7:20-23. In order that we might better understand the role of manumission in this passage, let us investigate briefly the process of manumission in Roman society.

MANUMISSION

Manumission was an integral part of the Roman slave institution. In considerably higher numbers than their Greek counterparts, Roman slave masters manumitted their slaves.[74] This historical datum has fascinated classicists and historians, and in the history of scholarship on Roman slavery, this phenomenon has led some scholars to believe that as the Roman empire progressed, the institution of slavery became more benevolent.[75]

---

[73]*Digest* 48.19.28.16.

[74]A. M. Duff, *Freedmen in the Early Roman Empire* (Oxford: Clarendon Press, 1928), 12-13.

[75]One sees the residue of the belief that manumission was deeply rooted in altruism in both Duff's and Treggiari's classic treatments of freedmen. Neither of these scholars is naive enough to discount the benefits of manumission for masters, but they certainly do not strongly suggest that manumission's primary cause was its value to the masters. See, for example, Treggiari, 14 and Duff, 19. Though nearly 75 years old,

It is certainly feasible that from time to time individual Roman slave masters may have felt some moral or emotional compulsion to manumit their slaves. Yet, in the light of the preceding definition and description of slavery, I am hard pressed to think that manumission was primarily motivated by the warm feelings of masters towards their slaves. More than being the rite of passage to freedom for individual slaves, manumission, as we shall see, was a constituent feature of slavery and worked in the master's favor. Before exploring the larger role of manumission in maintaining slavery, we turn to a brief discussion of the mechanics of manumission.[76]

Two types of Roman manumission are commonly identified: formal and informal. Formal manumission brought with it the concomitant gift of Roman citizenship, whereas informal manumission did not. Whether the manumission was formal or informal, the decision to manumit was primarily at the discretion of the slave owner.[77] David Daube, however, contended that the *censor*, the Roman magistrate responsible for the Roman census, had the power to act contrary to the wishes of a master and enroll a slave as a freed person on the

---

Duff's work is still considered a standard treatment on freedmen in the imperial period. As a twenty-first century (postmodern) reader, I am fascinated by the uncritical manner in which Duff seems to share the aristocratic assumptions of the Roman elitist sources. See, for example, Duff, 11 and 13-14.

[76]For fuller treatments, see Buckland, 437-597; Treggiari; Duff; Bradley, 154-173; Daube, "Two Early Patterns of Manumission," *Journal of Roman Studies* 36 (1946): 57-75, and Gardner, 7-51.

[77]This was one of the primary facts upon which Bartchy built his investigation and exegesis of 1 Corinthians 7:21-24, namely, that the slave did not have any input with respect to his/her manumission. See, for example, Bartchy, 96-120. Whereas Bartchy's assessment is, in the main, accurate, I do not think that this aspect of slavery (i.e., which party has the authority to start the manumission process) of necessity impacts greatly the exegesis of the passage. Paul's advice for the slaves to take freedom whenever the opportunity arises (if this is actually what Paul is saying) is not affected if the opportunity comes from the master or is created by the slave. Paul can be aware of many of the important, even technical aspects of Roman (slave) law, without pressing them into service at every turn.

census.[78] There were three types of formal manumission: manumission *censu*, manumission *vindicta*, and manumission *testamento*. A brief description of each will be useful.

Manumission *censu* was the least frequent, primarily because it could only be accomplished every five years when the census was taken. Once a (former) slave's name was listed on the roster of citizens, that person could no longer be regarded as a slave. Historians are not sure precisely when this form of manumission became passé, but it is generally agreed that by the imperial period this form of manumission was obsolete.[79]

Manumission *vindicta* involved a fictitious, juridical proceeding involving three or four persons, namely, the master, the slave, a local magistrate who represented the wishes of the state, and an independent party who suggested to the magistrate that the slave was a free person. Since the slave had no legal recourse, he needed someone to present his case for him, and this was the function of the independent party. Upon hearing the claim that the slave was free, the master would not offer a defense. Subsequently, the magistrate would award freedom to the slave and symbolize the slave's transfer from servile to free status by touching the slave with the rod, the *vindicta*.

By far the most common type of formal manumission was manumission *testamento*, or manumission by virtue of a will. Traditionally, a Roman slave master would make provision in his will to free a certain number of slaves upon his death, when the slaves would no longer be of service to him. It was not uncommon for the master, even in manumission *testamento*, to attach certain conditions to the will. The slave may have had to perform specific tasks in order to obtain manumission, or even after manumission; or pay a sum of money to the master's designated heirs. An indicator of the popularity of this form of manumission was the restriction on the number of slaves who could be manumitted at any one time, a restriction instituted by Augustus in the *Lex Fufia Caninia* in 2 BCE. This legislation

---

[78]Daube, 60-61.
[79]For a useful discussion of why this form of manumission became obsolete, see Buckland, 439-441.

created a formula detailing the number of slaves who could be released based upon the master's total number of slaves.

If a master owned between two and ten slaves, one-half could be bequeathed their freedom in the master's will. If the master owned between ten and thirty slaves, one-third could receive their liberty upon his death. If the master owned between thirty-one and 100 slaves, one-fourth could be set free. If the master owned between 100 and 500 slaves, only one-fifth could be set free.[80]

I contend that it is precisely in the area of manumission *testamento* that we see most clearly the notion of slavery as *social* death. Slaves freed by the will of their masters were referred to as *orcini*, since "they belonged, as it were, to *Orcus*, the realm of the dead."[81] These slaves were freedmen of the dead man. Only upon the death of the master could the social life of the slave begin; as long as the master was still alive, the slave was still (socially) dead.

As for informal manumission, the procedure was less rigid. A slave who was manumitted informally was juridically free and under no further obligation to work for his master. Yet, unlike formal manumission, where all three forms had the potential of providing the freedman with citizenship, informal manumission had no immediate prospect for citizenship. Informal manumission could be accomplished by letter from the master or in the company of friends.[82]

Having dealt with the mechanics of manumission, we now offer some brief reflections on the motives of masters to manumit their slaves. As suggested above, manumission might well occur because of a master's goodwill toward his slave, or because of a familial bond that developed between a master and his slave. Even so, there is good reason to believe that manumission, just like slavery, often operated primarily for the master's benefit.

Manumission benefited the master in a number of tangible and intangible ways. First, the promise of manumission served

---

[80]Gaius, *Institutes* 1.42-46.
[81]Duff, 25.
[82]Buckland, 444.

as a useful psychological deterrent on undesirable slave behavior. As the ultimate "carrot-on-the-stick," manumission was bound to insure docility and good behavior.[83]

Second, even though manumission was the supposed pathway to freedom, it reinforced the master's sense of domination over his slaves. Manumission was never to be looked upon as a right or privilege of any slave. Whenever it was granted, it was an act of graciousness on the part of the master.[84]

Third, by requiring money as a condition for release, the master insured himself against the loss of capital caused by the slave's departure; moreover, he also insured that he would have the requisite capital to purchase new slaves. Speaking poignantly to this economic reality, Hopkins writes, "As the adult slave grew older, the chances of death and sickness increased; insofar as release prices were related to market prices, it was better for the master at some stage to capitalize the slave's current value than to go on risking total loss or to keep on a declining asset."[85]

A fourth reason for manumission could have been the master's desire to marry a particular slave.[86] There were doubtless other reasons for individual masters to manumit

---

[83]Sometimes the psychological motivation of manumission would be held before a slave until the slave died. There was never any guarantee that a master would manumit a slave. For instance, in *The Satyricon*, mention is made of Scissa, a slave master, who was giving a dinner in honor of the slave whom she had manumitted on the slave's death bed. In this same passage, mention is made of the *vicesima libertatis*, the 5 percent liberation tax. See *The Satyricon*, 80.

[84]Bradley, 165.

[85]Hopkins, 147. In addition to the manumission price being a built-in way to "recapitalize" the master's investments, the *Digest* also suggests that the *peculium* was the master's insurance policy against law suits. In *Digest* 15.1.41 Ulpian contends, "Thus, a master may sue third parties for what they owe the slave, and he (i.e., the master) may be sued for what the slave owes them (i.e., third parties) up to the amount of the *peculium* and for any benefit thereby accruing to him."

[86]The *Lex Aelia Sentia* declared that a slave could not be manumitted until he was thirty years old. An exception to this law was granted to a master who wanted to marry his slave girl. See, for example, *Digest* 40.2.20.2 and 40.9.21.

slaves, but even manumission motivated by benevolence could have the practical effect of reinforcing the slave system. When one person was set free, surely another one was enslaved.

Having discussed the rationales for manumission, we now turn to the "sociological creation" resulting from manumission: the freedman (ἐλεύθερος, or *libertus*). If a slave was fortunate enough to receive freedom, he would become a part of the family of his former master, who would now become his patron. Upon receiving (formal) manumission, a freedman could take the three names (*tria nomina*) that typified that a person was a Roman citizen. Even if one was manumitted informally, one still took some form of the name of one's patron. This receiving of the family name *after* one's manumission only underscores the fact that the freedman in his previous state of slavery was beset with the burden of natal alienation.

Only upon receiving the gift of freedom could the slave become part of the family. In Rome and in some other larger cities of the Empire, such as Corinth, the freedmen population in the first century CE was as large, if not larger, than those claiming to be free-born Romans or free-born foreigners. The excessive number of freedmen is not an indication of the benevolence or graciousness of Roman slave masters. It is rather an indication of how pervasive Roman slavery was in the first place.

The freedman's relationship to his patron was regulated by law and custom. Often, as a prior condition of manumission, patrons could require freedmen to work a certain number of days for the benefit of the patron. The days of work were referred to as *operae*. The Roman law codes specified that the *operae* were to be performed solely for the benefit of the patron. *Digest* 38.1.9. says:

> Those [work obligations] which are in the nature of a duty are in the future and can be owed only to a patron, since the property in them resides in the person who performs them, and in him for whom they are performed. But skilled services or others are of a kind that can be discharged by anyone for anyone. But obviously if [the services] consist of skilled work, they can, on the patron's order, be performed for another.

If analyzed with some care, this legal ruling reveals provocative ideological insights about Roman slavery and manumission. To be sure, this law and similar ones were designed so that the manufacturing skills of freedmen could not be loaned out or even bequeathed unilaterally to one's friends or family. Duties that involved manufacturing could have a monetary value set upon them, and then the money could be bequeathed to other persons. The law also says that *officiales*, duties involving not just the freedman's skilled labor but more importantly the freedman's person, could only be provided to the patron. The law codes attest that a freedman literally owed his newly-found social life to the "generosity" of his former master and current patron.

Why would the law permit duties which involved the freedman's skilled labor or his actual person to be provided only for the patron? Such legislation publicly underscored that the former master was solely responsible for the freedman's new social life in the first place. Even though there were checks and balances on the *operae* that limited their abuse by patrons, they served as ideological sign posts. The *operae* constituted a publicly viewed social contract where the freedman, though now a legally-sanctioned actor and perhaps even a citizen, was, nonetheless, inextricably bound (usually for life) to a terribly unequal social relationship with his patron.

Not only did patrons require freedmen to enter into contracts which obligated them to work a number of days, they also expected *obsequium* from their freedmen. Noting the difficulty of translating *obsequium*, Gardner thinks of it as the socially acceptable acquiescence of freedmen toward patrons.[87] To employ distinctions used earlier, when speaking of *obsequium* one enters the realm of *mos* rather than of *lex*. This reverent acquiescence was at times difficult to enforce legally, but freedmen could well feel the force of social custom. In fact, the bitter venom for the "up-and-coming freedman," emitted by the Roman moralists, surely stemmed, at least in part, from an aristocratic perception that freedman had not offered the

---

[87]Gardner, 23-25.

requisite *obsequium* to patrons. A final indicator that manumission may have created a difference for the slave only in degree and not in kind is found in the laws concerning freedmen's testimony with respect to their patrons. Even though a slave had been freed, he was still unable to testify against his patron.[88]

For many slaves, manumission brought release from the physical and psychic indignities of slavery. Yet, we hear from the lips of a former slave himself that it would be a pure flight of fancy for a slave to place all his hopes in the quest for a better life after manumission. Epictetus writes:

> It is the slave's prayer that he be set free immediately. Why? Do you think it is because he is eager to pay his money to the men who collect the five per cent tax? No, it is because he fancies that up till now he is hampered and uncomfortable, because he has not obtained his freedom from slavery. "If I am set free," he says, "immediately it is all happiness, I shall pay no attention to anybody, I talk to everybody as an equal and as one in the same station in life, I go where I please, I come whence I please, and where I please." Then he is emancipated, and forthwith, having no place to which to go and eat, he looks for someone to flatter, for someone at whose house to dine. . . . And if he gets a manger at which to eat he has fallen into a slavery much more severe than the first. . . .[89]

Here, Epictetus, himself well acquainted with the indignities of slavery, vividly depicts how manumission could create an illusionary freedom which, in practice, became a new form of slavery. Even with all the "risks" of manumission, the hope for freedom still flickered in the minds of many slaves. As we shall see in the next section, this flame of hope may have been fanned by certain groups in the first century CE world.

---

[88]Gardner, 26.
[89]*Discourses* 4.1.33-36.

MANUMISSION, THE CHURCH, AND THE SYNAGOGUE

This dissertation desires to explore the complexity and ambiguity of 1 Corinthians 7:17-24 which emerge if one does not rush to premature resolution. The attempt to honor the richness of the passage has necessitated a full description of various social and cultural realities of the symbolic world. An implicit question of the investigation has been, what are the interpretive possibilities of this passage if one believes that Paul has in mind actual persons who are contemplating circumcision and uncircumcision and persons who are caught in the throes of Roman slavery?

In chapter three, I suggested that one way of taking seriously the social history of 1 Corinthians 7:18-19 was to position Paul's rhetoric against the backdrop of two very important institutions of the ancient world, the gymnasium and the synagogue. In the light of these institutions, Paul's language about circumcision/uncircumcision need not be read as a mere rhetorical digression or ornamental allusion. Instead, this language could give evidence of Paul's real concern, to posit the supremacy of the ἐκκλησία over other alluring social institutions. In a similar way, I would like to explore briefly the possibility of reading Paul's words about slavery in 1 Corinthians 7:21-23 against the backdrop of two concrete social institutions, the ἐκκλησία and the Jewish synagogue.

As discussed above, manumission was in the prerogative of individual slavemasters, and quite often a prerequisite for manumission was money. On some occasions, the master could require the slave's *peculium* (and even additional money) as a condition of manumission. In most cases, scholars of Roman slavery have assumed that the money for the slave's freedom came from the *peculium* or from the profits which occurred from the financial investments of the *peculium* by an industrious slave.[90] Keith Hopkins raises a query concerning this scholarly assumption. He remarks, "We may have been wrong to assume that all slaves paid for their own freedom. We cannot help but wondering whether money for the purchase of freedom was

---

[90]Watson, *Roman Slave Law*, 98.

sometimes put up by someone else."[91] In fact, there is strong evidence suggesting that third-parties sometimes supplied the money for manumission.

The Roman law codes indicate clearly that the financial capital for manumission may have originated somewhere other than the slave himself. Although it is noted in *Digest* 40.3.1 that the *collegia* did not have unilateral legal permission and authority to manumit until the time of Marcus Aurelius in the late second century CE, even before that time, other groups, municipalities, and individuals did have the right to manumit a slave. Offering legal advice concerning the slave's right to fulfill the previously arranged condition for manumission, the third century CE lawyer Ulpian remarks, "It matters little whether he [i.e., the slave] offers the money from his *peculium* or a sum received from a third party; it is accepted that the slave attains to freedom by giving money from his *peculium* whether he was directed to give it to the heir himself or to a third party."[92]

As suggested earlier, once the master set up the *peculium*, the slave could add to it through his own efforts or through gifts from outside sources, provided that the master was aware of the increase to the *peculium*.[93] Nothing prevented third parties from supplying the slave with financial gifts to increase his *peculium* in order to have enough money to buy his freedom when the opportunity emerged. In theory, according to Roman law, the person or persons who desired to finance the manumission of a slave would need the permission of the master because it was the master who held the *imperium* over the slave. Before discussing further the evidence and implications of third parties' buying persons from slavery, let us discuss briefly a traditional scholarly viewpoint concerning the ancient church's role in manumission.

Well documented[94] by scholars of ancient slavery is the practice of "ecclesial manumission" wherein Christian congregations released persons from slavery. Scholars

---

[91]Hopkins, 168.
[92]*Digest* 40.7.3.
[93]Watson, *Roman Slave Law*, 98.
[94]See, for example, Buckland, 449-451.

traditionally have given short shrift to this practice by relegating it, in the main, to the time of Constantine in the early fourth century. In dismissive fashion, Buckland remarks:

> It [so called ecclesial manumission] is of little importance in the general development of the law and therefore may be disposed of at once. . . . A constitution of Constantine, addressed in A.D. 316 to a certain bishop, and plainly reciting only earlier law, remarks that it has long been allowed for masters to give liberty to their slaves *in ecclesia catholica*. It must be done before the people in the presence of the priests, and there must be a writing signed by the *dominus, vice testium*. [95]

Buckland's understanding of the practice seems to presuppose that the master of the slaves in question was a leader or member of the particular church. Slaves in this case would be common slaves under the ownership of the church, and the church or the priest as "the master" of the slaves would have the right to manumit slaves at will.

There is other evidence, however, from a period long before Constantine suggesting the existence of another form of "ecclesial manumission" in the first two centuries of the Common Era. In this form of ecclesial manumission, the church or its leaders were not the master(s) of the slave but functioned instead as a third party acting in the slave's interest by attempting to manumit him. The church would mediate between the master and the slave, and with the master's permission, the church could manumit the slave.

Third-party manumissions were at least common enough for them to receive mention in the Roman law codes. The *Digest* 40.9.20 says, "If freedom has been given to someone else's slave without consent of the owner, the grant can have no legal force." That such a statute appears in the law implies that third-party manumissions happened with enough frequency to warrant legal clarification. Given the wording of the statute just quoted, it would be logical to assume that third-party

---

[95]Buckland, 449-450.

manumissions which *did* have the consent of the owner *would* have had legal force.

Having argued for the viability of third parties entering into the manumission process, I need to introduce the important concept of a *statuliber*. According to the Roman law codes, a *statuliber* was "one who has freedom arranged to take effect on completion of a period of fulfillment of a condition."[96] Often these conditions were placed in a master's will and were supposed to be met or fulfilled with respect to the master's heir(s). For example, in a will, a master could set a slave free at the time of the master's death, *on the condition* that the slave pay the son of the master a certain amount of money. Upon the death of the master, the slave would move from being a slave to being a *statuliber*. *Statuliber* is best understood as a hybrid social state, halfway between slave and freedman.

For all intents and purposes, the status of *statuliber* constituted a kind of two-stage manumission.[97] The first stage of manumission occurred when the master died, while the second and final stage of manumission took effect when the conditions for manumission stated in the master's will had been fulfilled, usually with respect to the master's heir.

As discussed above, it was not uncustomary for freedmen to have a certain number of obligations to fulfill for their

---

[96] *Digest* 40.7.1

[97] This custom of conditional manumission was not at all novel in the Greco-Roman world. In fact, conditional manumission found great and even earlier expression among the Greeks. Hopkins's work on the Delphic inscriptions has elucidated the process of two-stage manumission. Hopkins writes, "The [Delphic] inscriptions also cast light on a curious institution called *paramone*, which we translate rather loosely as conditional release; perhaps suspended release would be better. By this institution, slaves bought formal freedom but contractually bound themselves to stay with and to continue serving their former owners, even after they were freed, just as though they were still slaves, usually until the former owner's death. Conditional release was a twilight state of juridical freedom combined with slave-like service, a state which overlapped both slavery and freedom." Hopkins, 133. To be sure there were differences between the Greek practice of *paramone* and the Roman status of *statuliber*, but each social practice revealed that the process of manumission was by no means a simple, straightforward practice.

masters. Yet, even as freedmen fulfilled their *operae*, they were juridically free. Moreover, there were checks and balances in place to insure that patrons were not abusive to their freedmen. Although there were checks and balances on conditional manumission,[98] until the *statuliber* fulfilled the condition, he was technically a slave.[99] In this regard, conditional manumission differed from the full-fledged, one-stage manumission spoken of earlier. Regarding the slave status of *statuliberi*, *Digest* 40.7.29 declares, "*Statuliberi* hardly differ at all from the rest of our slaves. . . . Hence, too, in public trials they undergo the same penalties as the other slaves."

There are other aspects of the process of conditional manumission which are of considerable interest to us. *Statuliberi* could by law be sold to third parties by the heir who inherited the slaves. In the *Digest*, there are ambiguous rulings as to how this immediately affected the status of the *statuliber*.

Some Roman jurists[100] contended that the conditions which were to be fulfilled for the heir would transfer upon sale to the purchaser of the slave, and once the *statuliber* fulfilled those conditions for the new purchaser, he would then be fully manumitted. Other jurists[101] argued that the moment that a *statuliber* was sold by the heir to a third party he became a full-fledged freedman. In light of the above evidence, we can see that the Roman law codes paid more attention to the notion of third-party manumissions than is usually recognized by modern scholarship on Roman slavery.

---

[98] The *Digest* is very clear that all the conditions set for the *statuliber* must be met, although the heirs to whom the slave is bequeathed are expected to show flexibility and understanding as the *statuliber* fulfills the conditions. On the other hand, Roman law is equally clear that if the heir who is responsible for the *statuliber* attempts to thwart a *statuliber* from fulfilling the conditions, the *statuliber* would be free. For the relevant checks and balances on conditional manumission, see, for instance, *Digest* 40.7.3.

[99] One indication of the slave status of a *statuliber* is that, according to *Digest* 40.7.16, the child of a *statulibera* was considered to be a *slave* of the master's heir.

[100] *Digest* 40.7.6.

[101] *Digest* 40.7.3.17.

Not only do the Roman law codes give evidence of interest in third-party manumission, but there are also intimations in first and second century Christian literature[102] of Christians desiring to secure manumission for Christian slaves. One of the apostolic fathers, St. Clement of Rome, who was bishop of Rome from approximately 92-101 CE, wrote a missive from Rome to the Corinthian congregation during his episcopate.

Much like the founder of the Corinthian congregation had done some forty years earlier,[103] Clement, in his letter, addresses pastoral concerns in the life of the Corinthian congregation which are threatening to rob it of its vitality and harmony. Apparently, the chief concerns for Clement are the jealousy and strife in the Corinthian ἐκκλησία.[104] In place of this jealousy and strife, Clement urges upon the Corinthian Christians a life of concord and self-restraint.[105]

In the course of his missive, Clement appeals to examples of charity and compassion to bolster his case that the Corinthians should put aside their wrangling. Offering an example of charity and compassion known to him, in 1 Clement 55, he remarks, "We know of many among us who gave themselves up to fetters in order to ransom others. Many gave themselves up to slavery, and taking their (sale) price, they furnished food for others" (ἐπιστάμεθα πολλοὺς ἐν ἡμῖν παραδεδωκότας ἑαυτοὺς εἰς δεσμά, ὅπως ἑτέρους λυτρώσονται. πολλοὶ ἑαυτοὺς παρέδωκαν εἰς δουλείαν, καὶ λαβόντες τὰς τιμὰς αὐτῶν ἑτέρους ἐψώμισαν.) Clement's reference to "many among us" (πολλοὺς ἐν ἡμῖν) has been taken by commentators to refer to Roman *Christians* known by Clement. Thus, in 1 Clement 55, we are in the realm of the ἐκκλησία.

Clement claims to know Roman Christians who had been imprisoned so that others might be free and Roman Christians who had entered into slavery (παρέδωκαν εἰς δουλείαν). With

---

[102]Callahan, 113.

[103]J. B. Lightfoot dates 1 Clement to 95 or 96 CE. See Lightfoot, *The Apostolic Fathers: Clement, Ignatius, and Polycarp*, vol. 1 (Grand Rapids: Baker Book House, 1981), 27.

[104]1 Clement 6.

[105]1 Clement 30.

the money gained from fellow Christians selling themselves into slavery (τιμὰς αὐτῶν), other Christians have received concrete assistance, namely, food. The benevolent and self-sacrificial acts to which Clement refers could very well have been individual acts and not corporate or church-sponsored activities. Yet, it is interesting to note that in this text there are hints of Christians acting on behalf of one another in order to improve concretely the social situation of fellow Christians.

More specifically, 1 Clement 55 contains literary evidence of Christians using the money secured from selling themselves into slavery to benefit others. One could speculate that in other situations, the money gained from selling one Christian into slavery was used to purchase the manumission of another Christian. In 1 Clement 55, we certainly do not have any sort of "ecclesial manumission," but possibly it was this kind of concern in the ἐκκλησία for the social situations of fellow believers that would eventually lead the ἐκκλησία to become involved in communally-sponsored manumission.

There is, however, evidence about an ecclesial communal fund (for the purpose of manumission) in another early Christian text. Ignatius, the third bishop of Antioch, who was martyred in 110 CE, wrote an epistle to Polycarp, the Bishop of Smyrna. Ignatius's tone in this letter is warm and affectionate, and the occasion of the letter appears to be the giving of encouragement by an older church leader to a younger church leader. As Lightfoot[106] has noted, in this regard the letter to Polycarp resembles Paul's pastoral epistles.

In the fourth chapter of the letter to Polycarp, Ignatius directs his attention to particular issues in the congregation at Smyrna, and he offers his advice to the younger Polycarp. Ignatius writes, "Do not treat slaves, male or female, with disdain, but neither must they themselves become puffed up; on the contrary, for the glory of God they should render the better service so as to obtain a better freedom from God. Let them not desire to be set free from the common fund; lest they be found as slaves of their desires." (δούλους καὶ δούλας μὴ ὑπερηφάνει. ἀλλὰ μηδὲ αὐτοὶ φυσιούσθωσαν, ἀλλ' εἰς δόξαν θεοῦ πλέον

---

[106]Lightfoot, vol. 2, 229.

δουλευέτωσαν, ἵνα κρείττονος ἐλευθερίας ἀπὸ θεοῦ τύχωσιν. μὴ ἐράτωσαν ἀπὸ τοῦ κοινοῦ ἐλευθεροῦσθαι, ἵνα μὴ δοῦλοι εὑρεθῶσιν ἐπιθυμίας.)

The phrase of particular interest to us is μὴ ἐράτωσαν ἀπὸ τοῦ κοινοῦ ἐλευθεροῦσθαι. Why would slaves be desirous of being manumitted ἀπὸ τοῦ κοινοῦ? Could it be that such slaves in the church of Smyrna had heard of the Christian practice of using money available to the church to purchase the freedom of slaves in the congregation? In other words, Ignatius's prohibition against using the common fund in the ἐκκλησία in this way only makes sense if the money might have been used to manumit slaves in the first place.

Reading Ignatius's letter to Polycarp, one is struck by some similarities to 1 Corinthians 7. Although Ignatius in chapters four and five of his letter covers a variety of topics, two of the topics include the role of slaves and the role of sexuality and marriage in the Christian community; both topics, of course, occur prominently in 1 Corinthians 7. Also, Ignatius's belief that slaves will receive a better freedom from God might be understood to be similar to Paul's expression in 1 Corinthians 7:22, "for the slave called in the Lord is a freedman of the Lord." Finally, both Ignatius's letter to Polycarp and 1 Corinthians 7 seem to broach the topic of actual, concrete manumission. Ignatius states clearly that the slaves should not expect to be manumitted from the communal funds. On the other hand, Paul, on the issue of concrete manumission, is less than clear!

In this comparison, I am not suggesting that Ignatius's letter to Polycarp is an "interpretation" or trajectory of 1 Corinthians 7. By bringing Ignatius's letter into the interpretive discussion, I am simply illustrating the fact that early Christian communities, long before the age of Constantine, were at least aware of, if not themselves involved in, the manumission of slaves. Such historical realities disallow us from quickly relegating Paul's language in 1 Corinthians 7:17-24 to the realm of "theoretical digression." Perhaps, we should maintain the possibility that a similar situation might have existed in the mid 50's of the Common Era in a city like Corinth.

First century CE evidence of religious communities' involvement in manumission emanates not only from literary sources but also from archeological sources. This time it is not the ἐκκλησία but the synagogue that is involved. In the late 1980's, a Greek manumission inscription dating to 51 CE was discovered in the Black Sea region. A portion of the inscription reads, "freedom [to the sons] to be guaranteed by the guardianship of the Jewish community"[107] (συνεπιτροπευούσης δὲ καὶ τῆς συναγωῆς τῶν Ἰουδαίων). A second manumission inscription from the Black Sea region dating to 80 CE reads:

> During the reign of Tiberius Julius Rhescuporius friend of Caesar and of the Romans, dutiful in the 377th year the 12th of Peretou, I Chreste, formerly wife of Drusus, release to the *proseuche* my slave Heraclas, a free person once and for all according to my vow, he shall remain untouched and undisturbed by all my heirs as I have vowed. He may go where he wants unrestricted except that he adheres devoutly to the *proseuche*. This agreement is made by my heirs Heraclides and Kelikoniados, and the joint guardianship of the community of the Jews.[108]

---

[107]See D. I. Danshin, "Jewish Community of Phanagoria," *Vestnik Drevnei Istorii* 1: 58-73. Also cited in Robert S. Maclennan, "In Search of the Jewish Diaspora: A First Century Synagogue in Crimea?," *Biblical Archaeology* 22 (1996): 46. The word συναγωγή can be translated both as "community" and as "synagogue" (that is, synagogue in terms of a building). It has been suggested by scholars that in the first century CE world the word used to denote the physical building in which Jews gathered was προσευχή, and the word to denote the gathering itself was συναγωγή. Richard Oster, however, has reminded us that there is evidence that in a first century Diaspora community the actual building itself was referred to as a συναγωγή. See Oster, "Supposed Anachronism in Luke-Acts' Use of ΣΥΝΑΓΩΓΗ," *New Testament Studies* 39 (1993): 187. On the question of the meaning of συναγωγή and προσευχή, also see Irina Levinskaya, "A Jewish or Gentile Prayer House?: The Meaning of ΠΡΟΣΕΥΧΗ," *Tyndale Bulletin* 41 (1990): 154-159 and Lee I. Levine, "The Second Temple Synagogue: The Formative Years" in *The Synagogue in Late Antiquity* (Philadelphia: The American Schools of Oriental Research, 1987), 20-23.

[108]*Corpus of Jewish Inscriptions*, no. 683. For more recent collections of Jewish inscriptions in the Diaspora, see *Jewish Inscriptions of Graeco-Roman Egypt*, ed. William Horbury and David Noy (Cambridge: Cambridge University Press, 1992) and *Jewish Inscriptions*

According to this inscription, the *proseuche,* which was the Greek word used to connote the prayer house or synagogue in the first century, was the site of the manumission.

In both inscriptions, the synagogue was the guarantor of the manumission. Also, it is interesting to note that in the inscription from 80 CE the only condition or restriction placed upon the slave is that as a freedman he is to be devout with respect to the *proseuche.* In total, twelve manumission inscriptions[109] have been found in the Black Sea region, and as illustrated above, several of these inscriptions entrust the manumitted slave to the care of the Jewish community or synagogue. Thus, there is considerable literary and epigraphical evidence dating from as early as the mid-first century CE which suggests that both the ἐκκλησία and the synagogue played active roles in the manumission process.

The role of the ἐκκλησία and the synagogue in the manumission of slaves, in some sense, would come as no surprise to the Roman law codes. Interestingly, in the section of the *Digest* which treats *statuliberi* and conditional manumission, religious locales are mentioned as places where conditional manumissions occur. In *Digest* 40.7.4 we read:

> When the heir [for whom the conditions of manumission must be fulfilled] was absent on public business, the *statuliber* with the cash [ostensibly for manumission] must wait until the return of the person to whom the money is to be given, *or deposit it in a temple under seal, whereupon he attains freedom at once.*[110]

The origin of the role of temples in the manumission process may date back to a time when slaves could seek refuge at the shrines of various "pagan" gods. The slaves would, in effect, "be sold" to the gods who would then manumit them. In

---

of *Western Europe,* vol. 1, ed. David Noy (Cambridge: Cambridge University Press, 1993).

[109]For example, see nos. 684 and 690 in *Corpus of Jewish Inscriptions.*

[110]Emphasis mine.

the particular legal statute just quoted, the ancient practice of sacral manumission may not be in view. Nonetheless, for the Romans, religious shrines were important enough in the process of manumission that if a *statuliber* deposited his manumission money in a temple, he would immediately receive full manumission.

In the first century CE world, the ἐκκλησία and the synagogue may not have been "temples," as specified in the Roman law codes, but for their respective devotees these important social institutions may have functioned in a similar way, namely, as the locale and guarantor of the manumission of slaves. The historical evidence of differing types gives solid support that these two institutions, the ἐκκλησία and the synagogue, carried out such functions for slaves. This data, if brought to bear on 1 Corinthians 7, especially vv. 21-23, may enhance the richness of the interpretive possibilities of our passage. We now turn our attention to the exegetical implications of this data.

IMPLICATIONS FOR THE EXEGESIS OF
1 CORINTHIANS 7:17-24

Having amassed the above data from legal, literary, and archeological sources relating to first century Roman slavery, we now move from social description to social analysis. In what ways does this material help us resist the tyranny of exegetical resolution and thereby honor the rich complexity of this text? As we proceed, let us be reminded of the interpretive assumptions that guided our social analysis of circumcision in chapter three. In order to resist the tyranny of resolution, we are approaching 1 Corinthians 7:17-24 with the following assumptions:

a) Vv. 17-24 are neither tangential nor hypothetical observations but are integral (if only in Paul's mind) to the overall working of the letter's rhetoric;

b) Paul is not presenting a philosophy of maintaining the status quo per se. Instead he is reflecting on the radical nature of the call of God which creates the church.

Why does Paul in vv. 21-23 appeal to the social reality of slavery in the first place? The "obvious" answer (although not so obvious to many previous interpreters) is that he is speaking specifically *to slaves* in the Corinthian community. If Paul's words in this passage are not hypothetical but are addressed instead to actual slaves, what is he trying to impart to them?

In v. 20 Paul says, "Each in the calling in which he was called, in this let him remain." As we have contended, v. 20 represents a restatement of Paul's basic idea in v. 17. Paul seems to be saying that the responsibility of the Christian is to remain a Christian or more specifically to remain in the ἐκκλησία. Paul does not appear to advocate that a Christian who finds himself in the unfortunate state of being an actual slave should consider that state to be ordained of God.

As we have argued, the call does not create social states but instead creates the ἐκκλησία. Thus, to remain in the calling, as Paul urges in v. 20, is to remain in the ἐκκλησία. Paul then explores what remaining in the ἐκκλησία might mean for the slaves who undoubtedly are members of the Corinthian ἐκκλησία.

In v. 21ab Paul writes, "Were you a slave when called? Let it not be a care to you." The two words of v. 21a δοῦλος ἐκλήθης seem to indicate that the calling of God and one's social state are different realities. Otherwise, why would Paul ask if they were already slaves if the call itself makes them slaves in the first place? Paul's question is, was the person already a slave when he received the call of God?

7:21ab seems to suggest that one's social location as a slave existed prior to the call and was not the result of the call. If one were a slave at the time of entering the ἐκκλησία, that slave status vis-à-vis entering or participating in the ἐκκλησία should not be a concern to the slave. Paul does not seem to advocate that the slave status of the Christian is itself ἀδιάφορος. What is or should be a matter of indifference to the slave is his status as a condition of the call.

Paul's negative exhortation in v. 21b (μή σοι μελέτω) may indicate that the Corinthians slaves were, in fact, concerned about their status. It is quite obvious why a slave might have severe anxiety with respect to his status in general. Why would a *Christian* slave have anxiety about his slave status with respect to his call to the ἐκκλησία?

Answers to this question arise when one considers the practical workings of the first century ἐκκλησία.[111] It is now a consensus among New Testament scholars that in early Christianity, especially in its Pauline manifestations, the οἶκος[112] provided the concrete social setting for the gathering of the ἐκκλησία. Such private houses were provided by the more well-to-do members of the congregation for the occasional gatherings of the ἐκκλησία.

On certain occasions, the entire congregation, numbering perhaps as many as fifty persons, would gather in an especially large home of a Christian patron,[113] but on other occasions smaller meetings of the ἐκκλησία likely occurred in houses around the city of Corinth. In light of Paul's tenuous relationship with the synagogue, more than likely one of his primary tasks when entering a city may have been the selection of "patrons" who were both willing and able to provide hospitality for the meetings of the ἐκκλησία. When we

---

[111]Sixty years ago, Floyd Filson contended, "The New Testament church would be better understood, if more attention were paid to the actual physical conditions under which the first Christians met and lived." See Filson's classic article, "The Significance of the Early House Churches," *Journal of Biblical Literature* 58 (1939): 105-112.

[112]For further insight on "house churches," see Abraham J. Malherbe, "House Churches and Their Problems," in *Social Aspects of Early Christianity*, 2d edition (Philadelphia: Fortress Press, 1983), 60-91; Jerome Murphy-O'Connor, "House Churches and the Eucharist," *The Bible Today* 22 (1984): 32-38; Vincent Branick, *The House Church in the Writings of Paul* (Wilmington, DE: Michael Glazier, 1989), and Robert Banks, *Paul's Idea of Community*, revised edition (Peabody: Hendrickson Publishers, 1994).

[113]In the case of the Corinthian church, one of these larger houses may have been provided by Gaius. See Romans 16:23.

remember that the house church is the setting of the ἐκκλησία, we begin to see how anxiety and ambiguity might arise with respect to the status of slaves in the ἐκκλησία.

As discussed above, slaves performed myriad tasks in the Greco-Roman world. John Barclay,[114] however, has argued that domestic or household slavery would have been the version of slavery most familiar to Paul. The dilemma is immediately apparent. In Corinth, the οἶκος was the context in which slaves lived and worked, but also worshipped as part of the ἐκκλησία. How would slaves and masters differentiate between their usual societal roles and expectations and those of the ἐκκλησία?

Differentiation would have been especially difficult for those slaves of the patron in whose house the ἐκκλησία met.[115] Would such slaves be required to work in order to provide "hospitality" for the rest of their Christian brothers and sisters? Or since free persons called into the ἐκκλησία were supposedly "slaves of Christ," could the actual slaves in the ἐκκλησία expect that their master might assist them, if not actually serve them, when the ἐκκλησία met? One can only imagine the ambiguous social dynamics when a slave who had recently received corporeal punishment from his master came together in the ἐκκλησία to worship with that master.

For these and other reasons, the slaves in the Corinthian ἐκκλησία might have had great concern about their slave status. In light of these social tensions, the Christian slaves may have felt that their status as slaves and their participation in the ἐκκλησία were severely incongruous realities. Thus, in the minds of some slaves, to walk or remain in the call (i.e., staying in the ἐκκλησία) would necessitate a concrete change of status, namely, manumission. These slaves would in effect say to Paul, "You are exhorting us to remain in the calling, but in order for us to remain in the calling, we must change our social position."

---

[114]John. M. G. Barclay, "Paul, Philemon and the Dilemma of Christian-Slave-Ownership," *New Testament Studies* 37 (1991): 161-186.

[115]The many dilemmas and ambiguities concerning slavery that must have arisen in house churches are set forth clearly by Barclay, "Paul, Philemon and the Dilemma of Christian-Slave-Ownership," 175-180.

If the above reconstruction in any way resembles what occurred in Corinth, one could argue that such a position on the part of the slaves would be a natural outgrowth of Paul's teaching as reflected in the early portion of chapter seven. On several occasions in 1 Corinthians 7, Paul clearly gives persons permission to change their social positions if such changes will keep them from falling into more problematic positions. For example, the unmarried and the widows[116] are given permission to change their social states if such a change will guard them from falling into πορνεία. Additionally, although Paul seems opposed to divorce in principle, he, nevertheless, "allows" it, asking only that divorced persons stay divorced or be reconciled to their partners.[117] Finally, Paul not only allows but encourages divorce if the unbelieving spouse no longer wants to be in the marriage,[118] and Paul's apparent rationale for encouraging this change of status is that it would promote peace. Thus, in 7:1-16 Paul intimates that on occasion there is a greater "principle" than staying in one's current social situation. If such a situation would eventuate in πορνεία or disharmony, then change is in order.

Nowhere does Paul in 1 Corinthians 7 argue against change of status in principle. He seems to indicate that change of status is irrelevant in light of the call, but it is certainly not prohibited. In fact, to change one's status might be necessary to avoid more problematic situations. As should be evident by now, Paul's position on change of status is quite ambiguous. On the one hand, change of status is irrelevant in light of the call into the ἐκκλησία, but on the other hand, in order to avoid πορνεία or disharmony, qualities inconsistent with the values of the ἐκκλησία, one might need to change one's social status.

Without much difficulty, one can imagine that the slaves in the Corinthian ἐκκλησία may have picked up on this ambiguity. Given the ambiguity in Paul's language, slaves could have argued that slavery and membership in the ἐκκλησία were mutually exclusive. If the potential of falling into certain

---

[116]1 Corinthians 7:2 and 7:8-9.
[117]1 Corinthians 7:10-11.
[118]1 Corinthians 7:15.

problematic states like πορνεία and disharmony are justifications for changing one's social status, then could not the same be said of slavery? Christian slaves in Corinth could have argued that the call of God may be irrelevant with respect to being in the ἐκκλησία, but in order for them to participate meaningfully in the ἐκκλησία in the first place, they would have to be manumitted.

The slaves may have contended that just as the possibility of πορνεία was a hindrance for unmarried persons who wanted to be in the ἐκκλησία, so too slavery was a hindrance for slaves who wanted to be in the ἐκκλησία. If Paul allowed the unmarried and the widows to remove their burden by marriage, surely he would allow slaves to remove their burden by manumission. For some Christian slaves, manumission may have appeared to be a necessity for being or remaining in the ἐκκλησία.

In v. 21c Paul himself implies that the prospect of manumission is not inconsistent with membership in the ἐκκλησία. He writes, "But even if you are able to become free." There is absolutely no textual reason why the interpreter of these words should doubt that Paul has in mind real manumission. Paul begins this clause with the conjunction ἀλλά. It is almost as if he is trying to avoid being insensitive to the plight of the slaves. He has just told them that their slave status should not be a concern to them in light of the call into the ἐκκλησία. Lest the slaves in the congregation think that Paul is acquiescing to the system of slavery, in v. 21c he broaches the topic of actual manumission. In effect, Paul says to the slaves, "With respect to your participating in the ἐκκλησία, your status as slaves should not concern you, but if the opportunity to be manumitted presents itself. . ."

Without being too dramatic, one can imagine Paul hesitating as he attempts to fill in the blanks of the above ellipsis. Much was riding on what Paul would say next. If he suggested that the slave should forego the opportunity for manumission, he could be viewed as a supporter of the abusive and inequitable slave system. If he suggested that the slaves should seek manumission, then he could be understood as advocating manumission for all Christian slaves. Such a position would not put him in good stead with the Christians in the ἐκκλησία who owned slaves.

If joining the ἐκκλησία required masters to manumit their slaves, who would pay for these manumissions? Were masters expected to absorb these costs, or would such actions be supported by funds from the ἐκκλησία? If the news were noised abroad that joining the ἐκκλησία was a possible avenue to manumission, slaves might enter the ἐκκλησία in droves[119] (which would not necessarily have been a problem). On the other hand, masters might leave the ἐκκλησία or never join it in the first place, considering such widespread manumission to be too costly a price to pay.

Paul implies that some social relations in the Corinthian ἐκκλησία were already marked with tension.[120] The last thing he needed at this point was to lose the support of his patrons who provided their households (and slaves)[121] for the meetings of the ἐκκλησία. Furthermore, if slaves were manumitted because of their membership in the ἐκκλησία, then whose freedmen would these slaves be? Would they owe their patronage to their former masters? Or, if these slaves were *statuliberi*, and the church sponsored their manumission by helping them meet the financial conditions, would they be freedman of the ἐκκλησία?

Since Corinth was such a crossroads of the Roman world, it is not at all unlikely that Corinthian slaves had heard stories of how slaves in other parts of the Mediterranean world had been manumitted under the supervision of religious bodies such

---

[119]Barclay, "Paul, Philemon and the Dilemma of Christian-Slave-Ownership," 176.

[120]See, for example, 1 Corinthians 1:10-13.

[121]Barclay raises the often overlooked fact that Pauline house churches, in the most pragmatic way, were dependent upon patrons and their slaves. Ironically, in the very place where the baptismal proclamation ("their is neither slave nor free") should have been practiced, the prevailing social structures were reinscribed. See Barclay, "Paul, Philemon and the Dilemma of Christian-Slave-Ownership," 176.

as the Jewish synagogue.[122] If the synagogue would sponsor manumission, perhaps Corinthians slaves felt that the ἐκκλησία should follow suit.

Much was riding on Paul's words concerning the role of slavery and manumission with respect to the ἐκκλησία. On whichever side Paul landed, he would be both a winner and a loser. He was between the proverbial rock and a hard place. In such a situation, Paul did what many before him had done and what many after him would do. He retreated into the shadows of ambiguity.

Paul says to the slaves, "With respect to your participating in the ἐκκλησία, your status as slaves should not concern you, but if the opportunity to be manumitted presents itself. . . use *it* all the more" (μᾶλλον χρῆσαι). In v. 21d Paul uses the aorist imperative of the verb χράομαι, knowing full well that he needs to supply a noun in the dative case in order to specify what the implied "it" is. Previous attempts to untie this interpretive Gordian knot have proceeded as if somehow Paul accidentally neglected to fill in the blank of this exhortation with a noun in the dative case.

Great efforts[123] have been made to finish the work that Paul "inadvertently" left undone and to supply the missing

---

[122]The fact that Jewish synagogues were places where slaves could be manumitted might have been another enticement for (Christian) slaves to seek membership in the synagogue as well as the ἐκκλησία.

[123]For instance, Harrill adduces seventeen examples of the combined use of μᾶλλον and χράομαι. To be sure, his investigation is both noteworthy and exhaustive, but at the end of the day, it only yields probable parallels from a wide assortment of contexts and time periods. Ironically, Harrill sharply criticizes other scholars for using comparative materials on slavery from time periods either predating or postdating the first century CE. Yet, his solution to the *crux interpretum* utilizes the same comparative methodology. Harrill's suggestion that μᾶλλον χρῆσαι is an adversative not to its immediate protasis (i.e., if you are able to become free) but instead to the preceding apodosis (i.e., do not let it worry you) seems both awkward and forced. See, for example, Harrill, 108-128. I agree with Harrill that in 1 Corinthians 7 Paul does not advocate a socially conservative philosophy of "remaining in the status quo." As my survey of 1 Corinthians 7 in chapter one revealed, Paul makes many concessions towards social change. Yet, in each of those cases, though other aspects of Paul's advice may have been ambiguous,

dative for Paul. Rather than considering Paul's semantics in v. 21d as an accident, I contend that Paul purposefully left the phrase unfinished. The ambiguity is deliberate[124] because Paul does not know what to recommend concerning slavery and manumission with respect to the ἐκκλησία. Paul's ambiguity is not a problem in the text; *it is an intrinsic feature of the text!*

The ambiguity abounds in v. 22a. He writes, "For the slave called in the Lord is a freedman of the Lord." The phrase "called in the Lord" (ἐν κυρίῳ κληθείς) could be understood as entering the ἐκκλησία. Thus, Paul indicates that the slave who enters the ἐκκλησία is a freedman of the Lord. Some who heard Paul's words must have queried, "Exactly what does Paul mean by saying that slaves are 'freedmen of the Lord'?"

Is this a "spiritual" freedom which has nothing to do with the transformation of concrete circumstances? Or does Paul have something more literal in mind? If the church sponsors the manumission and enables a *statuliber*[125] to fulfill his conditions for manumission, then according to Roman law, such a person would quite literally be a freedman of the ἐκκλησία, that is to say, a "freedman of the Lord."

As indicated in chapter one, in v. 22b, it is clear that Paul has entered the arena of metaphor. He writes, "Likewise the free person called is a slave of Christ." It is, however, not clear precisely why Paul includes free persons in his discussion. Deming's contention that Paul in chapter seven uses a diatribe style of argumentation may be helpful. In such argumentation,

---

his advice concerning the potential change of status is relatively clear. Why is Paul not as clear about manumission as he is about change of status with respect to marriage, divorce or even circumcision/uncircumcision? Could it be that Paul himself is unclear as to what his position is with respect to manumission and the ἐκκλησία.

[124]A similar argument is made by Barclay in his exegesis of Philemon 15-16. Barclay contends that Paul's words in Philemon 16 (οὐκέτι ὡς δοῦλον ἀλλὰ ὑπὲρ δοῦλον, ἀδελφὸν ἀγαπητόν) are deliberately ambiguous and open-ended with respect to how Paul expects Philemon to respond to Onesimus. See Barclay, "Paul, Philemon and the Dilemma of Christian-Slave-Ownership," 174-175.

[125]See above the discussion of *statuliberi* and conditional manumission.

both sides of an issue are presented, but the speaker is only truly interested in one side of the statement. Perhaps, the real force of what Paul is saying is contained in v. 22a, and v. 22b is used by Paul to give balance to his statement. Even if we cannot ascertain exactly what Paul means by saying that free persons in the ἐκκλησία are slaves of Christ,[126] it is quite justifiable to think that in v. 22a he is still speaking to actual slaves in the ἐκκλησία.

In v. 23a Paul responds, "You were bought with a price." As noted in chapter one, Paul makes an identical assertion in 1 Corinthians 6:19 when dealing with πορνεία in terms of Christians having sexual relations with prostitutes. Because of this parallelism of the forms in 6:19 and 7:23, I suggested in chapter one that both assertions are metaphors, perhaps depicting the believer's ethical responsibility in light of the "spiritual" redemption effected by Christ. Yet, in light of our discussion of the role of the ἐκκλησία and the synagogue in the (conditional) manumission of slaves, a very different and quite literal meaning could have been attached to Paul's words.

One will recall that it was possible for third parties to purchase and manumit *statuliberi*. In some instances, if a *statuliber* were sold to a third-party, that *statuliber* was automatically manumitted. Furthermore, in one of the manumission inscriptions from the Black Sea, as a consequence

---

[126]Dale Martin's explication of 7:22-23 is less than satisfactory. His interpretation does not entertain the concrete social practice of (third-party) manumission. See Martin, *Slavery as Salvation*, 63-68. 1 Corinthians 7:22 poses a difficulty to his understanding of slavery as a positive or soteriological metaphor. His theory, which in many regards is quite compelling, rests however, on the assumption that whenever Paul uses this kind of language he has in mind a kind of imperial slavery. The slaves of Caesar may have had considerable status and upward mobility, but such slaves were the exception that proved the rule. Ancient Roman slavery carried so many valences that it is impossible to pinpoint the many ways that the phrase "slaves of Christ" may have been heard by the variety of persons in the Corinthian ἐκκλησία. For those, be they slaves or masters, who were intimately acquainted with the more typical and abusive manifestations of slavery, the designation "slaves of Christ" may have always been heard in a negative fashion.

of the synagogue's role in a slave's manumission, the manumitted slave was expected to show religious devotion to the *proseuche*. Thus, there is evidence that when religious groups participated in the manumission process those groups expected some kind of piety in return from the manumitted slave.

Thus, Paul's words "you were bought with a price" may carry the nuance of the slave's ethical responsibility as well as being a veiled allusion to the concrete practice of manumission. Allen Callahan offers an important syntactic observation supporting a more literal reading of v. 23a.[127] He argues that there is a similar structure between the "implied"[128] questions Paul asks in v. 18 and v. 21 and the "implied" question of v. 23a.

In v. 18 Paul queries, "Was anyone circumcised when he was called. . . .was anyone uncircumcised when he was called. . . ?" The intended answer to these questions is "yes." In v. 21a Paul's "implied" question is, "were you a slave, when called?" Again, the implied answer is "yes." 7:21a contains a noun and second person (singular) aorist, passive indicative verb (ἐκλήθης), and it is read as a question. Then, why cannot v. 23a, which contains a noun and a second person (plural) aorist, passive indicative verb (ἠγοράσθητε) be read in the same way? Thus, Callahan reads τιμῆς ἠγοράσθητε not as an indicative but as an implied interrogatory. "You were bought with a price, weren't you?" As in vv. 18 and 21a, the implied answer to the question of v. 23a would be "yes."

The real question is what kind of price does Paul have in mind here? Is this price (τιμῆς) a metaphorical allusion to the price that Christ paid by dying for the believer's sins?[129] Or does it refer to the price paid for manumission of slaves in the Corinthian ἐκκλησία? In this case, the price (τιμῆς) was a concrete monetary amount, as in the fee paid to release a *statuliber* from all the conditions for his manumission. If actual

---

[127]Callahan, 113.

[128]I use the word "implied" to indicate that Paul does not use the syntax of direct interrogatory.

[129]For an example of Paul's kerygma, see 1 Corinthians 15:3-4.

manumission is being referred to in v. 23a, is Paul supportive or neutral with respect to this kind of action?

Whether one reads v. 23a as a straightforward indicative statement or a type of implied question which expects a yes answer, the ambiguity abounds. It is not clear exactly what Paul means, and it is certainly not clear how the recipients of his missive would have heard this statement.

In v. 23b Paul continues with a negative exhortation. "Do not become slaves of people" (μὴ γίνεσθε δοῦλοι ἀνθρώπων). As with many of the other statements in this passage, this exhortation could be understood metaphorically. In that interpretation, Paul would be exhorting the Corinthians to avoid a "metaphorical" slavery. Dale Martin remarks, "Because they [Christians] are now slaves of Christ, they should not willingly become slaves of any human being."[130] Martin's understanding here begs the question. Obviously, Paul exhorts persons not to become slaves, but what kind of slavery does he have in mind? Only in passing does Paul mention free persons in this text (vv. 22b); so there is little to suggest that his focus here is the free person.

More than likely in v. 23b, Paul is still speaking directly to slaves. What is Paul's message to slaves when he says, "Do not become slaves of people?" By having concerns about their slave status with respect to their participation in the ἐκκλησία, have these actual slaves entered into another kind of "slavery"? Or is Paul's exhortation a subtle denunciation of the slave system, although this would be quite interesting given his extensive use of the rhetoric of slavery. In this case, he would be criticizing the institution using the very language of the institution. Yet, we have seen that Paul is not necessarily a social conservative with respect to change in one's status. There are some states that are so problematic (e.g., πορνεία or disharmony in marriage) that he would prefer believers to change their social status than fall into these states. Or should we understand v. 23b as Paul's support of manumission but his concern that it not be accomplished at the expense of other persons entering into slavery? If one seriously attempts to "embody" Paul's language

---

[130]Martin, *Slavery as Salvation*, 66.

with concrete social data, it becomes tortuously difficult to disentangle metaphor from concrete social situations.

Paul's concluding remark in v. 24 brings little clarity to the meaning of this passage. He suggests, "Each in the calling in which he was called, brothers, in this let him remain before God." The structure of v. 24 is quite similar to v. 20, with the exception of the phrase "before God" (παρὰ θεῷ). It is not at all clear[131] what the force of παρὰ θεῷ is.

Is παρὰ θεῷ tantamount to being in the ἐκκλησία? Thus, is this passage ending with an emphatic assertion that the only real status that matters is that which comes from being in the ἐκκλησία or being "before God?" If membership in the ἐκκλησία or life παρὰ θεῷ is the only status that matters, does that prohibit members of the ἐκκλησία from making concrete changes in their social status? In other words, one could respond in at least one of two ways to the potential claim that human social states are irrelevant. On the one hand, in light of their irrelevance, one could remain in one's current social location. On the other hand, one could attempt to change one's social location; such changes would not make any difference in one's standing in the ἐκκλησία, but they could make a substantial difference in one's standing outside of it.

In chapter one, I intimated that in vv. 17-24 Paul might be attempting to clarify his position concerning the irrelevance of human social status in light of the call to the ἐκκλησία vis-à-vis the prohibition of change of status in general. In chapter seven, Paul addresses this theme with directives about several areas of communal life including marriage, sexuality, and ethnicity. To different degrees, Paul is ambiguous on these issues. When the time comes for Paul to address the issue of the change of status with respect to slavery, the ambiguity increases almost exponentially. Nearly every phrase in vv. 21-23 can be read in different ways.

Even if one is disinclined to accept my argument of *deliberate* ambiguity, one must, nonetheless, agree that Paul's statements in 7:21-23 are intractably opaque. Whether the

---

[131]For insight on how some interpreters have resolved this ambiguity, see my discussion of v. 24 in chapter one.

ambiguity is *de jure* or *de facto*, intentional or unintentional, it is, nevertheless, very present. Orlando Patterson captures poignantly the ambiguity of 1 Corinthians 7:21-23. He writes:

> Thus Paul, when asked to give his views on manumission, made the following paradoxical reply: "Regarding the matter of which you wrote me, the slave who is called by the Lord is a freedman of the Lord, likewise the free man who is called is a slave of Christ. You have been bought for a price, be not slaves of men. Let each man, brothers, remain beside God in that status in which he was called." *This theological obscurantism left the early fathers utterly confused. Paul himself may have been none too clear about what he meant.*[132]

Paul himself admits that the Corinthians had a proclivity to misunderstand his teachings.[133] One can only wonder if this passage would have been added to the list of their misunderstandings of Paul!

CONCLUSIONS

Dissatisfied with previous understandings of the role of slavery in early Christianity, I attempted to "revalue" the actual social institution of slavery by using Orlando Patterson's diachronic sociological definition of slavery which contends that slavery in every society is a form of social death. The careful and systematic application of Patterson's definition, supported by appeals to the primary literature on Roman slavery, has provided a more realistic picture of this institution so integral to Greco-Roman society.

The attempt to treat this text seriously as a piece of early Christian rhetoric addressed to actual slaves then led to a discussion of manumission practices in the first century Roman world. In light of the information yielded, two social institutions, the synagogue and the ἐκκλησία, have come to view. With an understanding of the role of the synagogue and

---

[132]Patterson, *Slavery and Social Death*, 227 (emphasis mine).
[133]1 Corinthians 5:9.

the ἐκκλησία in the manumission of slaves in the first century, the probability is even greater that Paul is speaking to actual slaves about concrete manumission. Yet, even when one reads closely Paul's words in vv. 21-23 in light of all of the social data, one is unable to ferret out a clear message concerning Paul's position on slavery, manumission, and the ἐκκλησία.

As should be evident, Paul's use of the phrase μᾶλλον χρῆσαι is but a small piece of the passage's overall ambiguity. I have contended that the ambiguity in this section (vv. 21-23) is not a problem in the text to be solved as much as it is an explicit feature of the text. I am not presenting a Paul who is the quintessential twenty-first century postmodern playfully engaging in endless deconstruction. Instead, our investigation has yielded a Paul who to this point has unsuccessfully sorted out all of the concrete implications of his own kerygma, especially as it relates to the change of one's social status.

Clarifying the social contexts from which this rhetoric emanates, sharpening our focus of manumission practices, and adducing linguistic parallels to the rhetoric of this passage are all important exercises. Yet, to render 1 Corinthians 7:17-24 as a self-evidently lucid piece of communication is to do something that not even Paul himself was able (or willing) to do.

The final aspect of this study will be an exploration of the ideological nature of various interpretations of this text, especially when they prematurely resolve the text's ambiguity. That is, we must now move from textual and social concerns to ideological concerns. This will be the task of chapter five.

Chapter 5

IDEOLOGY AND INTERPRETATION

INTRODUCTION

I have attempted to look at this passage in the Corinthian correspondence from a variety of angles and in a variety of contexts in order to expose its complexity and ambiguity. In chapter one, I examined the complexities and ambiguities *in the text itself*. In chapter two, I analyzed the *social and cultural worlds* of the Corinthians and of Paul, paying particular attention to issues of ethnicity and social status. In chapters three and four, I permitted the data from the first two chapters to inform and reform my understanding of Paul's appeals to circumcision and slavery in 7:17-24. In chapter five, I will investigate this passage from still another angle: *the ideological*.

In recent years, the term ideology has been rehabilitated. The term is no longer solely understood in its more negative, exploitative connotations.[1] According to Terry Eagleton, ideology is "the ways in which what we say and believe connect with the power-structure and power-relations of the society we live in."[2] As I understand it, ideological analysis is the sophisticated, self-critical examination of the relationship between texts (or in Eagleton's language "what we say and believe") and society (or in Eagleton's language "the power-structure and power-relations of the society").

---

[1] Historically, ideology, in its more pejorative sense, has referred to the "ideas and beliefs which help to legitimate the interests of a ruling group or class specifically by distortion or dissimulation." See Terry Eagleton, *Ideology* (London: Verso, 1991), 30.

[2] Terry Eagleton, *Literary Theory: An Introduction* (Minneapolis: University of Minnesota Press, 1983), 14.

A similar and equally useful definition of ideology is "an integrated system of beliefs, assumptions and values, not necessarily true or false, which reflects the needs and interests of a group or a class at a particular time in history."[3] My understanding of ideology acknowledges readily that the writing of texts and the interpreting of texts by original and subsequent audiences are *political acts*—political in the sense that writers and readers have needs and interests and will attempt to muster *power* (of assorted varieties) to address those interests and meet those needs.

In short, to speak of ideology is to enter the realm of the practical application of texts by readers. Texts not only say something; they attempt "to do" something. My simple contention in this chapter is that the complexity and ambiguity evident in the other aspects of 1 Corinthians 7:17-24 manifest themselves in the ideological arena as well.

According to Vernon Robbins, there are several ways to expose the ideological texture of texts. One can investigate the ideology in texts, in authoritative traditions of interpretation, in intellectual discourse, and in individuals and groups.[4] For the purposes of this chapter, it will be sufficient to analyze the ideology in authoritative traditions of interpretation. I will also provide some cursory observations concerning the role of ideology in prevailing intellectual discourse concerning Paul. In that regard, this dissertation itself must be the object of ideological scrutiny.

The primary task of this chapter will involve an exploration of some traditions of interpretation of this passage. If, as argued above, ideology has to do with the practical application of texts, I can think of no instance more pragmatic than the use of 1 Corinthians 7:17-24 in the nineteenth century to support *and* to decry the institution of chattel slavery in America. There is no more compelling example of this passage's ambiguity than its overt use by *two ideologically opposed social groups*, slavery advocates and abolitionists, to support

---

[3]David Brion Davis, *The Problem of Slavery in the Age of Revolution 1770-1823* (Ithaca: Cornell University Press, 1975), 14.

[4]Robbins, *Tapestry*, 193.

completely opposite positions, namely, the perpetuation or abolition of slavery. The ambiguity sowed initially by Paul and cultivated by conditions in first century CE culture came to full bloom in a particular reception of this text by reading communities nineteen centuries later.

The final question of this chapter will be, does the ambiguity surrounding this passage in the first century and the nineteenth century have implications for our hermeneutics in the twenty-first century? In that regard, I must analyze the ideology of my own intellectual discourse in this dissertation. Before we tackle hermeneutical issues of the twentieth and twenty-first centuries, let us first visit the nineteenth century.

IDEOLOGY IN TRADITIONS OF INTERPRETATION

Introduction

The Bible's ideologically duplicitous role in nineteenth century American hermeneutics and politics concerning chattel slavery[5] is a well-rehearsed fact.[6] On the one hand, there were narratives such as the Israelites' exodus from Egyptian bondage which fascinated and fueled the literary,[7] the theological and

---

[5]The literature on Black slavery in the Americas is copious. For exhaustive bibliographies, see John David Smith, *Black Slavery in the Americas: An Interdisciplinary Bibliography, 1865-1980*, 2 Vols. (Westport, CT: Greenwood Press, 1982). Also for another useful bibliographic essay, see Charles H. Lippy, "The Religious Experience of Southern Blacks: Black-White Interaction in Southern Religion" in *Bibliography of Religion in the South* (Macon: Mercer University Press, 1985), 81-106. Also for a useful primer, see Timothy L. Smith, "Slavery and Theology: The Emergence of Black Christian Consciousness in Nineteenth Century America," *Church History* 41 (1972): 497-512.

[6]For concise, representative treatments, see Katie Geneva Cannon, "Slave Ideology and Biblical Interpretation" in *The Recovery of Black Presence: An Interdisciplinary Exploration*, ed. Randall C. Bailey and Jacquelyn Grant (Nashville: Abingdon Press, 1995), 119-128, and James H. Evans, Jr., "The Bible: A Text for Outsiders" in *We Have Been Believers: An African-American Systematic Theology* (Minneapolis: Fortress Press, 1992), 33-52.

homiletic,[8] and the musical[9] imagination of enslaved and free Africans in America who dared to believe that the *reality* of American social life would match the vaunted American *rhetoric* about social equality.

Yet, on the other hand, this same Bible contained equally straightforward mandates enjoining upon ancient (and therefore by extension modern) slaves passivity and contentment. One quickly calls to mind the Haustafeln[10] or so-called household codes in Colossians 3:22-25, Ephesians 6:5-8, and 1 Peter 2:18-25. These codes instruct slaves to be submissive and to realize that obedience to their earthly masters is, in actuality, a spiritual obedience rendered unto God. Therefore, the Bible has provided rhetorical tropes for the construction of an African American liberation theology. And simultaneously, the Bible has wielded an ideological dagger, assassinating the hopes of freedom with its command for contentment among slaves.

For this reason, African Americans have typically had a love/hate relationship with scripture and especially with Paul.[11] Historically, African Americans have been positively disposed to those strands of scripture which speak of concrete social

---

[7]For a sophisticated analysis of the use of Exodus motifs in African American literary and religious traditions, see Theophus H. Smith, *Conjuring Culture: Biblical Formations of Black America* (New York: Oxford University Press, 1994), 55-80.

[8]See, for example, Dwight N. Hopkins, "Slave Theology in the 'Invisible Institution' " in *Cut Loose Your Stammering Tongue: Black Theology in the Slave Narratives* (Maryknoll: Orbis Books, 1991), 13-15.

[9]Although it is more than twenty five years old, James Cone's little classic, *The Spirituals and the Blues*, is still well worth reading. See Cone, *The Spirituals and the Blues* (Maryknoll: Orbis Books, 1972,), 32-43.

[10]See Clarice J. Martin, "The Haustafeln (Household Codes) in African American Biblical Interpretation: 'Free Slaves' and Subordinate Women'" in *Stoney the Road We Trod: African American Biblical Interpretation*, ed. Cain Hope Felder (Minneapolis: Fortress Press, 1991), 206-231.

[11]In light of this antipathy for Paul in certain segments of African American religious culture, Amos Jones's book, *Paul's Message of Freedom*, is an attempt to "rehabilitate" Paul for African American church traditions.

emancipation. In some sense, the biblical text has been so integral to African American theology and religious practice that it has functioned as a "language-world" for African Americans. Vincent Wimbush remarks:

> For the great majority of African Americans the Bible has historically functioned not merely to reflect and legitimize piety (narrowly understood), but as a language-world full of stories—of heroes and heroines, of heroic peoples and their pathos and victory, sorrow and joy, sojourn and fulfillment. In short, the Bible became a "world" into which African Americans could retreat, a "world" they could identify with, draw strength from, and in fact manipulate for self-affirmation.[12]

Nevertheless, even as African Americans were retreating into the "world" of scripture, they discovered that parts of this "language-world" in the Bible were foreign, and even inimical, to their hopes for affirmation and freedom. Thus, the Bible was a world both to flee to and to flee *from*.

Certain Pauline statements were thought to be especially problematic. Consequently, Paul has been the target of much interpretive suspicion and enmity among African Americans. In traditional[13] African American interpretation, the scholarly distinction between the historical Paul and the "deutero-Paul" has held little influence. Thus, many African Americans believed that two of the three household codes, those found in Colossians and Ephesians, emanated from the hand of Paul. Anyone, even a

---

[12]Vincent L. Wimbush, "The Bible and African Americans: An Outline of an Interpretive History" in *Stony the Road We Trod: African American Biblical Interpretation*, ed. Cain Hope Felder (Minneapolis: Fortress Press, 1991), 83.

[13]When I use the word "traditional," I am referring primarily, but not exclusively, to that interpretation which has occurred in the context of the African American church. Unlike our white counterparts for whom the university has been a locus of interpretive activity, the locus of the majority of African American biblical interpretation has been the church. These interpretations have found expression in the homiletical, musical, abolitionist, and civil rights protest traditions. Regrettably, only in the last two decades has there emerged even a perceptible number of African American biblical interpreters who are located in academic contexts.

Christian apostle, who could encourage slaves to be submissive and content, was someone of whom to be wary.

The celebrated story of the grandmother of Howard Thurman, the African American philosopher and mystic, succinctly captures the pragmatic, yet ideologically sophisticated, suspicion many African Americans had for Paul. Thurman wrote:

> Two or three times a week I read the Bible aloud to her. I was deeply impressed by the fact that she was most particular about the choice of Scripture. For instance, I might read many of the more devotional Psalms, some of Isaiah, the Gospels again and again, but the Pauline epistles, never—except, at long intervals, the thirteenth chapter of first Corinthians. . . . With a feeling of great temerity I asked her one day why it was that she would not let me read any of the Pauline letters. What she told me I shall never forget. "During the days of slavery, she said, "the master's minister would occasionally hold services for the slaves. Old man McGhee was so mean that he would not let a Negro minister preach to his slaves. Always the white minister used as his text something from Paul. At least three or four times a year he used as a text: "Slaves be obedient to them that are your master. . . , as unto Christ." Then he would go on to show how it was God's will that we were slaves and how, if we were good and happy slaves, God would bless us. I promised my maker that if I ever learned to read and if freedom ever came, I would not read that part of the Bible.[14]

In short, in nineteenth century African American hermeneutics, African Americans did not have problems with Paul's theology but instead his politics. Paul's emphasis on the primacy of love and faith and his notion of the centrality of the Christ event resonated well with African American interpreters. His politics—that is, his understanding of concrete power

---

[14]Howard Thurman, *Jesus and the Disinherited* (Nashville: Abingdon Press, 1949), 30-31. For another fascinating anecdote concerning nineteenth century African American slaves literally walking out of a church service where a white preacher used a Pauline text to legitimize slavery, see Albert J. Raboteau, *Slave Religion: The "Invisible Institution" in the Antebellum South* (Oxford: Oxford University Press, 1978), 294.

relationships—was the cause of unrest. In the African American symbolic world, theology and politics have never been strange bedfellows, but indeed lawfully wedded spouses.[15] Thus, for many African Americans, hostility for Paul's politics was not canceled out by an affinity for his theology.

Undoubtedly, in the dominant, white (religious) symbolic world of nineteenth century America, the Bible also possessed an extremely prominent place. In the fierce debate concerning chattel slavery, white supporters of slavery and white abolitionists[16] mustered arguments from every quarter of human endeavor—history, geography, the classical literature of Greece and Rome, and even American jurisprudence. Yet, each group realized that the arguments for and against slavery would be ideologically anemic without appeals to the Bible. Carolyn Shanks contends, "Both sides [proslavery and abolitionists] felt

---

[15]For a classic treatment of the inextricable relationship between theology and political protest in African American religion, see Gayraud Wilmore, *Black Religion and Black Radicalism: An Interpretation of the Religious History of Afro-American People* (Maryknoll: Orbis Books, 1983). Also, see Vincent Harding, "Religion and Resistance among Antebellum Slaves, 1800-1860" in *African American Religion*, ed. Timothy E. Fulop and Albert J. Raboteau (New York: Routledge, 1997), 107-130.

[16]Even though I am mentioning white abolitionists, I am also aware of the tremendous role that *African American* abolitionists played in the nineteenth century. My research, however, has revealed that to the degree that African American abolitionists were appealing to the Bible, they were not appealing widely to Paul in general and to 1 Corinthians 7:17-24 in particular. Many of the arguments of the African American abolitionists were more of a theological, ethical, and political nature than they were of a purely exegetical nature. It is lamentable that in my research I have not, as of yet, discovered examples of exegetical appeals to 1 Corinthians 7:17-24 by either African American abolitionists or slaves. The proslavery and abolitionist materials among whites in the nineteenth century is more readily available and contains overt exegetical appeals to 1 Corinthians 7:17-24. For insights on the role and arguments of African American abolitionists, see Herman E. Thomas, *James W. C. Pennington: African American Churchman and Abolitionist* (New York: Garland Publishing, 1995), 103-143. Also, see Carol V. R. George, "Widening the Circle: The Black Church and the Abolitionist Crusade" in *African American Religion*, ed. Timothy E. Fulop and Albert J. Raboteau (New York: Routledge, 1997), 153-173.

that the Biblical arguments were the most potent that could be adduced, and both found in the Bible ample support for their opinions—unmindful that each, instead of deriving his case from the Bible, was trying to make the Bible subserve a ready-made system."[17] Even in the wake of the Enlightenment attack on the authority of the Bible, the Bible in many quarters of nineteenth century American life still had an important verdict to render on what constituted truth.

Although it is difficult to reduce to easily identifiable types the various ways scripture has been used by communities, certain patterns of use have been recognized by scholars. In his book, *The Uses of Scripture in Recent Theology*, David Kelsey maps at least three ways that theologians have viewed scripture: 1) the scripture as a book of doctrines whose authority stems from its nature as the inspired word of God; 2) the scripture as a narrative which recounts the acts of God or brings "to life" characters in the narrative; 3) the scripture as the depository of images and symbols that articulates the experience of divine revelation and potentially evokes subsequent revelation.[18] A full exploration of Kelsey's categories is beyond the scope of this study. Yet, they keenly express that the Bible is (and has been) appropriated in vastly different ways by different communities of readers—be they twentieth century academic theologians or nineteenth century slaveholders or slaves.

Some scholars have argued that African Americans interpreters, especially African American preachers,[19] have

---

[17]Carolyn L. Shanks, "The Biblical Anti-Slavery Argument of the Decade 1830-1840," *The Journal of Negro History* 16 (1931): 132-133.

[18]David H. Kelsey, *The Uses of Scripture in Recent Theology* (Philadelphia: Fortress Press, 1975).

[19]Concerning the narrative hermeneutic utilized by many African American preachers, Henry Mitchell remarks, "The Black preacher is more likely to think of the Bible as an inexhaustible source of good preaching material than as *an inert doctrinal and ethical authority.* . . . It [the Bible] provides the basis for *unlimited creativity in the telling of rich and interesting stories*, and these narrations command rapt attention while the eternal truth is brought to bear on Black experience and the struggle for liberation." See Mitchell, *Black Preaching* (Philadelphia: J. B. Lippincott, 1979), 113 (emphasis mine).

traditionally approached the Bible as a narrative. While this is a generalization in need of further nuance, it illumines the fact that different hermeneutical approaches may have been operative among African American and white interpreters in the nineteenth century. In the nineteenth century, the *stories* of liberation and of triumph over great odds instilled hope in oppressed African Americans—hope that what God had done in the ancient story would be duplicated in the contemporary context.[20]

In contradistinction, for many nineteenth century white interpreters (some of whom we will examine), it appeared that the Bible functioned more as a "book of doctrines." Thus, a pronouncement in the Bible for or against slavery carried considerable ideological weight among whites. Such statements concerning slavery, especially those in the New Testament, could not be easily dismissed. If they supported one's position, one's argument gained important credibility. If they contravened one's position, one had to explain not why the Bible was incongruous with one's position, but why one's position was incongruous with the Bible.

As will be demonstrated below, when either slavery advocates or abolitionists found themselves at odds with a particular passage in the Bible, they mounted ideologically impressive (if not persuasive) arguments to explain the disparity. The length to which interpreters would go to explain these disparities between the Bible and their position on slavery is an indicator of the Bible's sway in nineteenth century white religious culture.

It is in this curious and ideologically charged matrix that Paul's directives concerning slavery in 1 Corinthians 7:21-23 were interpreted in nineteenth century America. In an antebellum America, the question concerning the existence,

---

[20]One could argue that traditional African American interpretation has been a combination of categories two and three in Kelsey's typology. African Americans have found inspiration in the Bible's narratives of liberation. They have also viewed the stories as symbols pointing to the possibility of a fresh revelation of God—the revelation of freedom and equality for oppressed people in the contemporary world.

roles, and status of African American slaves would prove so divisive that it would eventually split the nation. In a very real sense, it was the slavery issue that created the (modern) "eschatological moment" predicted by the Bible when father would turn against son and mother against daughter.[21] In such a volatile atmosphere, the ability to locate ideological support for one's position for or against slavery was an important undertaking.

To have the Bible, and more specifically the apostle Paul, who was thought to have penned half of the New Testament, on one's side would be valuable ideological capital. In a particularly poignant way, exegesis of Pauline passages on slavery in the nineteenth century American context was a decidedly political act. Before investigating representative appeals to 1 Corinthians 7:17-24 by slavery advocates and abolitionists, a sketch of salient features of the religious[22] arguments of each group might prove useful.

Proslavery and Abolitionist (Religious) Arguments

As intimated above, the Bible was a major weapon in the arsenal of slavery advocates. Many nineteenth century proslavery ideologues were facile biblical interpreters because they were so well-versed in their Bibles. If they could find nothing else in their Bibles, they could at least cite relevant biblical texts in defense of slavery. One does not read nineteenth century proslavery literature long before being inundated with scriptural references. As Larry Morrison rightly observes, "The foundation upon which the slaveholding ethic and the proslavery argument was built was the scriptural defense of

---

[21]Luke 12:53.

[22]Slavery advocates and abolitionists proffered a number of economic and political arguments as well. The role that these kind of arguments played in the construction of proslavery and abolitionist ideologies is beyond the scope of this current investigation.

slavery. Nearly every proslavery pamphlet, article, and speaker made at least some reference to a biblical sanction of slavery."[23]

Through appeals to the Bible, slavery advocates affirmed that the slavery of African Americans was ordained of God. In fact, this very concept, the existence of slavery being God-ordained, is the title of a fascinating piece of nineteenth century proslavery ideology written by the Reverend Fred Ross, a Presbyterian minister. Very simply, Ross's book is entitled *Slavery Ordained of God*.[24] To be sure, slavery advocates were not above distorting scripture,[25] but they found a basis for their appeals because materials in the biblical text supporting their cause were available.

One of the first hermeneutical moves slavery advocates made was to cite the so-called curse of Noah in Genesis 9. When Noah awoke from his wine-induced slumber and realized what his youngest son Ham had done to him, he condemned Ham's progeny by addressing the following curse to Ham's son, Canaan: " 'Cursed be Canaan; lowest of slaves shall he be to his brothers.' He also said, 'Blessed by the Lord my God be Shem; and let Canaan be his slave. May God make peace for Japheth, and let him live in the tents of Shem; and let Canaan be his slave.' "[26] When slavery defenders read this text, they saw it as a foundation for constructing a racial geography.

---

[23]Larry R. Morrison, "The Religious Defense of American Slavery Before 1830," *The Journal of Religious Thought* 37 (1980): 16.

[24]Fred Ross, *Slavery Ordained of God* (Philadelphia: J. B. Lippincott, 1859; reprint New York: Negro Universities Press, 1969).

[25]In her article, "Slave Ideology and Biblical Interpretation," Katie Cannon focuses almost exclusively on the ways in which the Bible was distorted by slavery advocates. She does not entertain the degree to which these apologists for slavery at times had solid, exegetically plausible arguments. Not every appeal to scripture in support of slavery required ideological distortion. Eugene Genovese might be correct in intimating that on historical and theological grounds the proslavery appeal to the Bible was more convincing than the abolitionist appeal to it. See Genovese, " 'Slavery Ordained of God': The Southern Slaveholders' View of Biblical History and Modern Politics" (Gettysburg: Gettysburg College, 1985), 19-20.

[26]Genesis 9:25-27.

They understood the curse on Canaan to extend backwards to his father Ham. Accordingly, they read the Table of Nations in Genesis 10 to mean that Ham, after being cursed with the burden of slavery, traveled to central Africa. Shem, who was not cursed but instead blessed, went to Asia. Japheth, who for the slavery apologists was most blessed of all, went to Europe. Thus, the possession of African slaves by the European descendants of Japheth was, for the proslavery advocates, a modern continuation of a biblical "doctrine."

A second hermeneutical move was to point to respected biblical characters who themselves held slaves. The contention was that if biblical notables such as Abraham, the father of the faithful, could possess slaves, slavery could not be inherently sinful. Larry Morrison observes:

> Clearly, the favorite example [of the slavery advocates] was Abraham. . . "this spotless patriarch who constantly obeyed the voice of God—kept his charge, his commandments, his statues, and his laws, and moreover found such acceptance with him as to be admitted to familiar conferences with Jehovah." Yet among the deeds of Abraham is found "the transaction of buying bondsmen for money." However, not "the least mention" is given "by any of the inspired writers that Abraham's conduct. . . was in the most distant manner discountenanced by any private admonition or public suggestion of God's displeasure for such contract or acquisition."[27]

When using Abraham, slavery advocates also appealed to the story of Abraham owning the Egyptian slave Hagar.

As a third hermeneutical tactic, slavery supporters used biblical "arguments from silence." They insisted that the Bible did not expressly forbid slavery. Interestingly, although some slavery advocates could bring themselves to consider slavery a social *evil*, they did not consider it to be a *sin*. For example, the nineteenth century slavery ideologue Frederick Ross understood sin to be committing acts which God expressly forbade in the

---

[27]Morrison, 20. (The quotation marks throughout this paragraph are contained in the original. It is not clear from what source Morrison is citing.)

Bible.[28] Since God did not expressly prohibit this trafficking in humans, slavery was not inherently a sinful act. As an *evil* but not *sinful* institution, Ross and other slavery supporters could "tolerate" slavery in a way that they "could" or "would" not if slavery were shown to be truly a *sin*.

Undoubtedly, there were other ideological pillars erected by nineteenth century religionists, but one final argument must be mentioned. One constant refrain among slavery supporters was the claim that the abolitionist movement had abandoned the Bible altogether.[29] This criticism of abolitionists had at least two parts. First, abolitionists ignored the clear fact that the Bible contained no prohibitions against slavery. Second, by ignoring the testimony of scripture, the abolitionists showed they were bereft of an important source of divine illumination. This enabled slavery supporters to accuse the abolitionists of simply walking in darkness.

The abolitionists, however, realizing the argumentative significance of appeals to the Bible's authority, would not so easily concede the biblical terrain to slavery supporters. They developed an array of biblical arguments against slavery. One of the most interesting was philological in nature.

They contended that δοῦλος, like its Hebrew equivalent עבד, had a wide range of meanings that included "servants in families, servants of God, servants of Christ, servants among the Pagans, servants among Christians. . . ."[30] In effect, the abolitionists criticized the slavery advocates for radically reducing the base meaning of δοῦλος, thereby preventing it from being used in scripture as a synonym for "free service." Thus, the abolitionist George Cheever declared, "If at any time it [the New Testament] refers to slaves it is with no intimation of any sanction of slavery but rather (as in 1 Tim. vi., 1, 2) in the supposition that only out of the church of Christ, only among

---

[28]Ross, 15 and 30.

[29]Ross, 37.

[30]George B. Cheever, *The Guilt of Slavery and the Crime of Slaveholding Demonstrated from the Hebrew and Greek Scriptures* (Boston: John P. Jewett & Co., 1860; reprint New York: Negro University Press, 1969), v.

pagans and unbelievers, can there be found persons who will hold slaves."[31]

The abolitionists also countered the appeal to Abraham made by proslavery advocates. They freely granted that Abraham possessed servants (but they refused to call these persons *slaves*). But even if it were granted that Abraham possessed *servants*, this did not imply approval of slavery, since Abraham also engaged in other questionable activities such as lying and concubinage. Abraham may have been an example of faith, but his owning servants, having concubines, and lying were not thereby exemplary.

A third anti-slavery argument held that slavery was in direct violation of the eighth commandment from Sinai, "Thou shall not steal." The effectiveness of this argument can be seen in the strenuous proslavery efforts to discredit it. Slavery advocates argued, for example, that the *original sin* of stealing the slaves *did not transfer* to the subsequent buyers of the slaves. Thus, later slave owners were not thieves, but legitimate property owners, who had not violated the eighth commandment.

Often slavery advocates contended that even though the slaves were stolen originally, this theft was actually in the best interest of the Africans. It was a beneficent theft, where a moral end was achieved by an immoral means.[32] Yet, abolitionists rightly insisted that Africans *had been stolen* from foreign shores, and the abolitionists had none other than the lawgiver Moses on their side.

Of the many passages to which the abolitionists appealed, Colossians 4:1 received special attention. Here Paul says, "Masters, treat your slaves justly and equally, for you know that you also have a Master in heaven." Ironically, this passage is part of a household code which could easily be interpreted as an ethical and theological rationale for slavery, or, at least, used as an argument against slave disobedience or to discourage slaves' efforts to be manumitted.

---

[31]Cheever, 5.
[32]See, for example, Ross, 153-159.

Abolitionists seized upon two key words in Colossians 4:1, "justly" and "equally," to show that Christianity itself was morally opposed to such an institution. These two words, they argued, were crucial indicators of Paul's implicit opposition to slavery. Alluding to Colossians 4, the abolitionist George Cheever wrote:

> And when an apostle by divine inspiration commands masters everywhere to give unto their servants that which is just and equal, it is not merely that which the natural conscience, uninstructed by the divine word, affirms or intimates to be just and equal, which would be a rule unreliable, uncertain and variable in the extreme, differing according to every man's moral character and notion of expediency, but that which the word of God declares and defines to be just and equal, that which the Old Testament Scriptures reveal and enjoin on this very subject as the will of God. And the very first article of that justice and equality or equity is, that no man shall hold or treat any other man as property, that no human being shall make merchandise of man.[33]

Abolitionists realized that on the plain surface the Bible seemed to offer substantive support to the proslavery position. They saw that, to use a Pauline phrase, "the letter could kill." Thus, they looked for creative (and sometimes fallacious) ways to unleash the "spirit of scripture" to bring life and strength to their arguments. They wanted to take seriously the meaning of "justly" and "equally," yet find ways to get at the "spirit" of scripture.

Having provided a précis of nineteenth century American biblical hermeneutics concerning slavery, I will now consider a few examples of how nineteenth century interpreters on both sides of this ideological divide grappled with the complexity and ambiguity of 1 Corinthians 7:17-24.

---

[33]Cheever, 342-343.

Nineteenth Century Appeals to 1 Corinthians 7:17-24

Nellie Norton

As the Civil war moved into its final phases and as the ink was still drying on Lincoln's Emancipation Proclamation, a white minister from Macon, Georgia, the Reverend E. W. Warren, would, in 1864, pen one of the most intriguing pieces of proslavery propaganda. Dissatisfied to address such an important topic as slavery and abolition in a straightforward and purely discursive manner, Warren sought a creative way to publish his view that slavery was ordained of God and thoroughly supported by the Bible. Mindful that many books on this topic had been written but not read, Warren desired a wide, popular audience. Rather than systematize his views in formal, logical proofs, he couched his ideology in the universally appealing format of narrative.

Warren composed a fascinating fictional account of Nellie Norton, a young lady raised and educated in a college in the North, who travels to the south to visit her uncle, Mr. Thompson.[34] Nellie is accompanied on this trip by her mother, Julia. Both Nellie's mother Julia and her uncle Mr. Thompson had been reared in the north, but Mr. Thompson had subsequently moved to the south and become a slaveowner. Nellie and her mother, having remained in the north, had become champions of abolitionists' views. Mr. Thompson, however, had long since overcome those views and fully adopted the stance that slavery was ordained of God.

---

[34]E. W. Warren, *Nellie Norton: or Southern Slavery and the Bible: A Scriptural Refutation of the Principal Arguments upon which the Abolitionists Rely: A Vindication of Southern Slavery from the Old and New Testaments* (Macon: Burke, Boykin & Company, 1864). Interestingly, one of the copies of this book with which I worked is housed in the Library of Congress's Rare Books Reading Room. This particular copy was confiscated by the Union army when it captured the Confederate army in Richmond, Virginia, towards the end of the Civil War. Thus, in more ways than one, this book is an interesting piece of "Americana."

In short, the two initial main characters in the novel, Nellie and Mr. Thompson, are "straw figures" representing the abolitionist and proslavery positions respectively. Nellie longed to see her uncle, but in traveling to his southern plantation, she would be forced to encounter chattel slavery which she considered "the sum of all villainies."[35] Her uncle, Mr. Thompson, "had come South with the usual prejudice against slavery which northern birth and education instill,"[36] but now his benevolent objective was to demonstrate to his niece from the scriptures how he could equate his standing as a Christian with the possession of human property.

The Reverend Warren punctuates his narrative with intriguing (albeit stereotypical) details of plantation life, even including accounts of a slave wedding[37] and a slave religious service.[38] This historical verisimilitude could easily lead one to speculate that such vivid details were not figments of Warren's imagination but could have come from scenes actually witnessed on *his* own plantation among the slaves he owned. Notwithstanding my speculation, clearly all the supporting elements in this narrative—setting, plot, and characterization— are in service of Warren's argument for divine and biblical sanction of slavery.

Most important for our purposes is the plot of the story. During the course of Nellie's visit on her uncle's plantation, she and her uncle engage in countless conversations concerning religious, and specifically biblical, arguments for or against slavery. In order to persuade his niece, Mr. Thompson musters every conceivable biblical argument in favor of slavery. In the course of their discussion, Mr. Thompson travels from Genesis to Revelation, leaving no stones unturned.

Lest it appear in the novel that Mr. Thompson is taking advantage of *his biblically-illiterate* niece,[39] the author introduces into the story Nellie's pastor, Dr. Daniel Pratt, a

---

[35]Warren, 3.

[36]Warren, 8.

[37]Warren, 17-19.

[38]Warren, 20-23.

[39]See above my discussion of the proslavery claim that the abolitionists had abandoned the Bible.

New England abolitionist, who under the advice of his physician, was traveling south for some warmth and relaxation. Dr. Pratt then champions the abolitionist cause, while Mr. Thompson defends the proslavery position. The remainder of the book details this "gentlemen's debate" in the home of Mr. Thompson concerning the Bible's views on slavery.

In the course of the debate, Dr. Pratt, the abolitionist, marshals many of the typical abolitionist arguments discussed above, only to have Mr. Thompson refute them from the pages of scripture. As the debate in the narrative ensues, Mr. Thompson appeals, interestingly, to Paul's words in 2 Timothy 3:16. Thompson remarks:

> If the book of God is taken at all, it must all be taken; for "all Scripture is given by inspiration of God, and is profitable for doctrine, for reproof, for correction, for instruction in righteousness." Permit me to suggest, that the passages referred to, may have been given for the "correction" of the errors of the abolitionists, and for their "instruction in righteousness," since their tendency to depart from truth certainly needs a countering influence.[40]

Mr. Thompson's unwillingness to live with complexity and ambiguity in the Bible, especially concerning slavery, is clearly evinced in one of his rebuttals of Dr. Pratt. Mr. Thompson replies, "God has either enacted slavery, or He has not. He either countenances the institution, or He does not. He is not on both sides of the question, as you seem to think. He has not said and unsaid, done and undone. He has not given slavery to his people and then ordered its abolition. He is not so changeable, so fickle as that. 'I am God, and I change not.' "[41] For Mr. Thompson, every page of the Bible radiates the divine approval of slavery.

Towards the end of the novel, Mr. Thompson and Dr. Pratt scrutinize what the New Testament says about slavery. Their discussion concerning 1 Corinthians 7:17-24 is a

---

[40]Warren, 32.
[41]Warren, 41.

fascinating example of interpreters resolving the complexity of this passage. This discussion must be quoted in full:

> Dr. Pratt broke the silence by saying, "Mr. Thompson, you are frequently twitting me with a failure to produce Scripture or argument against slavery. I shall beg leave to dissent from the admission of Dr. Wayland,[42] 'that there is no precept in the New Testament against slavery,' and prove to you there is.
>
> I remember being in Baltimore a few years ago at a Christian convocation, and to have heard a Southern minister, perhaps Dr. Johnston, of South Carolina, ask one of our most celebrated divines, 'What he considered to be the strongest Scripture in the Bible against slavery.' Taking the New Testament in his hand, he turned to 1 Cor. vii:21, and read: 'Art thou called being a servant? Care not for it; but if thou mayest be made free, use it rather.'
>
> I hold, sir, that here is an inspired preference for the freedom of the slave. It is best, 'Use it rather,' it is for his development as a Christian, and therefore will promote his efficiency, and consequently is for the glory of his Savior. If all these good results are to follow the emancipation of a Christian slave, then every Christian master is under obligation to liberate his Christian slave."
>
> "Your quotation," said Mr. Thompson, "without the context, would seem to bear the construction you give it. If the master proposes to free his slave, and the slave is advised to accept it, there must be some reason for the advice which made the condition of freedom preferable. But let us go back and read the context, beginning at the 17th verse: 'But as God hath distributed to every man, as the Lord hath called everyone, so let him walk. And so I ordain in all the churches. Is any man called being circumcised? let him not become uncircumcised. Is any called in uncircumcision? let him not be circumcised. . . . Let every man abide in the same calling wherein he was called.'

[42]Dr. Wayland was a renowned nineteenth century abolitionist. For further insight on Wayland, see Francis Wayland, *A Memoir of the Life and Labors of Francis Wayland* (New York: Arno Press, 1972). Below, I will discuss Wayland.

Here, Doctor, is a key furnished by the inspired author of this language by which to reach his meaning. The Jew was called being a Jew; let him not desire to be a gentile. The gentile was called being a gentile, let him not at his conversion desire to be a Jew. The master was called being a master, and the slave was called being a slave. Then let neither of these be discontented with his condition, but 'abide in the same calling wherein they were called.' With this interpretation agrees Dr. Alford, who was himself an abolitionist. The early Fathers, as they are called, believed this passage favored slavery. Chrysostom says: 'If thou art called as a slave care nothing for it; nay, although thou canst become free, yet serve rather, for the believing slave is yet free in the Lord, and the free man a slave of Christ.' Your construction is of modern date, and owes its origins to abolitionism. Indeed, it seems to conflict with the great idea which occupied the mind of the Apostle when he wrote, to wit: That the gospel of Christ was not to unsettle the relations of human society. There is not the slightest intimation to the master that it is his duty to liberate his slave, not even a preference for it is hinted at, nor is the slave to *seek* his liberty. . . .

Your view [that is, the abolitionist view that Paul urges manumission] of this passage is not universally conceded by Biblical critics, even among abolitionists. Conybeare and Howson,[43] the former 'Late Fellow of Trinity College, Cambridge' and the latter 'Principal of the Collegiate Institution, Liverpool,' both learned critics and translators, give the passage in examination this version: 'Wast thou in slavery at the time of thy calling? Care not for it. Nay, though thou have the power to gain thy freedom, seek rather to remain content.' In the footnote these men say: 'The Greek here is *ambiguous*, and might so be rendered as to give directly opposite precepts (emphasis mine); but the version given in the text. . . agree best with the *kai* and *also with the context.' "[44]

Several aspects of the exegetical debate contained in this discussion deserve comment. Dr. Pratt, the abolitionist, renders the problematic phrase μᾶλλον χρῆσαι into English as "use *it* rather," but then he assumes that the "it" to which Paul refers is

---

[43]I will comment on Conybeare and Howson below.

[44]Warren, 168-170.

manumission. There is not even the slightest acknowledgment by Dr. Pratt of the complexity of this verse. Dr. Pratt, however, is not alone in his efforts to render the ambiguous as clear.

Mr. Thompson urges consideration of the context in order to properly understand 7:21. This is clearly a solid exegetical move. Yet, Mr. Thompson's contextual analysis only extends back to v. 17 and does not take into consideration the many concessions and changes of status that Paul allows throughout chapter seven.

Second, Mr. Thompson seeks to solidify the persuasiveness of his claim by an (ideological) appeal to history and tradition. On the one hand, he cites ancient patristic evidence (i.e., Chrysostom) which agrees with his interpretation, and on the other hand, he criticizes the abolitionist reading supporting manumission as a "modern" fascination. Thus, since the proslavery reading, in his estimation, is the more ancient reading, it must be more in line with the original intention of its author.

Third, Mr. Thompson's reading also completely removes any equivocation in Paul on this matter of slavery and manumission. According to Mr. Thompson, Paul did not want the gospel of Christ "to unsettle the relations of human society." On the one hand, Mr. Thompson could support this understanding of Paul as the guardian of the status quo with other Pauline passages such as Romans 13:1-7 where Paul *seems* to enjoin a philosophy of extreme social conservatism.[45]

Yet, on the other hand, even within 1 Corinthians Paul contends that in light of the gospel and the impending apocalyptic moment, Christians should seek changes in their lifestyles[46] and also in their attitudes about their lifestyles.[47] In

---

[45]In some detail Neil Elliott wrestles with the problems of Paul's words in Romans 13:1-7. Interestingly, Elliott also explores how previous interpreters of Romans 13:1-7 have read a status quo interpretation into Romans 7 based on their "status quo" reading of 1 Corinthians 7. See Neil Elliott, 211-214.

[46]Paul may have been so radical in his teaching about how the gospel affects human relations that he needed to actually modify his claims. See 1 Corinthians 5:9.

[47]1 Corinthians 7:29-31.

other words, Mr. Thompson's reading is "flat" and lacks the tension between accommodation to the world and transformation of the world which energizes much of Paul's writings.[48]

Fourth, Mr. Thompson cites the exegetical observations of two English commentators, W. J. Conybeare and J. S. Howson, who admit that the Greek is ambiguous,[49] but contend that 7:21 should read, "Wast thou in slavery at the time of thy calling? Care not for it. Nay, though thou have the power to gain thy freedom, *seek rather to remain content*."[50] Of course, the interpretation "seek rather to remain content" is a very "loose" rendering of μᾶλλον χρῆσαι, but such a rendering gives credence to Mr. Thompson's belief that Paul encouraged a gospel of social conservatism.

Though it is a fictional account, *Nellie Norton* shows us the debate generated among nineteenth century interpreters, as they used 1 Corinthians 7 to argue for or against slavery. The same exegetical energy can also be seen in other nineteenth century writings as well. Let us now investigate an actual nineteenth century debate on slavery which has been preserved for us in letters.

---

[48]As examples of Paul's belief that the implications of the gospel will not only unsettle but completely disrupt social conditions, see 1 Corinthians 1:18-25, 2:6-8, 11:17-22, and 15:24-28.

[49]See W. J. Conybeare and J. S. Howson, *The Life and Epistles of Saint Paul*, The People's Edition (Hartford, CT: S. S. Scranton and Company, 1869), 43, note 6.

[50]In the 1869 edition of Conybeare and Howson, 7:21 is translated, "Wast thou in slavery at the time of thy calling? Care not for it. Nay, though thou have the power to gain thy freedom, *rather make use of thy condition*." Though the change is slight, it is, nevertheless, a noticeable shift. The phrasing of the 1869 edition more clearly urges slaves to remain in their slavery. In this quotation in *Nellie Norton*, there are no notes to indicate the edition of Conybeare and Howson to which Mr. Thompson is referring.

Domestic Slavery[51]

In November, 1845, the Reverend Richard Fuller of Beaufort, South Carolina, wrote a letter which was published in *The Christian Reflector*. In the letter, Fuller, a slavery advocate, maintained that the Bible condemned the abuses of slavery but not the institution itself.[52] In the course of this published letter, Fuller took strong exception to the views of the abolitionist, Francis Wayland. Fuller's remarks galvanized Francis Wayland to write a response, which, in turn, prompted a response from Fuller. Again, Wayland replied to Fuller's response. This series of letters contains, in pithy form, many of the most characteristic proslavery and abolitionist biblical arguments.

More than a decade after the commencement of this epistolary debate, Fuller and Wayland agreed to collect and publish their letters in one volume "in order that both of the views taken of this subject might be presented together both at the North and the South."[53] Like the fictional debate between Mr. Thompson and Dr. Pratt in *Nellie Norton*, this actual debate between Fuller and Wayland possessed an air of civility. It had all the appearances of a "gentlemen's debate," since each man, though adamant in his views, attempted to fight fairly with his opponent.

Although Wayland, the abolitionist, examined many New Testament passages in his letters to Fuller, he offered no exposition on 1 Corinthians 7. Fuller, however, did appeal to 1 Corinthians 7 in support of his claim that the Bible sanctions slavery. Once again, it will be useful to quote the passage at length:

> The passage I allude to, you at once recollect. It is very fine indeed, and when you remember the condition of a slave then, under a heathen master, there is in it a simple grandeur of thought, compared with which all the vaunted

---

[51]Richard Fuller and Francis Wayland, *Domestic Slavery Considered as a Scriptural Institution: In a Correspondence between the Rev. Richard Fuller and the Rev. Francis Wayland* (New York: Sheldon & Company, 1860).

[52]Fuller and Wayland, 4.

[53]Fuller and Wayland, iv.

sublimity of Homer is unutterably mean. "Is any man called," says the apostle, "being circumcised? Let him not become uncircumcised. Is he called in uncircumcision? Let him not be circumcised. Circumcision is nothing, and uncircumcision is nothing, but the keeping of the commandments of God. Let every man abide in the same calling wherein he was called. *Art thou called being a servant? Care not for it*; but if thou mayest be made free, use it rather. For he that is called in the Lord, being a servant, is the Lord's freeman: likewise, also, he that is called, being free, is Christ's servant." 1 Cor. vii 18-22.

His ardent soul on fire with the great salvation, and the anticipations of the glory to be revealed, Paul declares that the true spirit of the gospel, instead of interfering with social relations, should cause the believer to soar above them; and that the advantages and disadvantages of all earthly conditions ought to be forgotten and swallowed up in the thought of these transports and raptures to which he is hastening.

In the verse just copied, while he says that liberty is to be preferred to slavery, yet he adds that, in the light of faith, the soul alone has true value, and even the hardest bondage is nothing at all, not worth a thought, if the slave had been called to the glorious liberty of the gospel. And he classes the distinction between master and servant in the same list with circumcision and uncircumcision, which made no sort of difference.

"Hast thou been called," says Chrysostom, "being a slave? Care not for it. Continue to be a slave. Hast thou been called, being in uncircumcision? Remain uncircumcised. Being circumcised, didst thou become a believer? Continue circumcised. For these are no hindrances to piety. Thou art called, being a slave; another with an unbelieving wife; another, being circumcised. Astonishing! Where has he put slavery? As circumcision profits not; and uncircumcision does no harm, so neither doth slavery, nor yet liberty."[54]

What gives peculiar importance to this passage is, that it was written in answer to a letter from the Corinthian church touching certain matters, and among them, the

---

[54]See *The Homilies of St. John Chrysostom on the First Epistle of St. Paul the Apostle to the Corinthians* (Oxford: John Henry Parker, 1839), 252-253.

duty of Christians sustaining to each other the relation of master and slave. Now here, if slavery be a heinous crime, would not these inquirers been told so? But we see the answer which the apostle, or rather which the Holy Spirit returns.[55]

Fuller uses his exegesis of 1 Corinthians 7 to support his own views of social conservatism. He rightly alludes to the apocalyptic aspects of 1 Corinthians 7 when he mentions the influence of Paul's "anticipations of the glory to be revealed." According to Fuller, Paul, in light of this imminent apocalyptic moment, enjoins social contentment upon slaves, since "the true spirit of the gospel, instead of interfering with social relations, should cause the believer to soar above them." As was the case in *Nellie Norton*, this proslavery interpretation completely removes the tension in Paul's writings concerning the proper relationship between the believer and various social exigencies in the world.

Fuller's "spiritualizing" of the passage also obscures the social realities with which Paul was struggling. According to Fuller, Paul pacifies the Corinthian slaves by suggesting that "the soul alone has true value, and even the hardest bondage is nothing at all, not worth a thought, if the slave had been called to the glorious liberty of the gospel."

Fuller's exegesis also treats Paul's directives concerning social change in 1 Corinthians 7 as a univocal exhortation to remain in one's social condition, since conditions such as slavery are, "no hindrances to piety." Paul's willingness to permit or even encourage social changes when he considers certain social states as potential threats to piety is ignored by Fuller. When he suggests that Paul is opposed unilaterally to social alterations, he is resolving an ambiguity implicit within the text.

Lest one assume that the premature resolution of this passage's ambiguity was merely an obsession among proslavery exegetes, let us consider an example from the abolitionist side of the struggle.

---

[55]Fuller and Wayland, 189-191.

The Guilt of Slavery

Unwilling to surrender the terrain of scripture to slavery supporters without a fight, George Cheever, a nineteenth century pastor of a Puritan congregation, sought to demonstrate the iniquity of slavery by appealing to the Bible. According to Cheever, slavery was not only iniquitous, but it was also a stumblingblock to the foreign missionary efforts of American Christians. How could Christian evangelists compel "the heathen" abroad to accept the gospel message, when the very missionary boards sponsoring these evangelists supported and participated in slavery on domestic shores? Cheever directly attacked the immorality of slavery, declaring, "The relation of slaveholding must be sentenced by the church as in itself an immoral relation, and the claim of property in man must be presented as it stands in God's word, as a moral guilt equivalent with the crime of murder."[56]

Cheever then set out to examine all relevant passages in the Bible that spoke to the slavery question. Cheever's proposed method included philological, legal, historical, and moral arguments based on scripture.[57] Towards the end of his book he comments on 1 Corinthians 7. Interestingly, he discusses the interpretation of Conybeare and Howson, the two commentators to whom Mr. Thompson, the slavery advocate, had appealed in *Nellie Norton*. Again, it will be useful to quote the passage at length:

> They [the English commentators Conybeare and Howson] have taken the bad and lowest signification of the terms, from Pagan usage, in regard to *slaves*, and applied *that slavish signification*, to the highest, freest, most honorable and voluntary commission and work of Christ's servants among mortals! They have gone so far as to render 1 Cor. vii., 23, "Christ's slave, for he has paid a price for you all." And they have translated Paul's injunction to use freedom, thus: "Nay, though thou have power to gain thy freedom, seek rather to remain content;" at the same time acknowledging that "the Greek might be so rendered as to

---

[56]Cheever, xx.
[57]Cheever, i.

give directly opposite precepts." Whence then this preference for slavery, and this dreadful attempt to foist it in, and fasten it upon, the blessed words and doctrine of divine inspiration?

1 Cor. vii., 21-23: "Art thou called being a servant? δοῦλος. Care not for it; but if thou mayest be made free, use it rather. For he that is called in the Lord being a servant, δοῦλος, is the Lord's freeman; likewise also, he that is called, being free, is Christ's servant, δοῦλος. You are bought (redeemed, ἠγοράσθητε,) with a price; be not ye the servants, δοῦλοι, of men?"

The argument here is the same as that in regard to a wife who is called, but is the wife of an unbelieving husband. If he pleased to dwell with her, let her not leave him, for she may be the means of saving him. But if he depart, she is not under bondage, she is free from him, and from all obligations to him. So if a servant is called, being a servant, he is not to be troubled by that condition of bondage, as if it were obligatory upon him, for if he may be made free, if he *can* be made free, or become free (εἰ καὶ δύνασαι ἐλεύθερος γενέσθαι), he is at liberty to avail himself of that, he is commanded to become free, rather than remain a slave. Several things are to be considered.

1. It is not merely a permission, but a command, *Use it rather.*

2. The reason, the ground, of this command is, that the slave, when converted, is the Lord's freeman; but if he uses the privilege of his freedom from men, he is still Christ's servant.

3. He is redeemed by Christ, and must not be the slave of men.

4. If the state of freedom is his privilege and duty, then, on the other hand, it follows incontrovertibly that it is the duty of every master to yield to him that privilege, to let him go free. If, as a Christian, he is free, and is commanded to use his freedom rather than remain in bondage, then much more it is the duty of his master, as a Christian, not to restrain him of that freedom, not to prevent him from that duty, not to deny him that privilege. If the state of freedom is so much better for the servant, or slave, that he is bound to use it, if he can become free, then by the same

obligation his master is bound to give it to him, as justice and equality, as his due, bound to do to him as he would have him do to himself. This acknowledgment, or gift of freedom, is the first thing considered in the obligation of masters giving to their servants that which is just and equal. The first thing, and without which nothing can be just and equal, is to treat them as free, to yield to them their freedom, and to deal with them as free.

5. It is to be marked that while a general command is issued to converted persons to remain in the same calling in which they were found when called to the knowledge of Christ, one exception is made, and only one is mentioned, that of slavery. Out of that calling a man is to hasten as soon as possible, and as being the Lord's freeman; and for plain reasons, not only of natural and Christian right, but because the state of slavery is so infinitely disastrous and degrading to the moral being, so unfavorable to piety, so inevitably interfering with a man's duty to God. That a man may hope to keep his Saviour's commandments, and grow in grace, he must, as quick as possible, get out of the state of slavery. If thou *canst* be made free, use it rather. Deliver me from the oppression of man; so I will keep thy precepts. Deliver me, that I may keep them.[58]

Several aspects of Cheever's reading demand comment. First, Cheever's philological suggestion concerning the meaning of δοῦλος is less than persuasive. He intimates that previous commentators have imported "slavish signification" into this term, and that it should be rendered "servant." In light of our analysis of first century slavery in chapter four, it is most likely that by δοῦλος Paul in every way meant "slave" and not "servant." Moreover, regardless of what shade of meaning one gives to the term, Paul more than likely was addressing some persons in the Corinthian congregation who stood completely outside of the system of honor and power. Thus, in this case whether one chooses to call them "slaves" or "servants" is immaterial.

Second, Cheever maintains that μᾶλλον χρῆσαι is not a "permission" or a Pauline preference but instead a "command." Yet, he does not acknowledge the ambiguous nature and

---

[58]Cheever, 387-389.

decidedly weak tone of the command. If this were Paul's statement of principle concerning the right of manumission for (all) Christian slaves, Paul would have been more forceful. One might ask Cheever, How effective are unclear "commands"? Paul himself, in another context, intimated that "unclear trumpets" (i.e., commands) do not rally troops for warfare.[59] Similarly, one wonders if Paul's ambiguous words mustered a great battlecry for manumission among slaves and masters in Corinth.

Third, Cheever's reading of 1 Corinthians 7 is heavily influenced by Colossians 4:1. Paul's command in Colossians for masters to give to their slaves that which is just and equal is superimposed on Paul's statements in our passage. As we saw earlier, whether Colossians 4:1 can be understood as a subtle exhortation by Paul for masters to manumit slaves is a point of contention. Moreover, even if that were the case in Colossians, one cannot necessarily assume that this was Paul's message also in 1 Corinthians 7.

Finally, Cheever claims that Paul makes only one exception concerning his principle of remaining in the same social state, namely, slavery. As we have demonstrated, it is dubious to consider Paul's words in 1 Corinthians 7 as a doctrine of the status quo, and Paul allows more exceptions for change of status than just slavery. Thus, on many accounts, Cheever's exegesis of our passage is forced and eliminates many of the complexities and ambiguities we have discussed.

Conclusions

This synopsis of nineteenth century appeals to 1 Corinthians 7:17-24 has demonstrated how the ideological concerns of nineteenth century America caused many interpreters of this passage to ignore its complexity.[60] In light of the prevailing

---

[59]See 1 Corinthians 14:8.

[60]For another interesting nineteenth century proslavery appeal to 1 Corinthians 7, see Albert Taylor Bledsoe, *An Essay on Liberty and Slavery* (Philadelphia: J. B. Lippincott & Co., 1856), 214-222. For another

political and cultural climate of antebellum America, interpreters of this passage turned to 1 Corinthians 7 for ideological support of their positions. Regardless of the text's ambiguity, they found in this passage what they needed and discounted the rest. Ironically, this text about slavery and manumission has been held captive by the ideological needs of its would-be liberators. Has this passage fared any better among twentieth century interpreters? To this and other (ideological) issues, we now turn.

IDEOLOGY IN INTELLECTUAL DISCOURSE

This dissertation must finally address the issue of how contemporary scholars approach certain aspects of the interpretation of 1 Corinthians 7, especially vv. 17-24. How one interprets a passage is seen as a function of hermeneutics. Yet, as should be evident from the above discussion, the way one interprets a text is also an ideological matter, for the interpretation of texts is a decidedly political act, involving the (sometimes competing) needs and interests of various groups and the interpreters who belong to those groups.

The particular group upon which I now reflect is the academy of biblical scholars. Analyzing the ideology of intellectual discourse among biblical scholars who interpret 1 Corinthians 7, I raise the following questions: What ideological presuppositions have informed the approaches to the exegesis of this passage, and what ideological presuppositions have informed my approach to this passage?

In a very cogent essay, Fernando Segovia provides a useful overview of the competing modes of intellectual

---

fascinating eighteenth century abolitionist appeal to 1 Corinthians 7, see Granville Sharp, "An Essay on Slavery: Proving from Scripture its Inconsistency with Humanity and Religion" in *Tracts on Slavery and Liberty: The Just Limitations of Slavery in the Laws of God, The Law of Passive Obedience, The Law of Liberty* (London: 1776; reprint Westport, CT: Negro Universities Press, 1969), 32-38.

discourse in contemporary biblical scholarship.[61] According to Segovia, there are three primary modes of discourse in biblical scholarship: traditional historical criticism, literary criticism broadly conceived, and cultural criticism broadly conceived. In his analysis of the waning relevance of traditional historical criticism, Segovia basically discounts the theoretical appeal of this form of exegesis. Segovia remarks:

> Indeed, the historical-critical model may even be described as defunct from a theoretical point of view but not from a practical point of view. From a theoretical perspective, the method is so defunct that it has been unable to mount a serious and informed defense of its own methodological principles or reading strategy and underlying theoretical orientation. From a practical perspective, the method is alive, though at various stages of health: while its grasp in the United States has slipped considerably, its dominance in Europe is still very much in evidence, though with dangerous cracks beginning to appear here and there as well.[62]

Segovia's provocative remarks overstate the case, but he points to some serious issues within the current debate. He rightly calls our attention to the infusion of new and modified methods in biblical studies over the last two decades. The book for which Segovia's essay is the introduction provides

---

[61]Fernando F. Segovia, "And They Began to Speak in Tongues": Competing Modes of Discourse in Contemporary Biblical Criticism" in *Reading from This Place*, vol. 1, ed. Fernando F. Segovia and Mary Ann Tolbert (Minneapolis: Fortress Press 1995), 1-32. I am grateful to Professor Brian Blount for sharing with me his useful and even-handed treatment of the strengths and weaknesses of *Reading From This Place*. His paper, "Response to *Reading From This Place*, Volumes 1 and 2 and *Teaching The Bible*" was delivered at the Annual Meeting of the Society of Biblical Literature in the Committee of Underrepresented Racial and Ethnic Minorities in the Profession, Orlando, Florida, November 21-24, 1998. Also, for a similar accounting of modes of discourse in contemporary biblical scholarship, see Robbins, *Texture*, 106-110. Kevin Vanhoozer also provides a useful overview of the three major hermeneutical periods in the last three centuries. See Vanhoozer, *Is There A Meaning in This Text?* (Grand Rapids: Zondervan Publishing House, 1998), 25-29.

[62]Segovia, 7-8, note 9.

substantial testimony to the rise of "social location" exegesis. Yet, in the interpretation of Pauline texts such as 1 Corinthians 7:17-24, the intellectual orientation of most exegesis is still decidedly historical.[63] I dare say that the majority of interpretations of 1 Corinthians 7:17-24 seek to clarify the linguistic and social contexts of this passage in order to ascertain more clearly the meaning that Paul intended, its so-called "original meaning."

Two of the more celebrated efforts to grapple with this passage, the studies of Bartchy and Harrill, are firmly situated within historical-critical scholarship. Other studies (such as Dawes's) employ rhetorical analysis, but this rhetorical analysis is also in service of a more accurate understanding of Paul's original meaning. This dissertation has regularly employed, though not exclusively,[64] the insights and methods of historical-critical exegesis in order to clarify the cultural, social, rhetorical, and ideological contexts from which this passage emanates. In short, historical exegesis is by far still the dominant intellectual discourse employed in the exegesis of 1 Corinthians 7:17-24.

Undeniably, historical-critical approaches to the text have yielded substantial clarifications. The detailed insights on first century Greco-Roman manumission practices explicated by both Bartchy and Harrill have reminded us of the importance of an

---

[63]For historical and methodological background on the historical-critical method, see, for example, Edgar Krentz, *The Historical-Critical Method* (Philadelphia: Fortress Press, 1975). Also see, Morgan, *Biblical Interpretation*, 44-132.

[64]In my discussion of ethnicity in chapters two and three, I have also used insights which might be called social-scientific. Also, my interest in Pauline ambiguity and in the uses of this text in the nineteenth century are informed by postmodern and ideological concerns. In this dissertation, I have been unashamedly eclectic. For a critique of biblical scholarship's preoccupation with method, see Steven J. Kraftchick, "Facing Janus: Reviewing the Biblical Theology Movement" in *Biblical Theology: Problems and Perspectives*, ed. Steven J. Kraftchick, Charles D. Myers, Jr. and Ben C. Ollenburger (Nashville: Abingdon, 1995), 75-77. Also for a fascinating discussion of the need for eclectic methodologies in postmodern (African American) biblical interpretation, see Osayande Obery Hendricks, "Guerrilla Exegesis: 'Struggle' as a Scholarly Vocation," *Semeia* 72 (1995): 73-90.

in-depth investigation of the practices and characteristics of Greco-Roman slavery. Furthermore, both studies have compelled interpreters of this passage to admit the possibility that Paul may have the actual practice of manumission in mind, rather than some spiritual, abstract manumission. Yet, in spite of the fruitful yields of historical approaches to this text, there are some ideological presuppositions inherent in most historical-critical investigations which, in the case of 1 Corinthians 7:17-24, may actually hinder us from achieving the best exegetical results.

There are three basic, closely related presuppositions which underlie many historical approaches to the exegesis of Pauline texts in general and our passage in particular. First, such approaches assume that ancient texts are basically lucid pieces of human communication. Consequently, obscure features in a text are to be considered exceptions which prove the rule. Surely, historical approaches acknowledge that the texts under consideration were written in a different time and cultural milieu, but generally historical approaches contend that these differences can be overcome, if not eliminated, when the interpreter gains the proper knowledge of requisite ancient languages and cultural practices.

A second presupposition is that if persistently obscure features in a text do not yield their insights, the application of more refined (historical) critical tools will eventually illumine the enigma. Although many of the studies of 1 Corinthians 7:17-24 gloss over some of the other difficulties of chapter seven, they do acknowledge the difficulty of understanding μᾶλλον χρῆσαι. Yet, the unspoken assumption is that this textual ambiguity is more apparent than real. Most exegetes assume that Paul *was* clear, and if the right historical data are applied, the enigma will be eliminated. With enough time and proper historical information about manumission practices or ancient literary parallels of the use of μᾶλλον χρῆσαι, the exegete can and will resolve the ambiguity.[65]

---

[65]One wonders to what degree the very nature of academic writing contributes to this need to render the ambiguous as clear. Academic writing, and certainly dissertation writing, is built on the premise that

A third presupposition is that Paul *must* be clear. This notion derives less from the belief in the inherent lucidity of Paul's letters than the compulsion to solve the riddles in this passage because of the canonical status of this text. For many, this passage is *Scripture!* Therefore, its dictates carry a special ideological force. Regardless of an individual interpreter's belief or disbelief in the religious authority of this passage, one cannot deny or ignore that much of the appeal of this passage for interpreters has been the assumption that it contains Paul's— and by extension a divinely inspired—view on "the slavery question."

Unlike our nineteenth century interpretive counterparts for whom the slavery question was a live issue, twenty-first century American interpreters have the luxury of having had this question decided for us. The abolition of chattel slavery in America has significantly lessened the ideological exigencies of this passage. Yet, clarifying Paul's stance on slavery is, nonetheless, an important contemporary intellectual (if not overtly political) exercise for those who would enlist or dismiss Paul as a friend or foe in various current struggles for liberation. Thus, the ardent contention that this passage *must* make sense is itself fueled by ideological convictions.

At this point, I do not take issue necessarily with historical-critical exegesis as much as I do with some of its presuppositions. Could it be that interpretive methodologies, such as historical-critical exegesis, should work in an *inverse* way in the case of 1 Corinthian 7:17-24? Accordingly, the more we refine the linguistic, social, cultural, and ideological features of this text, the more *ambiguous* the text becomes. Typically "good" exegesis brings clarity. In this case, however, "good" exegesis might amplify the complexity and ambiguity, precisely

---

the writer is contributing "new" knowledge to the discipline or solving heretofore unresolved problems. This dissertation is not immune from this feature of academic writing, but it is attempting to be more forthcoming about its presuppositions. My "new" insight may be that certain ambiguous elements of this passage may not be eliminated by methods of critical exegesis, because to do so is to actually ignore certain features of the text, and to hold the text captive to the interpreter's needs.

because complexity and ambiguity may have been original features of the text.

To speak of ambiguity as an original feature of the text is to open up two horizons. First, one may suggest that Paul, intentionally or unintentionally, was responsible for this ambiguity. Second, literary critics have argued that in some sense there is no text without a reader and that readers are themselves producers of textual meaning.[66] Thus, to speak of complexity and ambiguity as original features of the text is also to open up the possibility that the first recipients of Paul's missive may have been befuddled by some of his statements and thus may have construed them in ways other than Paul intended. One may assume that in some sense and on some issues, Paul intended to be clear and may have failed. In other instances, Paul may have intended to be unclear and expected his readers to fill in the lacunae.

I am not alone in arguing for the presence of intentional ambiguity in 1 Corinthians. In a sophisticated treatment of 1 Corinthians 9:19-23,[67] Mark Given argues that Paul's self-avowed ambiguous strategy of "being all things to all people" is not an insincere tactic of accommodation and manipulation but rather a thoughtful expression of Paul's understanding of God's nature and purpose. Given intimates that Paul may have thought that at times both the nature and the purpose of God

---

[66]The literature on reader-centered approaches to interpretation is vast, varied, and complex. For representative treatments of these approaches and their presuppositions, see Roland Barthes, "Death of the Author," in *Authorship from Plato to Postmodernity*, ed. Seán Burke, 125-130 (Edinburgh: Edinburgh University Press, 1992); Stanley Fish, *Is There A Text In This Class?* (Cambridge, MA: Harvard University Press, 1980); Wolfgang Iser, *The Act of Reading: A Theory of Aesthetic Response* (Baltimore: Johns Hopkins University Press, 1978); Susan R. Suleiman and Inge Crossman, eds., *The Reader In the Text: Essays on Audience and Interpretation* (Princeton: Princeton University Press, 1980), and Edgar V. McKnight, *Postmodern Use of the Bible: The Emergence of Reader-Oriented Criticism* (Nashville: Abingdon Press, 1988).

[67]Mark D. Given, "True Rhetoric: Ambiguity, Cunning and Deception in Pauline Discourse" in *Society of Biblical Literature Seminar Papers* (Atlanta: Scholars Press, 1997), 526-550.

are hidden and inscrutable. Thus, the opaque nature of some of Paul's declarations was an imitation of "God's concealed wisdom" which could be discerned only by the "in crowd" who had true knowledge.[68]

Yet, Paul's ambiguity is not always a reflection of his understanding of the inscrutable nature of divine revelation. There are times when Paul simply has not made up his mind. Given rightly observes that "Paul often expresses himself by saying both 'yes' and 'no' to an issue, especially a controversial one."[69] In fact, twentieth century interpreters such as Given are joined by a company of first century persons who considered Paul's words to be less than clear. Paul himself indicates that his hearers misunderstood him[70] and that his critics charged him with duplicity. For instance, in 2 Corinthians 1:16-18 Paul may be defending himself against a charge of ambiguity. Paul retorts:

> I wanted to visit you on my way to Macedonia, and to come back to you from Macedonia and have you send me on to Judea. Was I vacillating when I wanted to do this? Do I make my plans according to ordinary human standards, ready to say, "Yes, yes" and "No, no" at the same time? As surely as God is faithful, our word to you has not been "Yes and No."

On some occasions, Paul's words were not "Yes and No." On other occasions, Paul's words were intentionally "Yes and No." And if his words were not intentionally "Yes and No," they certainly could be interpreted as his saying, "Yes and No."

The history of interpretation of 1 Corinthians 7:17-24, however, is replete with exegetes who have been terribly dissatisfied with a Paul who says both "Yes *and* No," especially on an issue as controversial as slavery. Thus, many nineteenth and twentieth century interpreters have "persuaded" Paul to say either "Yes" *or* "No." By resolving the tension, such interpreters may have unwittingly reduced Paul to a form of interpretive slavery or exegetical tyranny. They have compelled

---

[68]Given, 550.
[69]Given, 536, note 37.
[70]See, for example, 1 Corinthians 5:9.

Paul to say things that he was unprepared or unwilling to say. Ironically, previous interpreters may have paid less attention to what Paul really said and more attention to what they wanted Paul to say.

CONCLUSIONS

In this study, I have endeavored to provide both a critical investigation of 1 Corinthians 7:17-24 and of some of the presuppositions which have informed approaches to this passage. I have suggested that in our grappling with this text we may have subjected it to an interpretive tyranny by insisting on resolving complexities and ambiguities. On many occasions, I have offered variant readings of aspects of the text and of the text's social and cultural world. I have not done this to delimit meaning, or supplant all previous readings with *the* new reading, but rather to demonstrate the polyvalence in this passage. If I claimed to have *the* reading of this text, my critics could rightly exclaim, "Physician, heal thyself." If my study has further "problematized" the interpretation of this passage, then in some small way, I may have contributed to the *manumission* of this passage from the hands of overly confident interpreters.

Although my presuppositions, if not always my discourse, might be classified as postmodern, I am no archenemy of hermeneutical realism. I *do* believe that there are many biblical passages whose meanings are reasonably clear, and in those cases, to claim otherwise might be a blatant ignoring of the evidence.

I began this study, however, firmly convinced that texts may conceal as much as they reveal. I equally believe that there are other texts where the intended meaning and all other subsequent meanings[71] are complex, ambiguous, and conflicted. When interpreting those kinds of texts, one's hermeneutical goals should be modified. The pursuit of fixed, textual meaning need not necessarily be abandoned as an outdated vestige of

---

[71]Of course, texts have countless meanings which the author never intended. The author may, intentionally or unintentionally, prescribe a trajectory for a text, but there is no guarantee that subsequent interpreters will follow that trajectory.

Enlightenment philosophy. Instead, a meaning of such texts might be that all ultimate claims to know *the* meaning of that text are themselves problematic.

In many ways, this study is the product of the marriage of certain modern presuppositions (i.e., that clarifying or hypothesizing about the meanings of this text for its initial author and audiences is an important intellectual exercise) and certain postmodern presuppositions (i.e., that complexity and ambiguity are not inherently problems to be solved but indeed indicators of our "situatedness" in competing communities). Like all "children," this dissertation has taken a little from each parent. The trait of modernity is the interest in original contexts. The trait of postmodernity is the unflinching confession that (some of) this ambiguity may not be the result of deficiencies in our interpretive methods, but rather may be an intractable feature of the text. Postmodern assumptions about this text might actually move us closer to the text's original situation.

I wholeheartedly agree with Robert Robinson's estimation of the hermeneutical task, when he writes:

> Interpretation is a messy business, subject to contrary currents of value and interests, both conscious and unconscious, to the serendipity of the information available, to contrasting pressures to conform to contemporary standards and to break new ground, to conventions governing what features of a text may be taken to be meaningful, to appraisals of the audience and its interests, to a judgment of what the interpretation hopes to accomplish, why it is undertaken, *to desire to let the interpretation mimic the richness of the text*. And much more. Interpretation is messy, and that messiness resists and subverts theoretical consistency, often in subtly ironic ways.[72]

The goal of this interpretation has been to "mimic the richness" of the tensions, and even the ambiguities in this text. In order to effect such an interpretation, I have asked certain implicit and explicit questions: What if this passage is not a

---

[72]Robert B. Robinson, "Introduction to Textual Determinacy: Part Two," *Semeia* 71 (1995): 9 (emphasis mine).

"theoretical digression"? What if Paul is not advocating a doctrine of the social status quo? What if he is reflecting on the radical nature of the call of God? What if the language about circumcision and uncircumcision has some basis in the concrete exigencies of life in Corinth? What if the gymnasium and the synagogue are viewed by Paul as potential enticements to his converts? What if Paul is unintentionally obscure on some points and intentionally ambiguous on others? These and other questions have guided and arisen in the course of this study.

Certain elements of my exegetical approach could be called a (post)modern hermeneutics of suspicion. Quite simply, I *suspect* that Paul is conflicted as he works out the concrete social implications of his kerygma. Kevin Vanhoozer rightly suggests that suspicion is a chief tenet of postmodernism.[73] He is incorrect when he too broadly defines the object of the suspicion. He contends that a chief characteristic of postmodernism is "incredulity toward meaning."[74] This may be the case in some, but not all, postmodern thought. My postmodern thought in this dissertation can be characterized not as incredulity toward meaning per se, but instead incredulity toward our methods of arriving at meaning—methods that must "extract" meaning from a text at all cost.

To say that a text contains ambiguity is, of course, not to say that a text is devoid of meanings. Perhaps, one meaning of 1 Corinthians 7, to employ words uttered elsewhere by Paul, is that Paul himself is working out the implications of his kerygma with "fear and trembling."[75] Interpreters who are uncomfortable with a hesitant Paul, who stutters and stammers to say the right words, have often said things for Paul. Ambiguity may not always be inherent in Paul's writings; yet, it may also be an important, even intentional feature of his texts. Thus, some of the textual ambiguity may not be an unfortunate reality to be explained away, but instead an invitation to the messy, but magnificent, work of interpretation.

---

[73]Vanhoozer, 16-17.

[74]Vanhoozer, 16.

[75]I allude to and amend Paul's words in Philippians 2:12.

The ability to appeal to Paul and other authoritative traditions in our ethical conversations and to say with assurance that we have found *the* meaning of a Pauline passage may, on certain occasions, abridge and impair such conversations. When we honestly admit that some of the ancient (and modern) texts upon which we work are complex, conflicted, and ambiguous, it reminds us that the composers of these texts were themselves not immune from the strain of interpretation and moral discernment.

Sustaining ambiguity is difficult. The ethical exigencies of our lives regularly force us to amplify or choose one side of (textual) ambiguity. When we resolve the ambiguity in order to get on with the business of living, we must readily acknowledge that some times our claims to have found *the* (or even a) meaning of the ambiguity may be useful and even necessary fictions, but *fictions* nonetheless. I would prefer for this passage to be released from the tyranny of premature resolution. If Paul were asked whether this passage should seek an opportunity to be manumitted or continue in its present state of exegetical slavery, I imagine he would "confidently" declare, "μᾶλλον χρῆσαι!"

BIBLIOGRAPHY

Ani, Marimba. *Yurugu: An African-Centered Critique of European Cultural Thought and Behavior*. Trenton: African World Press, 1994.

Ascough, Richard S. *What Are They Saying about the Formation of Pauline Churches?* New York: Paulist Press, 1998.

Badian, E. "Figuring Out Roman Slavery." *Journal of Roman Studies* 72 (1982): 164-169.

Baird, William. *History of New Testament Research: From Deism to Tübingen*. Vol. 1. Minneapolis: Fortress Press, 1992.

Balch, David L. "1 Cor 7:32-35 and Stoic Debates about Marriage, Anxiety, and Distraction." *Journal of Biblical Literature* 102 (1983): 429-439.

Banks, Robert. *Paul's Idea of Community*. Homebush West, Australia: Anzea Publishers, 1979. Revised Edition, Peabody: Hendrickson Publishers, 1994.

Barclay, John M. G. "Paul, Philemon and the Dilemma of Christian Slave-Ownership." *New Testament Studies* 37 (1991): 161-186.

――――. "Thessalonica and Corinth: Social Contrast in Pauline Christianity." *Journal for the Study of the New Testament* 47 (1992): 49-74.

――――. *Jews in the Mediterranean Diaspora: From Alexander to Trajan (323 BCE-117 CE)*. Edinburgh: T & T Clark, 1996.

Barrett, C. K. *The First Epistle to the Corinthians*. New York: Harper & Row, 1968.

――――. *Essays on Paul*. Philadelphia: Westminister Press, 1982.

――――. *Paul: An Introduction to His Thought*. Louisville: Westminster/John Knox Press, 1994.

Bartchy, S. Scott. *ΜΑΛΛΟΝ ΧΡΗΣΑΙ: First Century Slavery and the Interpretation of 1 Corinthians 7:21*. Missoula, MT: Scholars Press, 1973.

Barth, Fredrik. "Ethnic Groups and Boundaries." In *Process and Form in Social Life*, 198-227. London: Routledge & Kegan Paul, 1981.

Barthes, Roland. "Death of the Author." In *Authorship from Plato to Postmodernity*, ed. Seán Burke, 125-130. Edinburgh: Edinburgh University Press, 1992.

Barton, Stephen C. "Paul's Sense of Place: An Anthropological Approach to Community Formation in Corinth." *New Testament Studies* 32 (1986): 225-246.

Bassler, Jouette M. "Paul's Theology: Whence and Whether." In *Pauline Theology: 1 & 2 Corinthians*. Vol. 2, ed. David M. Hay, 3-17. Minneapolis: Fortress Press, 1993.

Baur, Ferdinand Christian. *The Church History of the First Three Centuries*. London: William & Norgate, 1878.

Beker, J. C. *Paul the Apostle: The Triumph of God in Life and Thought*. Philadelphia: Fortress Press, 1980.

———. "Recasting Pauline Theology: The Coherence-Contingency Scheme as Interpretive Model." In *Pauline Theology: Thessalonians, Philippians, Galatians, Philemon*. Vol. 1, ed. Jouette M. Bassler, 15-24. Minneapolis: Fortress Press, 1991.

Berger, Peter L. *The Sacred Canopy: Elements of a Sociological Theory of Religion*. New York: Doubleday, 1967.

Berger, Peter L., and Thomas Luckmann. *The Social Construction of Reality*. Garden City: Doubleday & Company, 1966.

Betz, H. D. *Galatians*. Philadelphia: Fortress Press, 1979.

———. "The Problem of Rhetoric and Theology according to the Apostle Paul." In *L'Apotre Paul: Personnaliteé, Style et Conceptions du Ministere*, ed. A. Vanhoye, 16-37. Leuven: Leuven University Press, 1986.

Bickerman, Elias. "The Maccabean Uprising: An Interpretation." In *The Jewish Expression*, ed. J. Goldin, 66-86. New Haven: Yale University Press, 1976.

———. *The God of the Maccabees: Studies on the Meaning and Origin of the Maccabean Revolt*. Leiden: Brill, 1979.

Bilde, Per, Troels Engberg-Pedersen, Lise Hannestad, and Jan Zahle, eds. *Ethnicity in Hellenistic Egypt*. Aarhus: Aarhus University Press, 1992.

Bizzell, Patricia, and Bruce Herzberg, eds. *The Rhetorical Tradition: Readings from Classical Times to the Present*. Boston: Bedford Books, 1990.

Blass, F., and A. Debrunner. *Greek Grammar of the New Testament and Other Early Christian Literature*. Chicago: University of Chicago Press, 1961.

Bledsoe, Albert Taylor. *An Essay on Liberty and Slavery*. Philadelphia: J. B. Lippincott & Co., 1856.

Blount, Brian K. "Response to Reading From This Place, Volumes 1 and 2 and Teaching The Bible." Paper delivered at Annual Meeting of the Society of Biblical Literature in the Committee of Under-represented Racial and Ethnic Minorities in the Profession, Orlando, Florida, November 21-24, 1998.

Boadt, Lawrence. *Reading the Old Testament: An Introduction*. New York: Paulist Press, 1984.

Bockmuehl, Marcus. *The Epistle to the Philippians*. London: A & C Black, 1997.

Boers, Hendrikus. *What Is New Testament Theology?* Philadelphia: Fortress Press, 1979.

————. *The Justification of the Gentiles: Paul's Letters to the Galatians and Romans*. Peabody: Hendrickson Publishers, 1994.

Boissevain, Jeremy. *Friends of Friends: Networks, Manipulators and Coalitions*. Oxford: Basil Blackwell, 1974. Quoted in Vernon K. Robbins, *Exploring the Texture of Texts: A Guide to Socio-Rhetorical Interpretation*, 100. Valley Forge: Trinity Press, 1996.

Borgen, Peder. "Observations on the Theme 'Paul and Philo': Paul's Preaching of Circumcision in Galatia (Gal 5:11) and Debates on Circumcision in Philo." In *The Pauline Literature and Theology*, ed. Sigfred Pedersen, 85-102. Aarhus: Forlaget Aros, 1980.

————. "Philo of Alexandria: A Critical and Synthetic Survey of Research since World War II." In *Aufstieg und Niedergang der römischen Welt* 2.21.1, 98-154. New York: Walther de Gruyeter, 1984.

Bound, J. F. "Who Are the 'Virgins' Discussed in 1 Corinthians 7:25-38?" *Evangelical Journal* 2 (1984): 6-7.

Bousset, Wilhelm. *Kyrios Christos: A History of the Belief in Christ from the Beginning of Christianity to Irenaeus.* Translated by John E. Steely. Nashville: Abingdon Press, 1970.

Boyarin, Daniel. *Intertextuality and the Reading of Midrash.* Bloomington: Indiana University Press, 1990.

———. *A Radical Jew: Paul and the Politics of Identity.* Berkeley: University of California Press, 1994.

Bradley, Keith. *Slavery and Society at Rome.* Cambridge: Cambridge University Press, 1994.

Branick, Vincent. *The House Church in the Writings of Paul.* Wilmington, DE: Michael Glazier, 1989.

Broneer, Oscar. "The Apostle Paul and the Isthmian Games." *Biblical Archaeologist* XXV (1962): 3-31.

Brunt, P. A. "Aristotle and Slavery." In *Studies in Greek History and Thought.* Oxford: Clarendon Press, 1993.

Buckland, W. W. *The Roman Law of Slavery.* Cambridge: Cambridge University Press, 1908.

Bultmann, Rudolf. "New Testament and Mythology." In *Kerygma and Myth*, ed. Reginald Fuller, 1-44. London: SPCK, 1953.

———. "Ist die Apokalyptik die Mutter der christlichen Theologie?: Eine Auseinandersetzung mit Ernst Käsemann." In *Apophereta Festschrift für Ernst Haenchen zu seinem siebzigsten Geburtstag am 10. Dezember 1964.* Berlin: Verlag Alfred Töpelmann, 1964.

Cadbury, H. J. "Erastus of Corinth." *Journal of Biblical Literature* 50 (1931): 42-58.

Callahan, Allen. "A Note on 1 Corinthians 7:21." *The Journal of the Interdenominational Theological Center* XVII (1990): 110-114.

Cannon, Katie Geneva. "Slave Ideology and Biblical Interpretation." In *The Recovery of Black Presence: An Interdisciplinary Exploration*, ed. Randall C. Bailey and Jacquelyn Grant, 119-128. Nashville: Abingdon Press, 1995.

Cantarella, Eva. *Pandora's Daughters: The Role and Status of Women in Greek and Roman Antiquity.* Baltimore: The Johns Hopkins Press, 1987.

Carcopino, J. *Daily Life in Ancient Rome*. New Haven: Yale University Press, 1940.

Cartlidge, David R. "1 Corinthians as a Foundation for a Christian Sex Ethic." *Journal of Religion* 55 (1975): 220-234.

————. "Review of *Paul, The Worldly Ascetic*." *Journal of Biblical Literature* 108 (1989): 355-357.

Castelli, Elizabeth A. *Imitating Paul: A Discourse of Power*. Louisville: Westminster/John Knox Press, 1991.

————. "Allegories of Hagar: Reading Galatians 4:21-31 with Postmodern Feminist Eyes." In *The New Literary Criticism and the New Testament*, ed. Elizabeth Struthers Malbon and Edgar V. McKnight, 228-250. Sheffield: Sheffield Academic Press, 1994.

Chadwick, H. "All Things to All Men." *New Testament Studies* 1 (1955): 261-275.

Cheever, George B. *The Guilt of Slavery and the Crime of Slaveholding Demonstrated from the Hebrew and Greek Scriptures*. Boston: John P. Jewett & Co., 1860. Reprint, New York: Negro University Press, 1969.

Chow, John K. *Patronage and Power: A Study of Social Networks in Corinth*. Sheffield: JSOT Press, 1992.

Cohen, Shaye J. D. *From the Maccabees to the Mishnah*. Philadelphia: Westminster Press, 1987.

————. " 'Those Who Say They Are Jews and Are Not': How Do You Know A Jew in Antiquity When You See One?" In *Diasporas in Antiquity*, ed. Shaye D. Cohen and Ernest S. Frerichs, 1-45. Atlanta: Scholars Press, 1993.

Collins, John J. *Between Athens and Jerusalem: Jewish Identity in the Hellenistic Diaspora*. New York: Crossroad, 1983.

————. "A Symbol of Otherness: Circumcision and Salvation in the First Century." In *"To See Ourselves as Others See Us": Christians, Jews, "Others" in Late Antiquity*, ed. Jacob Neusner and Ernest S. Frerichs, 163-186. Chico, CA: Scholars Press, 1985.

Cone, James H. *The Spirituals and the Blues*. Maryknoll: Orbis Books, 1972.

Conybeare, W. J., and J. S. Howson. *The Life and Epistles of Saint Paul, The People's Edition*. Hartford, CT: S. S. Scranton and Company, 1869.

Conzelmann, Hans. *A Commentary on the First Epistle to the Corinthians*. Philadelphia: Fortress Press, 1975.

Csillag, Pál. *The Augustan Laws on Family Relations*. Budapest: Akádemai Kiadó, 1976.

Danshin, D. I. "Jewish Community of Phanagoria." *Vestnik Drevnei Istorii* 1 (1993): 58-73.

Daube, David. "Two Early Patterns of Manumission." *Journal of Roman Studies* 36 (1946): 57-75.

Davies, W. D. *Paul and Rabbinic Judaism*. London: SPCK, 1948.

——. "Paul and Judaism." In *The Bible in Modern Scholarship*, ed. J. Philip Hyatt, 178-186. Nashville: Abingdon Press, 1965.

Davis, David Brion. *The Problem of Slavery in Western Culture*. Ithaca: Cornell University Press, 1966.

——. *The Problem of Slavery in the Age of Revolution 1770-1823*. Ithaca: Cornell University Press, 1975.

Dawes, Gregory W. "But if you can gain your Freedom: 1 Corinthians 7:17-24." *Catholic Biblical Quarterly* 52 (1990): 681-697.

Dawson, David. *Allegorical Readers and Cultural Revision in Ancient Alexandria*. Berkeley: University of California Press, 1994.

De Boer, Martinus C. "The Composition of 1 Corinthians." *New Testament Studies* 40 (1994): 229-245.

Deissmann, Adolf. *Light from the Ancient East*. New York: G. H. Doran, 1927.

Deming, Will. *Paul on Marriage and Celibacy*. Cambridge: Cambridge University Press, 1996.

——. "The Unity of 1 Corinthians 5-6." *Journal of Biblical Literature* 115 (1996): 289-312.

de Saussure, Ferdinand. *Course in General Linguistics.* Translated by Roy Harris. LaSalle, IL: Open Court, 1986.

Dill. S. *Roman Society from Nero to Marcus Aurelius.* New York: Meridian Books, 1956.

Dodd, C. H. "The Mind of Paul: I and II." In *New Testament Studies.* Manchester: Manchester University Press, 1953.

Doty, William G. *Letters in Primitive Christianity.* Philadelphia: Fortress Press, 1973.

Doughty, Darrell. "The Presence and Future of Salvation in Corinth." *Zeitschrift für die neutestamentliche Wissenschaft* 66 (1975): 61-90.

Duff, A. M. *Freedmen in the Early Roman Empire.* Oxford: Clarendon Press, 1928.

Dulau, P. "The Pauline Privilege: Is It Promulgated in the First Epistle to the Corinthians?" *Catholic Biblical Quarterly* 13 (1951): 146-152.

Dungan, David L. *The Sayings of Jesus in the Churches of Paul: The Use of the Synoptic Tradition in the Regulation of Early Church Life.* Philadelphia: Fortress Press, 1971.

Dunn, James D. G. " 'A Light to the Gentiles,' or 'The End of the Law': The Significance of the Damascus Road Christophany for Paul." In *Jesus, Paul and the Law: Studies in Mark and Galatians.* Louisville: Westminster/John Knox, 1990.

————. "Who Did Paul Think He Was?: A Study of Jewish-Christian Identity." Paper presented at the Society for New Testament Study, Copenhagen, Denmark, July 1998.

Eagleton, Terry. *Literary Theory: An Introduction.* Minneapolis: University of Minnesota Press, 1983.

————. *Ideology.* London: Verso, 1991.

Eilberg-Schwartz, Howard. *God's Phallus: And Other Problems for Men and Monotheism.* Boston: Beacon Press, 1994.

Elliott, John H. *What Is Social Scientific Criticism?* Minneapolis: Fortress Press, 1993.

Elliott, Neil. *Liberating Paul: The Justice of God and the Politics of the Apostle*. New York: Orbis Books, 1994.

Eriksson, Anders. *Traditions as Rhetorical Proof: Pauline Argumentation in 1 Corinthians*. Stockholm: Almqvist & Wiksell International, 1998.

Evans, James H., Jr. "The Bible: A Text for Outsiders." In *We Have Been Believers: An African-American Systematic Theology*. Minneapolis: Fortress Press, 1992.

Fee, Gordon D. *The First Epistle to the Corinthians*. Grand Rapids: William B. Eerdmans Publishing Company, 1987.

———. *Paul's Letter to the Philippians*. Grand Rapids: William B. Eerdmans Publishing Company, 1995.

Feldman, Louis. "How Much Hellenism in Jewish Palestine?" *Hebrew Union College Annual* 57 (1986): 83-111.

———. "Josephus' Attitude toward the Samaritans: A Study in Ambivalence." In *Jewish Sects, Religious Movements, and Political Parties*, ed. Menachem Mor, 22-45. Omaha: Creighton University Press, 1992.

———. *Jew and Gentile in the Ancient World: Attitudes and Interactions from Alexander to Justinian*. Princeton: Princeton University Press, 1993.

———. "Diaspora Synagogues: New Light from Inscriptions and Papyri." In *Sacred Realm: The Emergence of the Synagogue in the Ancient World*, ed. Steven Fine, 48-66. Oxford: Oxford University Press, 1996.

Ferguson, Everett. *Backgrounds of Early Christianity*, 2d ed. Grand Rapids: William B. Eerdmans Publishing Company, 1993.

Filson, Floyd. "The Significance of the Early House Churches." *Journal of Biblical Literature* 58 (1939): 105-112.

Finley, M. I., ed. *Slavery in Classical Antiquity: Views and Controversies*. Cambridge: W. Heffer & Sons, 1960.

———. *Ancient Slavery and Modern Ideology*. New York: Viking Press, 1980.

Fish, Stanley. *Is There A Text In This Class?* Cambridge, MA: Harvard University Press, 1980.

Fishbane, Michael. *Biblical Interpretation in Ancient Israel*. Oxford: Clarendon Press, 1985.

Fitzgerald, J. T. *Cracks in an Earthen Vessel: An Examination of the Catalogue of Hardships in the Corinthian Correspondence*. Atlanta: Scholars Press, 1988.

Foerster, Werner. "σῴζω." In *Theological Dictionary of the New Testament*. Vol. 7, 989-998. Grand Rapids: William B. Eerdmans Publishing Company, 1971.

Ford, J. M. "Levirate Marriage in St. Paul (1 Cor vii)." *New Testament Studies* 10 (1963): 361-365.

Fredriksen, Paula. "Judaism, the Circumcision of Gentiles, and Apocalyptic Hope: Another Look at Galatians 1 and 2." *The Journal of Theological Studies* 42 (1991): 532-564.

Frei, Hans. *The Eclipse of Biblical Narrative: A Study of Eighteenth and Nineteenth Century Hermeneutics*. New Haven: Yale University Press, 1974.

Friedländer, L. *Roman Life and Manners under the Early Empire*. London: Routledge and Kegan Paul, 1907.

Froehlich, Karlfried. " 'Always to Keep to the Literal Sense in Holy Scripture Means to Kill One's Soul': The State of Biblical Hermeneutics at the Beginning of the Fifteenth Century." In *Literary Uses of Typology*, ed. Earl Miner, 20-48. Princeton: Princeton University Press, 1977.

Fuller, Richard, and Francis Wayland. *Domestic Slavery Considered as a Scriptural Institution: In a Correspondence between the Rev. Richard Fuller and the Rev. Francis Wayland*. New York: Sheldon & Company, 1860.

Furnish, Victor Paul. "Corinth in Paul's Time—What Can Archaeology Tell Us?" *Biblical Archaeology Review* Vol. XV (1988): 14-27.

Gager, John G. "Functional Diversity in Paul's Use of End Time Language." *Journal of Biblical Literature* 89 (1970): 325-337.

———. "Jews, Gentiles, and Synagogues in the Book of Acts." *Harvard Theological Review* 79 (1986): 91-99.

Garnsey, Peter. *Social Status and Legal Privilege in the Roman Empire*. Oxford: Clarendon Press, 1970.

Garnsey, Peter, and Richard Saller. *The Roman Empire: Economy, Society and Culture*. London: Duckworth, 1987.

Genovese, Eugene. " 'Slavery Ordained of God': The Southern Slaveholders' View of Biblical History and Modern Politics," 7-29. Gettysburg: Gettysburg College, 1985.

George, Carol V. R. "Widening the Circle: The Black Church and the Abolitionist Crusade." In *African American Religion*, ed. Timothy E. Fulop and Albert J. Raboteau, 153-173. New York: Routledge, 1997.

Given, Mark D. "True Rhetoric: Ambiguity, Cunning and Deception in Pauline Discourse." In *Society of Biblical Literature Seminar Papers*, 526-550. Atlanta: Scholars Press, 1997.

Goudriaan, Koen. "Ethnical Strategies in Graeco-Roman Egypt." In *Ethnicity in Hellenistic Egypt*, ed. Per Bilde, Troels Engberg-Pedersen, Lise Hannestad, and Jan Zahle, 74-99. Aarhus: Aarhus University Press, 1992.

Grant, Robert M. *A Short History of the Interpretation of the Bible*. Philadelphia: Fortress Press, 1984.

Green, Peter. "The Spread of Hellenism: Explorations, Assimilation, Colonialism; Or the Dog that Barked in the Night." In *Alexander to Actium: The Historical Evolution of the Hellenistic Age*. Berkeley: University of California Press, 1990.

Hall, Robert G. "Epispasm and the Dating of Ancient Jewish Writings." *Journal for the Study of the Pseudepigrapha* 2 (1988): 71-86.

Harding, Vincent. "Religion and Resistance among Antebellum Slaves, 1800-1860." In *African American Religion*, ed. Timothy E. Fulop and Albert J. Raboteau, 107-130. New York: Routledge, 1997.

Harrill, J. A. *The Manumission of Slaves in Early Christianity*. Tübingben: J. C. B. Mohr, 1995.

Hatch, Edwin, and Henry A. Redpath. *A Concordance to the Septuagint*, 2d edition. Grand Rapids: Baker Books, 1998.

Hays, Richard B. *The Echoes of Scripture in the Letters of Paul*. New Haven: Yale University Press, 1989.

——. *1 Corinthians*. Louisville: John Knox Press, 1997.

Hendricks, Osayande Obery. "Guerilla Exegesis: 'Struggle' as a Scholarly Vocation." *Semeia* 72 (1995): 73-90.

Hengel, Martin. *Judaism and Hellenism*. Philadelphia: Fortress Press, 1974.

Hock, Ronald. *The Social Context of Paul's Ministry: Tentmaking and Apostleship*. Philadelphia: Fortress Press, 1980.

Hock, Ronald, and Edward N. O'Neil, eds. *The Chreia in Ancient Rhetoric*. Vol I. Atlanta: Scholars Press, 1986.

Hodgson, Peter. *The Formation of Historical Theology*. New York: Harper & Row Publishers, 1966.

Holladay, Carl R. *The First Letter of Paul to the Corinthians*. Abilene: ACU Press, 1979.

——. "Jewish Responses to Hellenistic Culture in Early Ptolemaic Egypt." In *Ethnicity in Hellenistic Egypt*, ed. Per Bilde, Troels Engberg-Pedersen, Lise Hannestad, and Jan Zahle, 139-163. Aarhus: Aarhus University Press, 1992.

——. "Paul and His Predecessors in the Diaspora: Some Reflections on Ethnic Identity in the Fragmentary Hellenistic Jewish Authors." Paper presented at the Society for New Testament Study, Copenhagen, Denmark, July 1998.

Hopkins, Dwight N. "Slave Theology in the 'Invisible Institution.' " In *Cut Loose Your Stammering Tongue: Black Theology in the Slave Narratives*. Maryknoll: Orbis Books, 1991.

Hopkins, Keith. *Conquerors and Slaves: Sociological Studies in Roman History*. Cambridge: Cambridge University Press, 1978.

Hornblower, Simon, and Anthony Spawforth, eds. *Oxford Classical Dictionary*, 3d Edition. Oxford: Oxford University Press, 1996.

Horsley, Richard A. "1 Corinthians: A Case Study of Paul's Assembly." In *Paul and Empire: Religion and Power in Roman Imperial Society*. Harrisburg: Trinity Press, 1997.

Hurd, John Coolidge, Jr. *The Origin of 1 Corinthians*. New York: Seabury Press, 1965.

Iser, Wolfgang. *The Act of Reading: A Theory of Aesthetic Response*. Baltimore: Johns Hopkins University Press, 1978.

Johnson, Luke Timothy. *The Writings of the New Testament: An Interpretation*. Philadelphia: Fortress Press, 1986.

————. *The Acts of the Apostles*. Collegeville: Liturgical Press, 1992.

Jones, Amos, Jr. *Paul's Message of Freedom: What Does It Mean to the Black Church?* Valley Forge: Judson Press, 1984.

Judge, E. A. *The Social Pattern of Christian Groups in the First Century*. London: Tyndale, 1960.

Kaplan, L. "And the Lord Sought to Kill Him" (Exodus 4:24) Yet Once Again." *Hebrew Annual Review* 5 (1981): 65-74.

Käsemann, Ernst. "On the Subject of Primitive Christian Apocalyptic." In *New Testament Questions of Today*. London: SPCK, 1969.

Keener, Craig S. *And Marries Another: Divorce and Remarriage in the New Testament*. Peabody: Hendrickson Publishers, 1991.

————. *Paul, Women and Wives: Marriage and Women's Ministry in the Letters of Paul*. Peabody: Hendrickson Publishers, 1992.

Kelsey, David H. *The Uses of Scripture in Recent Theology*. Philadelphia: Fortress Press, 1975.

Kent, John Harvey. *The Inscriptions, 1926-1950. Corinth*. Princeton: American School of Classical Studies at Athens, 1966.

Kerkeslager, Allen. "Maintaining Jewish Identity in the Greek Gymnasium: A 'Jewish Load' in CPJ 3.519." *Journal for the Study of Judaism* XXVIII (1997): 12-33.

Kim, S. *The Origin of Paul's Gospel*. Grand Rapids: William B. Eerdmans Publishing Company, 1982.

Kloppenburg, John S., and Stephen G. Wilson. *Voluntary Associations in the Graeco-Roman World*. London: Routledge, 1996.

Koch, Klaus. "What is Apocalyptic? An Attempt at a Preliminary Definition." In *Visionaries and Their Apocalypses*, ed. Paul Hanson, 16-36. Philadelphia: Fortress Press, 1983.

Kraabel, A. T. "The Diaspora Synagogue: Archaeological and Epigraphic Evidence since Sukenik." In *Aufstieg und Niedergang der römischen Welt*, 19.1, 479-510. New York: Walther de Gruyeter, 1979.

———. "The Disappearance of the 'God-fearers.' " *Numen* 28 (1981): 113-126.

Kraftchick, Steven J. "Seeking a More Fluid Model: A Response to Jouette M. Bassler." In *Pauline Theology: 1 & 2 Corinthians*. Vol. 2, ed. David M. Hay, 18-34. Minneapolis: Fortress Press, 1993.

———. "Facing Janus: Reviewing the Biblical Theology Movement." In *Biblical Theology: Problems and Perspectives*, ed. Steven J. Kraftchick, Charles D. Myers, Jr., and Ben C. Ollenburger. Nashville: Abingdon Press, 1995.

Krentz, Edgar. *The Historical-Critical Method*. Philadelphia: Fortress Press, 1975.

Kruse, Colin G. *Paul, the Law, and Justification*. Peabody: Hendrickson Publishers, 1996.

Kubo, Sakae. "I Corinthians VII. 16: Optimistic or Pessimistic?" *New Testament Studies* 24 (1978): 539-544.

Lapin, Hayim. "Locating Ethnicity and Religious Community in Later Roman Palestine." Paper presented at Annual Meeting of the Society of Biblical Literature in the Constructs of Social and Cultural Worlds of Antiquity Group, San Francisco, CA, November 22-25, 1997.

Levine, Lee I. "The Second Temple Synagogue: The Formative Years." In *The Synagogue in Late Antiquity*. Philadelphia: The American Schools of Oriental Research, 1987.

Levinskaya, Irina. "A Jewish or Gentile Prayer House?: The Meaning of ΠΡΟΣΕΥΧΗ." *Tyndale Bulletin* 41 (1990): 154-159.

Lewis, Charlton T. *A Latin Dictionary*. Oxford: Clarendon Press, 1879.

Lewis, Naphtali, and Meyer Reinhold, eds. *Roman Civilization: Selected Readings*. Vol. 1, 3d edition. New York: Columbia University Press, 1990.

Lippy, Charles H. "The Religious Experience of Southern Blacks: Black-White Interaction in Southern Religion." In *Bibliography of Religion in the South*. Macon: Mercer University Press, 1985.

Longenecker, Richard N. *Galatians*. Dallas: Word Books, 1990.

Lüdemann, Gerd. *Early Christianity according to the Traditions in Acts*. Minneapolis: Fortress Press, 1989.

Macdonald, Margaret Y. "Women Holy in Body and Spirit: The Social Setting of 1 Corinthians 7." *New Testament Studies* 36 (1990): 161-181.

Mack, Burton L. *Rhetoric and the New Testament*. Minneapolis: Fortress Press, 1990.

Maclennan, Robert S. "In Search of the Jewish Diaspora: A First-Century Synagogue in Crimea?" *Biblical Archaeolgy Review* 22 (1996): 44-51, 69.

MacMullen, Ramsey. *Roman Social Relations, 50 B.C. to A.D. 284*. New Haven: Yale University Press, 1974.

Malherbe, Abraham J. "House Churches and Their Problems." In *Social Aspects of Early Christianity*, 2d edition. Philadelphia: Fortress Press, 1983.

———, ed. *Moral Exhortation: A Greco-Roman Sourcebook*. Philadelphia: Westminister Press, 1986.

———. "A Physical Description of Paul." *Harvard Theological Review* 79 (1986): 170-175.

———. "Determinism and Free Will in Paul: The Argument of 1 Corinthians 8 and 9." In *Paul in his Hellenistic Context*, ed. Troels Engberg-Pedersen, 231-255. Minneapolis: Fortress Press, 1995.

Malina, Bruce. *The New Testament World: Insights from Cultural Anthropology*. Louisville: Westminster/John Knox Press, 1993.

Manson, T. W. "The Corinthian Correspondence." In *Studies in the Gospels and Epistles*. Manchester: Manchester University Press, 1962.

Martin, Clarice J. "The Haustafeln (Household Codes) in African American Biblical Interpretation: 'Free Slaves' and 'Subordinate Women.' " In *Stoney the Road We Trod: African American Biblical Interpretation*, ed. Cain Hope Felder, 206-231. Minneapolis: Fortress Press, 1991.

Martin, Dale B. *Slavery as Salvation: The Metaphor of Slavery in Pauline Christianity*. New Haven: Yale University Press, 1990.

————. *The Corinthian Body*. New Haven: Yale University Press, 1995.

McEleney, Neil J. "Conversion, Circumcision and the Law." *New Testament Studies* 20 (1974): 319-341.

McKnight, Edgar V. *Postmodern Use of the Bible: The Emergence of Reader-Oriented Criticism*. Nashville: Abingdon Press, 1988.

Meeks, Wayne A. "The Christian Proteus." In *The Writings of St. Paul*. New Haven: Yale University Press, 1972.

————. "The Image of the Androgyne: Some Uses of a Symbol in Earliest Christianity." *History of Religions* 13 (1973): 165-208.

————. *The First Urban Christians: The Social World of the Apostle Paul*. New Haven: Yale University Press, 1983.

————. *The Moral World of the First Christians*. Philadelphia: Westminister Press, 1986.

Metzger, Bruce M. *A Textual Commentary on the Greek New Testament*, 3d edition. Stuggart: United Bible Societies, 1975.

Meyer, Paul W. "Pauline Theology: A Proposal for a Pause in its Pursuit." In *Pauline Theology: Looking Back, Pressing On*. Vol. 4, ed. E. Elizabeth Johnson and David M. Hay, 140-160. Atlanta: Scholars Press, 1997.

Meyer, Rudolf. "περιτέμνω." In *Theological Dictionary of the New Testament*. Vol. 6, 72-84. Grand Rapids: William B. Eerdmans Publishing Company, 1968.

Miall, David S., ed. *Metaphor: Problems and Perspectives*. Sussex, NJ: Harvester Press, 1982.

Mitchell, Henry H. *Black Preaching*. Philadelphia: J. B. Lippincott, 1979.

Mitchell, Margaret. *Paul and the Rhetoric of Reconciliation: A n Exegetical Investigation of the Language and Composition of 1 Corinthians.* Tübingen: J. C. B. Mohr, 1991.

Morgan, Robert. "New Testament Theology." In *Biblical Theology: Problems and Perspectives,* ed. Steven J. Kraftchick, Charles D. Myers, Jr., and Ben C. Ollenburger, 104-130. Nashville: Abingdon Press, 1995.

Morgan, Robert, with John Barton. *Biblical Interpretation.* Oxford: Oxford University Press, 1988.

Morrison, Larry R. "The Religious Defense of American Slavery Before 1830." *The Journal of Religious Thought* 37 (1980): 16-29.

Moule, C. F. D. *An Idiom Book of New Testament Greek.* Cambridge: Cambridge University Press, 1953.

Moulton, James Hope, and George Milligan, eds. *The Vocabulary of the Greek New Testament.* Grand Rapids: William B. Eerdmans Publishing Company, 1930.

Moxnes, Halvor. "Honor and Shame." In *The Social Sciences and N e w Testament Interpretation,* ed. Richard Rohrbaugh, 19-40. Peabody: Hendrickson Publishers, 1996.

Murphy-O'Connor, Jerome. "Works Without Faith in I Cor., VII 14." *Revue Biblique* 84 (1977): 349-361.

————. "The Divorced Woman in 1 Cor 7:10-11." *Journal of Biblical Literature* 100 (1981): 601-606.

————. *St. Paul's Corinth: Texts and Archaeology.* Wilmington: Michael Glazier, 1983.

————. "The Corinth that Saint Paul Saw." *Biblical Archaeologist* 47 (1984): 147-159.

————. "House Churches and the Eucharist." *The Bible Today* 22 (1984): 32-38.

————. "Corinth." In *Anchor Bible Dictionary.* Vol. I., 1134-1139. New York: Doubleday, 1992.

Neyrey, Jerome H. *Paul, In Other Words: A Cultural Reading of His Letters.* Louisville: Westminster/John Knox Press, 1990.

Nolland, John. "Uncircumcised Proselytes?" *Journal for the Study of Judaism* XII (1981): 173-194.

O'Brien, Peter T. *The Epistle to the Philippians*. Grand Rapids: William B. Eerdmans Publishing Company, 1991.

O'Day, Gail. "Jeremiah 9:22-23 and 1 Corinthians 1:26-31: A Study in Intertextuality." *Journal of Biblical Literature* 109 (1990): 259-267.

Orr, William F., and James Arthur Walther. *1 Corinthians*. Doubleday: New York, 1976.

Osiek, Carolyn. *What Are They Saying about the Social Setting of the New Testament?* New York: Paulist Press, 1992.

Oster, Richard E. "Use, Misuse and Neglect of Archaeological Evidence in Some Modern Works on 1 Corinthians: (1 Cor 7,1-5; 8,10; 11,2-16; 12,14-26)." *Zeitschrift für die Neutestamentliche Wissenschaft* 83 (1992): 52-73.

———. "Supposed Anachronism in Luke-Acts' Use of ΣΥΝΑΓΩΓΗ." *New Testament Studies* 39 (1993): 178-208.

Patterson, Orlando. *Slavery and Social Death: A Comparative Study*. Cambridge, MA: Harvard University Press, 1982.

———. *Freedom in the Making of Western Culture*. Vol. I. New York: Harper Collins, 1991.

Pitts-River, Julian. "Honor." In *Encyclopedia of the Social Sciences*, 2d edition, vol. 6. New York: Macmillan Company, 1968, 505. Quoted in Orlando Patterson, *Slavery and Social Death*, 80. Cambridge, MA: Harvard University Press, 1982.

Plummer, Reinhard. "Samaritan Synagogues and Jewish Synagogues: Similarities and Differences." In *Jews, Christians and Polytheists in the Ancient Synagogue: Cultural Interaction during the Greco-Roman Period*, ed. Steven Fine, 118-160. London: Routledge, 1999.

Pogoloff, Stephen M. *Logos and Sophia: The Rhetorical Situation of 1 Corinthians*. Atlanta: Scholars Press, 1992.

Poirier, John C., and Joseph Frankovic. "Celibacy and Charism in 1 Cor 7:5-7." *Harvard Theological Review* 89 (1996): 1-18.

Pomeroy, Sarah B. *Goddesses, Whores, Wives and Slaves: Women in Classical Antiquity*. New York: Schocken Books, 1975.

Procksch, Otto. "ἅγιος." In *Theological Dictionary of the New Testament*. Vol. 1, 88-97, 100-115. Grand Rapids: William B. Eerdmans Publishing Company, 1964.

Purvis, James D. "The Samaritans and Judaism." In *Early Judaism and Its Modern Interpreters*, ed. R. A. Kraft and G. W. E. Nickelsburg, 81-98. Atlanta: Scholars Press, 1986.

Raboteau, Albert J. *Slave Religion: The "Invisible Institution" in the Antebellum South*. Oxford: Oxford University Press, 1978.

Rajak, Tessa. "Jews and Christians as Groups in a Pagan World." In *"To See Ourselves as Others See Us": Christians, Jews, "Others" in Late Antiquity*, ed. Jacob Neusner and Ernest S. Frerichs, 245-262. Chico, CA: Scholars Press, 1985.

Ramsaran, Rollin A. *Liberating Words: Paul's Use of Rhetorical Maxims in 1 Corinthians 1-10*. Valley Forge: Trinity Press, 1996.

Richardson, Peter. " 'I Say not the Lord': Personal Opinion, Apostolic Authority, and the Development of Early Christian Halakah." *Tyndale Bulletin* 31 (1980): 65-86.

————. "Pauline Inconsistency: 1 Corinthians 9:19-23 and Galatians 2:11-14." *New Testament Studies* 26 (1980): 347-362.

Robbins, Vernon K. "The Social Location of the Implied Author of Luke-Acts." In *The Social World of Luke-Acts: Models for Interpretation*, ed. J. H. Neyrey, 305-332. Peabody: Hendrickson Publishers, 1991.

————. *Exploring the Texture of Texts: A Guide to Socio-Rhetorical Interpretation*. Valley Forge: Trinity Press, 1996.

————. *The Tapestry of Early Christian Discourse: Rhetoric, Society and Ideology*. New York: Routledge, 1996.

Robertson, Archibald, and Alfred Plummer. *The First Epistle of St. Paul to the Corinthians*. Edinburgh: T & T Clark, 1914.

Robinson, Robert B. "Introduction to Textual Determinacy: Part Two." *Semeia* 71 (1995): 7-16.

Ross, Fred. *Slavery Ordained of God*. Philadelphia: J. B. Lippincott, 1859. Reprint, New York: Negro Universities Press, 1969.

Rostovtzeff, M. I. *Social and Economic History of the Hellenistic World*. Oxford: Oxford University Press, 1986.

Rowland, Christopher. *The Open Heaven: A Study of Apocalyptic and Judaism in Christianity*. London: SPCK, 1982.

Runia, David T. "How to read Philo." In *Exegesis and Philosophy: Studies on Philo of Alexandria*. Brookfield: Variorum, 1990.

Sacks, Sheldon, ed. *On Metaphor*. Chicago: University of Chicago Press, 1978.

Saller, Richard. "Slavery and the Roman Family." *Slavery and Abolition* 8 (1987): 65-87.

Sanders, E. P. *Paul and Palestinian Judaism*. Philadelphia: Fortress Press, 1977.

———. *Paul, the Law and the Jewish People*. Minneapolis: Fortress Press, 1983.

Sanders, Jack T. "Paul Between Jews and Gentiles in Corinth." *Journal for the Study of the New Testament* 65 (1997): 67-83.

Sandmel, Samuel. "Philo Judaeus: An Introduction to the Man, his Writings and his Significance." In *Aufstieg und Niedergang der römischen Welt* 2.21.1, 3-46. New York: Walther de Gruyeter, 1984.

Sapir, J. David, and J. Christopher Crocker, eds. *The Social Use of Metaphor*. Philadelphia: University of Pennsylvania Press, 1977.

Sasson, Jack. "Circumcision in the Ancient Near East." *Journal of Biblical Literature* 85 (1966): 473-476.

Schäfer, Peter. *Judeophobia*. Cambridge, MA: Harvard University Press, 1997.

Schiffman, Lawrence. *Who Was a Jew?: Rabbinic and Halakhic Perspectives on the Jewish Christian Schism*. Hoboken: Ktav Publishing House, 1985.

———. *From Text to Tradition: A History of Second Temple and Rabbinic Judaism*. Hoboken: Ktav Publishing House, 1991.

Schlier, Heinrich. "ἐλεύθερος." In *Theological Dictionary of the New Testament*. Vol. 2, 487-502. Grand Rapids: William B. Eerdmans Publishing Company, 1964.

Schmidt, K. L. "ἀκροβυστία." In *Theological Dictionary of the New Testament*. Vol. 1, 225-226. Grand Rapids: William B. Eerdmans Publishing Company, 1964.

Schrage, Wolfgang. "Die Stellung zur Welt bei Paulus, Epiktet, und in der Apokalyptik: Ein Beitrag zu 1 Kor 7, 29-31." *Zeitschrift für Theologie und Kirche* 61 (1964): 125-154.

Schrenk, G. "ἐκλέγομαι." In *Theological Dictionary of the New Testament*. Vol. 4, 168-192. Grand Rapids: William B. Eerdmans Publishing Company, 1967.

Schüssler Fiorenza, Elisabeth. *In Memory of Her: A Feminist Theological Reconstruction of Christian Origins*. New York: Crossroad, 1983.

———. "Rhetorical Situation and Historical Reconstruction in 1 Corinthians." *New Testament Studies* 33 (1987): 386-404.

———. *But She Said: Feminist Practices of Biblical Interpretation*. Boston: Beacon Press, 1992.

Schweitzer, Albert. *The Mysticism of Paul the Apostle*. New York: Seabury Press, 1931.

Segal, Alan. *Paul the Convert: The Apostolate and Apostasy of Saul the Pharisee*. New Haven: Yale University Press, 1990.

Segovia, Fernando F. "And They Began to Speak in Tongues": Competing Modes of Discourse in Contemporary Biblical Criticism." In *Reading from This Place*, vol. 1, ed. Fernando F. Segovia and Mary Ann Tolbert, 1-32. Minneapolis: Fortress Press, 1995.

Seifrid, M. A. "In Christ." In *Dictionary of Paul and His Letters*, ed. Gerald F. Hawthorne, Ralph P. Martin, and Daniel G. Reid, 433-436. Downers Grove, IL: Intervarsity Press, 1993.

Shanks, Carolyn L. "The Biblical Anti-Slavery Argument of the Decade 1830-1840." *The Journal of Negro History* 16 (1931): 132-157.

Sharp, Granville. "An Essay on Slavery: Proving from Scripture Its Inconsistency with Humanity and Religion." In *Tracts on Slavery and Liberty: The Just Limitations of Slavery in the Laws of God, The Law of Passive Obedience, The Law of Liberty.* London: 1776. Reprint Westport, CT: Negro Universities Press, 1969.

Sherwin-White, A. N. *The Roman Citizenship.* Oxford: Clarendon Press, 1939.

————. *Roman Society and Roman Law in the New Testament.* Oxford: Oxford University Press, 1963.

Smallwood, E. M. "The Legislation of Hadrian and Antoninus Pius against Circumcision." *Latomus* 18 (1959): 334-347.

Smith, D. E. "The Egyptian Cults at Corinth." *Harvard Theological Review* 70 (1977): 201-231.

Smith, John David. *Black Slavery in the Americas: An Interdisciplinary Bibliography, 1865-1980.* 2 Vols. Westport, CN: Greenwood Press, 1982.

Smith, Jonathan Z. "Fences and Neighbors: Some Contours of Early Judaism." In *Imagining Religion: From Babylon to Jonestown.* Chicago: University of Chicago Press, 1982.

Smith, Theophus H. *Conjuring Culture: Biblical Formations of Black America.* New York: Oxford University Press, 1994.

Smith, Timothy L. "Slavery and Theology: The Emergence of Black Christian Consciousness in Nineteenth Century America." *Church History* 41 (1972): 497-512.

Soskice, Janet Martin. *Metaphor and Religious Language.* Oxford: Clarendon Press, 1985.

Speiser, E. A. *Genesis.* Garden City: Doubleday, 1983.

Stambaugh, John E. "Social Relations in the City of the Early Principate." In *Society of Biblical Literature Seminar Papers*, 75-99. Chico, CA: Scholars Press, 1980.

Stambaugh, John E., and David Balch. *The New Testament in its Social Environment.* Philadelphia: Westminster Press, 1986.

Stanley, Christopher. " 'Neither Jew nor Greek': Ethnic Conflict in Graeco-Roman Society." *Journal for the Study of the New Testament* 64 (1996): 101-124.

Ste. Croix, G. E. M. de. *The Class Struggles in the Ancient World from the Archaic Age to the Arab Conquest*. London: Duckworth, 1981.

Stein, R. H. "Jerusalem." In *Dictionary of Paul and His Letters*, ed. Gerald F. Hawthorne, Ralph P. Martin, and Daniel G. Reid, 463-474. Downers Grove, IL: Intervarsity Press, 1993.

Stendahl, Krister. "The Apostle Paul and the Introspective Conscience of the West." In *Paul Among Jews and Gentiles*. Philadelphia: Fortress Press, 1976.

Stowers, Stanley K. *Letter Writing in Greco-Roman Antiquity*. Philadelphia: Westminster Press, 1986.

Stuhlmacher, Peter. *Historical Criticism and Theological Interpretation*. Translated by Roy A. Harrisville. Philadelphia: Fortress Press, 1977.

Suleiman, Susan R., and Inge Crossman, eds. *The Reader in the Text: Essays on Audience and Interpretation*. Princeton: Princeton University Press, 1980.

Tcherikover, Victor. *Hellenistic Civilization and the Jews*. Philadelphia: Jewish Publication Society of America, 1959.

Theissen, Gerd. *The Social Setting of Pauline Christianity: Essays on Corinth*. Philadelphia: Fortress Press, 1982.

———. *Psychological Aspects of Pauline Theology*. Philadelphia: Fortress Press, 1987.

Thiselton, Anthony C. *New Horizons in Hermeneutics*. Grand Rapids: Zondervan Publishing House, 1992.

Thomas, Herman E. *James W. C. Pennington: African American Churchman and Abolitionist*. New York: Garland Publishing, 1995.

Thurman, Howard. *Jesus and the Disinherited*. Nashville: Abingdon Press, 1949.

Treggiari, Susan. *Roman Freedmen during the Late Republic*. Oxford: Clarendon Press, 1969.

Vanhoozer, Kevin J. *Is There A Meaning in This Text?* Grand Rapids: Zondervan Publishing House, 1998.

Van Unnik, Willem C. *Tarsus or Jerusalem: The City of Paul's Youth.* London: Epworth Press, 1962.

Vlastos, Gregory. "Slavery in Plato's Thought." In *Slavery in Classical Antiquity: Views and Controversies,* ed. Moses I. Finley, 133-149. Cambridge: W. Heffer & Sons, 1960.

Vogt, J. *Ancient Slavery and the Ideal of Man.* Oxford: Basil Blackwell, 1974.

Wallace-Hadrill, Andrew. "Patronage in Roman Society: from Republic to Empire." In *Patronage in Ancient Society.* London: Routledge, 1989.

Warren, E. W. *Nellie Norton: or Southern Slavery and the Bible: A Scriptural Refutation of the Principal Arguments upon which the Abolitionists Rely: A Vindication of Southern Slavery from the Old and New Testaments.* Macon: Burke, Boykin & Company, 1864.

Watson, Alan. "Roman Slave Law and Romanist Ideology." *Phoenix* 37 (1983): 53-65.

———, ed. *Digest.* Philadelphia: University of Pennsylvania, 1985.

———. *Roman Slave Law.* Baltimore: Johns Hopkins University Press, 1987.

Watson, Duane F. "Paul's Rhetorical Strategy in 1 Corinthians 15." In *Rhetoric and the New Testament: Essays from the 1992 Heidelberg Conference,* ed. Stanley E. Porter and Thomas H. Olbricht, 231-249. Sheffield: Sheffield Academic Press, 1993.

Wayland, Francis. *A Memoir of the Life and Labors of Francis Wayland.* New York: Arno Press, 1972.

Wedderburn, A. J. M. "Some Observations on Paul's Use of the Phrases 'in Christ' and 'with Christ.' " *Journal for the Study of the New Testament* 25 (1985): 83-97.

White, Michael L. "The Delos Synagogue Revisited: Recent Fieldwork in the Graeco-Roman Diaspora." *Harvard Theological Review* 80 (1987): 133-160.

———. *Building God's House in the Roman World.* Baltimore: Johns Hopkins University Press, 1990.

Wiedemann, T. *Greek and Roman Slavery*. Baltimore: Johns Hopkins University Press, 1981.

Wilken, Robert L. *The Christians as the Romans Saw Them*. New Haven: Yale University Press, 1984.

Willert, Niels. "The Catalogues of Hardships in the Pauline Correspondences: Background and Function." In *The New Testament and Hellenistic Judaism*, ed. Peder Borgen and Søren Giversen, 217-243. Peabody: Hendrickson Publishers, 1995.

Willis, Wendell. "An Apostolic Apologia: The Form and Function of 1 Corinthians 9." *Journal for the Study of the New Testament* 24 (1985): 33-48.

Wilmore, Gayraud. *Black Religion and Black Radicalism: An Interpretation of the Religious History of Afro-American People*. Maryknoll: Orbis Books, 1983.

Wimbush, Vincent L. *Paul, The Worldly Ascetic: Response to the World and Self-Understanding according to 1 Corinthians*. Macon: Mercer University Press, 1987.

————. "The Bible and African Americans: An Outline of an Interpretive History." In *Stony the Road We Trod: African American Biblical Interpretation*, ed. Cain Hope Felder, 81-97. Minneapolis: Fortress Press, 1991.

Winston, David. *Philo of Alexandria: The Contemplative Life, The Giants, and Selections*. New York: Paulist Press, 1981.

Wire, Antoinette. *The Corinthian Women Prophets: A Reconstruction through Paul's Rhetoric*. Minneapolis: Fortress Press, 1990.

Wisemann, James. "Corinth and Rome I: 228 B. C.-A. D. 267." In *Aufstieg und Niedergang der römischen Welt*, 7.1, 438-548. New York: Walther de Gruyeter, 1979.

Witherington, Ben. *Paul's Narrative Thought World: The Tapestry of Tragedy and Triumph*. Louisville: Westminster/John Knox Press, 1994.

————. *Conflict & Community in Corinth: A Socio-Rhetorical Commentary on 1 and 2 Corinthians*. Grand Rapids: William B. Eerdmans Publishing Company, 1995.

——. *The Paul Quest: The Renewed Search for the Jew of Tarsus*. Downers Grove, IL: Intervarsity Press, 1998.

Wuellner, Wilhelm. "The Sociological Implications of 1 Corinthians 1:26-28 Reconsidered." In *Studia Evangelica* VI, ed. E. A. Livingstone, 666-672. Berlin: Akademie, 1973.

——. "Greek Rhetoric and Pauline Argumentation." In *Early Christian Literature and the Classical Intellectual Tradition: In honorem Robert M. Grant*, ed. W. R. Schoedel and R. L. Wilken, 177-188. Paris: Editions Beauchesne, 1979.

——. "Biblical Exegesis in the light of the History and Historicity of Rhetoric and the Nature of the Rhetoric of Religion." In *Rhetoric and the New Testament: Essays from the 1992 Heidelberg Conference*, ed. Stanley E. Porter and Thomas H. Olbricht, 492-513. Sheffield: Sheffield Academic Press, 1993.

Yarbrough, O. Larry. *Not Like the Gentiles: Marriage Rules in the Letters of Paul*. Atlanta: Scholars Press, 1985.

Young, Brad H. *Paul the Jewish Theologian. A Pharisee among Christians, Jews, and Gentiles*. Peabody: Hendrickson Publishers, 1998.

PRIMARY TEXTS INCLUDING TRANSLATIONS

Acts of Paul and Thecla. In *New Testament Apocrypha*. Vol. 2, ed. Wilhelm Schneemelcher. Philadelphia: Westminster Press, 1964.

The Apostolic Fathers: Clement, Ignatius, and Polycarp. 2 Vols. Translated by J. B. Lightfoot. Grand Rapids: Baker Book House, 1981.

Aristotle. *The Art of Rhetoric*. Tranlated by John Henry Freese. Cambridge, MA: Harvard University Press, 1926.

——. *Politics*. Translated by H. Rackham. Cambridge, MA: Harvard University Press, 1935.

Artemidorus. *The Interpretation of Dreams*. Translated by Robert J. White. Park Ridge: Noyes Press, 1975.

Augustine. *On Christian Doctrine*. Translated by. D. W. Robertson, Jr. New York: Macmillan Publishing Company, 1958.

The Babylonian Talmud, ed. I. Epstein. London: Soncino Press, 1936.

Corpus of Jewish Inscriptions, ed. Jean-Baptiste Frey. Revised by Baruch Lifshitz. New York: Ktav Publishing House, 1975.

Corpus Papyrorum Judaicarum. 3 Vols., ed. Victor A. Tcherikover and Alexander Fuks. Cambridge, MA: Harvard University Press, 1957-1964.

Dio Cassius. *Roman Histories*. 9 Vols. Translated by Earnest Cary. Cambridge, MA: Harvard University Press, 1914-1927.

Dio Chrysostom. *Discourses*. 5 Vols. Translated by J. W. Cohoon. Cambridge, MA: Harvard University Press, 1932-1951.

Diodorus Siculus. 12 Vols. Translated by C. H. Oldfather et al. Cambridge, MA: Harvard University Press, 1933-1976.

Epictetus. *Discourses as reported by Arrian*. 2 Vols. Trans. W. A. Oldfather. Cambridge, MA: Harvard University Press, 1925-1928.

The Epistles of St. Clement of Rome and St. Ignatius of Antioch. Translated by James A. Kleist. New York: Paulist Press, 1946.

Gaius. *The Institutes of Gaius*. 2 Vols. Translated by Francis de Zulueta. Oxford: Clarendon Press, 1946-1953.

The Greek New Testament. 4th revised edition. Stuggart: United Bible Societies, 1994.

Herodotus. *The Histories*. Translated by Aubrey de Sélincourt. New York: Penguin Books, 1972.

Jewish Inscriptions of Graeco-Roman Egypt, ed. William Horbury and David Noy. Cambridge: Cambridge University Press, 1992.

Jewish Inscriptions of Western Europe. Vol. 1, ed. David Noy. Cambridge: Cambridge University Press, 1993.

John Chrysostom. *The Homilies of St. John Chrysostom on the First Epistle of St. Paul the Apostle to the Corinthians*. Oxford: John Henry Parker, 1839.

Josephus. *Against Apion*. In *The Works of Josephus*. Translated by William Whiston, 773-812. Peabody: Hendrickson Publishers, 1987.

————. *The Antiquities of the Jews.* In *The Works of Josephus.* Translated by William Whiston, 27-542. Peabody: Hendrickson Publishers, 1987.

————. *The War of the Jews.* In *The Works of Josephus.* Translated by William Whiston, 543-772. Peabody: Hendrickson Publishers, 1987.

A New Eusebius: Documents Illustrating the History of the Church to AD 337, ed. J. Stevenson. London: SPCK, 1987.

The New Testament Background: Selected Documents, ed. C. K. Barrett. San Franciso: Harper San Francisco, 1987.

Novum Testamentum Graece. 26th Edition. Stuggart: Deutsche Bibelgesellschaft, 1991.

Ovid. *Metamorphoses.* Translated by Rolfe Humphries. Bloomington: Indiana University Press, 1983.

————. *The Art of Love and Other Poems.* Translated by J. H. Mozley. Cambridge, MA: Harvard University Press, 1969.

Pausanias. *Description of Greece.* Translated by W. H. S. Jones. Cambridge, MA: Harvard University Press, 1969.

Petronius. *The Satyricon.* Translated by J. P. Sullivan. London: Penguin Books, 1986.

Philo. *The Works of Philo.* Translated by C. D. Yonge. Peabody: Hendrickson Publishers, 1993.

————. *Works.* 12 Vols. Translated by F. H. Colson, G. H. Whitaker, and R. Marcus. Cambridge, MA: Harvard University Press, 1934-1961.

Plutarch. *Lives.* 11 Vols. Translated by B. Perrin. Cambridge, MA: Harvard University Press, 1914-1926.

————. *Moralia.* 15 Vols. Translated by F. C. Babbitt, W. Helmbold, et al. Cambridge, MA: Harvard University Press, 1927-1969.

Quintilian. *Institutio Oratoria.* 4 Vols. Translated by H. E. Butler. Cambridge, MA: Harvard University Press, 1920-1922.

The Septuagint with Apocrypha: Greek and English. Translated by Sir Lancelot C. L. Brenton. Peabody: Hendrickson Publishers, 1986.

Sibylline Oracle 3. In *The Old Testament Pseudepigrapha,* vol. 1, ed. James H. Charlesworth. New York: Doubleday, 1983.

Strabo. *Geography.* 8 Vols. Translated by H. L. Jones. Cambridge, MA: Harvard University Press, 1923-1932.

Suetonius. *The Lives of the Caesars.* 2 Vols. Translated by J. C. Rolfe. Cambridge, MA: Harvard University Press, 1914.

Tacitus. *Histories 4-5.* 3 Vols. Translated by Clifford H. Moore. Cambridge, MA: Harvard University Press, 1931.

Testaments of the Twelve Patriarachs. In *The Old Testament Pseudepigrapha,* vol. 1, ed. James H. Charlesworth. New York: Doubleday, 1983.